Intellectual Property, Pharmaceuticals and Public Health

Intellectual Property, Pharmaceuticals and Public Health

Access to Drugs in Developing Countries

Edited by

Kenneth C. Shadlen

London School of Economics and Political Science, UK

Samira Guennif

Université Paris 13, France

Alenka Guzmán

Autonomous Metropolitan University-Iztapalapa, Mexico

N. Lalitha

Gujarat Institute of Development Research, India

Edward Elgar

Cheltenham, UK • Northampton, MA, USA

Published by
Edward Elgar Publishing Limited
The Lypiatts
15 Lansdown Road
Cheltenham
Glos GL50 2JA
UK

Edward Elgar Publishing, Inc.
William Pratt House
9 Dewey Court
Northampton
Massachusetts 01060
USA

A catalogue record for this book
is available from the British Library

Library of Congress Control Number: 2011928597

ISBN 978 1 84980 014 3 (cased)
ISBN 978 0 85793 879 4 (paperback)

Typeset by Servis Filmsetting Ltd, Stockport, Cheshire
Printed and bound by CPI Group (UK) Ltd, Croydon, CR0 4YY

Contents

Contributors

Tatiana Andia is assistant professor (on leave) at the Interdisciplinary Center for Development Studies (CIDER) at Los Andes University in Bogotá, Colombia, and she is currently pursuing a PhD in Sociology at Brown University (USA). She holds an MSc in Development Studies from the London School of Economics and a BA in Economics and a BA in History from Los Andes University.

Mélanie Bourassa Forcier is a professor of law at the University of Sherbrooke (Canada) and a research associate at the CIRANO, an inter-university centre for research, liaison, and knowledge transfer on the analysis of organizations. Professor Bourassa Forcier holds a PhD in Law from McGill University (Canada), an MSc in International Health Policy from the London School of Economics and an LLM in Law and Biotechnology from the University of Montreal. She previously worked as a pharmaceutical patent policy analyst for the Canadian government. Her research interests are related to pharmaceutical and health products regulations as well as to policies that promote innovation in the field of life sciences.

Matthew Flynn teaches Sociology at the University of Texas at Austin, where he completed his doctorate in Sociology and was awarded the Andrew W. Mellon Fellowship in Latin American Sociology. His dissertation, entitled 'Pharmaceutical Governance in Brazil: Institutions, Globalization and AIDS', examines the impact of the Agreement on Trade-Related Aspects of Intellectual Property (TRIPS) on Brazil's universal AIDS treatment program. His publications include the following: 'The Evolution of Brazil's Public Production of AIDS Medicines, 1990–2008', *Development and Change*, 39, No. 4, 2008, 513–36; 'Between Subimperialism and Globalization: A Case Study in the Internationalization of Brazilian Capital', *Latin American Perspectives*, 34, No. 6, Nov. 2007, 9–27; and 'Brazilian Pharmaceutical Diplomacy: Social Democratic Principles versus Soft Power Interests', *International Journal of Health Services* (forthcoming).

Dr Padmashree Gehl Sampath is a well-known international expert on innovation, technology and development issues and is presently working at the United Nations Conference on Trade and Development, Geneva. She has a research specialization in institutional and development economics, and has contributed extensively to international and regional debates on these issues through research results from the various projects that she has led in the field. She has an extensive publications record, including several journal publications, chapters in books and authored books. Apart from an earlier book in 2005 (*Regulating Bioprospecting*, UNU Press), her recently published books include *Reconfiguring Global Health Innovation: Capacity for Disease of the Poor* (Routledge, 2010), *Latecomer Development: Innovation and Knowledge for Economic Catch up* (with Prof. Banji Oyeyinka; Routledge, 2009) and *The Gene Revolution and Global Food Security: Biotechnology Innovation in Latecomers* (with Prof. Banji Oyeyinka; Palgrave Macmillan).

Samira Guennif is an associate professor at Paris 13 University. She is currently affiliated with the Paris Nord Centre for Economics (CEPN), Research Unit UMR CNRS 7234. Her research interests intersect industrial organization and public health. She examines the impact of strong intellectual property rights regimes inherited from the TRIPS and Free-Trade Agreements on local production of drugs and their accessibility in emerging and developing countries such as India, Thailand, Brazil, South-Africa, Morocco and Algeria. In particular, she scrutinizes antiretrovirals accessibility in Southern countries hit by the HIV/AIDS epidemic, and the implementation of public health programs.

Alenka Guzmán is a full time research professor at the Metropolitan Autonomous University Iztapalapa, Mexico. She obtained her doctorate degree in Economics from the Université de la Sorbonne Nouvelle, Paris III, France in 1999. She is a member of the Mexican National Researchers System, Level 1. She has published more than 30 articles in academic journals, on textiles, iron and steel and pharmaceutical industries regarding innovation, productivity, competitiveness and technological gaps. She has written two books on iron and steel and edited one on the pharmaceutical industry and intellectual property. She has been visiting professor at the Université de la Sorbonne Nouvelle and the Maison des sciences de l'Homme, Paris, France.

Heinz Klug is Evjue-Bascom Professor of Law at the University of Wisconsin-Madison and is an Honorary Senior Research Associate in the School of Law at the University of the Witwatersrand, Johannesburg, South Africa. Growing up in Durban, South Africa, he participated in the anti-apartheid struggle, spent 11 years in exile and returned to South Africa in 1990 as a member of the ANC Land Commission and researcher for the chairperson of the ANC Constitutional Committee. He has on occasion served as a temporary adviser to the World Health Organization on legal issues concerning access to essential medicines. His research interests include constitutional transitions, constitution-building, human rights and access to essential medicines. His first book, *Constituting Democracy: Law, Globalism, and South Africa's Political Reconstruction*, was published by Cambridge University Press in 2000. Most recently he has published *The Constitution of South Africa: A Contextual Analysis* in Hart Publishing's Constitutional Systems of the World series.

Gaëlle Krikorian is a PhD candidate at the École des Hautes Études en Sciences Sociales and a member of the Interdisciplinary Research Institute on Social Issues, Social Sciences, Politics and Health (IRIS) in Paris. In the past 10 years, she has worked either as a consultant or as a researcher on intellectual property issues, first in the field of health and medical innovation and since 2004 more broadly on access to knowledge. She recently co-edited a book on social mobilizations in this field: *Access to Knowledge in the Age of Intellectual Property* (Zone Books Eds: New York).

N. Lalitha is a professor at Gujarat Institute of Development Research, a premier social science research institute in Ahmedabad, India. Her research interests are in development and regional economics. She has been focusing on intellectual property rights related issues in the field of pharmaceuticals and biotechnology.

Jean-Frédéric Morin is professor of international relations at the Université libre de Bruxelles where he teaches international political economy and global environmental politics. He has an interdisciplinary background, including a dual PhD in law and political science. His most recent research projects explore political dimensions of the international patent regime, such as the impact of capacity building, the influence of academics, and trust-building among stakeholders. Prof. Morin frequently advises decision-makers on these issues. His publications can be downloaded from http://repi.ulb.ac.be/en/membres_morin-jean-frederic.html.

Kenneth C. Shadlen is Reader in the Department of International Development, London School of Economics. He works on the politics of intellectual property and the politics of trade and integration. Some of his recent articles on these topics have been published in *Comparative Politics, International Studies Quarterly, Journal of Development Studies*, and *Politics & Society*. He is co-editor (with Sebastian Haunss) of *The Politics of Intellectual Property: Contestation over the Ownership, Use, and Control of Knowledge and Information* (Edward Elgar, 2009) and (with Diego Sánchez-Ancochea) of *The Political Economy of Hemispheric*

Integration: Responding to Globalization in the Americas (Palgrave, 2008). He is completing a book on the politics of patents, technology, and innovation policy in Latin America.

Luwen Shi is Professor and Head of the International Research Center for Medicinal Administration at Peking University. He works on medicinal research and pharmaceutical policies and education and medical work in China. Several works on the topics are published in journals in China. He contributed to *Encyclopedia of Pharmacology in China.*

Mariko Watanabe is Senior Research Fellow, Institute of Developing Economies. She works on applied micro-economics in contract theory, institutional design and industrial organization, and empirical work on China's institutions and industry. Her work on the pharmaceutical industry includes *Pharmaceutical Industry in China: Intellectual Property Protection, Pricing and Innovation* (Institute of Developing Economies, JETRO, 2007, co-edited with Luwen Shi) and two chapters in *Japanese Generic Pharmaceutical Market and Pharmaceutical Industries of India and China* (Institute of Developing Economies, JETRO, 2006, Kensuke Kubo ed.).

Acknowledgements

Organising a volume among four co-editors who live and work in four different countries is not a simple task. We wish to thank The Foundation Maison des Sciences de l'Homme, in Paris, for generously funding the collaborative project, Globalisation and Public Health in Developing Countries, that ultimately produced this book. We are extremely grateful to Jean-Luc Racine, director of the International Programme for Advanced Studies at the Foundation, for enthusiastically encouraging and supporting our efforts throughout the entire process, and to Josiane Ochoa for the administrative support she provided. As residents in Paris, in addition to the generous financial support we received from the Foundation, we were fortunate to be provided office space at the Columbia University Institute for Scholars – Reid Hall and accommodation at Maison Suger. We are grateful to Danielle Haase-Dubosc, director of Columbia's Institute for Scholars, as well as to Mihaela Bacou, Naby Avcioglu and the rest of the staff at Reid Hall (as well as the other scholars in residence) for limitless support and collegiality they extended to us during the April–June 2009 period. We also wish to thank the many people who attended and participated in the workshop that we organised on Globalisation and Public Health in Developing Countries. This workshop, which took place at Reid Hall in June 2009, marked an important milestone in the subsequent production of this book. Lastly, we are grateful to Jonathan Styles for his tremendous help in copyediting, and to the editors and staff at Edward Elgar for the early interest they took in this project, their patience with us, and the helpful guidance they have provided.

1. Globalization, intellectual property rights, and pharmaceuticals: meeting the challenges to addressing health gaps in the new international environment

Kenneth C. Shadlen, Samira Guennif, Alenka Guzmán and N. Lalitha

In this volume we examine national strategies for pharmaceutical development and the protection of public health in the context of two fundamental changes that the global political economy has undergone since the 1970s, the globalization of trade and production and the increased harmonization of national regulations on intellectual property rights (IPRs). The substantial increases in international trade and direct foreign investment (DFI) that the global economy has experienced since the 1970s are well-known phenomena. Along with these changes, globalization has entailed the emergence and growth of knowledge- and information-based industrial activities based on technological innovation. Competitiveness and growth in the new global economy, it is widely recognized, are driven by technological innovation and thus dependent on societies' capabilities for generating, absorbing, and using knowledge (Lundvall 1992; Nelson 1993; Nelson 2008; Malerba and Manil 2009).

The broad changes in the global economy are mirrored in the pharmaceutical industry, which is the principal subject of this book. Pharmaceutical exports have increased dramatically since the 1980s, as has foreign investment in the sector; supply chains are increasingly global and the sector's leading firms have enlarged their presence in production and distribution in many developing countries. Changes in trade and the location of production have also been accompanied by changes in technology and industrial organization. The emergence of a new technological paradigm based on biotechnology, genomic medicine and nanotechnology has influenced innovation dynamics in this industry (Landau et al. 1999).

In addition to these characteristics, the pharmaceutical sector is marked by two additional attributes of great importance. First, it remains intensely concentrated. In 2009, for example, ten firms from four countries accounted for 45.1 percent of global pharmaceutical sales (IMS data). With regard to production, by which we mean the value added at each stage of the manufacturing process (e.g. manufacturing of active ingredients in bulk from basic chemicals, formulation and preparation of finished new medical entities, repackaging imported generic ingredients to make finished branded or unbranded generic products), notwithstanding the broad changes indicated above the sector remains marked by geographic concentration. As of the late 1990s, 92.9 percent of world pharmaceutical production was located in high-income countries, while the shares in low- and middle-income countries were 2.6 percent and 4.5 percent, respectively (WHO 2004, p. 5).

A second attribute of the pharmaceutical sector is the central and important role played by intellectual property rights (IPRs), particularly patents. The high cost of research and development, combined with the relative ease of reverse-engineering, make originator firms intensely dependent on patents as a mechanism to ward off competition and thus appropriate the rents derived from technological innovation.[1] And here too the sector shows a remarkable level of concentration. As Table 1.1 indicates, more than 80 percent of pharmaceutical, pharmo-chemical, and biotechnological patent applications recorded by the World Intellectual Property Organization in the period 1995–2006 originated from just six countries (USA, Japan, Germany, France, UK, Switzerland).

The pharmaceutical sector's intense reliance on patents in the context of globalization leads us to the second major contextual change, namely the increased harmonization of national policies and regulations in IPRs. Prior to the 1990s, countries retained significant autonomy in setting national policies in this domain. In the area of patents, for example, although signatories of the Paris Convention were required to abide by basic norms of non-discrimination and national treatment, countries retained virtually complete autonomy with regard to the substantive aspects of national patent law. Countries could declare certain technological areas ineligible for patents, and many countries refused to grant patents on pharmaceutical products and/or processes. When patents were available, countries could – and did – exhibit a great deal of variation in terms of the strength,

---

[1]   Pharmaceutical firms are also dependent on trademarks to preserve market shares in the absence of patents, but this concern is not just relevant to originator firms but can also pertain to producers of off-patent drugs (i.e. "branded generics").

Table 1.1 WIPO patent applications by country of origin, 1995–2006

	Pharma-ceuticals, % (824,759)	Pharmo-chemicals, % (773,231)	Biotech-nology, % (519,287)	All, % (2,117,277)
USA	39.5	32.4	45.0	38.3
Japan	11.3	18.7	14.1	14.7
Germany	10.3	15.5	9.1	11.9
China	9.7	4.4	6.6	7.0
France	5.6	7.8	4.2	6.1
UK	5.4	4.9	4.9	5.1
Switzerland	4.7	5.0	2.8	4.4
South Korea	1.8	2.4	2.7	2.2
Canada	2.5	1.4	2.8	2.2
Sweden	2.5	1.9	1.1	2.0
Netherlands	1.6	2.0	2.1	1.9
Italy	2.0	1.9	1.1	1.7
Belgium	1.9	1.7	1.3	1.7
Russia	1.8	0.9	1.9	1.5
Denmark	1.3	1.0	1.7	1.3
Australia	1.1	0.6	1.7	1.1
Israel	1.1	0.7	1.0	0.9
India	1.0	1.0	0.4	0.8
Spain	0.9	0.8	0.6	0.8
Austria	0.7	0.6	0.6	0.6
Finland	0.5	0.4	0.4	0.4
Ireland	0.5	0.3	0.2	0.3
Norway	0.4	0.2	0.3	0.3
Hungary	0.3	0.3	0.1	0.3
Ukraine	0.4	0.1	0.1	0.2
Brazil	0.3	0.2	0.2	0.2
New Zealand	0.2	0.1	0.2	0.1
Poland	0.1	0.2	0.1	0.1
Singapore	0.1	0.0	0.2	0.1
South Africa	0.1	0.1	0.1	0.1

Note: The countries are sorted in descending order of the final column (All).

Source: WIPO.

duration, and enforcement prospects of the rights of exclusion conferred by patents (Lerner 1999; Dutfield 2003; May and Sell 2005).

The Uruguay Round of multilateral trade negotiations, and the subsequent coming into effect of the World Trade Organization's (WTO)

Agreement on Trade-Related Aspects of Intellectual Property Rights (TRIPS), yielded a radically different scenario. TRIPS introduces important changes on each of the dimensions noted in the previous paragraph: all countries must make patents eligible for pharmaceutical products and processes (indeed, patents must be available for inventions in virtually all fields of technology); and the rights of exclusion are much stronger and for longer duration. TRIPS granted countries transition periods for implementing their new obligations, in that developing countries had until 2005 to begin introducing pharmaceutical patents and WTO members classified as Least Developed Countries have until 2016, yet ultimately what TRIPS establishes is a world of "universal" pharmaceutical patenting, in which patents will be available in all countries that are WTO members.[2] TRIPS, thus, marks a major and unprecedented step toward international harmonization, with particular relevance to pharmaceuticals.[3]

In this volume we aim to understand what the changing economic, industrial, and political contexts mean for developing countries' pharmaceutical industries, health policies, and access to medicines. We are of course not the first authors to point to the broad changes that have occurred in the global economy, the pharmaceutical industry, and international regulatory frameworks (Moatti et al. 2003; Harrison 2004; Coriat 2008). Yet this volume advances the debate by treating these phenomena as an integrated whole, and embedding case studies of national experiences in a common framework. Not only do globalization and the harmonization of IPRs give unprecedented importance to the development of capabilities for knowledge use and technological innovation, but these changes also reveal the existence of stark gaps among countries in terms of such capabilities. Moreover, these dynamics occur in the context of daunting disparities among countries and deficiencies within countries in the areas of health indicators and access to healthcare services. The contributors to this book share this starting point, and then provide detailed examinations of national policy responses from the Americas, Africa, and Asia.

---

[2]   We qualify "universal," because countries that are not members of the WTO are not bound by TRIPS. It is also worth keeping in mind that even where patents are available, they may not be obtained, so what is being universalized is "patentability" rather than patenting per se.

[3]   As is well-known, the transnational pharmaceutical sector played a major role in pushing for the adoption of new, global IPR rules that included the mandatory patentability of pharmaceutical products and processes (Braithwaite and Drahos 2000; Matthews 2002; Sell 2003). Indeed, while the sector's reliance on patents helps explain the *motives* for seeking new rules such as universal pharmaceutical patenting, the dominance of the sector by a small number of gigantic firms helps explain its *means* for doing so.

The remainder of this brief introductory chapter has four sections. First, to provide broader context, we review debates about IP, innovation, and growth. Second, we consider the challenges that must be met in terms of global health needs. Third, we review the principal policy alternatives that countries have to achieve health goals under the new international regime. Fourth, we provide brief overviews of the chapters in the volume.

PATENTS, INNOVATION, AND PHARMACEUTICALS

The effects on developing countries of the movement toward international patent harmonization have been the subject of significant debate. Some observers fear that TRIPS will further the gap between developed and developing countries by raising the cost of essential technologically intensive goods (UNDP 2003: Chapter 11; Correa 2005a, 2005b). Others, in contrast, point to the possibility that universally stronger IPRs can, by creating new incentive structures, yield widespread benefits through the creation and diffusion of knowledge and technology (Maskus 2004; Arora et al. 2005; Falvey and Foster 2005; Maskus et al. 2005). While the empirical evidence in support of either of these positions remains limited and inconclusive (Mazzoleni and Nelson 1998; Kortum 2005; Archibugi and Filipetti 2010), it is worth considering the underlying logics informing debates over IPRs.

In theory, granting and protecting patents can yield benefits through at least three channels. First, patents can serve as an inducement for private innovation: by granting temporary monopolies to innovators and thus allowing them to appropriate the benefits derived from their inventions, patents can provide a solution to the public-goods characteristics of knowledge generation. Second, once generated, the commercialization and thus diffusion, dissemination, and use of new technologies and knowledge-based products can raise productivity throughout the economy. Third, even if stronger IPRs do not, directly, induce more domestic innovation or yield the diffusion of more indigenous innovations, they may be associated with the introduction of more technology in the country via DFI and trade. It is important to consider the interactions among these channels. To be sure, the granting of exclusive rights – and thus permission to the patent-owner to secure monopoly rents – imposes static costs on society. But these costs can, hypothetically, be compensated for by the dynamic benefits that are derived from the introduction of new products and technologies and the ability of all actors to use and build upon the new knowledge and technologies induced by patents.

Countries differ, of course, in their levels of innovative and also absorptive capabilities. These differences mean that the abilities of actors both to respond to the incentives offered by patents and to take advantage of opportunities generated by the existence and introduction of new knowledge and technologies are likely to vary. In wealthier countries, which typically feature more public and private expenditure on research and development, exhibit more advanced scientific and technological infrastructures, and possess legal institutions that support vibrant markets in technology, patent systems can stimulate new knowledge and facilitate knowledge- and technology-diffusion through each of the channels referred to above. Not surprisingly, the wealthier countries were not only the principal protagonists of TRIPS but widely regarded as the main beneficiaries as well. In poorer countries, however, the inducement effect that patents have on indigenous innovation may be minimal, and what the patent system may amount to might simply be the granting of private rights of exclusion to foreign patent-holders. Furthermore, in developing countries, public and private actors' abilities to absorb knowledge and technology and thus exploit the externalities generated by others' innovations may be less advanced as well.

These differences have traditionally formed part of the rationale for poorer, developing countries having weaker systems for the establishment and protection of IPRs. But only a part of the rationale – for the justification of weaker IPRs in developing countries has been based not solely on negative or weak static effects (i.e. patents leading to a transfer of resources from local, knowledge-users to foreign knowledge-owners without leading to more technological uptake) but also on concerns with the dynamic accumulation of capabilities as well. After all, weak IPRs can facilitate reverse-engineering and technology adaptation, activities that can contribute to local actors' acquisition and accumulation of capabilities. Thus, in late developing countries, where industrial and scientific activities generally are not oriented toward innovation at the technological frontier, but rather learning the appropriate and efficient ways to use existing technologies, the role of patents as inducements for innovation and instruments of technology dissemination has generally been regarded as minimal. To the contrary, weaker IPRs (i.e. minimal and weakly enforced patents) have historically contributed to national strategies for technological learning.[4]

---

[4] Over time, however, the accumulation of technological capabilities can allow local actors to advance beyond absorption and imitation and undertake their own innovative activities, at which point actors who previously benefited from weaker IPR systems may develop an interest in stronger IPRs to protect their own innovations. This trajectory of weaker IPRs facilitating capability-

In the case of pharmaceuticals, the rationale for weaker IPRs in developing countries has, historically, been particularly acute, simply because of the comparative ease of reverse-engineering and thus its utility as an instrument for technology absorption and transfer in this sector. Where technology transfer depends on the participation of the technology's owner, then limiting patents may have minimal impact on local actors' ability to benefit from new technologies: the absence of patents may leave knowledge "freely" available in the public domain, but local actors may be unable to unlock and acquire the essential knowledge on their own. In pharmaceuticals, however, removing patent protection eliminates the most important barrier to technology transfer. Thus, many countries' domestic pharmaceutical industries were built on the basis of reverse-engineering and imitation in the context of weak or non-existent systems of patent protection. Conversely, however, establishing product patent regimes in pharmaceuticals, as required under TRIPS, erects a new set of legal barriers designed to block local actors from acquiring patented knowledge without the consent and participation of the patent-owners.[5]

If imitation is prohibited (at least for newer products, if not retroactively), then pharmaceutical development in the new international environment depends on innovation; not merely replicating existing molecules and drugs but creating new ones. The establishment of a global patent regime that includes pharmaceuticals brings to stark contrast differences in countries' capabilities for innovation in this sector. A number of indicators illustrate these differences. Consider, for example, differences in national pharmaceutical sectors' tendencies to invest in research and development. Guzmán and Gomez (2008) estimate national pharmaceutical R&D efforts, calculated as R&D expenditures as a percentage of value added in the sector, for a set of sixteen countries over the period 1980–2005. As Figure 1.1 shows, in many industrialized countries the sector's R&D expenditures exceed one quarter of the sector's output; in most (though not all) this ratio has increased over time. To be sure, some developing countries have experienced increases as well, but even the most advanced developing countries where R&D expenditures are increasing

---

development and capability-development generating a demand for stronger IPRs was experienced by Korea and Taiwan when developing strong local firms in a set of sophisticated industries, and more recently we see evidence of this in the cases of China and India. See Cimoli et al. (2005). See also the case studies in Odagiri et al. (2010).

[5] Indeed, that was the whole purpose behind TRIPS, at least from the perspective of the transnational pharmaceutical sector which mobilized so strongly for the agreement and, in particular, the mandatory patentability of pharmaceuticals.

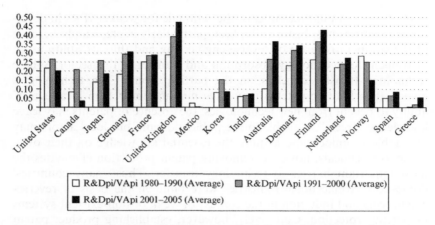

Source: Value added: OCDE, STAN Database, for India: Statistical Yearbook and the million of dollars of current prices were deflated to 1990 prices. R&D: OCDE, R&D Expenditure in Industry, several years.

Figure 1.1   Pharmaceutical R&D effort: R&D/value added in pharmaceutical industry by average period, 1980–2005

remain quite some distance from the OECD norm. For example, in India, the country with arguably the most advanced pharmaceutical sector in the developing world, R&D expenditures amount to roughly 6 percent of the sector's value-added. And in some instances, e.g. Mexico, the level of pharmaceutical R&D effort has decreased since the 1980s.

Different levels of R&D expenditures are reflected in patenting trajectories as well, as reflected in the concentration of patenting activities in a handful of countries referred to above (Table 1.1). Guzmán and Gomez (2008) also calculate countries' pharmaceutical inventive coefficients, defined as the number of patents granted to nationals in the United States per each one million inhabitants (Figure 1.2). Although a number of developing countries are experiencing growth in this measure (the top number is larger than the bottom number, even if the bars are too small to register), the clear and unmistakable take-away from these data are that the gaps are immense – and growing.

The question of countries' abilities to participate in global pharmaceutical innovation is addressed by a number of chapters in this volume, particularly in the cases of China (Watanabe and Shi), India (N. Lalitha), Mexico (Guzmán), and South Africa (Klug). Others, however, focus more on national strategies of adaptation as users of pharmaceutical innovations.

Taking a step back, the chapters in this volume point to two important – but different – issues, or mismatches, in the realm of global health.

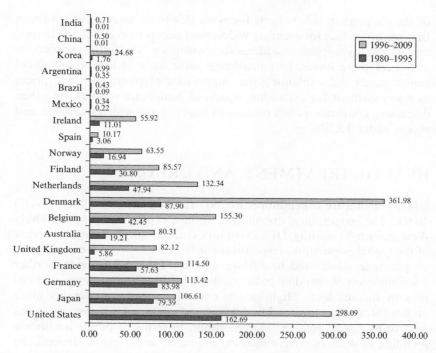

Source: USPTO classes 514, 424, 435 and 800 from 1980 to *October 2010 and United Nations database.

Figure 1.2 *Pharmaceutical inventive coefficients: patents per million inhabitants granted by USPTO in the bio-pharmaceutical field, 1980–2009*

The first regards the mismatch between global health needs and the orientation of global health spending and research. This is a deficiency in global health innovation, often referred to as the "neglected disease problem," in that the overwhelming amount of resources dedicated to healthcare research is directed toward diseases of people in wealthier countries; in contrast, "tropical diseases," i.e. diseases that disproportionately affect poor people in poor countries, receive minimal attention (Lanjouw 2001; MSF 2001; Morel 2003; Ito and Yamagata 2005). The second mismatch is between developing countries' health needs and their healthcare capabilities. The challenge being identified here is not so much one of developing relevant treatments that currently do not exist, but rather about improving health promotion on the basis of already-existing drugs (and health technologies more generally). Most of the chapters in this volume focus on this latter issue – the obstacles that countries face for securing widespread access to essential medicines, and national strategies to address such obstacles. The following sections introduce these issues, first providing some basic indicators of global health needs and explaining the importance of pharmaceutical prices as a key element for expanding access to healthcare services, and then discussing countries' policy options to improve and widen treatment and access under TRIPS.

HEALTH, TREATMENT, AND DRUGS

Global healthcare expenditures in 2007 reached US$4.1 trillion (WHO 2007).[6] The geographical distribution of these expenditures is remarkably skewed, with 30 wealthy, OECD countries, accounting for only 20 percent of the global population, responsible for 90 percent of total expenditures on pharmaceuticals and healthcare services. Table 1.2 provides further discrimination of spending patterns, distinguishing among types of countries by income level. High-income countries spend considerably more on healthcare than low- and middle-income countries, whether expressed relative to size of total economic output, in terms of public healthcare spending as share of government expenditures, or per capita. Indeed, the gaps in per capita spending are breathtaking, with the average person in a high-income country benefiting from roughly 68 times more healthcare spending than the average person in a low-income country. Note also that government health expenditures tend to be much less universal in poorer countries, often restricted to public sector employees, so private spending as a share of total health expenditures is larger in poorer countries – and because of limited insurance coverage "private" in this context generally means "out-of-pocket."

To appreciate the implications of these disparities, consider the global epidemiologic situation. The leading cause of death in the world is related to non-communicable diseases, e.g. heart conditions and cancer, responsible for six out of ten deaths. Communicable diseases like HIV/AIDS, malaria and tuberculosis are the second main cause of mortality, responsible for three out of ten deaths (WHO 2004). Yet while wealthier countries are affected disproportionately by non-communicable diseases, poorer, developing countries are hit by both non-communicable and communi-

---

6   This figure is for healthcare products and services, not money allocated toward health and biomedical research.

Table 1.2   Health expenditure ratios and aggregates, 2006

	Income group			
	Low	Lower middle	Upper middle	High
Total expenditure on health as % of GDP	4.3	4.5	6.3	10.0
General government expenditure on health as % of total government expenditure	5.9	8.2	9.8	17.1
Per capita total expenditure on health at international dollar rate	57	181	707	3848
General government expenditure on health as % of total expenditure on health	36.2	43.2	55.1	60.7
Private expenditure on health as % of total expenditure on health	63.8	56.8	44.8	39.3
External resources for health as % of total expenditure on health	16.9	0.8	0.2	0.0
Social security expenditure on health as % of general government expenditure on health	7.0	40.3	40.4	41.6
Out of pocket expenditure as % of private expenditure on health	85.4	85.7	70.0	36.2
Private prepaid plans as % of private expenditure on health	2.8	5.9	25.7	54.3
Per capita government expenditure on health at international dollar rate	21	78	389	2335

Source: WHO (2009).

cable diseases (Table 1.3). As a result, countries from Africa and South-East Asia bear the largest share of the global burden of disease. More than 50 percent of global disability-adjusted life years (DALYs) lost affects these countries, which gather 37 percent of the world's population and absorb only 2 percent of the global resources on health.[7] Though featured by smaller population and lower disease burden, high-income countries use more global health resources. In particular, OECD countries-members bear less than 10 percent of global disability-adjusted life years lost and consume up to 90 percent of global health expenses. Definitely, developing countries need more resources while advanced countries need in contrast to question the efficiency of their health system.

---

[7]   The disability-adjusted life year (DALY) is a metric developed by the WHO and is based on years of life lost from premature death and years of life lived in less than full health.

Table 1.3   Leading causes of death by income group, 2004

Disease or injury	Deaths (millions)	% of total deaths	Disease or injury	Deaths (millions)	% of total deaths
World			**Low-income countries**		
1. Ischaemic heart disease	7.2	12.2	1. Lower respiratory infections	2.9	11.2
2. Cerebrovascular disease	5.7	9.7	2. Ischaemic heart disease	2.5	9.4
3. Lower respiratory infections	4.2	7.1	3. Diarrhoeal diseases	1.8	6.9
4. COPD	3/0	5.1	4. HIV/AIDS	1.5	5.7
5. Diarrhoeal diseases	2.2	3.7	5. Cerebrovascular disease	1.5	5.6
6. HIV/AIDS	2.0	3.5	6. COPD	0.9	3.6
7. Tuberculosis	1.5	2.5	7. Tuberculosis	0.9	3.5
8. Trachea, bronchus, lung cancers	1.3	2.3	8. Neonatal infections	0.9	3.4
9. Road traffic accidents	1.3	2.2	9. Malaria	0.9	3.3
10. Prematurity and low birth weight	1.2	2.0	10. Prematurity and low birth weight	0.8	3.2
Middle-income countries			**High-income countries**		
1. Cerebrovascular disease	3.5	14.2	1. Ischaemic heart disease	1.3	16.3
2. Ischaemic heart disease	3.4	13.9	2. Cerebrovascular disease	0.8	9.3
3. COPD	1.8	7.4	3. Trachea, bronchus, lung cancers	0.5	5.9
4. Lower respiratory infections	0.9	3.8	4. Lower respiratory infections	0.3	3.8
5. Trachea, bronchus, lung cancers	0.7	2.9	5. COPD	0.3	3.5
6. Road traffic accidents	0.7	2.8	6. Alzheimer's and other dementias	0.3	3.4

Table 1.3   (continued)

Disease or injury	Deaths (millions)	% of total deaths	Disease or injury	Deaths (millions)	% of total deaths
Middle-income countries			High-income countries		
7. Hypertensive heart disease	0.6	2.5	7. Colon and rectum cancers	0.3	3.3
8. Stomach cancer	0.5	2.2	8. Diabetes mellitus	0.2	2.8
9. Tuberculosis	0.5	2.2	9. Breast cancer	0.2	2.0
10. Diabetes mellitus	0.5	2.1	10. Stomach cancer	0.1	1.8

Source: WHO (2008).

In light of these trends, it is not surprising that addressing healthcare gaps is prominently featured in the United Nations' Millennium Development Goals (MDGs). In particular, the MDGs place a special focus on addressing communicable diseases such as HIV/AIDS, malaria, and tuberculosis. Each of these three disease epidemics has profound impacts on development processes. AIDS and AIDS-related infections kill roughly 2–3 million people annually. In addition to high levels of mortality, a number of studies have shown a link between the spread of the epidemic and reduced economic output and, more generally, the devastating effects of the epidemic on nations, regions, towns, and families (Bonnel 2000; Dixon et al. 2002; Barnett and Whiteside 2006; UNAIDS 2008). Malaria, which the WHO estimates to be prevalent in more than 100 countries, kills nearly a million people each year, the majority being children under five years (WHO 2008a). The disease appears to have the strongest effect in sub-Saharan Africa, due to the abundance of a more lethal form of the parasite in combination with fragile and poorly resourced health systems. TB is a major cause of illness and death as well. The WHO reports 9.2 million new cases of TB in 2006, with 55 percent in Asia and 31 percent in Africa, and 1.7 million deaths attributed to the disease; and prevalence is increasing sharply in many regions of the world.[8]

Strategies to combat these epidemics have included efforts to slow the spread of the diseases and also to widen the availability of treatment.

---

[8]   TB and HIV/AIDS are closely related. In 2006 roughly 15 percent of the new TB cases were among HIV-positive people, and roughly 12 percent of deaths from TB were among people infected with AIDS (WHO 2008b).

With regard to HIV/AIDS, for example, prevention measures have been progressing among high-risk populations (e.g. female sex workers, men having sex with men, injecting drug users), and the percentage of people with HIV/AIDS in need of treatment that receive antiretrovirals increased from less than five percent in 2002 to over 42 percent by the end of 2008.[9] Likewise, combating malaria has entailed increased distribution of insecticide-treated bed nets and ramping up treatment campaigns, with the latter including both increased use of existing treatments and greater reliance on more effective – but also more expensive – artemisinin-based combination therapies. And the fight against TB has featured the implementation of Directly Observed Treatment, Short-course (DOTS).[10]

While progress has been made on each of these fronts, the enormous disparities pointed to above mean that significantly more effort is essential. Adequately confronting the challenges will require significant increases in the amount of money allocated to health in developing countries, both in terms of international funding and domestic resource allocation. Such resources will need to be used to strengthen healthcare infrastructures and to enable the provision of more healthcare options to more people. And to the extent that resources will be allocated toward healthcare provision, then the availability and price of drugs is of utmost importance.

Before proceeding, it is worth making two observations about the importance of drugs and drug prices for healthcare delivery. First, though effective healthcare treatment depends on many factors, the availability of the essential medicines is absolutely indispensable because drugs are irreplaceable. Functional – if not optimal – substitutes can be found to address inadequacies in other components of treatment: different sorts of infrastructure can be made suitable, alternative healthcare providers can be deployed, and so on. But no amount of managerial creativity can substitute for medicines. If drugs are not available, treatment is impossible, full stop. The second observation regards the relationship between drug

---

[9]   The figures cited are from the WHO's annual HIV/AIDS Progress Reports (http://www.who.int/hiv/pub/progressreports/en/). The WHO measures coverage as the estimated number of people receiving ARV therapy as a share of the estimated number of people age 0–49 in need of ARV therapy. Given the wide range of uncertainty regarding the number of people in a given country that have HIV/AIDS, and the further uncertainty in estimating how many of the people with HIV/AIDS at any given time are in need of ARV therapy, the figures for coverage are extremely rough. Yet the increase is unmistakeable. See Shadlen (forthcoming).

[10]   This is a strategy combining diagnosis of tuberculosis, registration of each patient detected, the secure supply of anti-tuberculosis drugs for all patients in treatment, and cohort evaluation to monitor overall program performance in terms of observance and drug resistances.

prices and healthcare infrastructure. After all, drug prices are far from the only relevant issue; even if drugs were free many countries would nevertheless be unable to extend treatment widely on account of inadequate healthcare infrastructures. Yet the interaction between drug prices and infrastructure ought not to be neglected: for public health ministries operating with scarce resources, the incentives to invest in the development of the infrastructure that is essential for widening treatment is logically related to the price of drugs. Low prices can encourage resource mobilization, while high prices can discourage such mobilization. Why bother investing in infrastructure that will go unused on account of the essential drugs being too expensive?[11] In short, because the availability of affordable drugs can make improving healthcare infrastructure a more useful investment, lower drug prices can free resources and also create incentives to invest in necessary infrastructure, i.e. they can help countries escape from "price-infrastructure traps" (Shadlen 2004).

The next question becomes what steps can be taken by developed and developing countries in the area of pharmaceutical policies to address these serious challenges and secure access to affordable, high-quality medicines. Unquestionably, adhering to the TRIPS Agreement in the pharmaceutical sector poses important challenges for developing and least developed countries in this regard. What are the options available to mitigate the negative effects that the onset of universal pharmaceutical patentability may have on access to medicines? To what extent can the use of such policy options help countries meet their public health objectives? Many of the chapters address these questions in some detail. In the following section we provide a brief overview of some of the most relevant health-related flexibilities in the TRIPS Agreement.

FLEXIBILITIES IN THE TRIPS AGREEMENT TO PROTECT PUBLIC HEALTH[12]

TRIPS requires all countries to make patents available for pharmaceutical products and processes. As discussed above, however, the agreement

---

[11]   The existence of such an interactive effect rests on the fact that many expenditures are disease-specific. After all, if investments in infrastructure are useful for healthcare provision more generally, then governments might find these worth making regardless of the availability of particular drugs.

[12]   For more detailed discussion of the policy flexibilities discussed here, in addition to the texts referenced below, see Correa (2000); CIPR (2002); UNCTAD-ICTSD (2005); Musungu and Oh (2006).

contains specific transition periods for complying with the new obligations in the area of pharmaceuticals. Specifically, developing countries had
until 2005 to begin granting pharmaceutical patents, and Least Developed
Countries have until 2016.[13] Within these overarching constraints the
agreement leaves countries with space to use discretion in implementing
their new obligations. In the following paragraphs we focus on three areas:
the procedures for examining and granting patents, the procedures that
regulate the exercise of patent rights and establish the balance of rights
between owners and users, and additional IP-related regulations that
affect the marketing of generic drugs.

The granting of a patent establishes a right of exclusion over the use
of knowledge. Such rights are established only when the knowledge and
innovations that are defined to be patentable subject matter are judged
to be novel, inventive, and industrially useful. Note that there are two
separate issues here, establishing the range of patentable subject matter
and putting into place the administrative processes for evaluating whether
any given innovation warrants a patent. TRIPS leaves countries some
leeway on these dimensions. Article 27.1 requires that patents be available for inventions in all fields of technology, but the agreement does not
define what an invention is, so countries can stipulate what is and is not
regarded as an "invention." Though an exceptionally limited definition
that excludes patents to a general class of products would almost certainly be a violation of TRIPS, countries can declare that certain types
of pharmaceutical innovations (e.g. new uses of existing molecules) are
not "inventions" and therefore not eligible for patents. Even if something
is patentable, in principle, any particular invention may not deserve a
patent if adjudged to lack novelty, inventiveness, or utility. These criteria
for patentability are ambiguous, however, they must be operationalized
in national patent examination guidelines and practices (Basheer 2005;
UNCTAD-ICTSD 2005; Correa 2007; Shadlen 2011). Lastly, countries
can introduce mechanisms that allow additional actors to have inputs
into the patent examination process (Amin 2011). In the case of observation systems, non-interested parties (e.g. firms, civil society organizations)
are permitted to submit materials to the patent office challenging a given
patent application. In the case of pre-grant opposition systems, these
external challenges may be treated in a more formal way by the patent

---

[13]   The 2005 period only applied to countries that were founding members
of the WTO, not post-1995 accession countries. The date of 2016 for LDCs was
not part of the original TRIPS agreement but an outcome of the 2001 Doha
Declaration on TRIPS and Public Health.

office. In sum, how countries set the scope of patentability, apply standard patentability criteria, and go about examining patent applications can affect how many and what sorts of pharmaceutical patents are granted.

With regard to the regulation of patent rights, two key policy areas regard parallel importation and compulsory licenses (CLs). Parallel importation consists of allowing patented goods to enter the market once patent-holders have placed the goods on the market elsewhere. So, for example, if a patent-holder markets a drug in Argentina for more than it markets the drug in Bolivia, parallel importation would allow actors in Argentina to import the lower-priced drug from Bolivia without infringing on the Argentinian patent. This step can help ensure affordability of patented products by facilitating arbitrage and thus constraining patent-holders' ability to set monopoly prices. TRIPS allows countries to engage in parallel importation by adopting *international* doctrines of patent exhaustion, i.e. once products are placed on the international market, patent-holders' exclusive rights are exhausted. If a country adopts a national doctrine of exhaustion, however, then parallel importation would be prohibited.

The policy issue that has received the most attention since TRIPS came into effect is compulsory licenses (CLs). CLs allow domestic entities (public or private) to import, produce, and distribute patented goods without the patent-holders' consent. TRIPS allows countries to determine the grounds on which they grant CLs, provided that a set of procedural conditions are met. These conditions include, for example, prior negotiations with the patent holder and the payment of royalties. Specifying the procedural conditions in terms of national law leaves countries with significant room for national differentiation. For example, countries retain leeway regarding how much negotiation for a voluntary license is required before a third party can legitimately request a compulsory license from the state. Third parties must attempt to gain authorization from the patentee, and the state may only grant a compulsory license if negotiations are not successful within a "reasonable period of time," but the determination of "reasonable" is left to individual countries. Likewise TRIPS requires that "adequate remuneration" be paid to the patentee, but countries establish their own definitions of "adequate."[14]

Beyond the issue of how countries implement the procedural obligations are the grounds for countries issuing CLs. Here it is important to emphasize that TRIPS is silent: countries can issue CLs for whatever

---

[14] During the Uruguay Round negotiations, the US sought to include a requirement to "compensate the right-holder fully" (Watal 1999: 114), but this language is not included in TRIPS.

reasons they choose. Again, TRIPS stipulates some of the conditions to be met for governments to issue CLs – but it leaves the grounds for doing so as matters of national policy. What this means is that so long as the procedural conditions – defined and operationalized locally – are met, countries establish their own grounds for issuing CLs. In fact, in the case of CLs granted during times of national emergency or for government use, known as "public utility" or "government use" licenses, countries are released from the obligation of prior negotiations.[15]

Developing countries' rights to issue CLs were confirmed in the Doha Declaration on the TRIPS Agreement and Public Health (WTO, 2001). Paragraph 5.b., for example, affirms that "each member has the right to grant compulsory licences and the freedom to determine the grounds upon which such licences are granted." Thus, developing countries are only required to abide by the conditions. Furthermore, even some of these conditions can be waived in the context of national emergencies, and paragraph 5.c. of the Doha Declaration stipulates that "each member has the right to determine what constitutes a national emergency or other circumstances of extreme urgency."

While the Doha Declaration confirmed developing countries' rights to issue CLs, it also acknowledged the limited utility of this instrument for less developed countries that lack the ability to produce drugs locally. For most countries, the ability to use CLs to lower the price of drugs depends on the ability to *import* generic versions from somewhere else. But doing so is difficult, on account of the restrictions that TRIPS places on compulsory licenses in *exporting* countries. Quite simply, importing a good presupposes someone else exporting that good, and TRIPS requires that goods produced in one country under a compulsory license be "predominantly" for domestic use (Article 31.f). To the extent that new drugs become patented in export-capable countries, as most certainly will in the post-2005 environment, this requirement could hamper provision of generic versions of such drugs to developing countries. Most developing countries lack the capacity to produce drugs locally, which makes threats to issue compulsory licenses for local production empty threats – but so too are threats to issue compulsory licenses for import, if potential exporters in more-industrialized developing and developed countries are hamstrung by TRIPS.

---

[15]   This provision, that when CLs are issued on grounds of national emergency countries are released from procedural obligations, is often misrepresented to suggest that countries can only issue CLs in national emergencies. To repeat: countries can issue CLs on whatever grounds they establish in national legislation, but in times of national emergency (and government use) they can do so without entering into negotiations.

Paragraph 6 of the Doha Declaration recognized the special problems faced by developing countries that lack local manufacturing capacity and called on the TRIPS Council to address the problem. In August 2003, WTO members agreed to a partial waiver of Art. 31.f, accompanied by a set of detailed regulations for issuing CLs for export to poor countries (including extensive safeguards against the exported drugs being redirected back into wealthier markets). The August 2003 agreement, along with a supplementary statement from the Chair of the WTO's General Council (WTO 2003a, 2003b), also included a list of developing and developed countries that pledged not to use the system as importers. Both the agreement and the supplementary statement were formalized as a permanent amendment to TRIPS in December 2005. A number of export-capable countries have since revised their patent laws to incorporate the waiver of Article 31.f (Matthews 2006). Canada was the first to do so, and Canada remains the only country to have granted a CL-for-export under this provision (see Morin and Bourassa Forcier, this volume).

Finally, additional areas that are important for health policy regard regulatory issues that affect the entry of generic drugs. Here it is worth flagging three issues that emerge in the subsequent chapters: early working provisions, linkage, and the treatment of test data.

When patents expire, new actors gain rights to participate in markets that were reserved for patent-holders. One factor that affects how quickly new actors may enter markets, and the subsequent competitive effects are felt in terms of reduced prices, is whether a country has "early working" provisions that allow firms to use patented knowledge and produce generic versions of patented drugs to obtain marketing approval prior to the expiration of the patent.[16] Without such provisions firms might be infringing patents by producing generic versions prior to the patents' expiration. Yet if firms must wait until patents expire to produce generic versions and apply to health authorities for authorization, patent terms are effectively extended by the amount of time it takes to complete these not-insignificant steps. Early working provisions, then, by allowing generic firms to use patented knowledge to prepare for market entry, can expedite competition at the point that patents expire. Such provisions, which are permissible under TRIPS, do not shorten patent terms but rather eliminate the effective extension of terms that is yielded by leaving a single firm with market exclusivity despite its patent's expiration.

Some pharmaceutical firms opt to launch generic versions prior to the end of patent terms, believing that their follow-on products do not infringe

---

[16] These are often referred to as "Bolar" provisions, after a US legal case.

existing patents or that the patents in question are invalid. Since marketing drugs depends on authorization from health authorities, the subsequent question is whether and how the activities of IP and health officials are coordinated. TRIPS does not address this, but subsequent to the closure of the Uruguay Round the transnational pharmaceutical industry has pushed for a form of coordination known as "linkage," whereby health authorities consult with IP authorities and deny registration to drugs when patents are in force. While this form of coordination seems unproblematic on the face of it (if the drug is patented, then the sale of generic versions would be illegal), many developing countries resist pressures to proceed in this direction, arguing that linkage inappropriately transfers the burden of defending patents from the private rights-holder to the public. Although linkage is not required by TRIPS, it has become an obligation for many countries that have negotiated trade agreements with the US and EU.

Generic competition is also affected by the treatment of test data that originator firms provide to local health authorities to receive market authorization. To obtain approval to market drugs, pharmaceutical firms submit clinical trial data to demonstrate the effectiveness of their products. Can manufacturers of generic medicines use these data to secure regulatory approval for their own drugs? If access to the data is prohibited, then generic firms must conduct their own clinical trials, a costly and time-consuming process that delays the onset of price competition.[17] TRIPS leaves developing countries significant leeway with regard to how they treat test data (Correa 2002; Reichman 2009). According to Article 39.3, countries must protect data that is obtained through "considerable effort" against disclosure and against "unfair commercial use." These requirements are strikingly vague. It is not clear what data are privy to protection (i.e. what is "considerable effort"). Nor does TRIPS specify a term of protection. Most critically, the article does not address whether regulatory authorities can, without disclosing the data, *rely* on the data submitted by one firm for the sake of approving new products. According to many legal scholars, doing so does not amount to "unfair commercial use" and is an acceptable option available to all countries under TRIPS.[18] Indeed,

---

[17] The emphasis here is on cost. Obviously there would also be critical ethical issues raised by the replication of clinical trials with control groups.

[18] Reichman (2009: 17–22) discusses the negotiating history on this issue. The US proposals, which would have prohibited not only disclosure but the use of the data by governments and third parties, were included as bracketed text in a 1990 draft of the agreement, the so-called "Brussels draft." But the bracketed text was omitted in its entirety from the subsequent text that formed the basis of the final agreement, the "Dunkel Draft of 1991" and from the TRIPS agreement itself.

the fact that there is no uniformity in the way test data are treated by different countries suggests that countries have a wide degree of flexibility in this regard.

In conclusion, how TRIPS affects health outcomes in developing countries will depend, in part, on the extent to which countries exploit the policy options that remain in the new international environment. In order to secure an adequate supply of essential medicines to address the health gaps identified in this chapter, it may be necessary to use all of the flexibility options mentioned here. The chapters in this volume examine national experiences.

ORGANIZATION OF THE BOOK

The country-based chapters that follow are organized by region. We begin with two case studies from Africa. Heinz Klug analyzes the case of South Africa. He shows how South African governments, both under the Apartheid regime and since democratization in the 1990s, have struggled with meeting the dual objectives of increasing local production capacity and reducing the prices of essential medicines. He places special emphasis on the post-Apartheid period, where the political environment has given greater prominence and urgency to social policy, but such changes occur in the context of TRIPS, the global reorganization of the pharmaceutical industry, and intense pressures on the part of transnational pharmaceutical firms and foreign governments to pressure countries into prioritizing the granting and protection of intellectual property rights. Klug's chapter thus analyzes South Africa's IP policies in a global perspective, and integrates the analysis into an examination of changes to the country's health and pharmaceutical regulatory regimes.

Gaëlle Krikorian examines the complex subject of IP and IP-related regulatory issues that affect access to medicines in Morocco. She focuses on the tensions between two seemingly paradoxical trends in government policy, introduction of new laws and administrative practices to increase the protection of intellectual property rights in the pharmaceutical industry, and significant efforts to increase coverage of and access to healthcare services (including pharmaceutical products). She examines the ways that Morocco has exceeded its obligations under TRIPS and thus introduced few of the policy options discussed in the previous section, and how the negotiation of a bilateral trade agreement with the US furthered the countries' "TRIPS Plus" trajectory. Importantly, Krikorian does not just examine the legal provisions, but offers a detailed analysis of how the countries' new international commitments affect the practices of the

Moroccan patent office in terms of pharmaceutical patent prosecution. Krikorian also examines Morocco's new health regulations, such as the country's early initiation of an AIDS treatment program. In doing so Krikorian points to the lack of coordination between IP and health policies, and subsequently the risk that the former may undermine the latter.

We then turn to the Americas. Tatiana Andia analyzes the effects of patents and additional regulatory changes on drug prices and access to medicines in Colombia. Andia's chapter examines two complementary trends in the pharmaceutical regulation in Colombia since the 1990s: (1) the trade-related increase in Intellectual Property Rights (IPRs) protection; and (2) the weakening of price controls and the introduction of a new regime of health regulation for biotech drugs. The chapter shows that the first of these trends, regarding IPRs protection, has been highly visible and strongly contested, mainly by health NGOs and the local pharmaceutical industry. As a result, the effects of Colombia taking on new IPR commitments as part of trade agreements have been less problematic than one might fear. Yet the chapter also shows that the broader health regulations, in stark contrast, have been mostly overlooked and weakly challenged, leading to increases in prices. The result of these different political and economic trajectories, Andia shows, is that the beneficial impacts of Colombia's cautious IPR policies have been overwhelmed by the harmful impacts of the "invisible" regulatory changes.

Alenka Guzmán examines the pharmaceutical industry in Mexico, in the context of the increasingly strong IPR system and stringent health regulations adopted since the 1990s. She shows that the absence of a significant sectoral R&D effort and the lack of an articulated industrial policy have prevented Mexico from capturing the potential benefits of knowledge spillovers derived from the intense activities of multinational pharmaceutical firms in this country. The high price of medicines consumes a significant share of public (and private) health expenditures. Thus, despite introducing a new IP system and new health regulations, vast shares of the Mexican population continue to lack access to essential medicines.

Matthew Flynn studies the case of Brazil, a leader in exploiting TRIPS flexibilities to lower the price of antiretrovirals for HIV/AIDS treatment. He points to the social conditions, in both state and society, that have created fertile ground for the introduction of health-oriented patent policies. Flynn's chapter suggests that the establishment of strong, autonomous health agencies, committed to universal public healthcare, can empower health officials to press for changes in national IP legislation. In the case of Brazil, Flynn argues that this state activism accounts for the incorporation of more TRIPS flexibilities in national laws and the use of humanitarian safeguards.

Kenneth Shadlen's comparative analysis of Brazil and Mexico presents an explanation that is complementary to – but different from – Flynn's. Shadlen contrasts the experiences of Brazil and Mexico in terms of their utilization of TRIPS flexibilities. Although both countries introduced pharmaceutical patents in the 1990s, in subsequent years Brazil adjusted the patent system to ameliorate the effects that patents can have on drug prices while Mexico introduced measures that reinforce and intensify these effects. To explain these differences Shadlen focuses on the actors pushing for reform and subsequent patterns of coalitional formation and political mobilization. In Brazil, the government's demand for patented and expensive drugs made health-oriented IP reform a high priority, and the existence of an autonomous local pharmaceutical sector allowed the Ministry of Health to build a coalition in support. In Mexico, the government's demand made IP reforms less urgent, and the fundamental transformations of the pharmaceutical sector allowed the reform project to become commandeered by IP owners. The findings suggest that the existence of indigenous pharmaceutical capacities may be beneficial not just for industrial development, but also for promoting public health by broadening the political coalitions that underpin health reforms.

Lastly, rounding out the Americas section, Jean-Frédéric Morin and Mélanie Bourassa Forcier examine the case of Canada, a developed country that, prior to the 1990s, had IP and pharmaceutical policies that many observers hold up as models for developing countries to emulate. The authors show the important changes that Canada introduced, as part of its commitments under both TRIPS and the North American Free Trade Agreement, but highlight efforts to retain coherence between the new and stronger IP policies and the commitment to control the price of drugs and facilitate generic competition. To that end the authors place particular emphasis on Canada's changing compulsory licensing regime (including the scheme to facilitate the exportation of generic drugs produced under compulsory licenses) and early working exceptions, as well as the critical role of drug price regulations.

We then turn to four Asian case studies. N. Lalitha examines a set of key policy issues that emerge from India's implementation of a pharmaceutical patent regime as required by TRIPS. Like other authors in this volume, she focuses on both IPR and broader regulatory issues that have an impact on access to drugs. Though production of drugs is not an issue in India, access to drugs is an issue of concern since private healthcare coverage is limited to a small percentage of the population. Hence, the Indian government addresses this issue through (1) drug price control mechanisms (2) provision of drugs in government healthcare and (3) selling generic drugs through retail outlets set up in government health-care. N. Lalitha also discusses the Indian pharmaceutical industry's R&D efforts, which since the mid 1990s have been oriented toward improving the standards of production to comply with international standards and to arrive at non-infringing processes to enter the regulated markets. The chapter also provides evidence of instances where India has effectively utilized the flexibilities included in the amendments made to the Indian Patent Act, particularly the provisions designed to ensure access to generic drugs and minimize patents on non-deserving incremental innovations.

Mariko Watanabe and Luwen Shi examine the demand for and supply of medicines in China in an institutional framework. They analyze the challenges presented by China's growing demand for healthcare services – and, moreover, drugs – in the context of changes to the country's patent system and health regulatory regime. The authors focus on the effects that the country's newly introduced patent system, system of drug licensing, and preferential pricing policies linked to the structure of hospitals, have had on firms' strategies and, subsequently, the rates of innovation and prices of drugs. While local pharmaceutical innovation in China has increased remarkably, Watanabe and Shi indicate that drug prices remain high, and beyond the coverage of medical insurance plans. The authors thus point to the challenge facing the Chinese government of settling upon a financially sound strategy for expanding access to healthcare services.

Samira Guennif analyzes access to essential medicines in Thailand. Like other authors in this volume, Guennif also focuses on the interface between patent policies and broader health regulatory policies. The Thai case shows that patents as well as standards aimed at improving the efficiency, safety and quality of drugs influence the development of national industrial capabilities in the pharmaceutical sector and, relatedly, the accessibility of essential drugs.

Padmashree Gehl Sampath analyzes pharmaceutical innovation in Bangladesh. As a least developed country Bangladesh has until 2016 to enter into full compliance with TRIPS in the area of pharmaceuticals, and Gehl Sampath considers the possibilities for Bangladesh emerging as a new source of generic medicines in the new international environment. Can Bangladesh's pharmaceutical sector gradually evolve to provide high-quality, low-cost alternatives to important patented drugs to other developing and least developed countries in the short or mid-term? To address these questions Sampath analyzes the strengths and weaknesses of Bangladesh's pharmaceutical sector, capacities for innovation, and the current patent landscape.

REFERENCES

Amin, Tahir. 2011. "Re-Visiting the Patents and Access to Medicines Dichotomy: An Evaluation of TRIPS Implementation and Public Health Safeguards in Developing Countries." In Obijiofor Aginam, John Harrington and Peter K. Yu, eds, *Global Governance of HIV/AIDS: Intellectual Property and Access to Essential Medicines*. Cheltenham, UK and Northampton, MA, USA: Edward Elgar.

Archibugi, Daniele and Andrea Filipetti. 2010. "The Globalization of Intellectual Property Rights: Four Learned Lessons and Four Theses." *Global Policy* 1, no. 2 (May): 137–149.

Arora, Ashish, Andrea Fosfuri and Alfonso Gambardella. 2005. "Markets for Technology, Intellectual Property Rights, and Development." In Keith E. Maskus and Jerome H. Reichman, eds, *International Public Goods and Transfer of Technology Under a Globalized Intellectual Property Regime*. New York: Cambridge University Press.

Barnett, Tony, and Alan Whiteside. 2006. *AIDS in the Twenty-First Century: Disease and Globalization*. 2nd edition. Basingstoke: Palgrave.

Basheer, Shamnad. 2005. "Limiting the Patentability of Pharmaceutical Inventions and Micro-Organisims: A TRIPS Compatibility Review." IPI Working Paper.

Bonnel R. 2000. "HIV/AIDS and Economic Growth: A Global Perspective". *South African Journal of Economics*, 68, no. 5.

Braithwaite, John and Peter Drahos. 2000. *Global Business Regulation*. New York: Cambridge University Press.

Cimoli, Mario, João Carlos Ferraz and Annalisa Primi. 2005. "Science and Technology Policies in Open Economies: The Case of Latin America and the Caribbean." Serie de Desarrollo Productivo y Empresarial, ECLAC-UN, Santiago, Chile.

CIPR. 2002. *Integrating Intellectual Property Rights and Development Policy*. London: Commission on Intellectual Property Rights.

Coriat, Benjamin, ed. 2008. *The Political Economy of HIV/AIDS in Developing Countries: TRIPS, Public Health Systems and Free Access*. Cheltenham, UK and Northampton, MA, USA: Edward Elgar.

Correa, Carlos. 2000. *Intellectual Property Rights, the WTO and Developing Countries: The TRIPS Agreement and Policy Options*. London and New York: Zed Books.

Correa, Carlos. 2002. "Protection of Data Submitted for the Registration of Pharmaceuticals: Implementing the Standards of the Trips Agreement." Geneva: Southcentre. Available at www.southcentre.org/publications/protection/protection.pdf.

Correa, Carlos. 2005a. "Can the TRIPS Agreement Foster Technology Transfer to Developing Countries?" In Keith E. Maskus and Jerome H. Reichman, eds, *International Public Goods and Transfer of Technology Under a Globalized Intellectual Property Regime*. New York: Cambridge University Press.

Correa, Carlos. 2005b. "The TRIPS Agreement and Transfer of Technology." In Kevin Gallagher, ed., *Putting Development First: The Importance of Policy Space in the WTO and IFIs*. New York: Zed Books.

Correa, Carlos. 2007. "Guidelines for the Examination of Pharmaceutical Patents: Developing a Public Health Perspective." WHO-ICTSD-UNCTAD Working

Paper. Available at: http://www.iprsonline.org/resources/docs/Correa_ Patentability%20Guidelines.pdf.

Dixon S., S. MacDonald and J. Roberts. 2002. "AIDS and Economic Growth in Africa: A Panel Data Analysis". *Journal of International Development*, 13, 411–426.

Dutfield, Graham. 2003. *Intellectual Property Rights and the Life Science Industries: A Twentieth Century History*. Dartmouth: Ashgate.

Falvey R. and N. Foster. 2005. *Intellectual Property Rights, Economic Growth and Technology Transfer*. Vienna: United Nations Industrial Development Organization.

Guzmán, Alenka, and Horensia Gomez. 2008. "Technological Gaps and Converging Processes Between Emerging and Industrialized Countries in Bio-Pharmaceutical Industry." Presented at the GLOBELICS 6th International Conference 2008, 22–24 September, Mexico City, Mexico.

Harrison, Christopher Scott. 2004. *The Politics of the International Pricing of Prescription Drugs*. Westport, CT: Praeger Publishers.

Ito, Banri, and Tatsufumi Yamagata. 2005. "Who Develops Innovations in Medicine for the Poor? Trends in Patent Applications Related to Medicines for HIV/AIDS, Tuberculosis, Malaria and Neglected Diseases." Discussion Paper No. 24, Institute of Developing Economies, April.

Kortum, Samuel. 2005. "TRIPS and Technology Transfer: Evidence from Patent Data." In Keith E. Maskus and Jerome H. Reichman, eds, *International Public Goods and Transfer of Technology Under a Globalized Intellectual Property Regime*. New York: Cambridge University Press.

Landau, R., B. Achilladelis and A. Scriabine. 1999. *Pharmaceutical Innovation*. Philadelphia: Chemical Heritage Press.

Lanjouw J.O. 2001. "A Patent Policy Proposal for Global Diseases." The Brookings Institution. Available at: http://www.brookings.edu/papers/2001/0611develop-ment_lanjouw.aspx.

Lerner. Josh. 1999. "150 Years of Patent Protection." Unpublished Working Paper, Harvard University.

Lundvall, B.A. 1992. National Systems of Innovation: Towards a Theory of Innovation and Interactive Learning. London: Pinter.

Malerba, F. and S. Manil. 2009. *Sectoral Systems of Innovation and Production in Developing Countries*. Cheltenham, UK and Northampton, MA, USA: Edward Elgar.

Maskus K.E. 2004. *Encouraging International Technology Transfer, UNCTAD-ICTSD Project on IPRs and Sustainable Development*. Issue Paper no. 7, May.

Maskus, Keith E., Kamal Saggi and Thitima Puttitanun. 2005. "Patent Rights and International Technology Transfer Through Direct Investment and Licensing." In Keith E. Maskus and Jerome H. Reichman, eds, *International Public Goods and Transfer of Technology Under a Globalized Intellectual Property Regime*. New York: Cambridge University Press.

Matthews, Duncan. 2002. *Globalising Intellectual Property Rights: The TRIPs Agreement*. London: Routledge.

Matthews, Duncan. 2006. "From the August 30, 2003 WTO Decision to the December 6, 2005 Agreement on an Amendment to TRIPS: Improving Access to Medicines in Developing Countries?" *Intellectual Property Quarterly* 10, No. 1, 91–130.

May, Christopher, and Susan K. Sell. 2005. *Intellectual Property Rights: A Critical History*. Boulder: Lynne Rienner.
Mazzoleni, Roberto and Richard R. Nelson. 1998. "Economic Theories about the Benefits and Costs of Patents." *Journal of Economic Issues* 32, No. 4 (December), 1031–1052.
Moatti J.P., B. Coriat, Y. Barnett, Y. Souteyrand, J. Dumoulin and P.Y. Flori, eds, 2003. *Economics of Aids and Access to HIV/AIDS Care in Developing Countries: Issues and Challenges*. ANRS, Collection Sciences Sociales et Sida.
Morel, Carlos. 2003. "Neglected Diseases: Under-funded Research and Inadequate Health Interventions: Can we Change this Reality?" EMBO reports 4, Special Issue 6, S35–S38.
MSF. 2001. "Fatal Imbalance: The Crisis in Research and Development for Drugs for Neglected Diseases." Available at: www.msfaccess.org.
Musungu, Sisule and Cecilia Oh. 2006. "The Use of Flexibilities in TRIPS by Developing Countries: Can they Promote Access to Medicines?" Geneva: South Centre and WHO.
Nelson, Richard R. 1993. *National Systems of Innovation: A Comparative Study*. Oxford: Oxford University Press.
Nelson, Richard R. 2008. "What Enables Rapid Economic Progress: What Are the Needed Institutions." Research Policy 37, No. 1 (February), 1–11.
Odagiri, Hiroyuki, Akira Goto, Atsushi Sunami and Richard R. Nelson, eds, 2010. *Intellectual Property Rights, Development, and Catch Up: An International Comparative Study*. Oxford: Oxford University Press.
Reichman, Jerome. 2009. "Rethinking the Role of Clinical Trial Data in International Intellectual Property Law: The Case for a Public Goods Approach." *Marquette Intellectual Property Law Review* 13, 1–68.
Sell, Susan K. 2003. *Private Power, Public Law: The Globalization of Intellectual Property Rights*. London: Cambridge University Press.
Shadlen, Kenneth C. 2004. "Challenges to Treatment: The Price–Infrastructure Trap and Access to Medicines." *Journal of International Development* 16, No. 8 (December), 1169–1180.
Shadlen, Kenneth C. 2011. "The Political Contradictions of Incremental Innovation: Lessons from Pharmaceutical Patent Examination in Brazil." *Politics & Society* 39, No. 2 (June), 143–174.
Shadlen, Kenneth C. forthcoming. "Is AIDS Treatment Sustainable?" In Obijiofor Aginam, John Harrington and Peter K. Yu, eds, *Global Governance of HIV/AIDS: Intellectual Property and Access to Essential Medicines*. Cheltenham, UK and Northampton, MA, USA: Edward Elgar.
UNAIDS. 2008. *Report on the Global AIDS Epidemic 2008*. Available at www.unaids.org (last visited July 2009).
UNCTAD-ICTSD. 2005. *Resource Book on TRIPS and Development: An Authoritative and Practical Guide to the TRIPS Agreement*. New York: Cambridge University Press. Available at http://www.iprsonline.org/unctadictsd/ResourceBookIndex.htm.
UNDP. 2003. *Making Global Trade Work for People*. London: Earthscan.
Watal, Jayashree. 1999. "Implementing the TRIPS Agreement on Patents: Optimal Legislative Strategies for Developing Countries." In Owen Lippert, ed., *Competitive Strategies for the Protection of Intellectual Property*. Vancouver: The Fraser Institute.

World Health Organization. 2004. The *World Medicines Situation*. Geneva: World Health Organization.

World Health Organization. 2007. *World Health Statistics 2007*. Geneva: World Health Organization.

World Health Organization. 2008a. *The Global Burden of Disease, 2004 Update*. Available at www.who.org, (last visited July 2009).

World Health Organization. 2008b. *World Malaria Report 2008*. Available at www.who.org, (last visited July 2009).

World Trade Organization. 2001. "Doha Declaration on the TRIPS Agreement and Public Health." WT/MIN(01)/DEC/W/2. Available at www.wto.org/english/thewto_e/minist_e/min01_e/mindecl_trips_e.htm, 2001.

World Trade Organization. 2003a. "Implementation of Paragraph 6 of the Doha Declaration on the TRIPS Agreement and Public Health: Decision of the General Council of 30 August 2003." WT/L/540. Available at http://www.wto.org/english/tratop_e/trips_e/implem_para6_e.htm.

World Trade Organization. 2003b. "The General Council Chairperson's Statement." Available at http://www.wto.org/english/ news_e/news03_e/trips_stat_28aug03_e.htm.

2. Pharmaceutical production and access to essential medicines in South Africa

Heinz Klug

Access to affordable essential medicines has become a central public policy issue in post-apartheid South Africa, particularly in the context of the country's HIV/AIDS pandemic. While it is clearly true that drug prices are not the only issue limiting access to essential medicines, the cost of medicines remains a central concern because unlike the broader structural goal of upgrading the health care system or more immediate concern to monitor treatment adherence among HIV/AIDS patients, there are just no substitutes or alternatives to the provision of these particular drugs. To this extent the cost of the medicines is in fact the "inelastic" part of the essential medicines equation. This is particularly the case in South Africa which is not a significant producer of pharmaceutical products and does not produce over 90 percent of the active ingredients of medicines. Lacking the capacity to credibly threaten to issue compulsory licenses and if necessary reverse-engineer patented drugs, as have Brazil and Thailand, South Africa's bargaining power is limited to a moral claim that access to essential medicines is a constitutional and humanitarian necessity to address the severe disease burden in the region, including HIV/AIDS, TB, malaria and other diseases.

However, in response to both market and public incentives, from the government's 2003 decision to provide antiretroviral treatment in the public sector to the United States government's program to fund access to antiretroviral medicines in Africa (PEPFAR), a significant generic medicines industry has emerged in South Africa since the late 1990s. While this industry remains dependent on the importation of active ingredients as well as licensing from the global pharmaceutical industry, there are hopes that this development might provide a sustainable source of supply of affordable medicines to address the continuing health crisis in South Africa and the region. This emerging pharmaceutical industry is however faced with competing public policy objectives that have shaped the industry's restructuring since the advent of democracy in South Africa. On the one hand, the government has been concerned to obtain a supply of drugs for the public health system at the lowest possible cost, whether from local or international sources, while on the other hand, there has been some support for the creation of a domestic pharmaceutical industry. Even if these goals were compatible, the task of building local pharmaceutical manufacturing capacity is subject to other conflicting priorities such as the push to strengthen intellectual property laws as a means to increase confidence among both international and domestic investors in the context of the post-TRIPS global trade and intellectual property regime. In addition, government policies to promote local employment and black economic empowerment, while not directly aimed at pharmaceutical production, have significant implications for policy formulation and decision-making affecting the industry.

Domestically, the supply and pricing of medicines in the public and private health sectors has been a major source of contention in post-apartheid South Africa and has closely tracked the broader conflict over health reform. Committed to improving public health, the government has adopted new legislation to govern the provision of health care (National Health Act, 2003), to regulate health insurance (Medical Schemes Act, 1998) and new law (Medicines and Related Substances Control Amendment Act,1997) and regulations to regulate medicine pricing (Regulations Relating to a Transparent Pricing System for Medicines and Scheduled Substances, 2004). These changes are geared to simultaneously expand access to health care and reduce costs as well as narrowing the gap in quality between the now overburdened public health system and the very high quality private health sector. In the case of medicines this means that manufacturers are free to set their own prices, but the 1997 amendment to the Medicines Act introduced three mechanisms to ensure greater transparency in the setting of prices. First, the Act placed restrictions on the use of incentives – such as discounts and rebates – which the drug companies had historically used to promote their products among doctors and other dispensers of medicines. Second, the legislation authorized the Minister of Health to establish a pricing committee to advise the minister on pricing. Third, pricing regulations promulgated in April 2004 implemented the idea of a single exit price, requiring manufacturers to sell their products for a single price to anyone, except the state. Subsequent regulations consolidated this new pricing regime by creating a system of international benchmarking to ensure that the manufacturer's prices are not vastly different to prices in comparable countries where these medicines are sold.

Since 1997 these legal changes have been consistently challenged. On the one hand, challenges were brought that had direct implications for local production, while on the other hand the most contentious legislation was that which directly addressed pricing but focused on the distribution chain rather than on production. While the pricing regulations give the Director-General of Health the power to investigate whether the price set by the manufacturer was reasonable, this is a fairly limited authority and the most consequential powers involve the ability to regulate wholesaler, distributor and dispensing fees of pharmacists and dispensing doctors. It was this latter power to set the level of dispensing fees for pharmacists that became the focus of legal attack. Although the High Court upheld the regulations, on appeal the regulations were declared unconstitutional by the Supreme Court of Appeal (SCA) which argued that the fees set were inadequate to protect the economic interests of dispensers and thus threatened access to medicines (*Minister of Health NO v New Clicks South Africa (Pty) Ltd*, 2005). When the Constitutional Court ruled on the case in September 2005 it reversed the decision of the SCA and upheld the government's authority to regulate medicine prices. However, while the Constitutional Court accepted the validity of the regulatory structure and the idea of a single exit price, it did not find the dispensing fee "appropriate" and required the pricing committee to accept further submissions and to reconsider an appropriate fee so as to ensure "that the right to health care is not prejudiced by driving . . . pharmacies out of the market" (*Minister of Health NO v New Clicks South Africa (Pty) Ltd (Treatment Action Campaign and Another as Amici Curiae)*, 2006, para 19).

Despite dramatic change in the regulatory environment producers of medicines are today allowed to set a comparable "international" price for their products in the private market in South Africa. But the structure of the local market, where the state remains the most important buyer in terms of volume, has important implications for local production. At the same time, the process of centralization that has characterized the restructuring of the global pharmaceutical industry, as well as the globalization of intellectual property rules, also affects the ability of local producers to engage in higher levels of production, particularly the production of active ingredients. As a result the question of pharmaceutical production and access to medicines in South Africa is less an issue of relative comparative advantage and more a problem of local capacity to challenge either the multinational pharmaceutical corporations or the system of global patent and trade rules. To understand this tension between production and access to medicines in South Africa this chapter will first provide a brief history of pharmaceutical production in the country and then explore the changing regulatory system as well as the legal and political responses to these changes that were introduced by the first democratic government. Finally, the chapter will describe the relationship between the structure of South

Africa's pharmaceutical market and its capacity to locally produce afford-able medicines as a way to evaluate ongoing policy debates over access to essential medicines and local production.

THE HISTORY OF PHARMACEUTICAL PRODUCTION IN SOUTH AFRICA

The history of modern pharmaceutical production in South Africa is intimately linked to the internationalization of the global pharmaceutical industry through the twentieth century. A number of concerns shaped the early globalization of pharmaceutical production, especially the bureau-cratic and regulatory frameworks within which the supply of medicines was embedded. In developing their multinational strategies pharmaceutical companies had to take into consideration "the structure and operation of national health systems, the nature of government product registration processes, formal and informal demands for local self-sufficiency in speci-fied products, and countless other national pressures" (Davenport-Hines and Slinn, hereinafter D-H&S, 1992: 226) in different countries. In the case of South Africa most of the pharmaceutical companies active in the country in the first half of the twentieth century simply employed distri-bution agents who "were responsible for the actual physical distribution, storage and invoicing of goods" (id.: 317). By the end of the 1950s however there were about eighty companies competing in South Africa's "rela-tively small ethical market" (id.: 315) (after the era of "patent medicines" pharmaceutical companies referred to their own products as ethical drugs, since they were only made available by doctor's prescription).

While 70 percent of the medicines were imported, 32 of these compa-nies "were South African subsidiaries of foreign multinationals . . . while thirty-three foreign companies were locally represented by agencies or distributors" (D-H&S, 1992: 315–16). Of the sixteen leading producers in the country, "fourteen manufactured or processed their products under licence or patent right agreements" and "65 per cent of the raw material used was imported" (id.: 316). Still the total market for antibiotics limited the options for local primary production since only if the producer could be "assured of securing all business" would it be possible to justify "the smallest possible economic fermentation operation" (id.: 318). Economies of scale are an essential factor in the decision to initiate local production. Historically, the size of the medicines market in South Africa has been constricted by cultural, political and economic factors, from the challenge of alternate or herbal medicines prevalent in the system of indigenous medicine, to apartheid's economic impact on the purchasing capacity of most South Africans, and on to the limited integration of the regional economy that could have provided the economies of scale necessary to sustain local production.

While there were two main factors driving the allocation of global production – the industry's own prerogatives and local opportunities – the establishment of local production in South Africa was affected by a number of additional considerations. If on the one hand, the character of internationalization was shaped by the internal concerns of the industry, including research, marketing, economies of scale and quality control (D-H&S, 1992: 226) as well as its preference to centralize primary production and basic research, on the other hand, the introduction of "tariff protectionism" by the post-1948 Nationalist apartheid government forced foreign businesses "to invest in more local production" (id.: 335). In such circumstances the pharmaceutical companies tended to adopt the basic model established by Bayer's acquisition of the Hudson River Aniline and Color Company of Albany as its American subsidiary in New York in 1903, "to whom it supplied intermediates for the manufacture of phenacetin and aspirin" (Redwood, 1988: 28). This involved keeping primary production of the active ingredients highly centralized while exporting secondary production – tableting or filling of capsules – to the host nations if economic or political advantage could be obtained (D-H&S, 1992: 226). Thus despite pressure to increase local productive capacity the global pharmaceutical industry sought to retain centralized control over primary production and to outsource only secondary production or even more limited packaging and marketing activities.

The experience of the British multinational Glaxo, in South Africa in this period, exemplifies the issues framing the introduction of local pharmaceutical production. Considering whether to establish local production Glaxo approached the South African New Industries Committee and presented three alternatives: (1) erection of a "complete primary fermentation factory" in exchange for a monopoly on government orders; (2) to work up finished penicillin from the imported intermediate X cyclohexylamine salt; or (3) to do secondary sterile packing of "bulk imported finished antibiotics into dosage forms, with secondary production of suspensions, tablets, ointments and other formulations" using local packaging materials (D-H&S, 1992: 319–20). While the first option would have created local productive capacity Glaxo would only do so if guaranteed bulk orders that would secure its economies of scale. The second option introduced limited productive capacity but required a far lower investment and less need for a guaranteed bulk market. The third option provided even less productive capacity. The government was thus given the choice of either working towards self-sufficiency in antibiotics by giving Glaxo a monopoly in public sector procurement or to continue to take advantage of "the prevailing system of cut-throat open tendering" (id.: 319).

When the government refused to guarantee a monopoly Glaxo opted for the third option and opened a factory at Wadeville, Germiston, in 1954. Equipping the factory at Wadeville posed interesting problems as the Witwatersrand is at an altitude of around 6000 feet above sea level, experiences extremely low humidity in the winter and its distance from Glaxo's plants in the United Kingdom meant that the bulk intermediates had to be transported a long distance by ship and then overland by rail. Despite an investment of £60,000 when the British-made incubator in the Sterility Testing Laboratory was first put into operation "it steadfastly refused to reach 37 degrees centigrade" as a result of the altitude and it was only after "a special capsule for the incubator was air-freighted out from Britain that the factory finally began production" (D-H&S, 1992: 323). In the case of the bulk streptomycin which arrived in large aluminum canisters after twelve days at sea and three by rail, the static charge that had developed meant that when "the canister was attached to the filling machine in the Sterile Area the streptomycin dropped into the vial and immediately flew back up into the canister" (id.). While the company had decided not to engage in primary production "the opening of the first factory in Africa south of the Equator equipped to handle sterile filling and processing of antibiotics received considerable publicity" (id.).

Despite this early introduction of limited productive capacity, the pattern of pharmaceutical provision in South Africa remained largely unchanged over the next two decades. Addressing the Economic Society of South Africa in 1978 Professor W.F.J. Steenkamp, Chairman of the 1978 Commission of Enquiry into the Pharmaceutical Industry in South Africa noted that in 1975 foreign-owned companies "accounted for 85.8 per cent of the market for prescription medicines" (Steenkamp, 1979: 76) and that the country produced "only 13 per cent of the required active ingredients" (id.: 87) and even then "a large portion of the small number of active ingredients produced here [are] . . . manufactured from imported fine chemicals" (id.). The Steenkamp Commission defined five distinct stages in the development of a domestic pharmaceutical industry: "(a) importation of final products already packaged; (b) the packaging of final products imported in bulk; (c) the compounding of final products from imported final raw materials, known as active and inactive ingredients; (d) the production of final raw materials either from imported intermediates or local materials or both; and (e) the manufacture of new or improved medical preparations on the basis of local research and development" (Report of the Commission of Enquiry into the Pharmaceutical Industry, January 1978, 38/1978 paras 55–59). Applying this categorization the Commission concluded that South Africa in the mid-1970s remained highly dependent on international sources of modern medicines and that the South African pharmaceutical industry was "still in the third, assembling stage" (id.: para. 81ff).

With the Soweto uprisings in 1976 and growing international concern at South Africa's apartheid policies, the possibility of attracting more international investment and productive capacity only declined. While the apartheid structure of the health system and the abject poverty of the vast majority of South Africans limited the private market for modern medicines, the growth of the international anti-apartheid movement, including consumer boycotts and demands on multinational companies to divest their investments from South Africa, frustrated attempts by the regime to encourage the local production of medicines. The imposition of repeated states of emergency from the mid-1980s and the advent of economic sanctions, including limits on new foreign investment in the 1986 Anti-Apartheid Act passed by the US Congress, precluded the emergence of a local industry since any local production would remain dependent on the importation of the active ingredients. Thus, by the dawn of democracy in 1994 the pharmaceutical industry had made no further progress toward the development of local productive capacity.

THE EVOLUTION OF A REGULATORY ENVIRONMENT SINCE 1994

Despite the growth in the number of pharmaceutical companies and products in the local market, there was no regulation of pharmaceutical products or manufacturing in South Africa until nearly two-thirds of the way through the twentieth century. The adoption of the Medicines and Related Substances Control Act 101 of 1965 saw the establishment of a Medicines Control Council (MCC) and the introduction of rules requiring manufacturers to provide information on the safety and effectiveness of their medicines. Today the introduction and provision of pharmaceuticals in South Africa is governed by a complex set of laws that regulate not only the safety and effectiveness of medicines but also the property rights of the holders of proprietary products (under the Patents Act 57 of 1978), as well as regulations to ensure both competition in the market place (Competition Act 89 of 1998) and the management of public procurement (Public Finance Management Act 1 of 1999) which still accounts for the vast bulk of prescription medicines consumed in the country. Furthermore, this domestic legal framework is shaped, to an important degree, by the system of intellectual property laws adopted as part of the international trade regime after 1994. South Africa's post-apartheid legal framework for the regulation of pharmaceuticals is also the product of a number of conflicting goals including the attempt by Nelson Mandela's government to increase access to medicines, which quickly ran into opposition from the global pharmaceutical industry, and subsequent campaigns by social movements in South Africa to both challenge and use the law to ensure access to essential medicines in the face of a terrible HIV/AIDS pandemic.

All medicines in the South African market must be registered by the Medicines Control Council (MCC) which is a statutory body made up of up to 24 part-time appointees who are experts in pharmacology, pharmaceutical chemistry, pharmaceutics and the clinical management of disease (both human and animal diseases). The MCC is supported by a full-time secretariat which is located in the National Department of Health and while its members are not part of the civil service it is organized as a "cluster" known as the Medicines Regulatory Affairs (MRA) cluster (Hassim et al., 2007: 420). The chief director of the MRA cluster is also the Registrar of Medicines responsible for keeping a register of all medicines that may be legally sold in the country. The approximately 20,000 medicines registered are classified into nine categories – schedules 0–8 – which determine the extent of regulation each medicine is subject to, including who may prescribe, who may sell, and who may purchase the particular medicine. Apart from new applications – which may take over two years to process – the MCC is considering bringing the approximately 18,000 additional complementary medicines, such as indigenous or traditional herbal remedies and modern dietary supplements, available in the market "under effective regulatory control" (id.: 424).

The MCC, created after the passage of the 1965 Medicines Act, remained initially unchanged in the new South Africa but came under increasing pressure both as drug policy changed and the question of complementary medicines – from vitamin supplements to traditional herbal medicines – came to the fore. The replacement of the old leadership in 1998 provided a new opportunity but also additional challenges. First Helen Rees and then Precious Matsoso took the helm and the MCC suspended the clinical trials of Virodene, a product that was supposed to be a cure for HIV/AIDS and had the support of President Mbeki's government. At the same time the MCC attempted to address the issue of complementary medicines and in 2002 published an official Government Notice calling for the registration of these products, resulting in thousands of applications that flooded and overwhelmed the review process. At a briefing to the parliamentary portfolio committee on health in 2008 the newly appointed Registrar for Medicines, Mandisa Hela, revealed that the backlog in the number of applications for registration that had been received but not completed each year had increased from 28 percent in 2003 to a colossal 98 percent in 2007. She explained that the number of evaluators and committee members had not changed since the 1960s and the MCC continued to rely on part-timers (see Thom, 2010). Changes to the Medicines Act, including the legal framework for a completely new regulatory body – to be named the South African Health Products Regulatory Authority (SAHPRA) – and the introduction of regulations to separate the registration of complementary and alternative medicines from scientific medicines, led Stavros Nicolaou, Senior Executive of Aspen Pharmacare to note that "the Department of Health has commenced a process aimed at clearing the Medicines Control Council backlog and improving approval timelines. Whilst these are early days, initial progress with the process is encouraging and we look forward to completion of the process."

While normal registration costs approximately US$1,800 per product and can take over two years, a fast track process is available at double the cost and guarantees a response from the MCC within nine months. The introduction of the idea of an essential drugs list and its implementation in 2003 provided for an expedited process of registration of these drugs; however it is doubtful whether the MCC, with its part-time appointees, who meet once every six weeks to review applications that have been studied by expert committees, has the capacity to implement an effective "fast-track" process (see Hassim et al., 2007: 458). The fast-track process does hold the potential for a quicker registration of essential drugs by providing for an abbreviated submission in cases where the product "has already been registered by another regulatory authority trusted by the MCC" (id.: 425). Section 21 of the Medicines Act also provides for special approval to import or purchase an unregistered medicine within specific categories; however, such approval applies only to individual users for a limited time period. In addition, individuals – either residents or visitors – are allowed to enter the country with up to a month's supply of an unregistered medicine for their personal use, so long as they have proof that it was legitimately prescribed (id.: 427).

The embrace of generic medicines and the adoption of an essential drugs list also raised the potential for reducing some of the regulatory and cost barriers to medicines in the South African market. Not only has the legislature provided for a quicker registration process for essential medicines but it also adopted a 2003 Bolar-type amendment to the Patents Act which allows companies to register generic forms of patented medicines so that they may enter the market as soon as the patent expires. Since most new medicines are patented in South Africa the introduction of a Bolar exception, permitting generic producers to use the patented drugs to prepare for the production of the drug as soon as the patent period expires, is an important step towards encouraging the emergence of a local generic industry. At the same time the embrace of generic medicines has produced its own unintended consequences in the regulatory process. First, there has been the introduction of many duplicate "generic" applications as companies have adopted differential pricing strategies, offering the same product under different names. Second, according to a 2008 report produced by Professor Ronald Green-Thompson, an advisor to the then Minister of Health, the ratio of new clinical entity (NCE) applications to generic applications went from 16:508 in 2003 to 22:765 in 2007 (see Report of the Ministerial Task Team, 2008: 23–24). The resulting delay in registrations of new entities led to complaints from HIV/AIDS groups who argued that the delay in the registration of new ARVs was unconscionable.

Apart from the regulatory process there have been demands for the government to use its other statutory powers to increase access to essential medicines. Section 56 of the Patents Act, for example, allows for the issuing of compulsory licenses in cases of patent abuse, and section 78 empowers the Minster of Trade and Industry to acquire a patent on behalf of the state with agreement of the patent holder, but there has been little evidence to suggest that the government has been willing to effectively use these mechanisms to increase access to essential medicines. Instead, social movement actors and public interest lawyers have used the threat of litigation under section 56 of the Patents Act to obtain voluntary licenses in the case of Boehringer Ingelheim (see Hassim et al., 2007: 460) and have actively challenged the brand companies under South Africa's newly invigorated competition law regime (see *Hazel Tau v GlaxoSmithKline*, complaint to the Competition Commission 2002). While a subsequent challenge, claiming that "private companies providing essential laboratory services" were acting as a cartel failed (Hassim et al., 2007: 465), attempts by brand companies to use copyright law to argue that the shape and color of pills was protected by copyright (*Beecham Group v Triomed*, 2003) or that the wording of package inserts was protected (*Biotech Laboratories (Pty) Ltd v Beecham Group*, 2002) have also failed.

RESPONSES TO REGULATORY REFORM POST-1994

When Mandela's government took power in 1994 the South African health care system still reflected the impact of apartheid. Although 80 percent of the population relied on the public health system for access to "modern" medical treatment and 60 to 70 percent of pharmaceuticals (by volume) were consumed in the public sector, the private sector accounted for 80 percent of the country's total expenditure on drugs (Department of Health, 1996: 3). In response to this situation the government adopted a new National Drugs Policy that incorporated the WHO's essential medicines program with the goal of reducing the cost of medicines. One year later, in 1997, the legislature amended the existing Medicines Act to allow for the parallel importation of medicines and compulsory licensing among other measures to implement this agenda. Although the new law was designed in part to fundamentally change the distribution practices of the pharmaceutical manufacturers – prohibiting, for example, industry employees from serving on the Medicines Control Board, and blocking manufacturers and wholesalers from providing bonuses, rebates or other incentives to doctors – the key feature of the Amendment was the "measures to ensure supply of more affordable medicines." These measures included empowering the Minister of Health "to prescribe conditions for the supply of more affordable medicines . . . so as to protect the health of the public . . . notwithstanding anything to the contrary in the Patents Act"; and to "prescribe the conditions [under] . . . which any medicine which is identical in composition, meets the same quality standard and is intended to have the same proprietary name as that of another medicine already registered in the Republic" may be made available. The effect of these provisions would have been to allow the parallel importation of medicines, generic substitution without the consent of the prescriber, and the issuing of compulsory licenses to allow for the importation or local manufacture of medicines without requiring the approval of the patent owner.

Although the new law passed the South African parliament over the objections of the pharmaceutical industry and the United States government, and was signed into law by President Nelson Mandela in December 1997, implementation of the Medicines Amendment Act was soon put on hold and when it was finally implemented in 2003 it would not be in its original form. Led by the Pharmaceutical Manufacturers Association of South Africa (PMA), 42 parties, including local companies, subsidiaries of transnational corporations and the multinational corporations themselves, challenged the constitutionality of the 1997 Act (PMA Case). They made a number of constitutional claims but argued most specifically that the Act's provisions – empowering the government to determine the extent to which rights granted under a patent in South Africa shall apply, and allowing the government to prescribe conditions for the supply of more affordable generic medicines – together deprived owners of intellectual property in the affected pharmaceutical products of their constitutionally protected property rights. The claimants proceeded to engage a number of major private law firms, and government attorneys soon found themselves completely snowed under with the volume of filings and alternative lines of attack (author's interview, 1999). Not only did the plaintiffs initiate the litigation with a request for an interim interdict preventing the law from being implemented, they soon followed with a series of claims in alternative fora – to the Public Protector and the Competition Board respectively – challenging government statements about the cost of drugs and calling for an inquiry into an alleged anti-competitive attempt by pharmaceutical distributors to create a joint company to engage in the parallel importation allowed under the Act. The scale of this legal assault, facilitated by the financial resources of the multi-national corporations involved, was unique in the South African legal context.

In a notice of motion filed in the High Court of South Africa (Transvaal Provincial Division) in Pretoria on February 18, 1998, the plaintiffs articulated an extraordinary array of claims against the Act's validity. In addition to asserting that the Act violated their patent rights as well as South Africa's legally incorporated international obligations under the International Agreement on Trade Related Aspects of Intellectual Property Rights (TRIPS), the plaintiffs claimed that the powers granted the Minister of Health amounted to an unconstitutional delegation of legislative authority to the executive, because it failed to set out policy considerations or guidelines that would limit the Minister's power and instead merely empowered the Minister to discriminate against local manufacturers in favor of imported medicines. Plaintiffs also charged that various sections of the Amendment were unconstitutional as they violated the basic values and principles governing public administration. At the same time M.T. Deeb, the Chief Executive Officer of the Pharmaceutical Manufacturers Association, argued in her founding affidavit that section 15C of the Act – which empowered the Minister to grant compulsory licenses and allowed for parallel imports – was in conflict with the TRIPS Agreement and she went so far as to claim that "Parliament ought not to have made a law which is in conflict with South Africa's international obligations" (Deeb, 1998a: para 10.2.5). In effect she inverted the traditional claim that equal and sovereign states are bound only by their own consent to international obligations and instead argued that the authority of the democratically elected legislature of South Africa should be limited by global rules.

While many countries provide for the direct incorporation of their international obligations into their domestic legal systems, South African law requires the legislature to specifically incorporate any obligations into domestic law through the passage of national legislation directly applying any new rules to the domestic legal system. In this regard South Africa is characterized as a "dualist" system, as is the United States in most circumstances, while many civil law countries are "monist" systems in which international obligations are automatically incorporated into domestic law. Neither of these national legal forms alters the fact that the country has either accepted or declined to accept specific international obligations which it owes to other states in the international system, but the legal consequences at the domestic level are quite different. In a monist system it might be possible to argue that the government must refrain from taking action which violates the state's international obligations but in a dualist system like South Africa local litigants may only claim a violation of South African law if they can point to local statutes that have incorporated the specific international rule they are asserting. If Parliament, as the national legislature, chooses to adopt legislation that is constitutionally permissible yet infringes upon international obligations embraced by the government in international agreements, Parliament cannot be legally challenged even if the resulting law is in fact in breach of international rules embraced by the executive branch of government. Thus it is possible for a domestic law to be perfectly valid even if it violates the state's international obligations. The outcome is that a country is liable to other states for being in violation of its obligations but may choose to remain in violation depending on its own judgment of its national interests and its willingness to accept the resulting international consequences, if any.

This linking of domestic constitutional claims with international trade issues continued when, in a supplementary affidavit to the plaintiffs' amended particulars of claim filed on July 23, 1998, Deeb argued that the United States Trade Representative's (USTR) placing of South Africa on that country's Special 301 Watch list "demonstrates that the provisions in the Amended Act which affect intellectual property are seen to be at least potentially in conflict with South Africa's international obligations and hence I submit that it cannot be regarded as being in the public interest as it may lead to the imposition of sanctions against this country and in fact may already have led to an undermining of investor confidence in South Africa" (Deeb, 1998b: para 20.6). Here the pharmaceutical corporations' legal strategy was able to tie into the efforts of the United States government which entered the debate over South Africa's policies and law from an early stage when the US trade representative wrote a letter to South Africa's UN representative in April 1997 querying South Africa's implementation of TRIPS and raising questions about compulsory licensing. While the Amendment Bill was still being considered by the legislature the US Embassy in Pretoria formally presented the US government's objections to Parliament while the US Ambassador to South Africa made frequent public and private statements against the legalization of parallel imports.

South Africa also became the target of direct bilateral pressure. Within two months of the law's adoption, the Pharmaceutical Research and

Manufacturers of America (PhRMA) requested the USTR to designate South Africa a priority country under section 301 of the US Trade Act 1974 because "South Africa has become a 'test case' for those who oppose the US government's long-standing commitment to improve the terms of protection for all forms of American intellectual property, including pharmaceutical patents" (Consumer Project on Technology, 1999). Bristol-Myers Squibb specifically complained about South Africa's decision to permit registration of a generic form of the cancer drug Paclitaxel (BMS brand name Taxol), an issue which the USTR took up directly during a WTO Trade Policy review a year later in Geneva. One month later, on May 1, 1998, the USTR put South Africa on the Special 301 Watch list. In June 1998, the White House announced that four items for which South Africa had requested preferential tariff treatment under the Generalized System of Preferences program would be put on hold until adequate progress was achieved in the protection of intellectual property rights in South Africa. At the end of October the US Congress passed an omnibus appropriations bill containing provisions cutting off US aid to the South African government pending a Department of State report outlining its efforts to "negotiate the repeal, suspension, or termination of section 15C of South Africa's Medicines and Related Substances Control Amendment Act No. 90 of 1997" (see Consumer Project on Technology, 1999).

United States pressure on the South African government increased when at the end of April 1999 the USTR scheduled an "out-of-cycle" review for South Africa under Special 301, arguing that South Africa's barriers to trade included: parallel imports, compulsory licensing, registration of generic forms of Taxol, and taking a leading role at the World Health Assembly (WHA). According to the USTR: "During the past year, South African representatives have led a faction of nations in the World Health Organization (WHO) in calling for a reduction in the level of protection provided for pharmaceuticals in TRIPS" (Consumer Project on Technology, 1999). Thus, from the perspective of the USTR the problem was not only the protection of patent rights in South Africa but also the position South Africa was taking in the international debate over TRIPS. From this perspective the South Africa/United States binational dispute in this period was fairly representative of the broader international struggle over the meaning of TRIPS, especially over the scope of, and exceptions to, internationally recognized intellectual property rights.

This globalized conflict over patent rights and access to medicines was muted by the Doha Declaration on TRIPS and Public Health agreed at the WTO's Doha ministerial conference on 14 November 2001 (WTO, 2001). Despite concerted opposition from multinational pharmaceutical corporations and a group of developed countries led by the USA, Switzerland,

and Japan, the 140 trade ministers gathered in Doha, Qatar, agreed that the TRIPS agreement "does not and should not prevent members from taking measures to protect public health . . . [and] that the agreement can and should be interpreted and implemented in a manner supportive of WTO members' rights to protect public health and, in particular, to promote access to medicines for all" (id.). Addressing what had been an intense debate within the TRIPS Council, the declaration specifically clarifies the right of members: to grant compulsory licenses; to determine what constitutes a national emergency or other circumstances of extreme urgency; and that each member is free to establish its own regime for the exhaustion of intellectual property rights. It also encourages developed countries to promote technology transfer to the least developed countries and extends the initial transition period for pharmaceutical products until 1 January 2016. Despite the active role of South African Minister of Trade Alec Erwin in achieving this compromise at Doha, the debate over access to medicines in South Africa would remain trapped in the conflict over AIDS denialism until at least 2003 (see Nattrass, 2007).

While the new National Drug Policy as well as the amendments to the Medicines Act were first held up by the legal and political challenges launched in 1997, efforts to implement these policies after regulations were finally issued in 2004 led to further delays as the decisions of the Pricing Committee were challenged before the courts. Effective implementation of these legislative changes thus only began in 2007, a decade after the passage of the original amendments to the 1965 Medicines Act. The MCC also suffered setbacks as it became embroiled in attempts to have supplements and complementary medicines as well as indigenous treatments registered, thus swamping the institution with thousands of applications and intense controversies about its inability to prevent various charlatans from claiming their products as cures for HIV/AIDS. Finally, with President Mbeki's resignation and the appointment of a new Minister of Health the MCC was able to begin a process of restructuring that has culminated in the appointment of new members, including former critics from civil society (see Appointment of Members of the Medicines Control Council, Government Notice 180, 12 March 2010).

THE PHARMACEUTICAL MARKET AND PRODUCTIVE CAPACITY

A key factor driving the debate over pharmaceutical production in South Africa remains the structure of supply and demand in which roughly 70 percent of demand by volume comes from the public sector while 70 percent of value derives from the sale of pharmaceutical products in the private sector. While the structure of the market is no longer defined by the formal racial divisions of apartheid, the division between public and private markets in health care and pharmaceutical sales reflects a class divide which in turn continues to have significant racial dimensions. Important too is the impact of government policy on reducing the price of medicines in both the public and private sectors, which has seen a growth in the production of generic medicines but not a growth in the value of the market, contributing to decisions by the multinational corporations to close factories and reduce their productive capacity in the country. While these decisions were driven as much by global developments in the pharmaceutical industry as opportunities in the local market, it is the demand in ANC resolutions and by some policy makers that government tenders be linked to the development of a local pharmaceutical industry, including even the possibility of creating a state owned pharmaceutical company, that links questions of market structure and productive capacity. At the same time, the very nature of pharmaceutical production – requiring skilled personnel, the refinement of fine chemicals and massive economies of scale to drive down costs – places constraints on the scope of interventions available to the South African government, even if it embraces the notion of a developmental state.

The Demand for Medicines

The demand for medicines in South Africa may be thought of in two distinct ways. First there is the traditional economic concept of demand which focuses on the marketplace and the economic value of the different sectors, public and private. Second, there is a human rights dimension which considers demand from a number of alternative perspectives including: need; the organized claims of social movements; and the imposition of legal duties through legislation or constitutional recognition. The demand-side of the pharmaceutical market in South Africa has been shaped by the interaction of these different factors. On the one hand, the retail cost of pharmaceutical products has been comparatively high and well out of the reach of the majority of South African consumers. On the other hand, the increasing need for medicines in the context of a high disease burden, social and political mobilization, as well as a state health system that still serves the bulk of the population, has driven the search for more affordable pharmaceuticals.

The pharmaceutical market in South Africa was valued at over US$2 billion in 2008 but is expected to grow to over US$3 billion by 2012 (Business Insights, 2010). Growth is premised on both a continuing health crisis and government policy changes, including: the decision to raise the CD4 count criteria, which determines when HIV-positive patients are treated with ARVs, from fewer than 200 to fewer than 350 cells per cubic millimeter, which will extend the provision of ARVs to nearly 80 percent of HIV+ individuals; the establishment of a national health insurance scheme that will provide greater access to medicines; and regulatory developments that are predicted to speed up product approvals, bringing more medicines into the market (id.). Today the public sector accounts for approximately 21 percent of consumption by value, over 80 percent of which is generic medicines while the private sector consumes about 79 percent by value of which 70 percent is prescription medicines, representing approximately 55 percent of the value of the market (see Maloney & Myburgh, 2007: 28–29). Of these private prescriptions, only 22 percent, or 12 percent by value, are generic medicines (id.:29–30). The private over-the-counter market represents a further 24 percent of the market by value (id.:30). Of even greater significance is that "around 75 percent of this demand is met by imports" (Kgara & Barsel, 2010: 50). The overall picture thus remains the same as before: the country remains dependent on imports, particularly for active ingredients, and the bulk of medicines are consumed in the public sector yet demand in the private sector determines the real value of the market.

It is however the social demand for medicines, and affordable medicines in particular, that has driven the public debate and policy change. While this aspect of demand may have had some initial success domestically with the government's victory in the PMA case and internationally with the adoption of the Doha Agreement by the WTO, neither of these developments produced a lasting resolution to the problem of access to affordable medicines. Domestically the continuing HIV/AIDS pandemic and government failure to address the crisis led to a new phase of legal activity initiated by the Treatment Action Campaign (TAC) in 2002 and given impetus by the consolidation of a new broad-based social movement including TAC branches and the People Living with AIDS organization, with support from the trade union movement and communist party. This phase of the struggle for affordable medicines in South Africa is defined by two distinct legal challenges with litigation focusing on both the demand and supply side of the equation. The first challenged the government to provide mothers and their new-born babies access to Nevirapine, an antiretroviral which, when administered to both mother and child during birth and shortly thereafter, more then halved the rate of mother-to-child transmission of HIV (*Minister of Health et al. v Treatment Action Campaign et al.*, 2002). Second, the TAC brought a complaint before the Competition Commission alleging that a number of the major pharmaceutical corporations had colluded in maintaining the high price of particular medicines (*Hazel Tau v GlaxoSmithKline*, 2002). The impact of these two initiatives was to dramatically alter the debate over access to antiretroviral treatment and to set the stage for a major reduction in the price of medicines.

In the Mother-to-Child-Transmission (MTCT) case, the Constitutional Court essentially upheld a high court decision requiring the government to provide mothers and new-borns in public health facilities access to Nevirapine. Relying on the constitutional guarantee of a right to the progressive realization of access to health care services, the Constitutional Court held that, under the circumstances in which the cost of the drug and the provision of appropriate testing and counseling to mothers was less burdensome then the failure to provide Nevirapine, the government had a constitutional duty to expand its program beyond the eighteen test sites the health authorities had already planned. In the second case, the TAC, pursuing its aim to lower drug prices and thus expand access to ARV treatment, launched a complaint with the newly constituted Competition Commission against two of the major global pharmaceutical corporations active in South Africa (GlaxoSmithKline [GSK] and Boehringer Ingelheim) accusing them of engaging in excessive pricing of medicines. After the Commission found that the companies had colluded to fix prices, the companies reached an out-of-court settlement with the government which included granting at least three generic pharmaceutical companies voluntary licenses on three major antiretrovirals, thus allowing more competition into the market and lowering the price of the drugs in the South African market (see AIDS Law Project and Treatment Action Campaign, 2003).

Despite these dramatic interventions and legal victories, the problem of access remained only partially solved. For the majority of South Africans, even the reduced price of drugs in the private market leaves most medicines unaffordable, and, until the government manages to establish a secure and sustainable public sector program, the majority of people in need of medicines will be denied access. The capacity of the government to meet these needs is in turn dependent on the supply of medicines.

The Supply of Medicines

In order to evaluate the stability of any policy or program to provide access to affordable essential medicines, it is important to briefly review the political pressures and sources of supply that have brought down the cost of these medicines over the last few years. First, it was the offer by Indian drug producer Cipla, in March 2001, to provide the first generation ARV drugs for $350 per patient per year to developing countries, a fraction of the going price in the developed country markets, that brought about the initial fall in prices (Médecins Sans Frontières (MSF), 2007). Although Brazil had already managed to reduce the price from $10,000 per patient to around $2,800 per patient within its own public health system, this was based on the government-controlled industry's capacity to reverse-engineer and manufacture the relevant drugs. Second, it was the response of the multinational drug companies to the accusations of activists and the bad publicity they received after they sued the South African government and named President Nelson Mandela as the first defendant, that led to offers by these companies to supply drugs to some developing countries at vastly reduced costs, and in some cases at no cost, for certain periods of time and for specified classes of poor patients. Third, the establishment of the Global Fund, and later President George W. Bush's President's Emergency Plan for AIDS Relief (PEPFAR) initiative, provided a source of funding for anti-AIDS programs, including the provision of essential medicines in the public sector. Fourth, the entry of the Gates and Clinton Foundations as both funders and as a source of political co-ordination of efforts aimed at the procurement of cheaper drugs, bolstered the longstanding efforts of non-government organizations such as Doctors Without Borders, James Love's Consumer Project on Technology, the Canadian HIV/AIDS Legal Network and the AIDS Law Project in South Africa, as well as various AIDS-specific activist organizations, such as ACT-UP in the US and the South African-based Treatment Action Campaign. Finally, the establishment in 2006 of UNITAID, initiated by the governments of Brazil, France and Norway, promised a long-term source of funding through a type of Tobin tax on international airline ticket sales and an international organization committed to pooling demand and using the resulting bargaining power to obtain medicines at reduced cost in the international market.

While these different initiatives and strategies have very different protagonists and modes of operation, the underlying premise of all these strategies is the continued existence of an adequate supply of the required medicines at affordable prices. Already there have been a number of incidents in which the supply of ARVs has been interrupted with obvious consequences for individual patients and possible drug resistance if patients are unable to maintain their treatment programs. In the case of the ARV retonivir, for example, there were five occasions in 2004 when drug companies in South Africa were unable to supply the drug (see Berger, 2005), in either pediatric doses or adult capsules, forcing patients to switch their medications and leading the South African government to briefly halt the rollout of their public sector program for children. These incidents and concern over the cost of second-line drugs, as well as the WHO's new treatment guidelines which suggest the use of more expensive drugs (see MSF, 2007), all raise questions about the stability and sustainability of the supply chain of affordable drugs. In order to understand the magnitude of this problem, it is important to note two facts: first, that under normal conditions the cost of a patented drug drops by only 20 percent when the first generic enters the market at the end of the patent term; and second, it is only when there are three or more generic companies competing to supply a particular drug that the cost falls to anywhere between 70–90 percent below the original price of the patented drug (Pile, 2005: 18).

Until 2005, this was not a dramatic problem because Indian drug producers were able to produce generic versions of these medicines, so long as they were able to come up with a process of production that had not been previously patented. As a result, Indian pharmaceutical companies have in recent years been producing approximately one-fifth of the world's generic drugs (Stokes, 2005: 1146–50). The implementation of the TRIPS Agreement in India since January 2005, which required the reintroduction of product patents into Indian law, now precludes the possibility that these companies will be able to produce generic versions of the next generation of ARVs, and henceforth the only way these companies will be able to enter the market to provide generic forms of any new drugs, will be as licensed producers, whether under voluntary or compulsory licenses (see Shadlen, 2007). In South Africa this has indeed been the trajectory as brand name companies have increasingly licensed local manufacturers to produce their products for the local and regional market. Most prominent of the generic companies receiving licenses is Aspen Pharmacare, whose stated aim as a company is to acquire patent-expired medicines from multinational drug firms, and which now controls 35 percent of South Africa's generic drug market (Pile, 2005: 18). While the turn to local licensing may have been made in the face of growing international pressure and after settling the case against them before South Africa's Competition Commission, a number of the brand name companies, including GlaxoSmithKline (GSK), have now licensed Aspen to locally manufacture their products. Aspen has, in turn, succeeded in having its newly constructed oral solid dosage (OSD) plant in the Eastern Cape region of South Africa approved by a number of regulatory bodies, including the local regulator, the Medicines Control Council, and the American Food & Drug Administration and the UK's Medical Health & Regulatory Authority (id.: 19). This placed the company in a position not only to win the South African State Tender in 2004, producing R3.4billion in ARV drugs over three years, but also to potentially win large international aid contracts from PEPFAR and the Global Fund (id.: 20).

While the granting of licenses to generic companies has definitely increased the supply of medicines to the South African market, the economies of scale that would make local production profitable while securing affordable prices remain dependent upon the public sector's purchasing power since the bulk of prescription medicines are still consumed in the government health system. It is this link, between the economies of scale needed to produce affordable medicines and the scale of the public sector, that has always made the process of public tendering so central to the production of pharmaceuticals in South Africa. The country's ARV tender, which is due to be re-authorized in 2010, is the largest in the world and is valued at approximately $20 million. The distribution of this tender has profound effects on the local pharmaceutical industry and any defect in the process is subject to challenge. In a recent unreported case decided by Judge Prinsloo of the High Court of South Africa in Pretoria the court found that the June 2008 to May 2010 tender to supply ARV drugs was validly subject to attack as "there was a lack of procedural fairness in the process" (*Aurobindo Pharma v The Chairman State Tender Board et al.*, 2010: para. 51). Despite this finding the Court declined to declare the tender invalid as a matter of law since the tender had only a matter of months to run and a refutation of the tender would have profound effects on the supply of medicines. Instead the court issued an order for costs to be paid to the complaining party.

The case however reveals the deep interdependence of those engaged in the local production of pharmaceuticals and the state. One of the successful bidders, Adcock Ingram, argued to the court that it had invested R611 million to upgrade its factory in order to supply the drugs, and was awarded a government tax incentive grant of R458 million from the Department of Trade and Industry's Strategic Industrial Projects fund for this purpose (*Aurobindo Pharma*: para. 22.1). Furthermore, a refutation of the tender would mean that R25 million worth of equipment for the production of ARVs would be left idle, requiring the retrenchment of company employees (id.). The court also considered the fact that patients were dependent on the regular supply of the medicines and that approximately 500,000–650,000 patients in the case of Aspen and between 280,000 and 300,000 patients in the case of Adcock Ingram would suffer "disastrous consequences" if the supply of these medicines was interrupted (id.: para. 21.2). Thus, from the time when Glaxo first considered setting up local production and attempted to negotiate for a guaranteed monopoly to supply the public sector until the present, the question of whether to set up industrial production of any drug in South Africa, or to import it from outside, has depended on an interplay between at times conflicting government policies, as much as on the laws of supply and demand.

CURRENT POLICY DEBATES

After the initial attempt by Mandela's government to implement a new drug policy, based on the WHO's essential medicines model, ran into intense opposition from pharmaceutical companies and the US government (see Klug, 2005 and 2008) the question of access to medicines became a casualty of the political conflict over HIV/AIDS that tarnished the Mbeki government. It was only after the government changed policy in 2003 and decided to provide access to ARVs through the public health system that issues of drug supply and local production were once again on the policy agenda (see Full Report of the Joint Health and Treasury Task Team Charged with Examining Treatment Options to Supplement Comprehensive Care for HIV/AIDS in the Public Health Sector, 8 August 2003). Responding to this opportunity the Aids Law Project and the Legal Resources Center, both important public interest law centers, sent a joint memorandum to the National HIV/AIDS Treatment Task Team arguing that the government had a constitutional obligation to assure access to affordable medicines and calling on the state to engage in negotiations with multinational pharmaceutical companies to grant voluntary licenses to at least five local generic companies to either import or locally produce the required ARVs (see Berger, Hassan and Budlender, 2003).

While the subsequent government tenders in 2004 and 2008 clearly stimulated the emergence of local ARV production, this was premised on a massive influx of donor funding, particularly from the US President's Emergency Plan for AIDS Relief which in 2010 contributed R4.3 billion, nearly matching the government's own budget of R5 billion for ARV treatment (see Cullinan, 2010). Despite the growth in local production the question of pricing remained controversial, leading the Minister of Health to complain that South Africa was paying significantly higher prices for ARVs as compared to other countries and to threaten that "there is no choice. We must purchase ARVs at the lowest possible cost from whatever source that can guarantee us the lowest prices, whether it's inside the country or outside the country. We are going to have to do so" (see Keet, 2010). While local manufacturers objected the Minister argued that as the largest consumer of ARVs in the world South Africa should benefit from economies of scale and therefore the tender rules would be written to allow the government to secure the drugs at an affordable price from anywhere, whether locally or internationally (id.). It is in this context then that the recent debate over local production has been conducted.

In 2007 the government initiated a debate over the future of pharmaceutical manufacture in the country and what role the state should play in encouraging the development of a local industry. In addition to commissioning a study from a local consultancy, Genesis, which was subsequently leaked to the press, the government set up a National Economic Development and Labour Council (NEDLAC) steering committee including participants from the Departments of Trade and Industry, Science and Technology, and Health as well as representatives from industry and labor. While the consultants argued that supporting a local pharmaceutical industry would contribute to the government's goal of promoting high value knowledge-based development, others expressed concern that the massive public investment this would take was unlikely to produce significant employment opportunities. Despite these different goals and concerns it was the need for cheaper access to medicines that seems to have driven the debate over local production at the ANC's National Conference at Polokwane in December 2007. Voting on a resolution on Social Transformation the delegates included, in its section on health, the statement that: "The ANC should explore the possibility of a state-owned pharmaceutical company that will respond to and intervene in the curbing of medicine prices" (African National Congress, 2007).

While there are clearly competing interests and goals affecting the development of government policy, there are also a number of circumstances that are beginning to frame the options that will be available. First, South Africa remains dependent on the importation of nearly all the active ingredients of drugs which account for approximately 60–90 percent of the cost structure of any particular pharmaceutical. Second, Aspen, which won the first two tenders for ARVs, charged the government between 20 and 30 percent more than the price of cheapest comparable drugs on the international market, raising concerns about reliance on local production when the demand for treatment is projected to reach its peak in 2021 at an expected cost to the government of around R30 billion. Third, changes in the global pharmaceutical industry have led to an increasing concentration of production resulting in the closure of 34 manufacturing plants in South Africa between 1994 and 2004 and a consequent loss of over 7000 jobs as employment in the sector fell "from 16,885 in 1997 to 9500 by 2007" (Kgara and Barsel, 2010: 49). Fourth, while the expansion of generic production under license from the multinational pharmaceutical corporations has increased local production since 2004, South African owned pharmaceutical manufacturers obtained 70 percent of their "capital equipment from foreign suppliers and local multinational firms that import 90% of capital infrastructure from outside South Africa" (id.: 53). Finally, the country has significant human resource challenges with "a shortage of qualified management and technical specialists such as pharmacists trained in manufacturing, regulatory affairs managers, laboratory analysts, financial managers (particularly procurement), clinical research specialists, manufacturing equipment maintenance specialists as well as appropriately trained mid-level workers" (id.).

CONCLUSION

Given that nearly 75 percent of demand for pharmaceuticals is met by imports and that over 90 percent of the active ingredients of medicines are imported, the question of the relationship between different government goals and the decisions of private industry remains at the heart of the question of access to essential medicines in South Africa and the region. Despite their clear identification of the difficulties facing local producers, Sidney Kgara and Sheila Barsel (2010) argue that the government's Industrial Policy Action Plan, when linked to the Polokwane resolution and Cosatu's longstanding call for "government ownership and control of the manufacturing of active pharmaceutical ingredients (APIs)" (id.: 52), provides an "opportunity to rebuild this sector" (id.: 49).

The possibility of creating a state-owned pharmaceutical company as a means of providing access to affordable essential medicines and ARVs in particular is however quite remote. Unlike Brazil and Thailand whose governments have threatened to issue compulsory licenses and whose well established industries can credibly threaten to reverse-engineer patented products, there is no equivalent capacity in South Africa to credibly threaten to reverse-engineer patented drugs or to produce the drugs so as to ensure the economies of scale necessary for the provision of affordable medicines. First, there is no public sector pharmaceutical production capacity and second, the existing local South African producers are intimately linked to the multinational companies through licensing agreements and investment and show very little ability or wish either to challenge these companies or to reverse-engineer their products. Even in the context of ARVs, where economies of scale based on local and regional need is sadly possible, it is clear that the local producers are dependent on both foreign funding and licensing. Despite the dream that South Africa may become a niche producer in those pharmaceutical products in greatest demand to address HIV/AIDS, TB and malaria in the region, the need to ensure the supply of all other medicines means that there is little space for directly confronting the multinationals. Instead, the government's efforts to regulate the industry and to stabilize prices through both regulation and tender bargaining offers a more immediate hope of South Africans obtaining increased access to essential medicines at an affordable price.

REFERENCES

African National Congress (ANC) (2007), 52nd National Congress: Resolutions, Social Transformation, paragraph 64, 20 December. Available at: www.anc.org.za/show.php?include=docs/res/2007/resolutions.html&ID=2536.

AIDS Law Project and Treatment Action Campaign (2003), "The Price of Life: Hazel Tau and Others versus GlaxoSmithKline and Boehringer Ingelheim. A Report on the Excessive Pricing Complaint to South Africa's Competition Commission," ALP and TAC, 2003. Available at: www.alp.org.za/modules.php?op=modload&name=News&File=article&sid=222.

Berger, Jonathan (2005), AIDS Law Project, Letter to Angelo Kondes, CEO Abbot Labs, South Africa re shortages of Ritonavir, dated February 14, 2005.

Berger, Jonathan, Adile Hassan and Geoff Budlender (2003), Submission to the National HIV and AIDS Treatment Task Team: "Reducing the Prices of Antiretroviral Drugs", September 8.

Business Insights (2010), "The South African Pharmaceutical Market Outlook to 2014: Policy environment, market structure, competitive landscape, growth opportunities." Summary available at: www.articlesbase.com/health-articles/south-african-pharmaceutical-market-outlook-to-2014-policy-environment-market-structure-competitive-landscape-growth-opportunities-2871883.html.

Consumer Project on Technology (1999), Cptech, Appendix B: Time-Line of Disputes over Compulsory Licensing and Parallel Importation in South Africa. Available at: www.cptech.org/ip/health/sa/sa-timeline.txt August 5.

Cullinan, Kerry (2010), "SA becomes a victim of its own ARV treatment success," South African Health News Service, September 1, 2010. Available at: www.health-e.org.za/news/article.php?uid=20032913.

Davenport-Hines, R.P.T. and Judy Slinn (1992), *Glaxo: A History to 1962*, Cambridge University Press.

Deeb, M.T. (1998a), Founding Affidavit, High Court of South Africa. February 18.

Deeb, M.T. (1998b), Supplementary Affidavit, High Court of South Africa. July 25.

Department of Health (1996), *National Drug Policy for South Africa*. Available at: www.doh.gov.za/docs/policy/drugsjan1996.pdf. Retrieved May 21, 2010.

Full Report of the Joint Health and Treasury Task Team Charged with Examining Treatment Options to Supplement Comprehensive Care for HIV/AIDS in the Public Health Sector, August 8, 2003.

Hassim, Adila, Mark Heywood and Jonathan Berger (2007), *Health & Democracy: A Guide to Human Rights, Health Law and Policy in Post-apartheid South Africa*, SiberInk: Cape Town.

Keet, Jacques (2010), "Govt wont be 'blackmailed' over ARVs says Minister," *Mail and Guardian*, April 13. Available at: www.mg.co.za/article/2010-04-13-govt-wont-be-blackmailed-over-arvs-says-minister.

Kgara, Sidney and Sheila Barsel (2010), "IPAP and the Need for a State-owned Pharmaceutical Company," *African Communist*, Special Issue: Towards a New Growth Path, Issue No. 180, 2nd and 3rd Quarter 2010.

Klug, Heinz (2005), "Campaigning for Life: Building a New Transnational Solidarity in the Face of HIV/AIDS and TRIPS," in *Law and Globalization from Below: Towards a Cosmopolitan Legality*, De Sousa Santos, Boaventura and Cesar A. Rodriguez-Garavito (eds), Cambridge University Press.

Klug, Heinz (2008), "Law, Politics, and Access to Essential Medicines in Developing Countries," 36(2) *Politics and Society* 207.

Maloney, Christopher and Andrew Myburgh (2007), G:enesis: The Growth Potential of the Pharmaceuticals Sector in South Africa, 29 May. Available at: www.genesis-analytics.com/search_results_projects.asp.

Médecins Sans Frontières, Campaign for Access to Essential Medicines (2007), *Untangling the Web of Price Reductions: A Pricing Guide for the Purchase of ARVs for Developing Countries* (10th edition, July). Available at: www. accessmed-msf.org (last visited September 24, 2007).

Nattrass, Nicoli (2007), *Mortal Combat: AIDS Denialism and the Struggle for Antiretrovirals in South Africa*, Sottsville: University of KwaZulu-Natal Press.

Pile, Jacqui (2005), "Aspen Pharmacare: Clinical Coup," *Financial Mail*, 182(3), 18, July 15.

Redwood, Heinz (1988), *The Pharmaceutical Industry: Trends, Problems and Achievements*, Felixstowe, UK: Oldwicks Press.

Report of the Ministerial Task Team on the Restructuring of the Medicines Regulatory Affairs and Medicines Control Council and Recommendations for the New Regulatory Authority for Health Products of South Africa, 25 February, 2008. Available at: www.info.gov.za/view/DynamicAction?pageid=607&id=0.

Report of the Commission of Enquiry into the Pharmaceutical Industry, January 1978, 38/1978.

Shadlen, Kenneth (2007), "The Political Economy of AIDS Treatment: Intellectual Property and the Transformation of Generic Supply," *International Studies Quarterly* 51(3), 559–581.

Steenkamp, W.F.J. (1979), "The Pharmaceutical Industry in South Africa," *The South African Journal of Economics* 47(1) 75–89.

Stokes, Bruce, (2005), "Pachyderm Pharma," *National Journal*, April 16.

Thom, Anso (2010), "Change at the MCC – too little, too late?" Available at: www.health-e.org.za/news/article.php?uid=20032808.

WTO, Doha Declaration on the TRIPS Agreement and Public Health, adopted on November 14, 2001, Available at: www.wto.org/english/thewto_e/minist_e/min01_e/mindecl_trips_e.htm.

CASES

Aurobindo Pharma v The Chairman State Tender Board et al., 2010, case number 59309/2008, unreported decision of the High Court of South Africa (North Gauteng High Court, Pretoria), decided May 19, 2010

Beecham Group v Triomed, 2003 (3) SA 639 (SCA)

Biotech Laboratories (Pty) Ltd v Beecham Group, 2002 (4) SA 249 (SCA)

Hazel Tau v GlaxoSmithKline, complaint to the Competition Commission 2002

Minister of Health NO v New Clicks South Africa (Pty) Ltd, 2005 (3) SA 238 (SCA)

Minister of Health NO v New Clicks South Africa (Pty) Ltd (Treatment Action Campaign and Another as Amici Curiae), 2006 (2) SA 311 (CC)

Minister of Health et al. v Treatment Action Campaign and Others, 2002 (5) SA 721 (CC)

STATUTES AND REGULATIONS

Appointment of Members of the Medicines Control Council, Government Notice 180, 12 March 2010, in Government Gazette No. 33006, 12 March 2010, p. 15
Competition Act 89 of 1998
Medical Schemes Act 131 of 1998
Medicines and Related Substances Control Act 101 of 1965
Medicines and Related Substances Control Amendment Act 90 of 1997
National Health Act 61 of 2003
Patents Act 57 of 1978
Public Finance Management Act 1 of 1999
Regulations Relating to a Transparent Pricing System for Medicines and Scheduled Substances, Government Notice R533 of 2004

3. Intellectual property and access to medicines: paradoxes in Moroccan policy

Gaëlle Krikorian

Important changes have taken place in Morocco regarding intellectual property rights and access to medicines in the past few years: changes in the legal and policy framework and in the practices of institutions and individuals. These developments follow at least two different logics: an increased range and protection of exclusive rights on the one hand; better access to health and medicines on the other.

Intellectual property law in Morocco has changed significantly in recent years. In 2004 and then in 2006, legislation incorporated the standards of protection required by the agreement on Trade-Related Aspects of Intellectual Property Rights (TRIPS) as well as higher levels of protection (TRIPS-plus). In the meantime, the Moroccan Office for Industrial and Commercial Property started to issue patents on medicines in December 2004 and has since been granting more and more of them, using patentability criteria which often do not seem to take into account Moroccan public health interests. Meanwhile, national policies on medicines and public health are facing challenges and changes. The local pharmaceutical industry, mainly producing generic medicines and partly working under multinational licenses, plays an important but declining role in supplying the domestic market for basic medicines. This industry recently made important investments in the modernization and increase of its manufacturing capacities in order to reach international production standards. Despite the absence of patents on pharmaceutical products until recently, prices of medicines are, on average, high in Morocco, particularly for newer products, which represents a barrier to access for the population. However, the national program for access to HIV antiretroviral medicines provides a good example of generalized access to relatively expensive medicines used against chronic disease. But this program is also facing increasing financial pressure. Morocco also launched in 2005 a universal health care coverage system to extend dramatically access to health care and medicines, most notably to reduce disparities between urban and rural areas, as well as between the north and south of the country.

Some of these policies and practices appear paradoxical from the point of view of their objectives: to provide increased protection for intellectual property rights holders that de facto limits access to affordable medicines on the one hand, and to develop better national coverage for health care and pharmaceutical products on the other. This chapter analyses the resulting tensions and challenges that the Moroccan government and its population face in considering health and intellectual property rules and their use "in a manner supportive of [Morocco's] right to protect public health and, in particular, to promote access to medicines for all".[1]

CHANGES IN THE INTELLECTUAL PROPERTY REGIME

In 2004, a new intellectual property law was adopted in Morocco to comply with the standards required by the World Trade Organization (WTO).[2] The new legislation, 17-97, was implemented on December 18, 2004, amending and reforming pre-existing provisions.[3] It includes levels of protection of intellectual property rights at least as high as those of the TRIPS agreement. In March 2006, a second legislative evolution led to the promulgation of the law 31-05, amending the previous law to introduce some of the requirements of the free trade agreement concluded with the United States in March 2004 and provisions from WIPO treaties ratified by Morocco. As a consequence, the current law on intellectual property in

---

[1] Doha Declaration, WTO, November 14, 2001.

[2] According to article 65.2 of the TRIPS agreement, Morocco, like other "developing" countries, did not have to apply most of the provisions of the TRIPS agreement until 1 January 2000. Moreover, like many countries at that time, Morocco did not protect pharmaceutical products per se by patent but only applied protection to fabrication processes prior to January 1, 1995. Following article 65.4 of the TRIPS agreement, developing countries that did not provide product patent protection in a particular area of technology when the TRIPS agreement came into force had up to 10 years to introduce this protection. In Morocco new legislation was passed in 2000 to comply with the TRIPS agreement. However, the legislation was not implemented until December 18, 2004. Unlike many countries, Morocco made full use of the extended deadline for TRIPS compliance.

[3] Two pieces of legislation governed intellectual property in Morocco during the pre-TRIPS era: one from June 23, 1916 that covered the former French area and was amended in 1941 and one from October 4, 1938 that applied in the former international area of Tangiers.

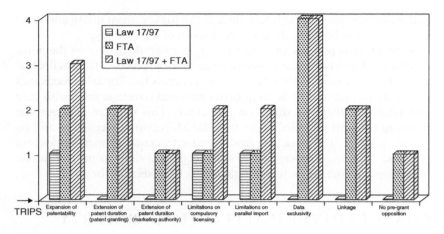

Source: Author.

Figure 3.1   Evolution of the level of intellectual property protection in Morocco

Morocco embeds two generations of restrictions that exceed the standards of the TRIPS agreement either by expanding and strengthening intellectual property protections or by undermining existing flexibilities left to overcome or bypass these protections.

Figure 3.1[4] shows the evolution of the levels of protection of intellectual property in Morocco. Through an analytical reading of the texts of the 17-97 law and the intellectual property chapter of the free trade agreement, the IPR level for each type of provision is qualified in terms of level of protection and a unit of protection is added for each provision that is more protective than the TRIPS standard. For example, patentability of new uses for existing medicines counts for one unit. This assessment of protection levels is partly subjective and as such is necessarily somewhat approximate, but it provides a valuable overview of the evolution of standards. Indeed, it shows clearly the cumulative effect of the first amendment of the intellectual property legislation and the provisions of the FTA and how they brought Morocco to adopt a level of protection that goes far above the WTO floor.

The law prevailing before the adoption of the law 17-97 had already set the duration of patent protection to 20 years after the filing date of the patent application. This duration was of course kept in the law 17-97

---

[4]   First published in Krikorian and Szymkowiak (2007).

(art. 17), however, the law 31-05 introduced the possibility to extend the duration of the patent protection "if the patent is granted after a period of four years from the filing date of the patent application" (art. 17.18).[5] This requirement corresponds to one of the provisions of the free trade agreement with the United States.[6] The duration of the protection can also be extended beyond the initial 20 years (art. 17.2). This was also included in the law because of a provision of the FTA with the US.[7] It is however stipulated in the Moroccan law that the extension can only be granted once for a given product and that it cannot exceed two and a half years (arts 17.3 and 17.4), while the request for extension must be made within three months after the granting of the market authorization.

The Moroccan law 31-05 uses the same definition as the TRIPS agreement of what constitutes an invention and fulfills the criteria of patentability (arts. 22, 26 and 28): it must be a "new invention", i.e. "not included in the state of the art", representing "an inventive step" and capable of a possible "industrial application". Following WTO requirements, the Law 17-97 introduced the patentability of pharmaceutical products, and not only production processes. However, the new law also included the protection of combinations or pharmaceutical compositions (art. 21) – it is interesting to note that this provision pre-existed the FTA with the US and was deliberately introduced by the legislator.[8] Moreover, the Moroccan legislation authorizes the granting of a patent on "new application[s]" and does not exclude the possibility to deliver patents for new uses of an already patented product – which may lead to the protection of all sorts of minor alterations of already well-known substances and the prolongation of the monopoly beyond the initial 20 years of patent protection.[9] This establishes very low criteria of patentability which facilitate the granting of questionable and unwarranted patents. On the other hand, the new law excludes the patentability of methods of surgical or therapeutic treatment, as well as diagnostic methods (art. 25) as provided for by article 27.2 of the

---

[5]   Translation by the author.

[6]   The FTA requires that patent extensions be granted to "compensate for unreasonable delays that occur in granting the patent" (art. 15.9.7).

[7]   The FTA requires that patent extensions be granted to compensate for "unreasonable curtailment of the effective patent term as a result of the marketing approval process" of pharmaceutical products (art. 15.10.3).

[8]   In the case of Morocco, these TRIPS-plus provisions included in the implementation of the TRIPS agreement do not seem to be US requirements but are the result of technical assistance from European countries.

[9]   The patentability of "new uses or methods of using a known product, including new uses of a known product for the treatment of humans and animals" is stipulated by article 15.9.2 of the FTA with the US.

TRIPS agreement. This was unchanged by the trade agreement with the US – contrary to other US FTAs in which it was required.

The Moroccan legislation does not include the possibility to oppose a patent before it is granted ("pre-grant opposition"). Such a provision was, however, introduced in the Moroccan law relating to trademarks on February 20, 2006. If Morocco were to decide that this represents a useful provision for patents as well – it has indeed proven particularly effective in countries like India – it would have to deal with the fact that it is forbidden by the FTA with the US (art. 15.9.5). Furthermore, a provision of the FTA restricts the grounds for revocation of a patent to the reasons that should have prevented it from being granted in the first place, such as "fraud, misrepresentation or inequitable conduct" (art. 15.9.5). Cases that can be considered as grounds for revocation under the TRIPS agreement, such as the absence of local production, the absence of exploitation of the patent, or reasons of public health are excluded.

The new law also forbids parallel importation, which the WTO leaves to the discretion of each country. Parallel importation allows nationals to buy from outside their country a good that is patented in their country. In other words, parallel importation is importation without the consent of the patent-holder of a patented product sold in another country either by the patent holder or with the patent holder's consent. Such a practice allows the procurement of products that are sold at a lower price abroad. It is based on the legal notion of "exhaustion of rights" according to which a right owner is correctly and definitively remunerated once the product is put on a market and has exhausted his/her intellectual property rights on the commercial exploitation of the good. The regime of exhaustion of rights allows a member state to define the territory over which patent rights apply (international, regional or national). Once patent holders, or any party authorized by them, have sold a patented product, they cannot prohibit the subsequent resale of that product since their rights in respect of that market have been exhausted by the act of selling the product. Article 6 of the TRIPS agreement explicitly states that practices relating to parallel importation cannot be challenged under the WTO dispute settlement system. The Doha Declaration has reaffirmed that members have this right, stating that each member is free to establish its own regime for such exhaustion without challenge. Thus the level of protection of the law adopted in 2004 clearly exceeds the WTO requirements.

As for compulsory licensing – one of the most important flexibilities allowed by the TRIPS agreement – the Moroccan legislation as it is now, and indeed as it already was at the end of the 1990s, contains a series of restrictions and sophistications that limit its use and make it harder to implement than it would be following the minimum requirements of the

TRIPS agreement. According to the latter, compulsory licensing may be requested only three years after the granting of a patent or four years after filing of the application. It can be invoked in several situations: if the patent owner is not exploiting the invention, if the product has not been commercialized in sufficient quantity for the national market, or if the patent owner has not exploited the patent or marketed the corresponding product for at least 3 years (art. 60). Those are extra requirements compared to the TRIPS agreement, which allows a wider set of grounds on which compulsory licensing can be granted and does not impose any minimum duration of prior exclusivity. According to the Moroccan law, a compulsory license can be granted only after an attempt to negotiate with the patent owner and if the party requesting the license can prove ability to fulfill domestic needs (art. 61), if it is non-exclusive and can serve only the national market predominantly (art. 62), in line with the requirements of article 31 of the TRIPS agreement on compulsory licensing. It can only be granted by a court that sets the appropriate royalties (arts. 62 and 63). Here again the law establishes a mechanism that is more restrictive than required by the TRIPS agreement.

However, "licences d'office", corresponding to the "governmental use" found in the legal environment of English-speaking countries, can be granted for pharmaceutical products through an administrative act, at the request of the administration in charge of public health, if it is required by public health (art. 67). This can apply when medicines are not available in sufficient quantity on the market or if the price is too high. No prior negotiation with the right holder is required. The decree passed in June 2004 to implement the law 17-97 established the administrative procedure to review and grant "licences d'offices".[10] According to this decree, the governmental authority in charge of health passes on the request for a "licence d'office" to the authority in charge of industry and commerce, and the latter notifies the rights owner of a request for exploitation. The rights owner has 15 days to react and send observations. After this period, the authority in charge of industry and commerce submits the request to a technical commission.[11] The commission has to provide an opinion within two months of the request being made, then exploitation of the patent is enacted by decree in response to a proposition from the authority in charge of industry and commerce and a request by the governmental

---

[10] Modifications were introduced in the decree no. 2-05-1485 of February 12, 2006.

[11] The composition and the functioning of this commission are to be defined by a joint decree from the authority in charge of industry and commerce and the commission on health.

authority in charge of health. Requests for exploitation from third parties are to be addressed to the authority in charge of industry and commerce and the authority in charge of health. A license can be granted to them by decree in response to a joint proposition from the authority in charge of health and the authority in charge of industry and commerce.

The setting-up of a commission dedicated to the issuance of licenses can be seen as a way to develop local expertise on this issue and on the use of such legal tools – which at the moment does not exist. And the fact that there is a deadline for this commission to render its opinion is a positive element because it prevents unlimited delays. However, unlike the system in many other countries, the procedure involves many different bodies and a succession of steps that can definitely make the procedure a long and arduous one. Besides, there is no time limit regarding the issuing of the decree by the governmental authorities.

The Moroccan law also stipulates that "licences d'offices" can be granted to meet "national economic needs" or "national defense needs" (section II of the June 2004 decree). However, in contrast to the TRIPs agreement, the language of the law does not include "situations of national emergency", "cases of public non-commercial use", or the need to "remedy a practice determined after judicial or administrative process to be anti-competitive"; and as a consequence the grounds for issuing a license are more limited than under the TRIPS agreement.

The "Bolar" provision, a provision that can be found in IP laws, including in the US, states that despite the existence of a patent covering an invention, third parties are allowed to work on it during the duration of the patent protection, without the agreement of the right owner. Among other things, this offers the possibility to generic manufacturers to prepare their product and conduct all the tests required by the regulatory authorities in order to obtain marketing authorization sooner once the patent has expired. The Moroccan law does not include such a provision. Article 55 of law 31-05 provides that rights conferred by patents do not apply to experimental acts using the invention, but it does not specifically mention the Bolar provision. However, a disposition has recently been added to the new pharmacy code in article 16 to make up for this omission, allowing an industrial pharmaceutical facility wishing to market a generic product to undertake any necessary trial or experimentation on the proprietary product before expiration of the patent.

With the free trade agreement, Morocco agreed to introduce into its legislation additional ways to create exclusive rights and monopolies. The FTA imposed exclusive rights on the data required for the registration of a medicine for a minimum of five years: "If [the] Party requires, as a condition of approving the marketing of a new pharmaceutical or agricultural chemical product, the submission of: (a) safety and efficacy data, or (b) evidence of prior approval of the product in another territory that requires such information" (art. 15.10.1). To obtain marketing approval for a new product, pharmaceutical companies must submit data proving the absence of toxicity and the effectiveness of the product. Such data are referred to as "registration data" or "marketing approval data" and result from tests and clinical trials on animals and human beings. When a company wants to market a generic version of a pharmaceutical product already on the market, the regulatory authorities do not ask it to undertake the same clinical trials (which would be unethical); they ask the company to provide the results of bioequivalent tests proving that its product is chemically equivalent and has the same action in the human body as the brand-name product. The authorities rely on the data on toxicity and effectiveness provided for the marketing of the first product to be registered. Data exclusivity establishes a marketing monopoly, since it prevents competitors from marketing their product unless they conduct new clinical trials.

Moreover, this provision can render the use of compulsory licensing to allow access to generic versions of patented products useless: even if a license is issued and the drug is produced or imported, it cannot enter the market. Even old products or unpatented products can benefit from a monopoly under this provision, as long as they have not already been marketed in Morocco. In the case of a product that is already on the market in Morocco, a provision (new in comparison to previous FTAs with the United States) in the FTA with the US introduced the possibility to obtain an exclusivity for three years (art. 15.10.2). Thus, on the basis of "new clinical information" provided for a new therapeutic use, it allows unlimited renewal of exclusive rights by permitting an additional data exclusivity period to cover the not-yet-approved use of already marketed products. The implementation of the FTA led to the adoption of a decree in 2006 that establishes the protection for five years of data produced through clinical trials and therefore proscribes the marketing of generic versions of the product based on these data.

Furthermore, the FTA establishes a link between the granting of marketing approval and patent protection (art. 15.10.4). It requires regulatory authorities to prevent third parties from granting marketing approvals for products which are protected by a patent, and to inform patent holders of the identity of third parties applying for marketing approvals during the patent term. Thus, the action of the regulatory authorities becomes dependent on patent laws and the action of the patent office. This can also prevent the granting of marketing approval for drugs that are produced or imported under compulsory licenses.

The new code of pharmacy, established in Morocco by the law 17-04 and adopted in June 2006, includes a provision stating that "the marketing of a generic product can only occur after the patent protecting the proprietary medicine of reference has expired" (art. 16).[12] This obligation required by the free trade agreement can prevent the efficient use of compulsory licensing by banning the marketing of a generic version of a drug legally produced and/or imported under compulsory licensing.

THE PRACTICE OF THE MOROCCAN OFFICE FOR INDUSTRIAL AND COMMERCIAL PROPERTY

An analysis was conducted of the pharmaceutical patents granted in Morocco from the 1970s until 2007 based on information found in the database of the Moroccan Office for Industrial and Commercial Property (OMPIC).[13] The purpose of this research was to get a general understanding of the number and type of patents existing in the pharmaceutical field at the time when Morocco implemented its new WTO-compliant legislation, the policy of pharmaceutical companies toward patent filing, and the management of patent granting by the OMPIC.

As it is not possible to search the database using key words defining inventions, as pharmaceutical products or as medicines, the search was conducted using names of pharmaceutical companies. The search included 80 companies; 43[14] of these had been granted patents in the pharmaceutical field during this period. This search was not intended to be exhaustive; other pharmaceutical patents may have been granted to companies that were not in the sample. Some firms have merged since the 1970s. For this reason, a patent that appears under the name of one company may at the time have been filed by another company, subsequently merged with or taken over by the other company. A patent may thus appear several times in the database. Cross-checking was carried out to avoid double counting.

---

[12]   Translation by the author. Original text can be found at: http://srvweb. sante.gov.ma/Reglementation/MedPharma/Pages/default.aspx.

[13]   Available at: http://www.ompic.org.ma/.

[14]   Actelion, Abbott, Agouron, Akzo Nobel, Alza Corporation, Amgen, AstraZeneca, Aventis, Bayer, Beecham, Boehringer, Bristol Myers Squibb, Celgene, Cephalon, Cipla Limited, Eli Lilly, Eisai, Galenix, Glaxo, Hoechst, Hoffmann, Janssen, Lambert, Merck, Millennium Pharmaceuticals, Novartis, Otsuka Pharmaceutical, Pfizer, Pharmacia, Pierre Fabre, Ranbaxy, Roche, Roussel, Sanofi, Schering, Servier, Smithkline, Synthélabo, Takeda, Upjohn, Unimed, Warner, Wellcome.

Because of the mergers and takeovers between companies, only 32 appear in the results instead of the 43 companies that were granted patents by the Moroccan office.

Cross-checking with the European patent office and US patent office was carried out to check priority dates and to identify the other countries in which each patent had been granted. The Food and Drug Administration database and the French AFSSAPS database were used to link chemical identities or medicines to the patents covering them.

Like other developing countries that did not grant patent protection for pharmaceutical products (but only to processes of preparation of products) when TRIPS came into force, Morocco had until January 1, 2005 to introduce such protection. In exchange, from January 1, 1995, it had to establish a 'mailbox' system. According to this system, applications for pharmaceutical product patents could be filed by rights holders and stored by the patent office which had to assess these applications by January 2005 at the latest. In the case of Morocco, the mailbox system ended on December 18, 2004, when the new WTO-compliant law allowing the patenting of pharmaceutical products came into force. If these applications satisfied the patentability and date criteria, a patent had to be granted for the remainder of the patent term.

Figure 3.2[15] shows the number of patents granted in the pharmaceutical field between the 1970s and December 18, 2004, when the new WTO-compliant law came into force – the figures given all concern our sample of 80 companies. 1497 patents were granted during that period. On December 18, 2004 alone, 436 patents were granted. This indicated that the mailbox system acted like a pipeline (the patents were systematically granted without evaluation provided that an original filing had been made elsewhere). Indeed, the office did not conduct examinations. It only registered the patents, and obviously granted as many as possible on the first working day after the new law came into effect. Between 1996 and 2004, 856 patents were granted. This represents patent requests that were submitted to the office through the mailbox system. They represent more than half the number of patents granted since the 1970s, which makes sense since the patentability criteria were relaxed. It also seems logical that pharmaceutical companies would be more willing to request patents as pharmaceutical products were now going to be patented and as the patentability criteria were widened by the new legislation. As the figure shows, between 1996 and 2006, 1325 patents were granted, representing 65 percent of the 2014 patents granted since

---

[15]   First published in Krikorian (2007).

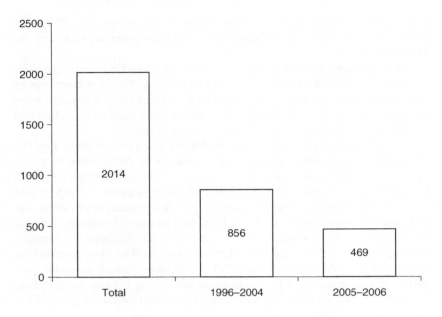

Figure 3.2   Patents delivered in the pharmaceutical field in Morocco since the 1970s

the 1970s. The figure presents more precisely the acceleration in patent granting from 1995. After 2004 the increase assumed new proportions and continued to grow.

The OMPIC is in charge of granting patents in the country. It was created in 2000 from the merger between a pre-existing office established in 1916 and the central register of commerce. Around 70 employees work for the OMPIC, which is financed only through its own revenues and does not receive any public subsidies. As its former director pointed out in 2006, its prices are rather low in order to attract rights holders.

The policy of the Moroccan office is straightforward: the number of patents granted is a reflection of the efficiency of the office. The more patents it registers, the better a job it is doing – and the richer it becomes. The OMPIC does not have patent examiners. According to the former director, in 2006 patent requests were not numerous enough to justify employing examiners qualified in all the various technological fields concerned. He also saw that it was very difficult for the Moroccan office to compete in terms of efficiency with the examining capacity of the European or US patent offices. In practice, the OMPIC bases the grant-ing of patents on the results of the examination conducted by these other offices.[16] If a patent has been granted elsewhere, the OMPIC registers the patent following the legal administrative procedure. It also relies on opinions given through the Patent Cooperation Treaty system of the WIPO.

The Patent Cooperation Treaty provides a patent owner with the possibility to file a single patent application for any or all countries that are PCT members – there are currently 141.[17] The PCT system does not grant patents, but it conducts a preliminary inquiry to assess if there is reasonable likelihood of patentability. This system does not exempt applicants from submitting individual applications to each patent office separately, but it establishes a "priority date" which is valid in all member states and automatically becomes the national filing date.[18] It also allows a delay (up to 30 months) before national filing procedures have to be initiated.[19] The Moroccan patent office sees the PCT system as a useful tool as it provides a partial examination. It clearly provides advantages to the rights holders and facilitates the granting of patents for their products. Such a policy

---

[16] Peter Drahos (2008a) explained how, through the assistance and training that the EPO provides for developing countries' patent offices, the latter become effectively convinced of the superiority and reliability of the EPO's granting decisions, and base their own decisions on this "technocratic trust".

[17] The Patent Cooperation Treaty (PCT) is an international patent treaty that provides a unified procedure for filing patent applications. It was concluded in 1970. Morocco ratified it in July 1999. In 2002, about 115,000 international applications were filed; they generated more than $120 million in fees. PCT fees provide 80 percent of WIPO's total income (http://www.grain.org/briefings/?id=159). The PCT is currently under reform and application procedures will be simplified. The US and other developed countries would like to take the opportunity to make PCT decisions binding on member states, in which case national patent offices would lose the freedom to assess the merits of international patent applications independently.

[18] The priority date, also sometimes called the "effective filing date" is the date on which the patent application was first filed at a patent office in any one of the countries signatory to the Paris Convention. The original priority date is the one considered for the examination of novelty and inventiveness or non-obviousness, which may then give rise to the granting of a patent. If the claimed invention is part of public knowledge before the priority date, it will not be eligible for a patent. In other words, any publication of the underlying research anywhere in the world prior to the priority date of the invention leads to the application being refused.

[19] Companies use these delays as strategic tools to extend their monopolies. As Drahos (2008b) notes: "Most applicants with global patenting strategies will begin the process by establishing a priority date in a major national office (e.g., the USPTO, JPO, EPO, German PO) and then move to the PCT. The national filing will give them a period of 12 months under the Paris Convention for the Protection of Industrial Property in which to file a PCT application, and from that filing applicants have about 18 months before the international application turns into a bundle of national applications."

explains why the OMPIC database contains patents that cannot be found in any other countries, according to the database of the World Intellectual Property Organization (WIPO).

Searching the Moroccan database also reveals patents on pharmaceutical components with priority dates prior to 1995, when the mailbox system was established, and even prior to the signing of the TRIPS agreement by Morocco. These patents should be revoked on the grounds that they should not have been granted in the first place.

Few new chemical entities appear on the US market every year. They represent active ingredients newly added to the products available for medical use. It is considered that the number of new chemical entities receiving approval from the Food and Drug Administration (FDA) in the US is around 25 per year. As the US market is the biggest worldwide, it is often the first country for which pharmaceutical companies apply for patents for new products, or at least the country in which they necessarily patent their products. Thus, it is reasonable to assume that there are no new chemical entities that are not patented in the US and 25 is the number of patents we could expect to see being granted in the US if only new chemical entities were to be granted patents. Similarly, from 1996 to 2004, the duration of the mailbox system in Morocco, we could expect to find 200 new patents in the database for pharmaceutical products corresponding to new chemical entities. However, we counted more than 800 patents granted to the 43 companies in our sample. This indicates that the patent office does not take advantage of the flexibilities provided by the TRIPS agreement and applies low standards of patentability.[20] Following the dominant trend in Western countries, where a large number of pharmaceutical patents protect processes of manufacture, formulations, systems of delivery and new uses of already known products,[21] the Moroccan database contains many patents on minor modifications of existing inventions or on new ways to present these inventions. Depending on the case, they cover crystalline forms, derivates, salts, new methods of treatments which should not be considered as fulfilling novelty criteria under a strict application of the TRIPS agreement's definition of patentability. The granting

---

[20]   The TRIPS agreement requires the patentability of any invention in any field of technology, but it authorizes certain exclusions from patentability, based on *ordre public* or morality grounds, especially with regard to protection of human, animal or plant life, or to prevent serious damage to the environment. WTO members are also free to exclude diagnostic, therapeutic and surgical methods for the treatment of humans or animals (other than micro-organisms) and plants.

[21]   On the contrary, the application of strict criteria helps prevent the patent thicket and its expansion.

of such trivial patents leads to 'evergreening' and the indefinite prolongation of the monopoly granted by the patent. This explains the fact that in some cases, for a single product, even a well-known and basic one, many different patents can be found in the database of the OMPIC; patents that create so many barriers to generic competition.

According to the director who ran the patent office until May 2007, if patents are not legitimate they can be challenged, and court decisions can provide a balance between protection and abuse. The adoption of such a strategy in a country where local producers of generic medicines and national courts have as yet no experience of dealing with patent revocation, seems at odds with local resources and needs. In such a context, it would seem more appropriate to start by taking advantage of the flexibilities provided by the TRIPS agreement and applying exceptions to patentability with a view to limiting the patent thicket before it arises, rather than aligning OMPIC practice with that of the European or US patent offices. As Timmermans (2005) notes, one of the first steps is to refrain from granting patents for "new uses" or marginal modifications of known products, such as polymorphs, dosage forms and drug formulations. And applying strict criteria for inventiveness and novelty would limit the volume and density of the patent thicket. Brazil provides an interesting strategy and mechanism of patent office regulation in the area of pharmaceuticals, involving the Brazilian Health Surveillance Agency (ANVISA) in the process of examining and granting patents. This arrangement gives ANVISA opportunities to prevent the granting of a patent if it concludes that the patent application fails to meet one or more of the criteria of patentability (Drahos, 2008a).[22]

PARADOXES IN POLICY

At the time of the negotiations, and in addition to political motivations at the highest levels of the Kingdom, the free trade agreement with the US was seen as a priority for some of the industries in Morocco. The textile industry and some agribusiness corporations were very committed to its signature. Representatives from these sectors were closely involved in the negotiations and backed it up politically. The expectation was to gain better and greater access to the US market (especially for textiles, the canning industry, fruits and vegetables), to attract new investment to

---

[22] Shadlen (2011) provides a detailed (and more pessimistic) assessment of ANVISA's role in pharmaceutical patent examination in Brazil.

the country and to put Morocco in a new strategic position between the US and Europe that would make it a very attractive place for foreign business to develop local production. These are the major reasons why there was such haste to sign the agreement and why health issues were relegated to lower priority.

If several Moroccan pharmaceutical producers feared the signature of a free trade agreement with the US, local players in this field also saw potential business opportunities in the agreement. And this is why the Moroccan Association for Pharmaceutical Industries (AMIP) campaigned for the new code of pharmacy in 2006 that liberalized the capital of pharmaceutical firms. Allowing local companies to open their capital to foreign investment was one of the benefits they expected from the signing of the FTA with the US.[23]

In the end, as we have seen, the free trade agreement with the US that was officially implemented in January 2006 led to a general strengthening of IP rights protection and the introduction of several TRIPS-plus measures into the Moroccan legislation through the IP law, separate decrees or the new code of pharmacy that created new potential barriers to the use of generic medicines.

The new code of pharmacy also states, in an amendment introduced at the last minute in article 16, that in case of need the minister of health is allowed to take any necessary measures despite what is required by other legal or regulatory requirements, including IP legislation. This indicates the existence of concerns among officials and legislators and their desire to ensure flexibilities for health authorities. However, the options offered by this article are rather limited. Article 16 explicitly mentions article 67 of the law 31-05 on "government use" and thus sets the waiver within this legal context. However, it also states that: "Despite all legal and regulatory provisions establishing any kind of system of protection on proprietary medicines, the administration is authorized to take all necessary measures to facilitate access to health care, for public health reasons in case of serious epidemic, or in case of extreme emergency or national calamity. The use of these provisions can only occur when the proprietary medicine

---

The previous code of pharmacy reflected the situation just after independence and had had very few modifications since then. At the time, the majority of pharmacists were foreign. There was no national diploma and the pharmaceutical industry consisted mainly of *comptoirs d'importation* for medicines. The debate on the adoption of a new pharmaceutical code took ten years. The first draft text was written in 1993. Many versions were written and debated after that date. The polemics centered on the dissatisfaction of pharmacists who were worried about losing their prerogatives.

concerned is provided to the public in insufficient quantity or quality or at abnormally high prices". Thus the government use would be limited to the same grounds as the compulsory licenses by virtue of this provision in the code of pharmacy. The idea of allowing authorities to waive extra TRIPS requirements such as data exclusivity through the use of a legal provision that resembles the mechanism of compulsory licensing is an interesting possibility for governments. However, the provision would have been more usable and effective if it had been formulated in more flexible terms, closer to TRIPS provisions and not introducing additional restrictions.

The legislation on IP establishes a new framework in which future Moroccan public health policies will be developed and implemented. The stakes are high, especially since Morocco has decided to adopt universal medical coverage. Compulsory Medical Insurance (AMO) and the Medical Aid Regime for the most vulnerable citizens (RAMED) were adopted in July 2005 and started gradually to be implemented in 2006. The objective is to extend access to primary health care and essential medicines across the country and to reduce the gap between urban and rural areas. In 2003, the WHO calculated that 35 percent of the 31 million inhabitants of Morocco did not have access to essential medicines (WHO, 2003; See also Ministry of Health, 2003), while medical coverage was estimated to be no higher than 17 percent of the population until recently (Repère Médical, 2006). With the AMO and the RAMED, the government seeks to provide partial to total medical coverage for more than 50 percent of the population in the coming years (Ministry of Health, 2005). The AMO should ultimately benefit approximately 10 million employees in the public and private sectors.[24] The RAMED should cover 9 to 12 million inhabitants (Belouas, 2006; 2007). The coverage of expenses that is currently 70 percent minimum for medicines should reach 100 percent for expensive chronic diseases (Dadès, 2006). Twenty diseases classified as serious pathologies (cancer, AIDS, diabetes, etc.) should be included in this program, which is intended to cover more than 1,600 health products, and 51 groups of pathologies.[25]

In this context, the high prices of medicines in Morocco represent a heavy burden on this system and a grave threat to its sustainability. A recent report from a commission of the Parliament indicates that drug prices in Morocco are particularly high, "abnormally high" according to

---

[24] According to information provided by the website of the Prime Minister, accessed in 2007.
[25] According to the Caisse Nationale de Sécurité Sociale, see http://www.cnss.ma/index.php?p=1975 (accessed on 27 October 2010).

those who conducted the survey.[26] Moroccan prices for brand name drugs, for example, are from 30 to 189 percent higher than in Tunisia, and 20 to 70 percent higher than in France. This situation was already indicated by a study conducted by Health Action International in 2004 which showed that the level of prices in Morocco was much higher than in most countries with comparable resources (HAI, 2004).[27] Medicines represent 40 percent of the total spending on health in Morocco.

The ten biggest companies in the Moroccan market do not face direct competition. And until now the country has not implemented a very aggressive policy to favor generic competition and promote the use of generic medicines. The efforts that have been made so far appear rather insufficient, while pharmaceutical companies for their part develop counter-strategies to undermine the use of generic medicines. Moreover, the way the prices are structured and established in Morocco favors high prices, for both brand name and generic products. At the same time, price control and price negotiation with the pharmaceutical companies are rather weak and show poor results.

The national program for access to HIV antiretroviral medicines provides a good of example of generalized access to relatively expensive medicines for chronic diseases. However, this program is also under increasing financial pressure due to the need to extend the therapeutic choice given to patients, highlighting the current challenges that Morocco is facing in the field of public health.

Morocco implemented a policy for access to medicines against HIV/AIDS very early on in comparison to most developing countries. National policy benefited from the impetus and experience of a local AIDS NGO, the ALCS.[28] The AZT monotherapy, which was the first antiretroviral drug prescribed against HIV/AIDS, was officially introduced in Morocco in 1990. The bitherapies, a combination of two drugs, started to be delivered in public facilities in 1995.[29] In 1996, as tritherapy was internationally acknowledged to be the most effective treatment, this started to be prescribed in Morocco, although it was only available to a very limited extent. The price of most of the antiretrovirals available in Morocco was,

---

[26] The survey report on the price of medicine in Morocco was presented by the Commission for Finances and Economic Development at the House of Representatives on November 3, 2009.

[27] Price of the less expensive generic medicines could reach more than 80 times the international price of reference and the price of the brand name drugs 200 times the internal price of reference.

[28] ALCS, Association de Lutte Contre le Sida, created in 1988.

[29] Either a combination of AZT+ddI or AZT+3TC.

however, out of reach of the vast majority of patients; the drugs were even more expensive than in France.[30] In 1999, a special government budget item was created for the procurement of medicines. Financial support from the International Therapeutic Solidarity Fund between 2000 and 2002, and later from the Global Fund against HIV/AIDS, Tuberculosis and Malaria after 2003 secured free access to medicines.

In 1998, when pharmaceutical multinationals started to offer price reductions for antiretroviral drugs to some of the African countries, the lobbying conducted by the ALCS enabled Morocco to benefit from 15 percent price reductions on a tritherapy.[31] In June 2002, after generic versions of several antiretroviral drugs were introduced on the global market, the price decreased again (falling to 2,000 dirhams per patient per month, around US$24). Drug supply is currently predominantly based on the procurement of brand name products. They are clearly more expensive than the cheapest product available on the international market. A generic version of the tritherapy can now be bought on the international market for approximately US$150–200 per patient per year. Generic medicines were introduced in Morocco in the past few years, but they also remain expensive.

Access to antiretroviral drugs is rather good in Morocco: out of 24,000 persons with HIV, more than 2,400 need medicines and only a few dozen do not receive treatment. Belated access in Morocco is usually due to clinical factors: anemia, hepatitis, opportunistic infections, etc.[32] However, the high prices limit the therapeutic options available to patients, as most of the recent drugs, which are patented, are too expensive to be purchased by the government. Increasing problems arise with the emergence of resistance to first-line treatment and the need for newer molecules.[33]

Thus, an overview of Moroccan policies in the fields of intellectual property and access to medicines brings several paradoxes to light. Morocco has an active policy on access to HIV antiretroviral drugs. The

---

[30] The tritherapy cost was 12,500 dirhams per patient per month – around US$1,500.

[31] The price for a triple therapy including a protease inhibitor fell from 12,500 dirhams to 6,500 dirhams per patient per month – around US$761.

[32] However, it is admitted that among people who live in rural areas, many are not aware of their HIV status.

[33] In Morocco as in any other country, over time, the viral strains of patients under treatment develop resistance to one or several components of the drug combinations they are taking, rendering this line of treatment ineffective against the spread of the disease. For this reason, they have to switch from what is called a "first-line therapy" to a new combination, called a "second line", then a "third line", and so on. In the absence of generic competition for the most recent regimes, these remain particularly expensive.

country is currently implementing universal medical coverage. A reform of the health system and hospitals is being prepared. At the same time, prices of medicines are extremely high. The government does not negotiate firmly with the industry and does not impose any price control. The patent office does not involve health experts in its decisions, nor does it try to avoid unnecessary patents on medicines. On the contrary, it seems to be aiming to grant as many as possible. The government could use compulsory licensing to balance the situation and allow the supply of cheap generics, but it has not done so yet. On the contrary, in the process of implementing the WTO standards and because of the FTA with the US, the country has adopted standards of intellectual property protection that are much more restrictive than those of the WTO, favoring the interests of patent holders against the interests of patients and public health policies. A possibility to waive IP barriers has been introduced in the new code of pharmacy, but it also contains unnecessary restrictions.

These contradictions are partly explained by the lack of integration of health concerns into the larger political agenda of the country, a problem that is fueled by insufficient communication and collaboration between institutions.

Many players are involved in the design and implementation of the policies and legislation that affect public health: pharmaceutical multinationals, local companies, associations of patients and health professionals, representatives of the ministry of health, of the Moroccan office for industrial property, of the ministry of commerce and industry, of the ministry of justice, of the ministry of foreign affairs, officials working with the King, etc. Individuals follow logics or cultures that vary from one institution to another; they act according to specific interests and focus on specific concerns. In recent years, certain interests (the protection of intellectual property, access to the US market for some local firms) have clearly prevailed over others (access to medicines, the sustainability of medical coverage). However, the local mobilization during the Morocco–US FTA negotiations, and for example actions such as the distribution of an analysis of the IP chapter of the agreement to all MPs by the ALCS, seem to have a positive impact in the longer run. At a time when health policies are moving to the forefront of government priorities, elements of analysis and criticism from health advocates finally appear as resources.

The current context shaped by the new legal environment of intellectual property, the implementation of universal medical coverage and the increasing burden of chronic diseases in Morocco are creating new tensions for the political institutions to arbitrate. The recent parliamentary commission on the price of medicines, whose goals are to ensure better access to medicines and the sustainability of the medical coverage system, is an example of the emergence of new issues in the political debate that may help to redefine the situation and modify the power relation between interests. The growing visibility of health imperatives and the accompanying political motivation lay the foundations for better collaboration between institutions and new mechanisms to facilitate this. One concrete option is, for example, the involvement of experts from the health ministry in the process of granting patents on pharmaceutical products. On this matter, the experience of other countries such as Brazil with the ANVISA provides interesting elements to inform reflection on the implementation of new mechanisms to improve collaboration between national institutions.

In response to the concerns raised about access to medicines during negotiation of the Morocco–US FTA, a letter of understanding was signed by the United States Trade Representative and the Moroccan Minister Delegate for Foreign Affairs and Cooperation. It states that: "The implementation of the provisions of Chapter 15 of the Agreement does not affect the ability of either Party to take necessary measures to protect public health by promoting access to medicines for all."[34] This certainly represents a legal avenue the Moroccan government could take advantage of to improve the balance of its laws and policies and reform its current legal and regulatory environment to protect public health and extend access to medicines throughout the country.

REFERENCES

Belouas, A. (2006), 'L'AMO des pauvres démarre en février 2007', La Vie Éco, 24 novembre.

Belouas, A. (2007), 'Le Ramed devrait coûter à l'Etat entre 1,2 et 3,4 milliards de DH par an', La Vie Éco, 31 janvier.

Dadès, H., (2006), 'Assurance Maladie Obligatoire: Quels tarifs pour la mise en oeuvre?' Le Reporter, 12 mars.

Drahos, P. (2008a), 'Trust Me: Patent Offices in Developing Countries', American Journal of Law & Medicine, 34(2–3), 151–74.

Drahos, P. (2008b), 'Regulating Patent Offices: Countering Pharmaceutical Hegemony', SCRIPT-ed, 5(3), 501–14.

Health Action International (HAI) (2004), 'Medicine Prices, a New Approach to Measurement', Enquête sur les prix du médicament au Maroc, April.

Krikorian, G. (2007), 'Évolutions récentes de la législation sur la propriété intellectuelle au Maroc et accès aux médicaments', KEStudies, 1, available at: http://kestudies.org/ojs/index.php/kes/article/viewPDFInterstitial/25/22 (accessed 27 October 2010).

---

[34] This letter is available on the USTR's website: http://www.ustr.gov/trade-agreements/free-trade-agreements/morocco-fta/final-text.

Krikorian, G. and D. Szymkowiak (2007), 'Intellectual Property Rights in the Making: The Evolution of Intellectual Property. Provisions in US Free Trade Agreements and Access to Medicine', The Journal of World Intellectual Property, 10(5), 388–418.

Ministry of Health (2003), 'Indicateurs de Santé', Royaume du Maroc, Ministère de la Santé, July.

Ministry of Health (2005), Press Statement, January, available at: http://www. sante.gov.ma/Leministre/Communique/2004/amo/signatureamo.asp (accessed 27 October 2010).

Repère Médical (2006), L'AMO en quelques chiffres, no. 5, November 2006, available at: http://www.repere-medical.com/article-51.html (accessed 27 October 2010).

Shadlen, K.C. (2011), 'The Political Contradictions of Incremental Innovation: Lessons from Pharmaceutical Patent Examination in Brazil', Politics & Society, 39(2), 143–74.

Timmermans, K. (2005), 'Health and Intellectual Property Rights: Thoughts on Ensuring Access to Medicines in 2005 and Beyond', World Health Organization, Indonesia, UNCTAD/ICTSD Regional Dialogue "Intellectual Property Rights (IPRs), Innovation and Sustainable Development", 8–10 November; Hong Kong, SAR, People's Republic of China.

WHO (2003), Country Cooperation Strategy for WHO and Morocco, 2004–2007, WHO-EM/ARD/005/E/L, World Health Organization Regional Office for the Eastern Mediterranean, Cairo, 2003.

4. The invisible threat: trade, intellectual property, and pharmaceutical regulations in Colombia

Tatiana Andia

As is the case in many other developing countries, since the mid-1990s Colombia has actively pursued an ongoing transformation of intellectual property rights (IPRs) and pharmaceutical legislation. Along with these legislative developments, other aspects of the IPRs and pharmaceutical sector have changed, including governmental agencies' functions and stakeholders'– NGOs and the local pharmaceutical industry – political strategies. There are two trends that loom large as key elements of the new pharmaceutical regulatory era in Colombia: on the one hand, the proliferation of international free trade agreement (FTA) negotiations, which include pharmaceutical intellectual property (IP) provisions, and, on the other hand, the recent rise of local non-IP and non-trade regulatory reforms regarding the marketing approval of drugs and price controls, which are meant to complement pharmaceutical IPR enforcement.

The first of these trends – the multiplication of FTAs negotiation – has been characterized by the increased public attention accorded to health issues and by the incessant lobbying exercised by the coalition of health NGOs and the local pharmaceutical industry against stronger IPR protection. In turn, these two factors helped prevent the country from granting higher IPR protection standards. In contrast, the second trend – the introduction of another type of pharmaceutical legislation, not trade or IP-related[1] – was confronted less effectively by the health NGOs and

---

[1] Some of these measures may respond to indirect trade-related pressures, such as those exercised in the context of temporary trade preferences acts such as the Andean Trade Preference Act–ATPA, but are not strictly trade related because they are not included in a formal and enduring free trade agreement. Such is the case of the Colombian data protection decree, which I will refer to later in the chapter. See USTR (2009).

local industry coalitions. Yet these regulations, neither IP- nor trade-related in a formal sense, have precluded improvement in the access to pharmaceuticals.

In this context, the Colombian case offers two new insights for the literature on IPRs and pharmaceuticals in developing countries. On the one hand, it demonstrates how a country, despite being considered trade-compliant, can also have an active civil society and a stable local pharmaceutical industry that advocates weaker IPR protection. On the other hand, the Colombian case also illustrates how a new 'age' of non-IP and non-trade pharmaceutical regulation may jeopardize the positive effects of 'similar drugs'[2] competition as well as civil society mobilization demanding access to health.

Therefore, the objective of this chapter is threefold: (1) to describe the two different, but complementary, trends in the Colombian pharmaceutical sector from the 1990s to the present, (2) to outline several effects of each trend, and (3) to suggest some of the political economy explanations for the difference in the outcomes of the two trends.

In the first section, I will describe the first trend – the IP-related and trade-related trend – as well as some of its results: the number of patents granted and the level of 'similar drugs' competition. In addition, I will describe some of the groups of stakeholders that have pushed, resisted and reacted to such legislative and regulatory initiatives. I will focus on health NGOs and local industries, since they represent a relatively coherent group of stakeholders that has confronted, and still confronts, the strengthening of pharmaceutical IPR protection.

The second section is devoted to depicting the non-IP and non-trade trend. I examine the enactment of additional regulations that were not embodied in trade agreements, but that may still have major effects on the access to treatment. I will refer particularly to two types of regulations: (1) price controls, which affect the affordability of all pharmaceuticals – chemical as well as biotechnological – and (2) biotechnology drugs registration requisites that create barriers to the introduction of 'biosimilars.' Furthermore, in this section I will assess the actual level of

---

[2]   I will use the term 'similar drugs' as an equivalent to what is usually called a 'generic' (i.e. any non-original product with the same active principle of the original, no matter if it is branded or not branded). Then I will use 'Brand-name generic' to talk about 'similar drugs' that use a brand name; and 'generic' to talk about 'similar drugs' that use the active principle name. It is worth clarifying that in Colombia 'generics' are interpreted to refer to products that are registered with nonproprietary names. Therefore, many of the drugs produced by the local pharmaceutical industry are not usually called 'generics' because they are branded, so they are called copies. See Homedes and Ugalde (2005).

price deregulation, its effect on pharmaceuticals' affordability, and the number of biotechnology products that were granted data exclusivity rights. I will also describe the role of the stakeholders described in the first part of the chapter, showing that contrary to expectations, their social mobilization strategies were ineffective in trying to thwart local non-IP and non-trade pharmaceutical regulations.

In the conclusion I suggest that the internationally induced increase of pharmaceutical IPR standards is closely related to the locally induced deregulation of pharmaceutical prices and the overregulation of bio-technology drugs. Furthermore, I will describe how the primary objective – curtailing competition and deregulating prices – is achieved. More suc-cinctly, I will argue that as is the case with the IPR chapters inherent in international trade agreements, the agenda of additional pharmaceutical regulatory reforms – usually overlooked by the literature, but nonetheless highly relevant[3] – is also shaped globally, except for the fact that the legal negotiations take place locally.

1. INTERNATIONAL PRESSURE FOR IPR PROTECTION: LOCAL PHARMACEUTICAL INDUSTRY AND CIVIL SOCIETY RESPONSE

The Legal IP Outcome of International Agreements

The first pharmaceutical IPR deliberations in Colombia date back to the introduction of international legislation during the 1990s. Indeed, the first regional agreement on the subject was conveyed in the Decision 311 of the Andean Nations Commission (ANC) in 1991, which allowed the patenting of pharmaceutical products for the first time. Thereafter, legislation was introduced in 1994, 2000 and 2002. These statutes essentially raised the levels of protection in order to comply with the WTO multilateral agreement

---

[3] Such as registration requisites, price controls, information systems, pharmaco-vigilance, among others. The literature on the strengthening of IPR protection in developing countries focuses principally on the legislative and prospective impact of multilateral and bilateral trade agreements (Correa, 2000, 2002; Drahos, 1997; Drahos and Mayne, 2002; Hoen, 2002; Nogués, 1990); some authors estimate the prospective economic impact of BTAs IP rules (Zuleta, 2000; Rocha, 2003; Cortes, 2004, 2009; Andia et al. 2009); some authors look at the political economy (Hoekman, 2002; Sell, 2000, 2003; Shadlen, 2005, 2007, 2008); and fewer research specific policy outcomes and local negotiation processes (Shadlen, 2009; Flynn, this volume, Chapter 6).

on Trade Related Aspects of Intellectual Property (TRIPS). Concurrently, bilateral trade negotiations advocating stronger IPR protection measures were held in 2003 and 2008 with the US and the EU, respectively.

An initial glance at the legislative output regarding pharmaceutical patents and data protection may lead to the conclusion that Colombia adopted a combination of TRIPS-'minimum' and TRIPS-'plus' approaches to the WTO agreement implementation (Deere, 2009, p. 12).[4] As a matter of fact, on the one hand, the Andean Decisions 344 of 1994 and 486 of 2000 did only what was necessary to comply with TRIPS, partially using the transition period and preserving the flexibilities associated with pharmaceutical patents, i.e. compulsory licenses, parallel imports and experimental use, among others. Also, although it may seem that the Andean Community introduced pharmaceutical patents too rapidly (in 1991), it did so by excluding pharmaceutical products that were included in the World Health Organization (WHO) essential medicines list and only eliminated such exceptions to fully comply with TRIPS in 2000. Moreover, in 1996 the Andean Community denied the retroactive recognition of patents – 'pipeline' protection – whereas other countries in the region such as Mexico (1991) and Brazil (1996) allowed it.[5] Therefore, it could be argued that these rulings were consistent with a TRIPS-'minimum' approach.

However, on the other hand, the same aforementioned Andean Decisions foreshadowed the upcoming data exclusivity statute – Decree 2085 of 2002 – that was introduced only in Colombia and went beyond TRIPS requirements. Decree 2085 stipulated a five-year data exclusivity term for new pharmaceutical entities entering the market and was implicitly demanded by the US government in exchange for the Andean Tariffs Preferences Agreement – ATPA. Consequently, with respect to data protection Colombia adopted a TRIPS-'plus' approach.

Either way, it is worth noting that Colombia has effectively never used TRIPS flexibilities, such as compulsory licenses or parallel imports. Only very recently, in 2008, the Colombian Ministry of Commerce, Industry and Tourism produced a decree (Decree 4302) specifying the compulsory-license issuing process, and in 2010 the Ministry of Social Protection produced

---

[4]   As explained by Carolyn Deere, the TRIPS level of implementation is related to: (1) the country's timing in complying with TRIPS – how far or close to the deadline; (2) the degree of the use of TRIPS flexibilities; (3) how internal IP laws were written; and (4) the country's IP enforcement provisions.

[5]   For a complete description of TRIPS implementation in developing countries in 1998 see Correa, 'Recent developments in the field of pharmaceutical patents: implementation of the TRIPS agreement', *Health Action International*, http://www.haiweb.org/campaign/novseminar/correa2.html.

another decree (Decree 1313) specifying the parallel imports authorization process, but none of the instruments has actually been used. Instead, I will show in this chapter that Colombia has gone beyond its own obligations by awarding five years of data exclusivity to most of the recently introduced high-cost biotechnology drugs, even though the data protection decree (Decree 2085) contemplates protection exclusively for chemical drugs.

After complying in full with TRIPS, Colombia entered a new era of pharmaceutical IPR protection debates, in which Bilateral Trade Agreement (BTA) bargains were the key elements. The first and most controversial BTA negotiated by Colombia was with the US. Negotiations began in 2003 – following the failure of the Free Trade Area of the Americas (FTAA) – and lasted almost three years until the agreement was finally signed on November 22, 2006. Nevertheless, after it had been signed, the Colombia–US Trade Promotion Agreement was rejected by the US Congress in July 2007. Subsequently, the agreement was modified in November 2007 – the IPR and labor chapters were mostly rewritten in order to better address access to health and labor rights concerns. Despite the fact that the agreement and its amendment protocol have already been endorsed by the Colombian Congress and Constitutional Court, US Congressional approval is still pending.

Following the US Trade Promotion Agreement, a new BTA negotiation with the EU began in 2008. Negotiations with the EU ended in 2010, but as at May 2011 approval is expected from the EU Council of Ministers and the European Parliament. In this case, health NGOs and the local pharmaceutical industry exerted pressure on the negotiations and as a result the riskier clauses regarding IPRs aimed at strengthening data protection and enforcement measures were reversed.[6] Briefly, if one takes only the pharmaceutical IPR legislative output and the texts of the FTAs into account, a trend of a gradual and slight increase in IPR protection measures is evident in Colombia. Yet, this gradual rise in IPR standards, coupled with the greater involvement of Colombia in bilateral trade negotiations, is by no means a unique trend in developing countries.

---

[6] What the EU proposed was an 11-year term of data protection granted to each new pharmaceutical product – not only to those that show 'significant effort' as the Colombian legislation states. The draft of the agreement also includes several new enforcement measures, such as port controls for pharmaceutical imports and stronger penalties in the case of rights violations. The last report disclosed by the Andean health NGOs alliance – following the 7th round of negotiations that took place in Brussels on September 21 – stated that after reversing all the EU requirements on patents, data protection and enforcement measures, the only dangerous clause that remained concerned biotechnology drug data exclusivity protection.

Furthermore, international pressures could have led Colombia to a TRIPS-plus scenario, increasing not only data protection standards, as actually occurred, but also expanding the scope of patent protection and curtailing the use of TRIPS flexibilities. This scenario was feasible, owing to the fact that in the first draft of the Colombia–US FTA 'second use' patents were included. This implied that if a new indication was identified for a drug already patented, this new indication could be the object of a second patent. On the contrary, until now Colombia has retained much of its pharmaceutical IP law.

The Real Output of IP Protection

Going beyond the 'black letter' IP law, we observe that despite the sharp rise in pharmaceutical patent applications,[7] the Colombian patent office has granted a consistent number of pharmaceutical patents over the past two decades (see Table 4.1).

Bearing in mind the fact that most patent applications submitted after 2000 are still being reviewed, it is not possible to assess whether the rate of successful applications – an average yearly output of 123 pharmaceutical patents during the 1990s – will increase substantially due to new incoming patents. Nevertheless, we can observe a similar trend – an increased number of pharmaceutical patent applications – during the second half of the 1990s. During that period we also observe the number of patents granted escalating less than proportionally to the increased number of applications.[8]

Accordingly, although 40 percent of the pharmaceutical patents were granted to 16 major transnational pharmaceutical companies (see Table 4.2), many of the so-called 'blockbuster drugs' were not patented in Colombia. This fact has allowed the local pharmaceutical industry to compete for the most profitable pharmaceutical market segments.

The Colombian patent office files reveal that it has acquired enough independence to deny many of the blockbuster patent applications on 'lack of novelty' grounds. For example, in the case of celecoxib (Celebrex®),

---

[7] In effect, pharmaceutical patent applications have risen from an average of 380 per year during the 1990s to an average of 653 per year between 2000 and 2008.

[8] In fact, while the number of pharmaceutical applications increased from an average of 253 per year between 1991 and 1995 to an average of 539 per year between 1996 and 1999, the average number of patents granted for the same periods remained almost equal – with on average 110 patents per year during the first half of the decade and 139 patents per year during the second half.

Table 4.1   Pharmaceutical patents granted in Colombia

Year of application	Applications		Patents granted	
	Total	Pharma	Total	Pharma
1991	612	184	425	116
1992	695	222	248	126
1993	907	239	280	102
1994	906	266	690	91
1995	1 155	357	365	117
1996	1 194	375	370	118
1997	1 592	486	505	151
1998	1 755	656	476	163
1999	1 786	640	590	126
2000	1 769	808	595	163
2001	497	167	363	15
2002	581	195	372	12
2003	1 209	627	291	37
2004	1 441	734	294	19
2005	1 761	814	256	9
2006	2 003	929	223	0
2007	1 976	838	222	0
2008	1 944	765	409	0
Total	23 783	9 302	6 974	1 365

Source: Superintendencia de Industria y Comercio.

the applicant, G.D. Searle & Co,[9] appealed the patent office's decision, building its argument on the basis of European and Peruvian patents for the same molecule. Nevertheless, the Colombian patent office ratified the patent refusal, stating that 'those patents [i.e. the European and Peruvian patents] are not binding for this office, just as the patents granted by this office are not mandatory for other countries'.

Furthermore, in the absence of strong patent protection, the Colombian pharmaceutical industry has managed to compete in profitable market niches. For instance, selecting four leading pharmaceuticals, including celecoxib (Celebrex®), omeprazole (Losec®), atorvastatin (Lipitor®), and clopidogrel (Plavix®) – used for arthritis, gastritis, and the prevention of cardiovascular diseases, respectively – it can be observed that each of these

[9]   Which is Pfizer, since G.D. Searle & Co was acquired by Monsanto, which later merged with Pharmacia & Upjohn. Finally, Pharmacia was acquired by Pfizer.

Table 4.2   Pharmaceutical patents granted

	Pharmaceutical applications						Pharmaceutical patents granted	
	1991–2008		1990s		2000s		1991–2008	
	Number	%	Number	%	Number	%	Number	%
Abbott	143	1.47	76	2.22	18	0.29	24	1.76
Astra-Zeneca	219	2.26	12	0.35	206	3.28	15	1.10
Bayer	302	3.11	77	2.25	218	3.47	40	2.93
Boehringer	316	3.26	87	2.54	224	3.57	45	3.29
Bristol-Myers Squibb	183	1.89	37	1.08	145	2.31	14	1.02
GlaxoSmithKline	281	2.89	111	3.24	164	2.61	40	2.93
SmithKline Beecham	443	4.56	241	7.03	202	3.22	59	4.32
Janssen Cilag	115	1.18	14	0.41	101	1.61	12	0.88
Merck	211	2.17	68	1.98	99	1.58	34	2.49
Novartis	360	3.71	71	2.07	289	4.60	50	3.66
Pfizer	716	7.38	285	8.32	425	6.77	105	7.68
Sanofi Aventis	249	2.57	58	1.69	191	3.04	46	3.37
Aventis	150	1.55	7	0.20	143	2.28	8	0.59
Schering-Plough	203	2.09	66	1.93	122	1.94	22	1.61
Wyeth	261	2.69	15	0.44	246	3.92	14	1.02
Totals	4152	43	1225	36	2793	44	528	39

Source: author's calculations using data from the Superintendencia de Industria y Comercio (SIC) (September 2009).

products has more than 20 local competitors.[10] Moreover, the four largest Colombian pharmaceutical manufacturers – Tecnoquímicas, Procaps, Lafrancol and Genfar – are among the 16 best-selling companies in the country.[11] They are able to produce both branded and unbranded 'similar drugs', and sometimes they conduct bio-bio studies[12] as well.

---

[10]   Author's calculations using data from the Vademecum Med-Informatica Versión Dorada con precios (September, 2009).

[11]   Tecnoquímicas was the first with sales of US$367 million; Procaps was the 8th after Baxter, Roche, Abbott, Bayer, Sanofi-Aventis, and Novartis, with sales of US$146 million; Lafrancol was the 12th and Genfar the 16th (ANDI, Encuesta Annual Manufacturera).

[12]   Bioequivalence and bioavailability are studies that demonstrate that two drugs are essentially the same. Usually 'similar drugs' that have proven equiva-

The co-existence of this prosperous local pharmaceutical industry alongside a weak patent protection system implies that a representative number of 'similar drugs' are available in Colombia for the most prevalent diseases. Nevertheless, as I will demonstrate later in this chapter, the Colombian case is an example of how more competition does not necessarily lead to lower prices – at least not as low as expected in some very competitive chemical drug market segments.

The Political Economy of IP Protection

In the early 1990s only local pharmaceutical industries were concerned about the possibility of increased IPR protection. They considered that international agreements on the subject threatened their subsistence; consequently, they decided to launch a vigorous lobbying strategy against them. During that period, public opinion was, for the most part, unaware of the characteristics and implications of the adoption of international IPR standards.

Evidence of this lack of public awareness can be found in the most widely read Colombian newspaper articles from 1991 to 2008.[13] The number of articles was much lower during the 1990s – with an average of 9 items per year – than during the 2000s, when the number of articles climbed to an average of 52 items per year, showing a peak in 2004 of 139 entries due to the Colombia–US FTA negotiation. Even more remarkable is the fact that none of the 1990s newspaper articles dealt with the impact of IPR protection on access to health. On the contrary, all of them referred to IPRs as a threat to local pharmaceutical manufacturers. On the other hand, since 2000, 96 percent of the articles dealt with IPRs with respect to access to pharmaceutical treatment and health issues.

This increased visibility of IPRs, and the association with access-to-health debates, was boosted primarily by media reports from South Africa and Brazil on access to HIV drugs as well as by local NGOs condemning stronger IPR protection. As a matter of fact, in 2001, 38 percent of the newspaper stories regarding IPR protection and pharmaceuticals mentioned the South African or Brazilian cases, with no reference to local

---

lence are called 'generics', but in Colombia these studies are not a prerequisite to obtaining market approval. Hence, many 'similar drugs' in Colombia could prove bioequivalence but they don't because they have not been required to do so; that is also why I called them all 'generics'.

[13] The newspapers and magazines consulted for the purpose of this chapter were: *El Tiempo*, *Revista Semana* and *Revista Dinero*.

health NGOs or activists. Only since 2003 were local civil society organizations or their leaders increasingly mentioned in the newspapers. In 2003, 32 percent of the newspaper entries mentioned at least one local health NGO or civil society leader; by 2006, the percentage climbed to 46, and in 2009, 95 percent of the IPR and pharmaceutical stories cited a local civil society organization or individual.

Moreover, the increasing public awareness about IPRs influenced the way in which many actors, i.e. government and industry representatives, presented themselves. Each of the actors involved in IPR debates perceived the necessity of explicitly addressing health access concerns. Consequently, transnational pharmaceutical corporations that prior to the 1990s had adopted the role of 'pharmaceutical product manufacturers'[14] presented themselves as key players in Colombia's economic development. By doing so, they downplayed their manufacturing power, highlighting instead the significance of their R&D investments. Furthermore, transnational pharmaceutical corporations stressed that without proper IPR protection, local patients would be excluded from benefiting from the most recent innovations.

Likewise, the local 'similar drugs' industry decided to steer public opinion not towards the national nature of their capital, but towards the possibility of guaranteeing more affordable treatments.[15] Moreover, local 'similar drugs' industries teamed up with civil society organizations in a win-win strategy. In this *quid pro quo*, the local industry's support partially relieved NGOs from their financial distress; in return, the NGOs' sympathy allowed the local pharmaceutical industry to apply some badly needed make-up to their public image.[16]

At the end of the day, local manufacturers and access-to-health advocates teamed up to resist any internationally induced attempt to strengthen

---

[14]   In fact, AFIDRO stands for Asociación de Fabricantes y Representantes Exclusivos de Productos Farmacéuticos, which means Pharmaceutical Products Manufacturers and Exclusive Representatives Association, but more recently they have identified themselves as R&D Pharmaceutical Laboratories Association – Asociación de Laboratorios Farmacéuticos de Investigación y Desarrollo in Spanish.

[15]   One of the most popular local pharmaceutical industry maxims coined during the Colombia–US FTA negotiations stated, 'the findings of all humanity at hand for everybody' (in Spanish 'los hallazgos de la humanidad al alcance de todos' by Genfar).

[16]   For example, Mision Salud – one of the most influential Colombian health NGOs today – was first created as the 'civil society arm' of the local pharmaceutical industry (interview with Germán Holguín, Director of Misión Salud, Oct. 2008).

IPR protection. They attended every round of trade negotiations, backed negotiation advisors,[17] made public statements, organized press conferences, established direct communication channels with government negotiators, and lobbied internationally by meeting politicians from their counterparts at the negotiation tables.

These campaigns against stronger IPR protection undertaken by health NGOs and the local pharmaceutical industry, sometimes with partial support from government representatives, can be considered to have been successful for the most part. This assertion is supported by three interconnected facts. First, during the last two decades there has been no major transformation of the TRIPS pharmaceutical IP law in Colombia. Second, the number of pharmaceutical patents granted has not increased significantly. Finally, the local pharmaceutical industry has managed to copy, survive and even identify profitable market niches.

2. LOCALLY INDUCED PHARMACEUTICAL REGULATORY REFORM: PRICE DEREGULATION AND REGISTRATION PROCEDURES OVERREGULATION

Together with the multiplication of international free trade agreements (FTAs) negotiations described in the first section of this chapter, other measures related to pharmaceutical regulation were undertaken in Colombia during the late 1990s and early 2000s. Although they are non-IP and non-trade related, these measures are pieces of the same puzzle of the global increase in IPR standards. Therefore, implementation of this more recent and less publicized trend of complementary measures looms large in pharmaceutical regulatory reforms, more specifically in two main fields: (1) drugs – chemical as well as biotechnological – price controls; and (2) marketing approval requirements and data protection for biotechnology drugs.

---

[17] For the Colombia–US FTA negotiations, Ifarma and Mision Salud backed Carlos Correa – a very well-known Argentinian IPR lawyer – as advisor for the Ministry of Health. Nevertheless, the transnational pharmaceutical companies' association (AFIDRO) and the US negotiators complained; although he was already being paid, he was marginalized from the negotiation process on the grounds that he was a foreigner (interview with Luis Guillermo Restrepo, Colombia–US FTA negotiator, June 2009). Colombian health NGOs also backed a new legal advisor for the Colombia–EU FTA negotiations – the Spaniard IPR lawyer, Xavier Seuba – but this time there were no complaints about his being a foreigner.

Price controls and biotechnology-product marketing approval policies are essential to fostering local pharmaceutical productive capacity and enhancing access to health care. Their importance is even more salient if we consider that in 2008, 24 percent of the amount invested by the Colombian government in drugs not included in the Basic Health Plan (*Plan Obligatorio de Salud, POS*) paid for only seven drugs, five of which were biotechnology drugs.[18] Moreover, the prices paid by the government for these products were in some cases five times higher than the reasonable market prices.[19]

Furthermore, Colombia's expenditure on pharmaceutical products experienced a sharp increase over the last decade – rising from 1.2 percent of GDP in 2001 to 1.3 percent in 2006, to 1.43 percent in 2008 – which threatened the Health System's financial sustainability.[20] As Figure 4.1 illustrates, only the costs of treatments not included in the Basic Health Plan paid by the tax-financed fund FOSYGA[21] escalated from US$2.8 million in 2001 to US$605.3 million in 2008.[22] This figure represents around 17 percent of the total governmental pharmaceutical expenditure and was primarily spent on expensive chemical and biotechnology drugs.

The fact that pharmaceutical expenditure increased so rapidly over the past decade is not surprising if we consider the prevalence of high-cost diseases in Colombia, such as cancer, HIV-AIDS, arthritis and diabetes. In fact, malignant tumors – especially stomach for men, and breast for women – are the second cause of death in Colombia after heart and circu-

---

[18]   Specifically, Mabthera®, Herceptin® and Avastin® by Roche; and Humira® and Sinagis® by Abbott. (Source: Boletín del Consumidor de Medicamentos No. 37, 2009).

[19]   This fact was made public by an economics magazine, *Portafolio*, that revealed some of the results of a study undertaken by AFIDRO that demonstrated the need for a top price list to control government pharmaceutical expenditures. *Portafolio*, 'Caprecom concentra medicinas No Pos', November 5, 2009.

[20]   Even more, considering the fact that according to the National Department of Statistics (DANE), the average increase of GDP between 2001 and 2008 was 5.7 percent. The data on pharmaceutical expenditure are derived from Zerda et al. (2001) and Cortés (2009).

[21]   FOSYGA stands for Solidarity and Guarantee Fund (Fondo de Solidaridad y Garantía). In Colombia drugs are paid for in two ways: by public and out-of-pocket expenditures. The public expenditure pays for drugs that are included in the essential medicines list, but it also pays for drugs that, although not included in the list, are necessary in order to guarantee the right to health for some individuals. These payments – for drugs not included on the essential medicines list – are those that are recouped from the FOSYGA.

[22]   Moreover, the amount paid by the FOSYGA reached US$790 million in 2009. These are data from the Ministry of Health.

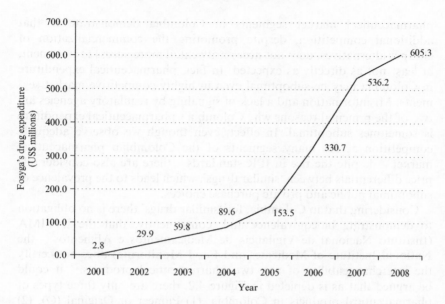

Source: Informe del Sistema de Información de Medicamentos – SISMED (July 2009).

Figure 4.1 FOSYGA's pharmaceutical expenditure (US\$ millions)

latory diseases.[23] Nonetheless, the problem of Colombian pharmaceutical expenditure is not only its frantic/exponential increase; even more important is the fact that most of Colombia's pharmaceutical expenditure is misspent due to the lack of competition and, where competition exists, due to the lack of proper price regulation.

Drug Price Deregulation

Concerns about excessive IPRs and data protection go hand in hand with worries related to insufficient market competition. Therefore, advocates of a less strict IPR and data protection regime view strong IPR protection as a barrier to the market entry of 'similar drugs' and assume that higher competition would lower monopolistic prices and, thus, pave the way for access to treatment.[24] However, what some highly competitive

---

[23] Instituto Nacional de Cancerología – INC, 2003.
[24] Many analyses of IPR protection welfare effects and economic costs are based on the assumption that competition works as an impetus for lowering prices.

pharmaceutical market segments in Colombia demonstrate is that additional competition, despite promoting the commercialization of cheaper alternatives, does not necessarily entail more access to treatment, at least not as directly as expected. In fact, pharmaceutical expenditure in Colombia may be suboptimal even in highly competitive market segments. Misinformation and a lack of signaling by regulatory agencies are two of the principal reasons why Colombia's pharmaceutical expenditure is sometimes suboptimal. In effect, even though we observe adequate competition across many segments of the Colombian pharmaceutical market – despite the rise in IPR standards – there are also considerable price differentials between 'similar drugs', which leads to the prevalence of suboptimal public and private purchase choices.

Considering that in Colombia, for 'similar drugs' there is no obligation to demonstrate bioequivalence and, consequently, that the INVIMA (Instituto Nacional de Vigilancìa de Medicamentos e Alimentos – the National Institute of Medicines and Food Monitoring) does not certify the interchangeability of any two pharmaceutical products,[25] it could be argued that as is depicted in Figure 4.2, there are only three types of pharmaceutical products in Colombia: (1) Pioneer or Original (O); (2) Brand-name Generic (BG); and (3) Generic (G).[26] These last two types of pharmaceutical products, i.e. Brand-name Generics and Generics, are, therefore, what elsewhere are called 'similar drugs'.[27]

There are two basic problems with these differential drug prices in Colombia: (1) the prices of the Os – monopolistic or not – are too high

---

For example, Danzon (1997); Danzon and Chao (2000); Attaran and Gillespie (2001); Attaran (2004); Borrell and Watal (2003); and Chaudhuri et al. (2003), among others.

[25]   In fact, the Decree 677 of 1995 states that a bio-bio study must be presented as a registration requisite only for products selected by the INVIMA. In particular, (a) anticonvulsivant drugs, (b) immunosuppressant drugs, and (c) other drugs that the INVIMA eventually considers high risk. Even though it was contemplated that the INVIMA would grant interchangeability certificates for commercial purposes, it has not. In fact, in a very renowned case when Pfizer sued Lafrancol (a local pharmaceutical company) for placing a label that said 'Eroxim® bioequivalent to Viagra®', the INVIMA did not back Lafrancol's position because although they approved the bio-bio studies presented by Lafrancol, they never certified the two products' interchangeability. See INVIMA, 'Demanda judicial Pfizer sobre Lafrancol, por violación de los derechos de marca.'

[26]   In this typology some of the Brand-name Generics and some of the Generics would have bio-bio studies, but some wouldn't.

[27]   For a description of the many different notations used in Latin American countries see Homedes and Ugalde (2005).

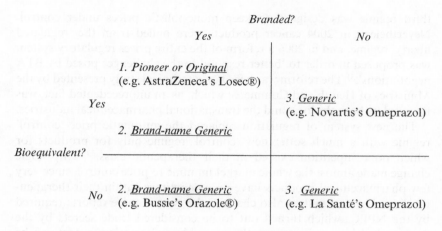

Figure 4.2   Taxonomy of 'generic' drugs in Colombia

compared to the rest of the Andean countries,[28] and (2) BGs and Gs, even when they have the same active ingredient and even when they are manufactured by the same laboratory, can be bought at prices that differ by up to 400 percent.[29]

The National Pharmaceutical Price Commission (NPPC) was created in Colombia in 1994 to correct these two types of market failure. Thus, in 1998, the NPPC established three regulatory regimes regarding pharmaceutical prices:[30] (1) 'liberty' – there is enough market competition and prices are unregulated but under watch; (2) 'observed and regulated liberty' – a top reference price could be established; and (3) 'control.' This last regime was intended for pharmaceuticals that were produced by fewer than three different suppliers, and that were, therefore, considered to be 'exclusive' or monopolistic. New chemical entities entering the market were automatically placed under price 'control' until enough copies – at least three – were made available.

The first two regulatory regimes were intended to prevent producers from charging unreasonable prices in competitive market segments. The

---

[28]   Cortés (2009). This study compares public and private prices in Colombia, Ecuador, Peru and Bolivia and finds that Colombian prices for original drugs are the highest in the region.

[29]   As is the case of clopidogrel (Plavix®) utilizing average prices.

[30]   The regimes already existed for all manufactured products by Law 81 of 1988; the NPPC only specified the 'control' regime characteristics in the case of pharmaceuticals.

third regime was designed to keep monopolistic prices under control. Nevertheless, in 2004 cancer products were pulled from the 'regulated liberty' regime, and in 2006 a reform of the entire prices regulatory system was proposed in order to 'better respond to the challenges posed by BTA negotiations'.[31] The reform was based on a technical study presented by the Ministries of Health and Commerce which, as an unprecedented fact, was financed by both the local and the transnational pharmaceutical industries.

The new system of regulation replaced the automatic price 'control' regime with a much softer new 'control' regime only for products for which no competition existed in their therapeutic class.[32] This single change made almost the whole market immune to price control, since very few pharmaceutical products have no competitors within their therapeutic class. The new system also changed the type of price reports required by the NPPC, which turned out to be considered trade secrets by the Andean legislation. Consequently, no public information system can be developed based on the information gathered. Furthermore, the order to disclose prices on pharmaceutical containers was rescinded, eliminating any possibility of market signaling for the consumer.

Although the 1998 pharmaceutical price control system was never fully operational, at least some information was available. Thanks to this availability of information, pharmaceutical companies were deterred by the possibility, however remote, of being sanctioned. In contrast, the 2006 regime is closer to complete deregulation.

This assertion can be substantiated if we consider the behavior of pharmaceutical market segments that, although competitive, lack consistency in their prices. By analyzing the cases of the four segments shown in Table 4.3, we can observe that there is enough competition. We can also note that for all of the cases, with the exception of Omeprazole, there are more Brand-name Generics (BG) available than Generics (G), which should not be a problem. However, it turns out that BG prices are at least twice, and sometimes even five times higher than Generic prices. Furthermore, taking a closer look (at Table 4.4) we find that some of the BG prices are almost equivalent to the price of the Pioneer.[33]

---

31   Call for proposal 'Estudio de la Política de Precios de Medicamentos en Colombia', Ministerio de la Protección Social, Ministerio de Comercio Industria y Turismo, Cámara Farmacéutica de la Andi, Asinfar, Afidro, 2005.
32   This means that even if a specific cancer pharmaceutical product has no more than one supplier, if there are other cancer products available, it is enough to avoid control.
33   This situation can partially be attributed to a problem of the incentives that local pharamaceutical companies have to inflate reported prices in order to

Table 4.3 '*Similar drugs' availability and prices*

Active ingredient	'Original' (O)	Company	Number			Average prices* (US$)		
			Generics total	Branded Generics (BG)	Generics (G)	O	BG	G
Atorvastatin	Lipitor 10 mg	Pfizer	24	13	11	33	18	5
	Lipitor 20 mg		20	11	9	36	25	8
	Lipitor 40 mg		5	4	1	36	33	16
Clopidogrel	Plavix 75 mg	Sanofi-Aventis	22	15	7	58	38	9
	Iscover 75 mg	Bristol-Myers Squibb				45		
Celecoxib	Celebrex 100 mg	Pfizer	13	7	6	22	12	5
	Celebrex 200 mg		12	7	5	22	13	5
Omeprazole	Losec 20 mg	AstraZeneca	54	25	29	52	17	4

Note: *The prices used are those reported to the NPPC for 2006 for the most common presentation.

Source: Author's calculations using data from the NPPC, Vademecum Med-Informática and INVIMA.

We can also find cases in which a product manufactured and commercialized by the same pharmaceutical company is sold with both a Brand name and a Generic name – as is the case of Glustar® and Atorvastatina (Table 4.4a), and Artroxil® and Celecoxib (Table 4.4b). In these specific cases, the Branded version prices are more than three times higher than the prices of the Generic alternatives.[34]

---

pretend that they are granting enormous discounts when they sell their products to health care providers.

[34] Even though these are examples, I have reviewed more than 45 different active principles/ingredients with competitive markets, and for 40 of them I identified at least one similar case. In fact, the majority of the local pharmaceutical companies have two business units, one devoted to Brand-name Generics and one devoted to Generics.

Table 4.4a Generics prices* and producers' examples

	Brand Name	Company	Price (US$)	Producer	Packing	Importer	Registry Owner
Atorvastatin 20 mg / 10 tabs							
Higher	Atorlip	Lafrancol	37	Lafrancol Colombia			Lafrancol Colombia
	Lipitor	Pfizer	36	Pfizer Brasil			Pfizer Colombia
	Glustar	La Sante	35	La Sante Colombia			Galeno Quimica Colombia
Lower	Atorvastatina	Expofarma	2	Bussie Synthesis Colombia	Expofarma Colombia		Expofarma Colombia
	Lipostan	Labinco	2	Labinco Colombia			Labinco Colombia
	Atorvastatina	La Sante	6	La Sante Colombia			La Sante Colombia

Clopidogrel 75 mg / 14 tabs

	Brand Name	Company	Price (US$)	Producer	Packing	Importer	Registry Owner
Higher	Plavix	Sanofi-Aventis	58	Sanofi Winthrop France		Sanofi Winthrop Colombia	
	Clopivas	Biotoscana	53	Cipla India		Biotoscana Colombia	
	Iscover	Bristol-Myers Squibb (BMS)	45	Sanofi Winthrop France	BMS Mexico		BMS Colombia
	Flusan	Farmacol	44	Farmacol Colombia			Farmacol Colombia
Lower	Clopidogrel	Tecnoquimicas	5	Tecnoquimicas Colombia			Tecnoquimicas Colombia
	Clopidogrel	Memphis	7	California Colombia			Memphis Colombia
	Clopidogrel	American Generics	7	Lafrancol Colombia			American Generics Colombia

Note: *Prices are those reported to the NPPC for 2006.

Source: Author's calculations using data from the NPPC, Vademecum Med-Informática and INVIMA.

Table 4.4b Generics prices* and producers' examples

| | Brand Name | Company | **Celecoxib 100 mg / 20 tabs and 200 mg / 10 tabs** | | | | |
			Price (US$)	Producer	Packing	Importer	Registry Owner
Higher	Celebrex	Pfizer	22	Pfizer Puerto Rico	Pfizer México		Pfizer Colombia
	Artroxil	Grufarcol	13	Tecnoquimicas Colombia			Grufarcol Colombia
	Cicloxx	Farmacol	13	Farmacol Colombia			Farmacol Colombia
Lower	Celecoxib	Tecnoquimicas	4	Tecnoquimicas Colombia			Tecnoquimicas Colombia
	Celecoxib	Farmacoop	4	Farmacoop Colombia			Farmacoop Colombia
	Celecoxib	American Generics	4	Lafrancol Colombia			American Generics Colombia

| | | | Omeprazole 20 mg / 14 tabs | | | |
Brand Name	Company	Price (US$)	Producer	Packing	Importer	Registry Owner
Higher Losec	AstraZeneca	51	AstraZeneca Suecia		AstraZeneca Colombia	AstraZeneca UK
Omeprazol	Novartis	40	Dr. Esteve España		Novartis Colombia	Sandoz Austria
Orazole	Bussie	35	Bussie Colombia			Bussie Colombia
Lower Omeprazol	AZ Pharma	1	Best Colombia	Best - Quibi Colombia		AZ Pharma Colombia
Omeprazol	Colmed	1	Procaps Colombia			Colmed Colombia
Omeprazol	La Sante	1	Alembic Limited – India			La Sante Colombia

Note: *Prices are those reported to the NPPC for 2006.

Source: Author's calculations using data from the NPPC, Vademecum Med-Informática and INVIMA.

These market practices are not exclusive to the 'similar drugs' pharmaceutical industry, as can be concluded from the cases of Plavix® and Iscover® (Table 4.4a). The cases of Plavix and Iscover indicate that transnational pharmaceutical companies implement the very same strategy, even if the differences between the reported prices are not as high as in the case of Brand-name Generics versus Generics. It is worth mentioning that differential pricing strategies based on trademarks are effective because of the widespread public perception of Generics as being less secure and efficacious products than branded drugs.[35] Nevertheless, although marketing based on trademarks usually leads to high prices and it is supposed to guarantee a premium to the seller, nothing seems enough to justify price differentials of up to 400 percent.

Thus, we can conclude that prices reported to the NPPC seldom reveal costs or quality information since they are systematically distorted by market practices. This fact might explain why price controls and information systems are needed to correct some of the pharmaceutical market failures.

In contrast, subsequent to the 2006 prices regulatory reform, the NPPC entered a period of inactivity that lasted until 2009, when under civil society pressure it finally placed one product, Kaletra, under price 'control,'[36] and seven other products on 'regulated liberty.' Nevertheless, Abbott appealed the Commission's decision regarding Kaletra on the grounds that Kaletra had numerous competitors in its therapeutic class.

Moreover, under the new 2006 price regulation system, none of the high cost chemical and biotechnology drugs protected with data exclusivity or patent are sold under price 'control'. It seems that, although patents and data exclusivity are, by definition, monopoly rights, under the Colombian prices regulatory regime, a patented product, or a product protected with data exclusivity, may still compete with several products in the market.[37]

---

[35] This belief is so widespread that in April 2009, the Colombian Congress organized a public session called 'The Truth about Generic Drugs'. There several patients' and doctors' associations expressed their doubts regarding generic quality controls, despite the technical presentations promoting generics made by the INVIMA and by academics from the Universidad Nacional and Universidad de Antioquia. Even the National Medical Federation had to produce a public statement supporting generics, entitled 'Seven truths about generic drugs in Colombia', in which it encouraged doctors to freely prescribe generic drugs.

[36] The price of Kaletra was controlled in response to a compulsory-license request made by the health NGO Ifarma and HIV patient associations that was denied by the government.

[37] Following this line of argument rituximab (Mabthera® by Roche) is not an 'exclusive' product because it is supposed to compete with all the other 'mono-

Biotechnology Drug Overregulation

In June 2008 the Colombian Ministry of Health and the INVIMA announced the completion of a draft version of a biotechnology drugs regulatory decree. The draft constituted an entirely new regulatory framework for biotechnology products.[38] Following the introduction of the draft, both governmental agencies staged two debates and one technical meeting, at which local and transnational pharmaceutical industries, doctors' associations and pharmaceutical chemists' associations came together.[39] The three meetings proved that striking a consensus about the draft was unlikely. This deadlock can be explained by highlighting two main characteristics of the proposed regulation: (1) it established that 'biologic products . . . are not generic products. Therefore, the registration application for a 'biosimilar drug' should include all the required studies of a new product, including clinical trials';[40] (2) it had a technical addendum devoted to specifying the operational characteristics that the laboratories should have in order to obtain authorization for manufacturing biotechnology products.[41]

These two features of the draft – clinical trials and operational requirements for laboratories – despite being proclaimed as a mean to secure drugs' quality, would inevitably create additional barriers to 'biosimilars' competition by raising the costs of market entry substantially.

It is worth noting that by 2009 none of the high cost biotechnology drugs available in Colombia had a 'biosimilar' in the market. Consequently, the implementation of the biotechnology drug decree would only serve to aggravate the lack of competition that the biotechnology market already evinces. Furthermore, the decree would obstruct the development of any local production capabilities.[42] In addition, although in Colombia very

---

clonal antibodies', that is, for example, trastuzumab (Herceptin® by Roche), among others.

[38]   It included registration requisites, quality controls and manufacturing practice controls.

[39]   The first two debates were sponsored by the National Academy of Medicine. The technical meeting was sponsored by the PAHO office; its main objective was to clarify biologic and biotechnology concepts. No civil society organizations were invited. Nevertheless, one of the health NGOs, Ifarma, showed up at the meetings without being formally invited, and many representatives of patients' associations sent letters expressing their opinions on the subject.

[40]   Decree draft (2008) at http://www.minproteccionsocial.gov.co/.

[41]   It did this by proposing a new indicator, with much higher requisites than those already in place for chemical products.

[42]   The decree has not yet been presented to Congress, but the Vice Minister of Health said that 'this decree was vital for Colombia's health access and that the

Table 4.5a   Entities with data exclusivity

From	Until	Active principles protected		
		Total number	Biotech drugs	Percentage
2003	2006	7	1	14
2004	2008	13	1	8
2005	2010	15	6	40
2006	2011	9	3	33
2007	2012	6	1	17
2008	2013	16	0	0
2009	2014	5	1	20
Total		71	13	18

few biotechnology drugs are protected by patents, 13 of them have been granted data exclusivity. In fact, as Table 4.5a indicates, 18 percent of the total entities that obtained data exclusivity between 2003 and 2009 are biotechnology drugs. Another 38 percent are used for cancer treatment and 23 percent for arthritis.

It should be mentioned that data protection for biotechnology products was not explicitly contemplated in the regulation introduced in Colombia's Decree 2085 in 2002. Nonetheless, the health regulatory authority granted data exclusivity protection to biotechnology products on the basis of their being 'new medications.' However, this decision contradicts the premises of the aforementioned biotechnology product decree, since the latter is based on the completely opposite premise – that biotechnology drugs are not the same as chemical drugs.

Furthermore, without additional debate, data exclusivity for biotechnology drugs might be included in the text of the BTA between Colombia and the EU. Oddly enough, during the seventh round of negotiations, after considering the fact that the INVIMA had already granted such protection without 'anyone objecting', the Colombian negotiators agreed to include data exclusivity for biologic and biotechnology products in the text of the agreement.[43]

In conclusion, even if Colombia's patent protection system preserves its current TRIPS 'minimum' levels, both data protection and the local

government will advance it no matter the cost' (Biofármacos – AFIDRO, at http://www.biofarmacos.org/noticia/54-regulacion-de-biotecnologicos--sigue-la-espera.html).

[43]   'Colombia–EU Trade Agreement: Report on the seventh round of negotiation', prepared by the Alianza CAN–UE (September 2009).

Table 4.5b   Biotechnology entities with data exclusivity and disease

From	Until	Active ingredient	Name	Laboratory	Disease
2003	2006	Adalimumab	Humira®	Abbott	Arthritis
2004	2008	Alemtuzumab	Mabcampath®	Ilex Pharma	Cancer
2005	2010	Cetuximab	Erbitux®	Merck	Cancer
		Nesiritide	Natrecor®	Janssen Cilag	Cardiac insuf
		Omalizumab	Xolair®	Novartis Pharma	Asthma
		Bevacizumab	Avastin®	Roche	Cancer
		Efalizumab	Raptiva®	Serono	Psoriasis
		Pegaptanib	Macugen®	Pfizer	Macular degeneration
2006	2011	Ibritumomab Tiuxetan	Zevamab®	Schering	Cancer
		Ranibizumab	Lucentis®	Novartis	Macular degeneration
		Dasatinib	Sprycel®	Bristol-Myers Squibb	Cancer
2007	2012	Abatacept	Orencia®	Bristol-Myers Squibb	Arthritis
2009	2014	Tocilizumab	Actemra®	Roche	Arthritis

Source: Author's calculations and classifications using data from the INVIMA.

registration requirements for biotechnology drugs could outweigh the gains obtained by health NGOs and the local pharmaceutical industry in their mobilization against IP measures during international trade negotiations.

The Contrasting Political Economy

With respect to the two regulatory issues described above – pharmaceutical prices and biotechnology registration requirements – civil society organizations and the local pharmaceutical industry were considerably less involved than in the IPR debates. In fact, neither the implementation of the new regulatory system for prices nor the data exclusivity rights granted to several biotechnology drugs engendered any public debate or protest. Nevertheless, the discussion of the biotechnology drug regulatory decree did raise concerns for some health NGOs and the local industries, but their strategies were significantly less effective than those implemented during the trade-related IPR negotiations.

During trade negotiation rounds, members of the health NGOs and local industry alliance seemed to agree upon a common strategy. However, during the biotechnology discussion meetings, the same actors demonstrated little coordination among themselves.[44] Furthermore, in facing trade agreement negotiations, health NGOs quickly obtained information and financial support to undertake prospective studies assessing the economic impacts of IPR protection.[45] Nonetheless, they have been unable to replicate the same strategy in facing the biotechnology drugs overregulation threat. Therefore, a question remains regarding the non-IP and non-trade trend of pharmaceutical regulatory reforms in Colombia: why did the health NGOs and their local pharmaceutical industry allies fail to react as effectively as they did in regard to the protection of pharmaceutical IPRs?

Three factors may address this question: (1) stakeholders' interest in the non-IP and non-trade pharmaceutical regulatory reforms did not converge as directly as they did in the IPR protection debates; (2) the public visibility of locally negotiated regulatory reforms was significantly lower than that of the IPRs; (3) health NGOs and local industry had financial, human and technical constraints that were not present when they mobilized against IPR protection.

Stakeholder interests

First, the lack of coordinated stakeholder interest is evident in the position that the local pharmaceutical industry took with respect to the 2006 price regulatory reform. In that context, and most unusually, the local pharmaceutical companies' association (ASINFAR) and the transnational pharmaceutical companies' association (AFIDRO) cooperated to finance and endorse the technical study that ultimately shaped the reform. This is atypical, but not surprising if we consider the fact that, as discussed previously in this chapter, a preponderance of both the local and the transnational pharmaceutical companies' profits are built upon price misinformation, lack of signaling by regulatory agencies and the lack of price control.

---

[44] Results of the participant observation exercised during the three discussion meetings sponsored by the National Medicine Academy and PAHO and the CAN–EU Alliance meetings.

[45] Both Mision Salud and Ifarma have produced several research documents assessing not only the economic impact of a stronger IPR protection, but also the more political and normative implications. Furthermore, Ifarma became the IPR economic impact 'calculator' for the entire Latin-American region. In fact, they have published primarily with the support of the WHO, PAHO and HAI impact studies for Colombia, Peru, Bolivia, and many Central American countries.

Moreover, by 2006 the local pharmaceutical industry already had a history of violations against the prior regulatory norms. In 2002, the NPPC sanctioned 32 pharmaceutical companies for failing to comply with previous rulings. Among them, 28 were local pharmaceutical companies and only three (Aventis, Merck and Roche) were transnational corporations.

Therefore, concerning price regulation, the alliance between health NGOs and local pharmaceutical industry did not last, and health NGOs preferred not to become involved in the debate. In fact, with the sole exception of the Colombian Medical Federation critique,[46] there were no public demonstrations against the pharmaceutical price regulatory reform.

In the case of biotechnology regulatory issues, interests could have easily converged, but the fact is that the coalition has yet not materialized. In fact, Mision Salud, one of the leading actors of the IPR campaign during FTA negotiations, did not participate in any of the biotechnology debates and seemed to become aware of their importance only after biotechnology data protection requirements were mentioned at one of the Colombia–EU FTA negotiation rounds.

Public visibility

As mentioned in the first part of this chapter, public awareness about the IPR debates increased over time, and was bolstered not only by health NGOs and local pharmaceutical companies' activities, but also by global events, such as the WTO Doha Round and the South African and Brazilian HIV cases. In contrast, price regulatory reforms are not an internationally fashionable topic; biotechnology drug regulatory issues remain to be fully understood by local actors, and among them, by the media. This fact can be easily corroborated by comparing the number of articles in the most widely read local newspapers. In fact, as Figure 4.3 illustrates, over the past two decades the average number of newspaper articles per year dealing with pharmaceutical prices or biotechnology drugs has been close to zero.

Furthermore, health NGO and local pharmaceutical industry public support was elusive, which was evident during the biotechnology discussion meetings. While during FTA negotiations, health NGOs and local industry provided some legitimacy as defendants of the public interests,

---

[46] The Federación Médica Colombiana, citing the principles expressed by the renowned Colombian pharmacologist, Enrique Nuñez Olarte, manifested their discontent with the deregulation of pharmaceutical prices and proposed an alternative pharmaceutical information system called SUIM (Propuesta de Política Farmacéutica Nacional, FMC).

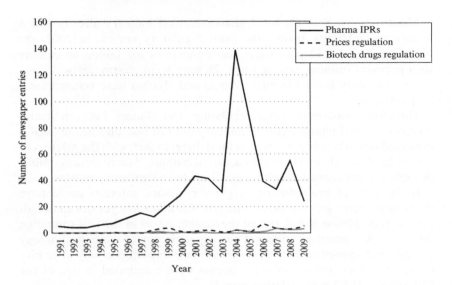

Source: Author's calculations based on archival research of the following newspapers: *El Tiempo, Revista Semana* and *El Espectador.*

Figure 4.3   Colombian newspaper articles

during the local negotiation of biotechnology regulation their legitimacy was constantly questioned. Moreover, letters from six high-cost-disease patient associations were read in public. They demanded stricter regulation of 'biosimilar' drugs, arguing that 'as far as they understand' 'biosimilars' are a threat to their health and that they have a right to be given the 'best' treatment option available.[47]

Financial, human and technical resources
For almost two decades, since the TRIPS agreement negotiations ended in 1994, health NGOs and the local pharmaceutical industry have been devoted to lobbying against stronger IPR protection.[48] As a result, a significant number of the health NGO financial and human resources available are already being consumed by the IPR campaigns. The local

---

[47]   These letters can be consulted at the Ministry of Social Protection website: http://www.minproteccionsocial.gov.co/vbecontent/NewsDetail.asp?ID=17769& IDCompany=3.

[48]   As mentioned by Germán Holguin, 'since then, IPR issues come up on a daily basis'. Interview with Germán Holguin, Mision Salud's director, October 2008.

pharmaceutical industry case is similar if we consider the fact that their presence in any public debate is almost exclusively handled by ASINFAR's director, Alberto Bravo, who has to deal with problems ranging from IPRs to biotechnology manufacturing procedures.

The health NGO and local industry's technical expertise, including the non-IP and non-trade reforms, especially biotechnology regulations, was much less evident than the IPR issues. This fact could be explained by both the complexity of the biotechnology topic and by the lack of previous international experience in the field that could have shed some light on the best course to follow.[49] Moreover, while for the trade-related IPR mobilization a substantial amount of financial and technical support was available via international institutions and NGOs, such as PAHO-WHO, Oxfam, MSF and HAI,[50] in the case of locally negotiated regulatory reforms, none of these resources is accessible to the NGOs.

Briefly, taken together these many factors seem to suggest that mobilizing against international pressures could be easier and more effective than locally negotiated initiatives. Furthermore, while strong IPR protection's negative effects have been clearly identified, first by local pharmaceutical industries and then by health NGOs, the threat posed by the new era of non-IP and non-trade regulatory reforms remained 'under the radar'.

CONCLUSION

After the TRIPS agreement had been signed and the implementation processes had begun throughout the developing world, only two alternatives seemed feasible: either to diligently submit to the regulations or to stubbornly resist. Nevertheless, a decade after the expiration of the deadline for compliance with TRIPS, the way IP rules have evolved in different developing countries varies substantially. In this context, the Colombian case illustrates that, although much attention has been given to the role FTAs played as the strategies used to strengthen IP rules beyond TRIPS requirements, there has been no interest in analyzing other concurrent local regulatory strategies (see Figure 4.4). Moreover, the Colombian case demonstrates how the latter strategies have severely aggravated the situation in the pharmaceutical and health sectors.

---

[49] In fact, the EMEA (European Medicines Agency) rulings are quite recent, and the US legislation is still being discussed.

[50] Oxfam and MSF support was more evident during the Colombia–US BTA negotiations. On the other hand, HAI has been very active mobilizing against the Colombia–EU BTA.

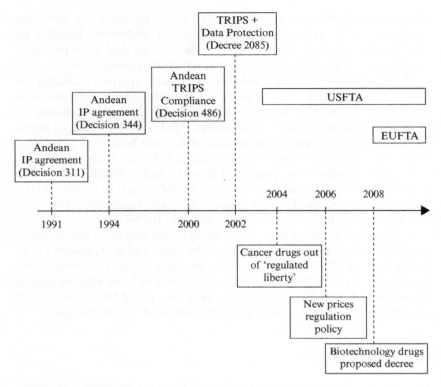

Figure 4.4   Colombian pharmaceutical IP and non-IP trends

The Colombian case also reveals how pharmaceutical prices and bio-technology regulatory reforms are closely tied to IPR protection initiatives, even if they seem to contradict them. In fact, on the one hand, the new Colombian prices regulatory system considers that a patented drug is not necessarily a monopolistic drug and, therefore, concludes that its price should not be controlled. This type of reasoning denies the fact that the purpose of a patent is precisely to grant monopoly rights to the owner of an invention; thus, the Colombian pharmaceutical price regulatory system ultimately increases the monopoly rights already granted by patent protection.

On the other hand, the Colombian biotechnology drug regulatory decree assumes that biotechnology drugs are completely different from chemical drugs and, therefore, that they should have special registration and production requirements. This logic contradicts the fact that, for the purpose of data protection, biotechnology drugs have been treated like every other chemical drug in Colombia; hence, they are not only giving additional regulatory privileges to biotechnology pioneers, but they are also extending to them the privileges of chemical drugs pioneers.

Nevertheless, this connection between the international IP and trade agenda and the local non-IP and non-trade agenda is not easily perceived by the health NGOs and local pharmaceutical industry that were so active in withstanding international IP pressures. Furthermore, the government has been completely passive as regards restraining the overcharges that the lack of proper regulations is creating. Ultimately, regulatory decisions, such as price control reforms and the enactment of biotechnology drugs regulatory norms, have become effective ways of restricting access to drugs and protecting pharmaceutical companies' profits.

Only very recently, non-IP issues have begun to become relevant, primarily because high pharmaceutical prices are threatening the financial stability of the health care system as a whole, and because the risk of being excluded from the biotechnology business became palpable for the local pharmaceutical industry and health NGOs. Nevertheless, until the government fully understands the challenges that pharmaceutical regulatory issues pose, not even the active mobilization of health NGOs and the pharmaceutical industry will help in resolving the structural shortcomings of Colombian pharmaceutical policy.

REFERENCES

Andia, T., M. Cortez, F. Rossi and I. Rodriguez (2009), 'Impacto de las Medidas Adpic-Plus sobre un Grupo de Madicamentos en Colombia: Implemenación del modelo IPRIM (Intellectual Property Rights Impact Micromodel) sobre los medicamentos anti-ulcerosos en Colombia', Informe de Investigación, Fundación IFARMA, March.

Attaran, A. (2004), 'How do patents and economic policies affect access to essential medicines in developing countries?', *Health Affairs*, **23**(3), 155.

Attaran, A. and L. Gillespie (2001), 'Do patents for antiretroviral drugs constrain access to AIDS treatment in Africa?', *Journal of the American Medical Association*, **286**(15), 1886–1892.

Borrell, J. and J. Watal (2003), 'Impact of patents on access to HIV/AID drugs in developing countries', Working Paper No. 92, Center for International Development, Harvard University.

Chaudhuri, S., P.K. Goldberg and P. Jia (2003), 'The effects of extending intellectual property rights protection to developing countries: a case study of the Indian pharmaceutical market', National Bureau of Economic Research, NBER Working Paper Series, Working Paper 10159.

Correa, C.M. (2000), 'Reforming the intellectual property rights system in Latin America', *The World Economy*, **23**(6), 851–872.

Correa, C.M. and South Centre (2000), 'Integrating public health concerns into patent legislation in developing countries', Geneva: South Centre.

Correa, C.M. (2002), 'Protection of data for the registration of pharmaceuticals: implementing standards', Geneva: South Centre.

Correa, C.M. and A. Yusuf (1998), *Intellectual Property and International Trade: The TRIPs Agreement*, London, Boston: Kluwer Law International.

Cortés, M. (2009), *Precio, Disponibilidad y Asequibilidad de Medicamentos y Componentes del Precio en Colombia*, Bogotá, Colombia: AIS LAC; IFARMA.

Cortés, M. and A. Zerda (2004), *Modelo Prospectivo del Impacto de la Protección a la Propiedad Intelectual Sobre el Acceso a Medicamentos en Colombia*, Bogotá, Colombia: PAHO; IFARMA.

Danzon, P. (1997), 'Price discrimination for pharmaceuticals: welfare effects in the US and the EU', *International Journal of Economics and Business*, 4(3).

Danzon, P. and L. Chao (2000), 'Does regulation drive out competition in pharmaceutical markets?', *Journal of Law and Economics*, **XLIII** (October).

Deere, C. (2009), *The Implementation Game: The TRIPS Agreement and the Global Politics of Intellectual Property Reform in Developing Countries*, Oxford, New York: Oxford University Press.

Drahos, P. (1997), 'Thinking strategically about intellectual property rights', *Telecommunications Policy*, **21**(3), 201–211.

Drahos, P. and R. Mayne (eds) (2002), *Global Intellectual Property Rights: Knowledge, Access and Development*, Basingstoke: Palgrave Macmillan.

Hoekman, B. (2002), 'Strengthening the global trade architecture for development: the pos Doha agenda', *World Trade Review*, 1, 23–45.

Hoen, E. 't (2002), 'TRIPS, pharmaceutical patents, and access to essential medicines: a long way from Seattle to Doha', *Chicago Journal of International Law*, **3**(1), 27–48.

Homedes, N. and A. Ugalde (2005), 'Multisource drug policies in Latin America: survey of 10 Countries', *Bulletin of the World Health Organization*, **83** (January), 64–70.

Nogués, J.J. (1990), 'Patents and pharmaceutical drugs: understanding the pressures on developing countries', Policy, Research, and External Affairs, International Trade, I. E. Department, World Bank.

Rocha, R. e. a. (2003), 'Efectos de la protección de la propiedad intelectual en el mercado farmacéutico en el marco de las negociaciones del TLC con los Estados Unidos', Bogotá, Centro de Estudios sobre Desarrollo Económico – CEDE, Universidad de los Andes.

Sell, S.K. (2000), 'Structures, agents and institutions: private corporate power and the globalisation of intellectual property rights' in R. Higgott, G. Underhill and A. Bieler (eds), *Non-state Actors and Global Authority in the Global System*, London: Routledge.

Sell, S.K. (2003), *Private Power, Public Law: The Globalization of Intellectual Property Rights*, Cambridge: Cambridge University Press.

Shadlen, K. (2005), 'Exchanging development for market access? Deep integration and industrial policy under multilateral and regional–bilateral trade agreements', *Review of International Political Economy*, **12**(5) (December), 750–775.

Shadlen, K. (2007), 'The political economy of AIDS treatment: intellectual property and the transformation of generic supply', *International Studies Quarterly* 51, 559–581.

Shadlen, K. (2008), 'Globalization, power, and integration: the political economy of regional and bilateral trade Agreements in the Americas', *Journal of Development Studies*, **44**, 1–20.

Shadlen, K. (2009), 'The politics of patents and drugs in Brazil and Mexico: the industrial bases of health policies', *Comparative Politics*, **42**(1), 41–58.

USTR (2009), 'Fourth report to the Congress on the operation of the Atpa', April 30.

Zerda, A., G. Velasquez, F. Tobar and J.E. Vargas (2001), 'Sistemas de seguros de salud y acceso a medicamentos – Estudios de casos de Argentina, Colombia, Costa Rica, Chile, Estados Unidos de América y Guatemala', http://apps.who.int/medicinedocs/en/d/Jh2958s/.

Zuleta, L. (2000), 'Incidencia del régimen de patentes de la industria farmacéutica sobre la economía colombiana', Informe de Investigación No. 002831, Fedesarrollo.

5. The challenges of constructing pharmaceutical capabilities and promoting access to medicines in Mexico under TRIPS

Alenka Guzmán

According to Pavitt's taxonomy (1984), the pharmaceutical sector has been classified as an intensively scientific industry, where technology depends basically on the basic sciences of R&D. The pharmaceutical firms maintain their leadership by using intellectual property rights (IPR – patents, industrial secrets and trademarks). Patent systems in particular are of great importance to the pharmaceuticals industry, given the permanent risk of copying through the use of low-cost processes.

In this section, we explain the analytical framework of the pharmaceutical industry whereby the health system and the intellectual property system are seen jointly, through both a national (Bell and Pavitt, 1993; Lundvall, 1993; Nelson, 1993; Kim, 1997) and a sectoral innovation approach (Edquist, 1997; Breschi and Malerba, 1997; Malerba, 2002, 2004). Both the factors of demand[1] and supply[2] that contribute to innovations in the pharmaceutical sector refer to the elements that make up the national innovation systems and the sectoral innovation systems (NIS and SIS, respectively).[3]

---

[1] The demand side includes the size and evolution of the market (Schmookler, 1966), which are influenced by economic factors and socio-economic factors and affected by government policies, price capping, health expenditure budget and preventive health programs (Agrawal, 2000: 24).

[2] The determining factors influencing the supply are identified as the costs, alongside the productivity of the research and development (R&D) sector linked to the technological opportunities (Mowery and Rosemberg, 1989).

[3] The government, through macro-economic policies, promotes foreign financing, and through fiscal policies, regulatory and IP policies establishes the base for institutional incentives of R&D private investment and thus embarks on the path of innovation. Moreover, the human capital contributes to the technological development but also in this process it gains knowledge and additional abilities. Progress in the different scientific fields generates technological opportunities asso-

Technological backwardness in the developing countries is associated with the absence of technological capabilities, low levels of technological transfer and a low GDP per capita, along with few, or no, R&D efforts (Lall, 2003).[4] Under these circumstances, the strength of the patents becomes a barrier to the entry of imitative activity due to the high costs related to patenting. Therefore, the divergent patent systems are characterized by their low level of domestic innovative activity and are associated with a limited expenditure in R&D, poorly trained human resources, limited private industry participation, weak enterprise–institution links, and low-tech-laden exports. Furthermore, the diffusion ratio (penetration in USPTO) is characterized as being low (Aboites and Cimoli, 2002). Concerning the pharmaceutical sector, some emerging countries have reasonable industrial capabilities for high-level chemistry and produce their own raw materials. Other developing countries maintain a reasonable capability for the formulation of drugs and for productive activities; however, they must import practically all the necessary raw materials. But there are also countries typically characterized as being small and having no local production; in these countries, finished drugs are imported, leaving enterprises with marketing activities only. This last case reveals there are no productive capabilities whatsoever (Frenkel, 1978; Cepal-Naciones Unidas, 1987; Palmeira and Pan, 2003).[5]

Taking into account this analytical framework, we aim to find out how Mexico has managed the tools of intellectual property rights (IPR) in order to develop the pharmaceutical sector, by considering the special features of national and sectoral innovation and the health systems. Although the initial imitation capabilities of the local pharmaceutical industry in Mexico have been fostered by demand factors, especially in association with the growing importance of the public health sector, its

---

ciated with a correct macro and intermediate environment, and will promote the R&D activities along with innovation (Agrawal, 2000).

[4] Lall proposes a classification based on a technology intensive index derived from the national technological activity using two variables: R&D financed by productive enterprises and the number of patents taken from USPTO. Both deflated by the population and adjusted by economic size.

[5] In contrast, countries characterized by a high R&D expenditure in relation to local GDP, a well-developed education system that trains high-quality human resources and provides networks, thus creating favorable synergies between enterprises and institutions, and whose exports have a high technological content, find favourable conditions for innovation activities within a strong intellectual-property framework (Lall, 2003); so they are in a convergent patent system (Aboites & Cimoli, 2002). Consequently, their pharmaceutical industries are capable of carrying out all the technological stages, going from basic research to the marketing of the drug (CEPAL, 1987; Frenkel, 1978; Palmeira and Pan, 2003).

development was characterized – during the import substitution industrialization (ISI) period (closed economy) – by the absence of several decisive supply factors. Indeed, there has been a lack of industrial regulation and IPR policies created with the objective of favoring R&D efforts to undertake steps on the path of innovation. The local pharmaceutical sector has not built up the necessary capabilities to integrate the industry by encompassing basic research, through the formulation and production of their own raw materials and drugs, to the marketing of the latter.

Within the export–industrialization pattern, the pharmaceutical sector is associated with a disarticulated national system of innovation in an unstable macro-economic and low-growth environment, with a prevailing lack of technological activities, insufficient human capital and marginal links between the universities and firms and cooperative networks. In this sense, we endorse the following hypothesis: the IPR reform seems to favor foreign companies since the multinationals own solid innovation capabilities and profit from the opportunities to increase their partial production of drugs and their intra-firm trade, whilst appropriating the R&D efforts carried out in their home countries. However, for local firms, the strengthening of patents could, in fact, deepen their technological dependence and impede higher development steps, unless this country undertakes an important effort to build national and sectoral systems of innovation, and most importantly, productive, export-oriented specializations.

The chapter is organized into four sections. Firstly, we proposed an analytical approach regarding national and sectoral innovation and health systems vis-à-vis the intellectual property system. Secondly (the next section), we characterize the Mexican pharmaceutical industry in the context of its intellectual property system and its health system. Thirdly, we identify the technological and innovative capabilities in the pharmaceutical industry in Mexico. Finally, we evaluate the impact on pharmaceutical innovation and performance along with access to drugs in Mexico, by considering the IPR system and analyzing the innovation framework of the pharma-health systems.

MEXICO'S PHARMACEUTICAL INDUSTRY, INTELLECTUAL PROPERTY SYSTEM AND HEALTH SYSTEM

Development Background

From the 1950s to the 1980s, industrial organization in Mexico's pharmaceutical sector was characterized by: i) the presence of a reasonable level of national capital in both the pharmaceutical and pharma-chemical sectors; ii) the absence of patents in the pharmaceutical area; iii) elevated tariffs on the importation of raw materials for the pharma-chemical sector; iv) priority of marketing approval to the medicines of local producers; and v) a significant increase in the number of medium sized and family structured national companies. This type of pharmaceutical and pharma-chemical model, which is orientated to the production of generic medicines and, in some cases, to the exportation of active ingredients of expired patents, is denominated as "later-follower" (Katz, 1997).

In the Mexican pharmaceutical industry, real imitation capabilities were developed to produce new pharmaceutical products, which allowed the country to cover its basic domestic demand for medicines (CEPAL, 1987).[6] Nevertheless, the Mexican industry never developed medicine exportation capacities, nor did the multinationals show any interest in exporting their products to other countries from their Mexican bases (Brodovsky, 1997). The knowledge and the abilities of the pharmaceutical companies came basically from two sources: licenses and (free) technology in the public domain, given the absence of a patent system in the pharmaceutical sector. In collaboration with public universities, important chemical synthesis laboratories developed basic research and, in some cases, achieved new molecules.[7]

Despite the Mexican inventive activity in the drugs and medical technological category, it remained highly incipient and marginal with respect to the industrialized nations, and patents formed no part of the development strategy. The USPTO granted, between 1963 and 1979, just 63 patents to Mexican holders in the drugs and medical category,[8] revealing the embryonic nature of the advance in the development of capabilities in the scientific and technological sectors of the country.

---

[6]   Medicinal imports were less than 2 percent of the whole national market consumption (Brodovsky, 1997).

[7]   The most relevant endogenous innovation, on an international scale, was the case of Syntex with the production of steroids (Gereffi, 1986). However, the strong technological dependence on foreign firms was constant in the local manufacturing plants in the pharma-chemical and pharmaceutical sectors.

[8]   The 63 patents granted by USPTO to Mexican holders in Drugs and Medical category between 1963 and 1979 reached 6.6 per cent of the all-sector total patents granted (956); this number has grown to 50 patents in 1980–1990 and to 71 from 1991 to 2002 (the period of adoption of TRIPS in Mexico). According to Jaffe and Trajtenberg (2002), the classification Drugs and Medical includes Drugs, Surgery and Medical Instruments, Biotechnology and Miscellaneous Drugs and Medical.

In Mexico, efforts to develop an integrated productive chain encompassing R&D related to the development of new molecules and the commercialization of new drugs were impeded by the technological intensity of the international sector and local firms' general incapacity to incorporate technological progress (Brodovsky, 1997). Moreover, the government failed to design adequate policies for the generation of a favourable macro-economic and institutional environment in which the development of scientific and technological capabilities would lead to innovation. This fragility was ever more apparent with the opening up of the economy, the dismantling of the protectionist structure and the strengthening of the patent system. In this new institutional environment, with the enormous technological and innovative gap in both scale and financial capacity, the local companies were pitted against the large, multinational pharmaceutical firms and thus registered ever increasing losses due to the increased competition combined with technological dependency.

The Importance and Industrial Organization of the Pharmaceutical Industry in Mexico

Currently, Mexico has almost a quarter of the resident population of Latin America and contributes 29 percent of the total regional GDP (CEPAL, 2008). The country's pharmaceutical market is classified among the "top ten" world markets and top in Latin America, with a value of 13.5 billion US dollars in 2006 (MOITI, 2006); its sales represent 37 percent of Latin America's total sales (Chávez, 2007). From 1994 to 2006, the pharmaceutical market registered an annual growth rate of above 10 percent (National Pharmaceutical Industry Chamber, CANIFARMA – Cámara de la Industria Farmacéutica). The dynamic growth of Mexico's medicines market is associated with, among other factors: i) an environment with a strong patent system for pharmaceutical processes and products since 1991; ii) commercial agreements signed with 33 countries, one of the most important being the North American Free Trade Agreement (NAFTA); iii) low production costs – 50 percent lower than in other countries; iv) the high professional qualifications of the personnel; v) related to the preceding factors, the strong growth in foreign direct investment (FDI); and vi) being the regional leader in the export of pharmaceutical products to European countries and the United States (calculated to be 1.5 billion US dollars in 2007).

The Mexican pharmaceutical industry represents 1 percent of the country's total GDP and 2.7 percent of manufacturing GDP. According to CANIFARMA, the industry is made up of 224 pharmaceutical laboratories owned by 200 companies, 46 of which are multinationals.[9] These companies generate nearly 50,000 direct jobs and an additional 47,000 indirect employment opportunities. Nearly three-fifths of the direct job total (57 per cent) are positions related to sales and administration, 37 percent are in production and R&D activities, whilst the remaining 6 percent are in other related activities (Mexican Pharmaceutical Industry Association – AMIF).

The pharmaceutical industry has a high market concentration, in which foreign companies account for 68 percent of the total market; local companies make up the remaining 32 percent. Of the 'top ten' companies in Mexico's pharmaceutical market, 9 are foreign multinationals (MNS), the most important being Pfizer, Bayer and Merck Sharp & Dohme, with sales of over 500 million US dollars in 2003; the only Mexican company in the "top ten" is Laboratorio Senosian, which registered sales of 131 million US dollars over the same period; of the nine foreign MNS, five are US based (Wyeth, Eli Lilly and the top three mentioned above), two are German (Boehringer Ingelheim Prometo and Merck), one is Swiss (Novartis) and the other is French (Sanofi-Synthélabo, now Sanofi-Aventis) (CANIFARMA; *El Asesor*, cited by WPM, 2005). The top 35 players in the Mexican market account for 80 percent of the total sales; among them there are six national participants, the rest being multinational pharmaceutical firms (Scripps Pharmaceutical Industry League Tables, 2004).

The market segmentation in relation to the private and public sectors is 80 per cent and 20 per cent, respectively. With regard to the public sector, Mexico's Ministry of Health has a total of 800 marketing approval medicines, of which 70 percent are national products distributed by ANAFAM. Four-fifths of the medicines acquired by the public health sector are generic products, the principal generic producers being national companies. Meanwhile, ANAFAM states that 80 percent are purchased from 50 national suppliers, whose sales to the government represented approximately 545,500 US dollars in 2006. Of the medicines included in the country's public-sector basic national basket, 776 are generic medicines, purchased on the basis of efficiency, quality, security and accessibility. The strong competition for this market can be seen in the fact that for each contract awarded there are 20 companies taking part in the bidding process and, in just 10 percent of this public market, 20 of the most

---

[9]   Other sources say that there were 390 domestic and transnational companies manufacturing pharmaceutical products (Massachusetts Office of International Trade & Investment – MOITI, 2006, www.mass.gov/moiti).

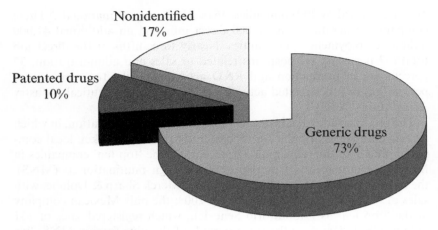

Nonidentified
17%

Patented drugs
10%

Generic drugs
73%

Source: Martínez (2010).

*Figure 5.1   Shares of generics and patented medicines in the Mexican
            public market by units, 2009*

important companies are represented (OECD, 2005: 66). The government allocates 56 percent of its drug procurement budget to medicines patented by the MNS, 29 percent to generics and 15 percent are not identified (Martínez, 2010). In terms of units, however, these financial resources buy 10 percent patented drugs, 73 percent generics and 17 percent are not identified (see Figure 5.1).

Public institutions like IMSS and ISSSTE allocate nearly one-third of their drugs expenditure to generics, representing three-quarters of total units bought. In contrast, they spend more than half their budget on patented drugs, representing only 10 percent of units on average. The case of Petróleos de México (PEMEX) is a little different because this institution spends more on generics and less on patented medicines. The public institutions belonging to the Social Security system (SS) spend mostly on patented medicines (89 percent), obtaining 63 percent in units, and less on generics (6 percent), obtaining 36 percent in units; this could be because those institutions have high therapeutic specialization and use new drugs to treat diseases and surgery interventions with efficacy. See Table 5.1.

Prescription drugs represent the largest share of the country's private medicine market, with 84.2 percent of total sales; meanwhile, over-the-counter products (OTC) account for the remaining 15.8 percent of total sales (World Pharmaceutical Markets, 2005). Associated with the importance of prescription medicine sales, patented medicines make up

Table 5.1   Shares of generics and patented drugs in the Mexican public market, 2009 (per cent)

	Units			Value		
	Generic drugs	Patented drugs	Non-identified	Generic drugs	Patented drugs	Non-identified
Public market	73	10	17	29	56	15
IMSS	74	8	18	32	50	18
ISSSTE	73	12	15	27	60	13
SS	36	63	1	6	89	5
PEMEX	70	23	7	49	44	7

Source: Martínez (2010).

87 percent of the total sales.[10] The generics market (denominated interchangeable generics) has relatively low market participation (2.7 per cent), while the non-bioequivalent drugs (known as "similar" generics) market share reached one tenth of total sales in 2002.[11]

The market for "similar" generics in Mexico was terminated in 2010, as new health regulations entered into force concerning the renewal of drug approvals procedures applicable to all pharmaceutical products every five-year period by the Federal Commission for the Protection against Health Risks (COFEPRIS – Comisión Federal para la Protección contra Riesgos Sanitarios), according to article 376 of the General Health Law. For the approval of medicines, the stringent regulations of COFEPRIS require: i) the official standards for good practice in the manufacture of medicines, NOM-164-SSA-1-1998; also, primary materials, especially active ingredients of the drugs, must follow the norms; ii) the bioequivalence and bioavailability tests, assuring the necessary concentration, stability, security and quality of production process and products;[12] iii) clinical trials which must verify the therapeutic efficacy; iv) conditions of quality,

---

[10]   The above probably explains the elevated prices of the medicines, much higher than those of the generics; nevertheless, the orientation of the health systems favoured the prescription of generically formulated medicines.

[11]   The interchangeable generic medicines are those that have proved their bioavailability and their bioequivalence, thus making them exactly the same as the originals. The "similar" products are generics that have not necessarily undergone the aforementioned studies.

[12]   The bioequivalence and bioavailability tests are going to be carried out by 'third party' laboratories under the authorization of the Ministry of Health.

efficacy and security must be maintained during the period of marketing of the product; and v) that COFEPRIS verify that the Mexican Intellectual Property Office (IMPI) has not, in the IMPI Gazette, published a patent on the chemical entity of the drug in question.[13]

In September 2005, COFEPRIS counted nearly 40,000 pharmaceutical products registered, of which 7,000 were on the market and only 3,100 were interchangeable generics. As a result of recent reforms, as of the end of 2010 there will no longer be any non-bioequivalent drugs on the market but only interchangeable generic products that meet the high requirements of the developed countries' pharmaceutical industry, and patented medicines.

Another important change in the pharmaceutical industry and health regulations is the cancellation of the "plant request" as a condition for the introduction of medicines into the Mexican market (9 August 2009).[14] COFEPRIS took this measure when the country was seen as one where HIV antiretroviral prices were among the highest in the world, during the World HIV/AIDS Conference in Mexico in 2008. According to the Mexican government, the goal of this measure is to facilitate the introduction of cheaper medicines, even through importation, and improve the sector's competitiveness. Therefore, for the assurance of the best production practices, quality and safety of drugs, COFEPRIS sends health supervisors to visit the foreign plants where the medicines imported into Mexico are produced. As a result of the cancellation of the "plant request", there have been some applications by pharmaceutical multinationals, which did not have production plants in Mexico, to market drugs in therapeutic categories for cancer and metabolic diseases. Although this new regulation favors access to cheaper medicines, it also contributes to deindustrializing this sector, reducing some MNS technological knowledge spillovers and reducing employment.

Foreign Direct Investment, Trade and Market Specialization

Mexico experienced a significant increase in foreign investment in the 1990s. Between 1999 and 2006, foreign direct investment (FDI) increased over 200

---

[13]   The adoption of the COFEPRIS–IMPI linkage on the renewal of the drug approval every five years has provoked a big debate among the local firms because it gives the possibility of delaying the entrance of generics in the domestic market. We analyze this issue later.

[14]   The plant request was a policy measure to incentivize pharmaceutical MNS to invest in Mexico. Through this requirement any company must have a production plant in Mexico to market their products.

percent, reaching US$346 million (Chávez, 2007). This investment came mainly from five of the most industrialized countries (the United States, 31 percent; the Netherlands, 10 percent; Germany, 9 percent; Switzerland, 8 percent and Spain, 6 percent) and was destined mainly for the capital, Mexico City, the State of Jalisco and the State of Mexico.

Mexico soon became a major player in the export of medicines not only to Central American and Caribbean nations, but also to industrialized countries such as the US and Germany. However, the importation of raw materials, along with final products, increased substantially. The latter represents 13 percent of total sales, of which a quarter came from the Unites States (World Pharmaceutical Markets, 2005 and 2006).

The specification of the type of imports has great relevance in the sense that it permits identification of the areas in which countries are self-sufficient or not, and thus the areas where they possess lesser productive and competitive capacities. Although the importation of retail medicines is relatively high (in 2004, 36 percent of total imports) the majority of the imports were concentrated in the medicine sector for OTC sales (60 percent), whilst the importation of semi-finished products was relatively marginal (4 percent). The importation of retail medicines was carried out by both local and foreign-based companies. With regard to final products, the majority of imports were purchased from affiliated multinational pharmaceutical laboratories, which indicates that several of these companies produce only certain products within the country and import the remainder.

In Mexico, the majority of the imported products arrive from the US or the European Union countries, which represent 86 percent of the total imports; a predominance of North American partners is evident. The remaining 14 percent of Mexico's imports come from China, India, Argentina and other countries.

Despite the important growth registered in Mexico's pharmaceutical markets in recent years, fragilities can be seen once the balance of trade is analyzed. Thus, although exports have registered substantial increases, imports have grown even more. As a consequence, the commercial balance with regard to pharmaceutical products, from 2000 to 2002, shows a deficit. In relation to the type of products, the deficit is greater regarding raw materials (55.8 percent). This implies that the greater part of the molecules, and active ingredients, necessary for the fabrication of medicines have registered net imports. This is associated with the closure of pharma-chemical plants. In Mexico, the net imports of active ingredients contributed with 55.8 percent of the total negative balance. In 2002, Mexico registered high negative commercial balances in raw materials related to vaccines, other antibiotics and tetracycline. The deficit in the semi-finished products represented 8 percent of the total negative commercial balance. The deficit

Table 5.2   Mexican trade balance in pharmaceutical sector, 2005

	Trade deficit (thousands of US$)	Per cent
Raw materials	–421,265	55.8
Semi-finished medicaments	–60,712	8.1
Retail medicaments	–272,711	36.1
Total	–754,688	100.0

Source: World Pharmaceutical Markets (2005).

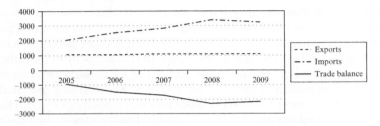

Source: Institute of Pharmaceutical Research & Innovation, A.C. with INEGI and Banxico databases.

Figure 5.2   Evolution of exports, imports and trade balance in Mexican medicines market, 2005–2009 (millions of US$)

regarding the antibiotics is of particular relevance. The negative balance of retail medicine sales is also substantial (36.1 percent); Mexico has a deficient production in hormones, other antibiotics and vitamins. See Table 5.2.

According to other sources, the negative trade balance in medicines was higher in 2005 (981.5 million dollars); moreover, it increased at an average annual rate of 21.97 percent from 2005 to 2009 because imports have risen faster than exports (see Figure 5.2). This loss tendency in the trade balance highlights the growing technological external dependency of the Mexican pharmaceutical sector. While in 2005 national production covered 90.0 percent of the apparent national consumption of medicines in Mexico, in 2009 it fell to 80.3 per cent.

Intellectual Property System

After several decades of a lax intellectual property rights (IPR) system, particularly in the pharmaceutical industry (products and processes),

Mexico carried out IPR reforms in 1991, just prior to the signing of the NAFTA, in 1992, which entered into force in January 1994 (Guzmán and Zúñiga, 2004). Although the entrepreneurs in the national pharmaceutical sector were instructed by the government in 1987 (the year in which Mexico joined the GATT) to develop their own generic production capacities within a period of ten years, along with the strengthening of the intellectual property rights, the principal players were taken by surprise by the premature adoption of the TRIPS-compliant Law on the Promotion and Protection of Industrial Property (LFPPI – Ley de Fomento y Protección de la Propiedad Industrial) (Guzmán, 2005). The Mexican government, under pressure from the American pharmaceutical companies, enforced IPR in this industrial sector, including the 20 years validity period. This new IPR environment would guarantee the flow of investment and commercialization within Mexico, even if the new products of pharmaceutical firms were always introduced into the Mexican pharmaceutical market, but now without the risk of imitation. And, as if this was not enough, the reform also included the "pipeline" system, which allowed for a retroactive period for product registration, even in cases where the knowledge was in the public domain, a fact that several companies exploited (De la Mora, 2005).[15] 'This was a requirement of NAFTA, which goes further than the limited marketing rights provided during the transition periods by TRIPS' (Maskus, 1997, cited by Moïse and Docteur, 2007: 10).

Also, this IPR reform included acceptance of a second therapeutic use of the molecules, which meant the implicit acceptance of the extension of the life period of the pharmaceutical patents. Suddenly, patent extensions are being demanded in developing countries as a compensation for the delays during the process of application and granting, but also for the length of time required for conducting clinical trials in order to obtain marketing authorization (Moïse and Docteur, 2007: 11). Faced with these new circumstances, and in the absence of an active industrial policy for the pharmaceutical sector, only a few companies entered into research and development (R&D) activities, in these cases strengthening the development of expired patents, or those in the public domain, or actually developing certain niche markets with regard to innovation.

By using compulsory licenses, Mexico could manufacture generic copies of patent medicines (Articles 70 and 77 of LFPPI). The compulsory license can be granted if the patented drugs have not been produced in Mexico

---

[15] According to article 12 of LFPPI, the applications for pipeline patents could be applicable to any pharmaceutical patent prior to 1991 in any country which has signed the Patent Cooperation Treaty.

within four years of the priority date or three years after the patent was granted. The compulsory license can be denied when the patent holder or a company licensed to import the drug has imported the product. With those requirements, under article 70 it becomes extremely difficult to obtain a compulsory license. In the case of a national emergency related to a health crisis or shortage of medicines, a compulsory license can be granted to another laboratory in accordance with Article 77 of LFPPI. Nevertheless, despite important cases of national health crisis in Mexico (especially the serious extent of the influenza AH1N1 since April 2009 in Mexico),[16] or the significant growth of public health expenditure on antiretroviral drugs to treat HIV/AIDS or other medicines for cancer and diabetes, among others, there has not been one compulsory license issued in Mexico over the last 14 years (Moïse and Docteur, 2007).

However, the adoption of a strong patent system was not enough for US companies to ensure that their Mexican counterparts would not infringe their patents. Through the Pharmaceutical Research and Medical Manufacturers of America (PhRMA), in 2003 they requested that the Ministry of Health and Assistance – Secretaría de Salubridad y Asistencia (SSA) – make drugs marketing approval conditional on the linkage of patents. Therefore the Regulation of Health Inputs of COFEPRIS amended article 167, adding 167 bis and also article 47 of the Patent Law of IMPI, adding 47 bis, both published in the Federation Official Gazette on September 19, 2003. According to article 167 bis, the linkage means that COFEPRIS will deny the generic medicine approval or license to market the drug in the event that a chemical entity patent exists. The request of linkage was finally incorporated into the reforms of marketing approval procedures in 2005 when the IMPI published the agreement of the rules to make up the list of the drugs to be published six-monthly in the IMPI Medicines Gazette regarding article 47 bis.[17] We must emphasize that article 6 of this agreement stipulates that the list will not include drug

---

[16]   The case of AH1N1 influenza in Mexico 2009 had important health repercussions not only in this country but also in other countries. Even though it was a new influenza strain and the vaccine wasn't yet developed, the medicine adequate for the immediate treatment of this influenza was the active ingredient ozeltamivir, known commercially as Tamiflu® and produced by Roche, the holder of the patent. The government could promote the production of the ozeltamivir generic version in the public or private laboratories through a compulsory license.

[17]   This IMPI Medicines Gazette was a *Publication of Drugs Patents in force according to 47 bis of Regulation of the Industrial Property Law*, not the ordinary IMPI Gazette which publishes all the patents monthly. In order to elaborate the list of allopathic drug patents in force at the time, the IMPI will consider the opinion of the CANIFARMA (Federation Official Gazette, February 4, 2005).

patents protecting product or formulation processes. The use of information from the drugs patents list will be used exclusively for COFEPRIS and IMPI linkage purposes (article 7).[18]

Although Mexican firms could not take advantage of the transition period for TRIPS compliance (as India and China did), because of the unexpected early IPR reforms of 1991, they agreed to respect the new IPR and more precisely the new Patent Law. But the reform of Patent Law in 2003, associated with the generic drugs approval, was seen by them as too stringent (even compared to those adopted in developed countries) and also as an entrance barrier to domestic generics. Indeed, since the 1990s, international innovation in molecules has decreased. The big pharmaceutical firms have followed a strategy of development by looking for new formulations, new uses, new dosages, new packaging or new chemical presentations in existing chemical entities. Nevertheless, even if there is an improvement in medicines and/or new findings in therapeutic uses, it does not signify the introduction of new molecules or chemical entities; the pharmaceutical companies extend the life of an existing patent or apply for a new patent. Consequently, the monopolistic price will be extended and the possibility of the general public and even the government accessing cheaper generic medicines, under a competitive environment, will be postponed even longer.

Additionally, drug approval applications meet with slowness and inefficiency. Many of them are not approved by COFEPRIS, owing to the lack of technological or IPR knowledge resulting from the absence of experts. Moreover, the lack of agreements between the ANAFAM (domestic firms) and AMIIF (MNS) associations, both belonging to CANIFARMA,[19] to establish jointly with the IMPI the list of patents protecting molecules, does not favor the right decisions. In this context, some MNS pharmaceutical firms have claimed in the courts or the Supreme Court of Justice the inclusion of patents which do not protect chemical entities and are excluded from the list of IMPI Medicines Gazette. Court decisions are frequently made with absolute ignorance in relation to the subject. The lack of judges skilled in IPR matters impedes the right

---

[18] Moïse and Docteur (2007: 11) point out that "The purpose of the Gazette is to reduce IMPI's burden in resolving pipelines cases by providing a link between the patents information on drugs that IMPI holds and the request for marketing authorization received by Ministry of Health."

[19] ANAFAM is the National Association of Drugs Manufacturers (Asociación Nacional de Fabricantes de Medicamentos); AMIIF is the Mexican Association of the Research-Based Pharmaceutical Industry (Asociación Mexicana de Industrias de Investigación Farmacéutica). Finally, CANIFARMA is the Chamber of the National Pharmaceutical Industry.

decisions being made; either the court calls for legal protection because the judges are convinced that the patent concerns a chemical entity[20] or suspends the unpublished patent in the Gazette on the grounds that it has been extended in other countries even though not in Mexico.[21] Sometimes during the litigation process the IMPI decides to include the patent in question in the Medicines Gazette, impeding the marketing approval. In other cases, COFEPRIS refuses or suspends the drug approval because of a lawsuit and this gives a practical extension to the patent concerned. Therefore, according to some local firms, almost one third of the drugs published in the Medicines Gazette do not belong to new chemical entities.

Health System

In 2007, life expectancy in Mexico rose to 76 years (73 years for men and 78 for women) (World Health Statistics – WHO, 2009).[22] The total expenditure on the health sector represented 6.6 percent of the country's GDP in 2005, which is one of the lowest levels of all the signature countries of the OECD (WHO, 2009). The government continues to make an important contribution to total health expenditure, although this is decreasing; its share dropped from 46.6 per cent in 2000 to 45.2 per cent in 2008. Still, health expenditure related to the activities of the Social Security system is substantial. Public health expenditure in 2006 reached 44.2 percent of total health expenditure and it was made up of 31.8 percent from the federal government, 6.2 percent from the states' governments and 62 percent from the Social Security institutes. Meanwhile, private sector health has increased its share in total health expenditure, rising from 53.4 to 55.8 percent between 2000 and 2006. Total health expenditure per capita, on average, was 527 US dollars in 2006 and 420 US dollars in 2008. In terms of dollar/peso purchasing power parity, total health expenditure per capita in the same year was 778 dollars; 55.8 per cent was private and 44.2 per cent public (WHO, 2009).[23]

---

[20]   This is the case with Terbinafina (Patent 182129) and Omeprazol (Patent 194930) among others.

[21]   This is the case with Clopidogrel (Patent 178820) and Micofenolato de mofetilo (Patent 177872).

[22]   According to OECD, life expectancy in Mexico increased from 63 years in 1970 to 70 years in 1980; and from over 74 years in 1990 to over 76 years in 2000 (OECD, Health Data 2004). Regarding child mortality rates, they stand at 20.5 percent and in the case of maternal mortality rates the figure is 65.2 percent, indicators superior to those of the average in the OECD countries.

[23]   The greatest differential in the calculation considered by the PPA may be related to the appreciation related to the peso/dollar exchange rate in the aforementioned years.

Nevertheless, although the Social Security system, and in particular the Ministry of Health, seem to have influenced decisively, among other factors, the increase in life expectancy, there is a significant level of backwardness in the coverage and financing of health, apparent in several indicators.

The creation of the national health system dates back to the post-revolutionary period and was linked to the need to have government intervention in social policies. Particularly, in the health sector the main objective was to improve hygiene in urban zones and to combat contagious diseases. In this context, the SSA was created. From the 1940s, the principal institutions that make up the present health-service sector were created.[24] Through this system, with social welfare adopted as the main focus, access to health services for an ever greater number of the country's poor was proposed, as well as the establishment of general public health policies and the administration of the Social Security system (SS) (including health services) for unionized workers or labor groups (IMSS). The SS was financed under a tripartite regime (government, employers, workers) and the allocation of resources and access to health services was based on the political and economical influences of distinct union groups (union cupolas) and were essentially based in urban zones. In contrast, the SSA was financed solely by the government and supplies health coverage to all those who had no right to services from the SS. The inequalities regarding the financing and the allocation of resources between the two systems was apparent in the differences in the services supplied, as was the significant lack of coverage in the rural zones of the country. As a result, from the 1960s, Mexico's health policies have been undertaken through several programs with different denominations: IMSS–COPLAMAR, IMSS–Solidaridad and currently IMSS–Oportunidades, aiming to reduce the unbalanced access to health services. Thus, the obligatory coverage of temporary and rural workers was extended, and there was also an increase in the partial access to loans from the Social Security Institute to groups based in rural areas and to players in the informal economy. Since the 1980s, there has been a concerted effort to decentralize the services supplied by the SSA towards the country's states, but this idea was severely affected by the economic problems suffered throughout that decade.

Once again, in the 1990s, efforts were made to continue the decentralization process involving the transfer of functions, responsibilities and

---

[24] In the 1940s, the Ministry of Health and Assistance (SSA) and the Mexican Social Security Institute (IMSS) were founded. In 1960, the Institute of Social Security Services of the State Workers (ISSSTE) was created.

financial resources to the states, especially in the context of the 1994–1995 financial crisis, during which the proportion of the Mexican population under the poverty line increased substantially, reaching 52 percent, and as a consequence the lack of medical coverage was much more evident. A further point is the incidence of nutritional problems in children below the age of 12 and in pregnant women, which severely affect both the physical development and emotional state of the victims.

The Reform Plan for Health Services 1995–2000 established, among other objectives, an increase in the coverage of health services supplied to the non-insured sector of the population through programs including the Program for Increased Coverage (PAC). The National Health Program 2001–2005 went further with the health coverage policies (OECD, 2005).

The Popular Health Insurance (SPS – Seguro Popular de Salud) was created as a pilot health program in 2001 to provide coverage for workers in the informal sector under the National Health Program 2001–2005. In 2004 the SPS became part of the system of Social Health Protection with the goal of being the main vehicle for assuring the entire social security coverage. The SPS proposes proportional, progressive coverage for a package of interventions and certain very costly treatments. The financial resources for this program are supplied by state and federal governments, alongside complementary payments by the families involved – on an income-based scale. With this voluntary health insurance scheme, the aim is to reduce the inequalities in the social security coverage throughout the country's states (OECD, 2005).[25]

SPS acquired relevance if we consider that 15 million people are self-employed, i.e. one-quarter of the working age population (OECD, 2005), around 20 million individuals are working in the informal sector (Ceballos, 2003) and 40 million people were uninsured in 2002. Nowadays the SPS relies on four main health programs, following the goals of the Millennium: 1) the Health Assurance for the New Generation, which concentrates on diseases and disabilities in children under 5 years old; 2) Healthy Pregnancy Strategy to assure the adequate care of pregnant women; 3) Catastrophic Expenditure Protection Funds assigned to cover the high speciality services; and 4) "Oportunidades" Program to give coverage to families in 266 medical interventions (including hepatitis, osteo-

---

[25] The financial sources of SPS are: i) social fee, 3.92 per cent of minimum wage of Mexico City – mwMC; ii) federal solidarity fee, 1.5 times the social fee (5.88 per cent of mwMC) and iii) state solidarity fee, 0.5 times the social fee (1.96 of mwMC). The federal and state governments' financial contributions are assigned: 89 percent to the affiliates by state; 8 percent to the catastrophic expenditures fund and 3 percent to the budgetary provision fund (Chertorivski, 2010).

Table 5.3   Numbers of people affiliated to Popular Health Insurance, 2004–2009

Year	People (millions)	Children (millions)*	Women**	Families (millions)***
2004	5.3			
2005	11.4			
2006	15.7			2
2007	21.8	0.82		2.5
2008	27.2	1.90	188	2.9
2009	31.1	3.00	568.3	3.2
2010 Feb	32.7	3.10	717.2	5

Notes:
*   Children affiliated to the Health Assurance Program for the New Generation
**   Women affiliated to the Healthy Pregnancy Strategy
*** Families affiliated to SPS receiving coverage of the Program "Opportunities"

Source: Chertorivski (2010).

porosis and arthritis). Although the number of people affiliated to SPS has increased, between 2004 and 2009 there has been a high turnover in the people affiliated, according to health needs. See Table 5.3.

Although the Popular Heath Insurance program was created to reduce backwardness in coverage with regard to health services and access to medicines, this program has some severe limitations. Firstly, this is due to the requirement for large quantities of additional financial resources in an environment of reduced economic growth, an absence of major fiscal reform that guarantees government income (not from the petroleum sector) and greater financial pressures from the country's pension scheme. Concerning the acquisition of low cost drugs, the SPS buys the generics by bidding at the lowest prices, but in the case of patented medicines they accept the monopolistic price. Secondly, the SPS only provides coverage for basic services and so has only limited control as regards potentially catastrophic risks. Recently, the SPS has included the treatment of HIV, diabetes, cervical and breast cancer, child and adolescent cancer, cataracts, bone-marrow transplants and intensive care for new-borns; in all these costly and serious areas, the SPS provided services to 60,561 persons in 2006 and 114,773 in 2009, spending 330.5 million dollars in the latter year. Thirdly, given the fact that the services of the program are provided in the same institutional premises as the Social Security, there is potential for differentiation in the quality of the services provided to those of the population with insurance coverage and those without SPS (OECD, 2005).

Epidemiology

In addition to the characteristic complaints resulting from under-development and poverty in Mexico, there are also illnesses associated with industrialized countries and that are common in the elderly population. The significance of these different illnesses is reflected in the size of the market within the therapeutic category in terms of sales of drugs. So, as can be seen in the magnitude of sales, expenditure is higher for medicines that correspond to the treatment of food/metabolism problems (which include illnesses found typically in poor countries – for example malnu-trition, including obesity problems;[26] and rich countries – for example diabetes,[27] bulimia), central nervous system and cardiovascular diseases. Smaller but no less important are the market segments that correspond to the categories of respiratory therapy and infectious diseases, which belong to the category of medicines used in the treatment of the everyday illnesses of a poor population (intestinal infections, malaria, tuberculosis, etc.).

Of the 31 OECD countries in 2006–2007, Mexico had the highest mortality rates, behind the eastern European countries (Estonia, Hungary, the Slovak Republic and Poland), the rates being estimated at between 138 and 178 per 100,000 inhabitants (see Gay et al., 2011, who quote OECD estimates). Illnesses related to the circulatory system have been identified as the principal cause of death in Mexico; in the year 2006, of the total number of deaths, 43.9 percent were associated with these types of illnesses. Other illnesses associated with a large number of deaths were: cancers (14.2 percent), infectious diseases (12.4 percent) and endocrine, nutritional and metabolic system diseases (5.9 percent). However, an alternative methodology has found endocrine, nutritional and metabolic system diseases to be the first cause of death (26 percent) (see Gay et al., 2011). The increase in the number of AIDS patients is of great concern owing to the high cost of care for this type of patient, given the fact that the latest generation of drug treatments have a greater effect and are patented. Among the illnesses related to poverty, in order of importance, are: influenza, diarrhea in both the under-5 age group and the over-5 age group, along with pneumonia. To conclude, Mexico is a country in which illnesses associated with under-developed countries are prevalent, but

---

[26] According to WHO (2010), Mexico ranks second globally in child obesity. This condition could increase several kinds of illness in the Mexican population, such as cardiovascular diseases and diabetes, and subsequently create financial burdens for government health spending.

[27] Mexico had 4 million people with diabetes in 1995, and 12 million people are expected to have diabetes by 2025 (IMS, 2010).

illnesses associated with the industrialized nations are also an important part of the equation.

TECHNOLOGICAL AND INNOVATION CAPABILITIES IN THE PHARMACEUTICAL INDUSTRY

In this section, we identify the technological and innovative capabilities of the pharmaceutical industry in Mexico. Our research is based on two innovation surveys carried out by the INEGI-CONACYT during the year 2000 and the years 2004–2005, with regard to applications and patents granted in the USPTO and those granted to residents and non-residents approved by the National Patents Bank (BANAPA) of the Mexican Institute of Intellectual Property (IMPI), alongside interviews held with qualified industry participants.

One of the first aspects of concern is: Who innovates and how much is devoted to innovation within the pharmaceutical industry? In Mexico in the year 2000, only 39 percent of the interviewed establishments reported undertaking R&D activities linked to at least one innovative project.[28] The proportion rose to 59.1 percent between 2004 and 2005, and just above half of those interviewed reported actual outcomes (56 per cent).[29] This important increase is, without doubt, related to the number of businesses with projects related to the bioequivalence and bioavailability sectors, with a view to accrediting generic medicines as interchangeable generic products.[30] Foreign firms carry out very little R&D and there seems to be no complementary work carried out between national and foreign companies. According to the Innovation Survey 2001, out of the total number of companies that carried out at least one innovative project, foreign companies accounted for 15 percent, while national companies registered the remaining 85 percent. Among the foreign companies, slightly over a third of them carried out R&D projects, while two-fifths of the national companies realized R&D projects. The percentage of turnover destined for R&D projects was very similar: 1.3 percent, in the case of multinational affiliated companies; meanwhile Mexican companies devoted 1 percent to this kind

---

[28] Innovation Survey – 2001, INEGI-CONACYT, Mexico.
[29] Innovation Survey – 2005, INEGI-CONACYT, Mexico.
[30] A new reform relating to the registration of medicines in Mexico requires all companies to undertake studies to prove the bioequivalence and bioavailability of generics in order for them to be accredited as interchangeable generics through the COFEPRIS, otherwise they lose their registration.

of project. This percentage is relatively marginal when compared to the substantial proportion of turnover that the pharmaceutical corporations devote, in their own countries, to the discovery and development of new ingredients and/or new therapeutic uses for existing products (Guzmán and Brown, 2004).

To understand the nature of innovation in this industry, we focus on identifying what type of innovation was being carried out and in which fields. Considering that the Mexican pharmaceutical industry is not noted for its discovery and development of new molecules, the innovative activities are divided into those carried out by the multinationals and those undertaken by national companies. In the first case, the multinationals that reported innovative activities divided their efforts into two areas: on the one hand, the clinical development of new molecules, the first R&D stages having been carried out in their country of origin and, on the other hand, the clinical trials, the adaptation and introduction of the MNS pharmaceutical drugs into the local markets (galenic research). In the second case, the national companies in general concentrate their innovative activities on the development of generic products, once the patent on a molecule has expired. Linked to these activities, the companies adopt new processes and machinery allowing the conduct of bioequivalence and bioavailability tests for the generics. In only a few cases are local companies involved in the discovery of new molecules. In both cases we can refer to the innovations in products and processes, but in the majority of cases the innovations are incremental, given that they correspond to adaptations carried out on the original molecules for the local markets.

According to the Innovation Survey 2004–2005, the innovations introduced in the fields of production, and the organization of the pharmaceutical establishments that responded to the survey, were directed principally towards the introduction of radically new technologies (28.6 percent), the use of new materials (26.7 percent) and new production techniques (23 percent); of lesser importance were activities related to organizational innovations (5.7 percent) or new, professional *software* (0.5 percent). In relation to the products, 24.2 percent of the companies focused on the introduction of new medicines, 28.8 percent on product improvements and 47 percent carried out no product improvements.

Weak technological development, insufficient human capital, and limited R&D has resulted in a low level of innovation and, therefore, a low rate of patents in the developing countries. In theory, the complementarity between internal R&D and the purchase of external technology transfer should generate a virtuous cycle for these companies. In industrialized countries, and some emerging East-Asian economies, the complementarity between internal R&D and technology transfer has been associated with an increase in technological development and innovation (license and technical assistance agreements, and tacit knowledge transfer).[31] In the case of Mexico, contrary to studies on industrialized countries and other industries, the purchase of foreign technology has a marginal effect on the R&D activities of the pharmaceutical firms and their investment decisions (Zúñiga, Guzmán and Brown, 2007). In addition, R&D efforts do not affect the purchase of technology. The absence of a complementary relation may be explained by the divergence of the companies' technological objectives. While company R&D investment is explained by its participation in export markets, the purchase of technology is determined, above all, by capital intensity and the size of the company.

Next, we identify the main sources of external knowledge along with the internal R&D activities within the Mexican pharmaceutical industry. According to the Innovation Surveys, the expenditure on R&D activities in the pharmaceutical firms in Mexico constitutes the largest expenditure directed towards activities of innovation, and by 2005 this field received almost half of total investment. Second, in investment terms, was innovation-related expenditure on the purchase of machinery and equipment (the majority being imported), increasing from around a quarter of total investment in 2001, to 37.1 percent in 2005, indicating a process of modernization in the production of medicines. In addition, 8 percent of total investment in 2001, and 3.1 percent in 2005, was allocated to the acquisition of other external technologies, whether related to products or processes. Investment in industrial design and the introduction of new and improved production processes, activities clearly considered as endogenous innovation, or the adaptation of foreign technology, fell in 2005. Meanwhile, resources set aside for training programs amounted to 7 percent of total investment in 2001 and fell to less than half that in 2005. Finally, 9 percent was spent on the introduction of technological innovations into the markets. According to this data, the purchase of incorporated and unincorporated technology, probably foreign, represented around a third of the total expenditure dedicated to innovation in 2001, whilst in 2005 the figure was closer to two-fifths of total investment. See Figure 5.3. For a comparison with other Latin American countries, see Guzmán and Guzmán, 2009.

---

[31] See: Katrack (1994) and Lee (1996). In turn, the hard or incorporated technologies are those derived from the use of products (for example, machines, materials, and other production technologies) in which the technology can be dismantled with the help of technical manuals.

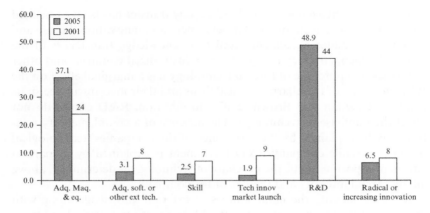

Source: Innovation Surveys, 2001, 2004–2005, Inegi-Conacyt, Mexico

*Figure 5.3   Mexico – distribution of pharmaceutical firms' innovation
expenditure, 2001–2005 (%)*

Importance of R&D as an Internal Source of Technological Knowledge

Considering the crucial role played by R&D in the assimilation and generation of new knowledge, we can see the order of priorities chosen by the pharmaceutical companies vis-à-vis innovation in each and every activity they carry out (see Figure 5.4). In two-fifths of these companies, R&D activities are highly significant; however, slightly over one-fifth of companies regard the activity as insignificant, or slightly significant, and just 28 percent see it as moderately significant, in fact 12 percent of these companies do not even have an R&D department. A similar percentage of the companies attribute a high level of importance, moderate importance and slight importance to their engineering department, although the number of companies that consider this department as insignificant is lower, while those with no engineering department are higher in the overall percentage. As for the departments of production and marketing, over half the companies consider them highly relevant and very few consider them unimportant. Just 4 percent admit to having no production department, while 14 percent possess no marketing department. This suggests that companies concentrate their innovative actions on the fields of production and marketing, and is probably linked to imitative actions, whereby R&D and engineering departments play a much less significant role. The production of generic medicines would explain, in part, this type of company strategy.

The fact that almost two-thirds of the pharmaceutical companies in

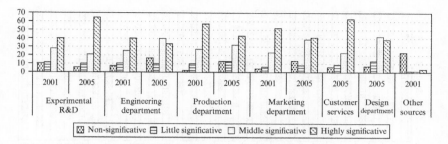

Source: Innovation Surveys, 2001, 2005.

Figure 5.4 *The importance of internal departments as a source of innovation in the Mexican pharmaceutical industry, 2001–2005 (%)*

Mexico have no R&D departments suggests that this sector does not orient its activities towards innovation, and yet their imitative activities are limited, in the sense that there is no development of the capacities necessary for the efficient absorption of knowledge. Additionally, the absence of an R&D unit complicates the life of the companies in the marketplace due to the need for bioequivalence and bioavailability tests for registration with the COFEPRIS, following the newly introduced health regulations. Sixty-three percent have no R&D unit, while 37 per cent do.

External Sources of Technological Knowledge

A further aspect relevant to the analysis of R&D and innovative activities in Mexico's pharmaceutical sector concerns the importance of external sources of information technology (IT) (see Figure 5.5). This is reflected in companies' strategies on technological acquisition with regard to their imitative and innovative activities. The sources of information considered most important by these companies are: their clients (three-fifths of businessmen), equipment, material and components suppliers (over two-fifths), industrial fairs and expos (almost half), whilst their competitors play a role in two-thirds of the cases. This implies that it is market information to which the businessmen in the pharmaceutical industry attach the greatest importance with regard to the generation of new ideas. However, although low in number, there are firms who place great importance on patent activity (10 percent), universities and other higher education establishments (10 percent) and non-profit, public and private investigation institutions (5 percent), which reveals the significant distance that exists between the players in Mexico's pharmaceutical sector and the institutions that generate the new scientific knowledge and, to the same extent, frontier

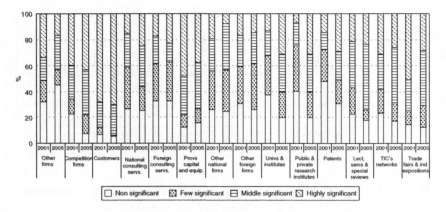

Figure 5.5   Importance of external sources of innovation in the Mexican pharmaceutical industry, 2000–2005 (%)

knowledge with regard to patent registration. Additionally, less than a third of companies consider that conferences, seminars and specialized magazines play a significant role in this field.

This low rate of interest in the information available in the field of patents, universities and institutions can be seen plainly in the fact that over half of the companies regard them as insignificant or of low significance. Other information sources, regarded by more than 50 percent of the companies as insignificant or of low significance, are those pertaining to national and international consulting companies, as well as other national and international companies in general. With regard to the importance placed on computerized information networks for innovative activities, the sector's businessmen have a heterogeneous opinion.

Finally, the financing for the development of innovation is of vital importance. Almost two-thirds of the companies which took part in the surveys said their R&D and innovation activities were self-financed; only a quarter received credits from the private banking sector, while 10 percent of the companies received financial help from subsidiaries or associated companies. It is striking that according to these surveys, there was an absence of help from governmental bodies, especially when considering that this is an industry requiring large amounts of investment.

Technology Transfer

Although there has been investment flowing into Mexico, there is no evidence that the local companies, in general, have taken into consideration the area of technology transfer, nor have they made any real effort in the field of R&D. The cases in which local companies have applied a specific strategy with regard to technological innovation can be counted on the fingers of one hand, as can the links between companies and universities with a view to participation in the competitive environment, since the introduction of the NAFTA and the stringent IPR system (Guzmán and García, 2009).

There is a relative difference in the importance attached to the different fields with regard to contracts for technology transfers among the national and international companies. It is evident that the affiliated pharmaceuticals companies based in Mexico do not undertake substantial activities related to R&D; technology transfer is essentially orientated to brands, patents and technological assistance. Although national companies also focus their transfer efforts on the acquisition of brands, patents and technological assistance, the field of industrial design is dedicated to the development of R&D activities undertaken by national companies.

Cooperation between Universities and Companies

In Mexico, four-fifths of R&D activities are carried out in-house. When they are externalized, this is generally due to the fact that there is no in-house R&D laboratory, so these companies establish a cooperation agreement with an external research institute or another company. The ratio between the two is: 83 percent in-house and 17 percent external. Added to which, only a quarter of the pharmaceutical companies have an engineering department, the actual figures being 74 percent with no engineering department for R&D purposes and 26 percent with. Even if there is certain international recognition for Mexican researchers in the bio-pharmaceutical field and their publications in journals classified in the International Scientific Index (ISI), the knowledge generation capabilities in science are still relatively low. Furthermore, academic strengths in the production of scientific knowledge are not reflected in the business world (Guzmán and García, 2009) and there is a scarcity of links between universities and firms, mainly due to the absence of institutional policies regarding intellectual property and active technological transfer which would encourage technological cooperation between the two parties. In the academic sphere, researchers have sufficient incentives to publish, but not to patent. The few examples of collaboration between academics and industry do not usually take place through the institutional university channels, due to the fact that the legislation is still at an incipient level and promotion is lax.

Human Capital Specialization in the Pharmaceutical Sector

In the industrialized countries, the training of PhD students is the result of a joint effort between public and private sector companies, along with governmental organizations, thus strengthening the academic infrastructure of the universities and research institutions. As part of their professional activities, PhD students carry out research and development work in research institutes, engineering companies and laboratories; also, in the academic field, in universities and higher education establishments, with the formation of new human resources at the level of higher education in the fields of science and technology. The efforts made in Mexico in terms of PhD training are low compared to the industrialized and newly industrialized countries.[32] There is a significant level of backwardness with regard to the number of researchers per 1000 labor force (R/1000 lf). Mexico had 0.9 R/1000 lf in 2007, which contrasts with 9.2 in the US, 7.6 in France, 7.2 in Germany and 7.9 in Canada. Among the emerging countries Portugal had 7.2, China 2.0 and Turkey 2.1. Nevertheless, from 2000 to 2007 the number of PhD graduates in Mexico increased from 6.8 to 13.5 per 1000 people working in the fields of science and engineering (CONACYT, 2009). In 2008, two thirds of PhD graduates working in these fields were working in scientific fields linked to the pharmaceutical industry.

Scientific Publications and their Importance

According to the International Scientific Index (ISI) classifications, there are eight scientific disciplines linked to the pharmaceutical industry: molecular biology, biology, biotechnology, pharmacology, immunology, medicine, microbiology and neurosciences. On a global scale, Mexico has a low production of scientific publications. The greatest capabilities in Mexico are in the fields of microbiology and pharmacology. Despite Mexico's low number of international publications in the field of medicine, in the context of the country and, particularly, in the scientific areas of health and natural sciences, articles related to this discipline have the highest relative importance, followed by those of biology.

A further indicator of the importance of scientific output, measured in

---

[32]   In 2001, the total number of researchers was divided mainly among the following geographical areas: Europe 34.3 percent, the United States 26.1 percent and Asia 33.3 percent. In the case of Asia, 13.7 percent were based in China. Meanwhile, Mexico contributed just 0.6 percent, even lower than Brazil, which was home to 1.3 percent of the total number of researchers.

terms of publications, is the *impact factor*.[33] By studying this indicator, we can appreciate that the average number of citations received by publications in the case of Mexico in 1999–2003 was higher than other Latin American countries in the fields of molecular biology, immunology and pharmacology, thus revealing that scientific research of an international standard has developed in Mexico, and does have a relative impact.

INDUSTRIAL PERFORMANCE AND ACCESS TO DRUGS

National and Foreign Patenting in Local Offices of Intellectual Property in Mexico

In Mexico, after the approved IPR reforms of 1991, the number of patent applications in the pharmaceutical area in the local offices increased dramatically, rising from 239 applications in 1990 to 3,164 patents in 2006, with an average annual growth rate of 15.2 percent. Of the 11,936 patents granted in Mexico between 1980 and 2006, 98.4 percent were granted to non-residents and just 1.6 percent to Mexicans. Contrary to the trend in foreign patents, local patents have been marginal, although there was an increase from 3 patents in 1980 to 35 in 2006. Almost half of all the patents granted to non-residents in Mexico between 1980 and 2006 were to North Americans, predominantly in the United States; meanwhile, European companies were granted almost two fifths of the approved patents and Asia represented 7 percent of the total, with Latin America representing less than 1 percent. According to the patents consulted, we identified that 91 percent of the non-resident patent acquirers were companies, with institutions and individuals representing just 6 percent and 3 percent, respectively. Among the companies with the largest numbers of non-resident patents granted in Mexico are those from the US and United Kingdom, which are characterized as the leaders on a global level and/or have been the object of mergers or takeovers, such as Pfizer, Pharmacia, GlaxoSmithKline, Eli Lilly, Merck, Johnson, Abbott and Bayer. The German companies Schering and Boehringer, the Swiss companies AstraZeneca and Novartis, along with the French company Sanofi-Aventis, also play an important role in innovative projects. Almost half of the patents granted to Mexican residents were granted to individuals,

---

[33] The impact factor is defined as 'the quotient between the citations and the number of articles in a determined time period' (CONACYT-INEGI, 2003, p. 70).

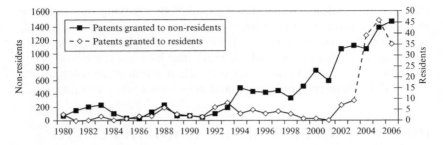

Source: IMPI (Industrial Property Mexican Institute), Banapa (National Bank of Patents). International class A61K.

Figure 5.6   Patents granted to residents and non-residents in Mexico by IMPI in pharmaceutical field, 1980–2006

less than a third to companies and close to a quarter to institutions. See Figure 5.6.

Patents Applied for and Granted in the USPTO within the Pharmaceutical Field: the Diffusion Rate

The number of Mexican patents applied for and granted by the United States Patent and Trademark Office (USPTO) has been extremely low for the past three decades, which is linked to the lack of resources devoted to R&D in the national pharmaceutical industry.[34] The diffusion rate related to the inventive activity in Mexico's pharmaceutical sector is almost zero and remains practically at a standstill. The high cost of making patent applications to the USPTO or through the PCT[35] mechanism and the weak patent culture in Mexico are factors which undoubtedly affect the rate of diffusion of innovative activities in these countries.

On analyzing the patents granted in the pharmaceutical area with regard to the type of process and product, it becomes obvious that inno-

---

[34]   Patents were consulted for the period 1980–2006 in this investigation from the USPTO in the classes 514 *Medicines and compounds for the treatment of bio-complaints of the body* and/or 424 *Drugs, bio-complaints and compounds for the treatment of the body*, for the pharmaceutical area. From the area of bio-technology, the consulted classes were 435 and/or 800. Considering that there are patents that can be in both classes of the USPTO, the search was carried out under the premise of *and/or*, so as to avoid duplication.

[35]   By way of the PCT mechanism, the agents may patent in several countries simultaneously for a period of one year.

vative activity is present in both, although in the majority of cases we are talking about incremental innovations. Mexico has obtained several patents in the field of products.

In the pharmaceutical area (classes 514 and/or 424), Mexico has a reduced level of claims: 10.5 per patent. With regard to Mexican agents with patents in the pharmaceutical area, granted by the USPTO, companies obtained the patents in less than two-fifths of the cases, whilst institutions and individuals had a similar level (29 percent) of ownership of the patents.

Regarding the nationality of the patent inventors, in almost all cases, they are Mexicans. Of the 59 inventors registered in Mexico, only one is from the United States, two are from the European Union, and three are from other countries. The foreign participation in the patents granted in Mexico may be due to agreements made with institutions, or companies, but it could also be explained by the companies in question hiring foreigners for their research projects. One interesting experience is that of the company Probiomed, which, after taking the decision to substitute foreign technological transfer, then met obstacles in collaborating with national university researchers; they decided to hire foreign researchers.

The number of inventors per patent partly reveals the way in which new knowledge is produced, in the sense that it indicates the size of the R&D laboratories and thus the organization of the research teams. In countries which have accumulated technological capacities with a significant amount of activity in the R&D institutes, there has been a trend towards research teams becoming more consolidated. The patents in these countries are generally the result of joint research and, in a few cases, the result of one individual researcher. In Mexico, there is participation of between 5 and 10 researchers in the invention area of the pharmaceutical sector.

Access to Medicines

From the point of view of some local firms, Mexico has always been a market where new world pharmaceutical products were introduced without delay, later followed by the generic versions, either through licensing of the patent or by means of reverse-engineering, during the period of lax patenting.[36] Nevertheless, the speed of Mexican firms' imitation capabilities was an important argument against the introduction of some new drugs. Consequently, American MNS pharmaceutical firms were

---

[36] This is the case for Ranicen by Glaxo, a generic version of which was produced very rapidly by Senosian, a Mexican firm.

instrumental in lobbying for the strengthening of IPR and especially the patent system in Mexico, prior to the NAFTA negotiations. Since 1991, the IMPI has registered an important growth in the number of foreign patent applications and patents granted. We deduce from the adoption of the TRIPS and the significant increase in patents applied for and granted that these firms had great expectations of introducing new medicines to Mexico under this new IPR environment. Therefore, the strong patent system seems to have favored the availability of new generation medicines in Mexico's pharmaceutical market. On the other hand, it has destroyed the possibility to introduce generic versions into the Mexican market, to the detriment of those involved in the procurement of medicines.

In 2009, almost half of the population receiving medical coverage through the IMSS and the ISSSTE had regular access to the prescription of medicines for the treatment of diseases and for other medical interventions. A further 45 percent of the population could access the medicines through other state or federal services, including Popular Health Insurance, and 5 percent by private means (IMS, 2010).[37] However, each social security service has its budget constraints; each has its own structured procedure to purchase medicines according to medical priorities. In the case of the SPS, this depends on the established guidelines and the financial capacity of the Ministry of Health. The expenditure of the public health institutions on medicines and medical inputs grew 60 percent between 2004 and 2010 (this last year is estimated). Although the budget allocated to drug procurement is higher, the affiliates do not always satisfy their needs completely from the institution and they must buy out of their own resources. As we have seen, the financial resources for purchasing medicines have increased as regards patented medicines, but with fewer units, and on the other hand, the share of the budget used for generics has decreased. Moreover, the deep problems of financial sustainability of the public health institutions and the regulations restricting the introduction of generics onto the market (associated with the drug approval procedures, as explained above), make it more difficult to assure the entire coverage of medicines needed by patients. As a consequence, for some illnesses, such as HIV/AIDS, the coverage of antiretrovirals (ARV) is almost complete – between 82 and 95 percent (CENSIDA-SS, 2010), but for other kinds of disease there are occasionally shortages or delays in supplies.

---

[37] According to the Health Law Reform (10 April 2007), 30 million people did not have access to medicines, 55 million had access through IMSS and ISSSTE and 15 million could have private consultations and purchased the medicines on their own. Only three percent of the Mexican population has private health insurance (Moïse & Docteur, 2007).

When patients have to follow a treatment without interruption, they will be forced to buy the medicines themselves in the private market or wait until the medicine becomes available again in the institution.

Of the total expenditure on medicines in Mexico in 2009, 64.7 percent was out-of-pocket, 2.4 per cent was from the private sector and one third from the public health institutions (17 percent from the IMSS, 6 percent from the ISSSTE and 10.2 percent from the Ministry of Health and SSP).

Prices

Historically, drug prices in Mexico have been lower than in other OECD countries.[38] In 1987, both the consumer prices index (CPI) and pharmaceutical consumer price index (PCPI) recorded inflation of three digits (more than 180 and 160 percent, respectively), which fell to two digits in 1988. From 1988 to 1990 the CPI rose faster than the PCPI. From 1991 (when Mexico adopted the stringent IPR reforms) to 1999 the price indexes on pharmaceutical products were higher than those of the CPI, following a policy of price flexibility. Since September 1996, there has been an agreement to regulate the prices of medicines by adopting the maximum-price regulation.

An analysis by the Ministry of Health (2002) found that in more than 43 percent of cases the retail sale prices were higher than maximum permitted retail prices (González-Pier and Gonzalez 2004). Therefore, in 2004, maximum price regulation was adopted. The pricing agreement was signed jointly by the Ministry of Economy and CANIFARMA (representing the members of AMIIF). The main points of this reform, administered by the Ministry of Health, are: i) the regulation applies only to patented medicines on the private market; ii) the manufacturers' participation is voluntary; iii) the international prices are taken as a reference to establish the maximum retail sales price; iv) in the case of new products, the manufacturers fix the prices, which can be re-evaluated three months after product launch; v) generic products and original products whose patents have expired are not considered for price regulation; vi) three different prices are considered in the price regulation: the international reference price; the reference price for retail sales and the maximum retail sales price.

As a consequence, PCPI inflation has slowed down to one digit since 2004, reaching the lowest figure in 2008 (2.7 percent) and lower than the

---

[38] In the early 1990s, prices of pharmaceutical products in Mexico were 5 times lower than in the United States and 3 times lower than in European countries (IMS Health, 2005, cited in Moïse and Docteur, 2007).

pharmaceutical producer price index (PPPI) (5 percent). The next year (2009), the producer price index remained higher than the consumer price index. A new study was conducted in 2005, revealing that in 73 percent of cases the maximum price of the 273 medicines in the sample was lower than the international reference price and in 2 percent of cases were equivalent. Another study on comparative pharmaceutical prices (Danzón and Furukawa, 2003) showed that Mexican prices in this sector were 80 percent of those in the United States and were lower than in Germany, Italy and the United Kingdom, but higher than in Canada and France. Generic prices in Mexico were higher than in the United States and patented medicine prices were lower. Commenting on these findings, Danzón and Furukawa underline that Mexicans pay higher prices if we take into account the comparative income level. The lower per capita income level of the country is probably not the only reason for the price elasticity of demand. Other factors that should be considered include income distribution preferences and the level of out-of-pocket payments for pharmaceutical purchases.

In the case of the public sector, the consumer price index figures of the basic listing medicines have significantly decreased, falling from 3.68 in 2004 to –24.5 in 2009. Meanwhile, private sector prices and the consumer price index recorded a high increase, with an important divergent trend.

Among the medicines in the public sector, the prices of some therapeutic classes fell on average between 2003 and 2009, probably linked to the introduction of more generics, although some patented medicines have been also included in the public sector. This was the case for ophthalmology (–79.1 percent), cardiology (–42.30), psychiatry (–38.02), infectious diseases (–18.11), gastrointestinal diseases (–11.89) and neurology (–0.27).[39] Otherwise, in the same period, the prices of other therapeutic classes of medicines have risen on average as follows: nutrition (45.33 percent), rheumatology (37.40), dermatology (11.16) and otolaryngology (4.9). The high inflation here suggests the existence of patented products.

The role played by Simi medicines, i.e. non-bioequivalent or "similar" generics, up until 2010 gave many people the opportunity to access drugs at hugely reduced prices, especially the lowest income and uninsured people. The lower people's income the higher is their propensity to buy Simi generics (IIIFAC). From 2003 to 2008, the sales of Simi pharma-

---

[39]   Sources: Pharmaceutical and Medical National Institute of the Public Sector – INEFAMSP, Spanish acronym of Instituto Nacional Farmacéutico y Médico del Sector Público; Pharmaceutical Research Institute – IIIFAC, Spanish acronym of Instituto Farmacéutico, A.C.

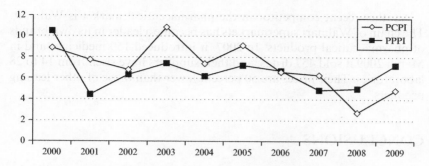

Source: Pharmaceutical Research and Innovation Institute, A.C., with Banxico and INEGI database.

Figure 5.7 *Consumer and producer prices index in drugs market in Mexico, 2000–2009*

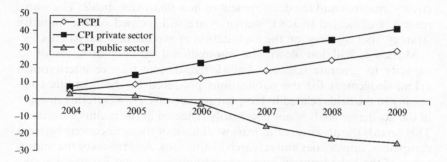

Source: Pharmaceutical Research and Innovation Institute, A.C., with Banxico and INEGI database.

Figure 5.8 *Accumulated inflation of the consumer, public and private sector of the basic listing of medicines in Mexico, 2004–2009*

ceutical products almost doubled in terms of units; basically they are inferior goods and the lower prices are also due to the fact that Simi has its own distribution chain of pharmacies throughout the whole country and they import low-price inputs from India and China, among other countries. As Simi products have increased their presence in the pharmaceutical market, their sales growth has fallen. After concentrating on the bioequivalence test to obtain marketing approval from the COFEPRIS, the Simi generics producers are now seeking to introduce products in new therapeutic classes and to bid in the public sector.

Another recent competitor in the pharmaceutical market is Walmart. The chain of Walmart supermarkets has become a leader in its own brands of pharmaceutical products. In 2007, it introduced 150 medicines and in March 2009 it sold 457 drugs, and their suppliers have risen from 14 to 28 laboratories. Their prices are 50 percent lower than those of other leading products.

CONCLUSIONS

The technological efforts in Mexico's pharmaceutical sector are still relatively low. Companies are still reluctant to assume the costs of R&D and of developing their own patents, considering it unnecessary. Although local companies have been forced to modernize and undertake the necessary tests, so as to have their interchangeable generic medicines approved, there are still very few that have increased their efforts in the areas of discovery, research and the development of new pharmaceuticals. The scarce resources dedicated to R&D activities are still focused on the imitative strategy, that is to say, on the exploitation of expired medical patents.

Mexico is still low down the international ranking in terms of its capacity to generate scientific knowledge, despite relative international acknowledgement for the publications produced by the scientific community in the fields related to bio-pharmaceuticals. However, this strength in the academic fields is not necessarily reflected in the realm of business. This reveals the absence, or at least weakness, of the connections between companies, universities and research institutions. Awareness of the importance of the links between business and universities has led to some successful cases. Alliances between companies are also scarce, which results in the work carried out by some companies being somewhat fragmented. Companies have had to organize themselves in the face of adverse economic policies, but this kind of organization has been lacking with respect to R&D projects.

Regarding the innovation model, in terms of the players that dominate the market, technological efforts and domination in the systems of intellectual property, we found that the pharmaceutical sector in Mexico is dominated by a multinational model; not because of the foreign companies spreading their technological and innovative efforts throughout the country, but rather because they have increased their control over the national market and have thus been the beneficiaries of the patent system, while local companies and institutions have made weaker technological and innovative efforts, thus leading to a limited level of market participation.

The type of patent system is characterized as being divergent. In effect, there is a high relative dependence, which implies that a greater number of foreign (non-resident) patents are being applied for at the local offices, when compared with the number of national (resident) applicants. In addition, the inventive coefficient level (patents per million inhabitants) is marginal. This suggests that the new technological knowledge (pharmaceutical products and processes) that is protected belongs to foreigners and, as a result, the beneficiaries of the monopolistic exploitation related to patents also remains in the hands of the foreign companies (multinational companies, in most cases).

Mexico's adoption of the TRIPS, in a context of meager economic growth, recurring economic and political crises and unfinished institutional changes, in conjunction with low levels of investment in R&D activities, does not provide any incentives to participate in innovation projects. These factors result in a status quo with regard to the low number of patents granted per year in comparison with the Asian countries. The adoption of the TRIPS in Mexico has favored the multinational companies, because the opportunities open to national companies are limited by their low capacity for imitative and innovative projects, concentrated in just a few local companies which have been able to develop some niche opportunities.

Given the strategic importance of the pharmaceutical industry in the health and well-being of the population, Mexico should strengthen this industry, focusing on innovation in specialized areas, whilst at the same time developing the country's capabilities in the production of interchangeable generic products. Good competitive performance also involves an improvement in the commercial balance, efficiency in public health policies and an increase in the scale of the knowledge-based economy. In recognition of the crucial importance of R&D and innovative activities, within an adequate macro, micro and institutional environment, Mexico must take up the challenge to achieve a modern and competitive industry, requiring the design of industrial, fiscal, financial and educational policies to allow the development and accumulation of technological capacities.

REFERENCES

Aboites, J. and M. Cimoli (2002), "Intellectual property rights and national innovation systems. Some lessons from the Mexican experience", *Revue d'Economie Industrielle*, 99, 2ème Trimestre: 215–232.

Agrawal, M. (2000), *Global Competitiveness in the Pharmaceutical Industry. The Effect of National Regulatory, Economic, and Market Factors*, Pharmaceutical Products Press, New York.

Bell, M. and K. Pavitt (1993), "Technological accumulation and industrial

growth: contrasts between developed and developing countries", *Industrial and Corporate Change*, 2 (2): 157–269.
Breschi, S. and F. Malerba (1997), "Sectoral innovation systems: technological regimes, Schumpeterian dynamics, and spatial boundaries" in C. Edquist, *Systems of Innovation Technologies, Institutions and Organizations*, Pinter, London.
Brodovsky, J. (1997), "La industria farmacéutica y farmoquímica mexicana en los años 90", in J. Katz (ed.), *Apertura económica y desregulación en el mercado de medicamentos*, Cepal-Alianza, Santiago.
Ceballos, D. (2003), "Labour-Mexico: 20 million informal sector workers", Interpress Service News Agency, www.ipsnews.net.inerna.asp?idnews=199946.
CENSIDA-SS (2010), Centro Nacional para la prevencíon y control del VIH/ SIDA, "Informe Nacional sobre los progresos realizados en la aplicación del UNGASS, México 2010", Secretaria de Salud, Mexico.
CEPAL (2008), *Statistical Yearbook for Latin America & the Caribbean*, Statistics & Economics Projection Division.
Cepal-Naciones Unidas (1987), "La industria farmacéutica y farmoquímica: desarrollo histórico y posibilidades futures", Argentina, Brasil and México, serie de Estudios e Informes de la Cepal No. 65, Santiago de Chile.
Chávez, S. (2007), "Mexican pharmaceuticals: strong FDI", August 20, http:// www.Latinbusinesschronicle.com.
Chertorivski, S. (2010), "El seguro popular y su cobertura en la salud", paper.
CONACYT (2009), Anexo estdístico del Informe General del Estado de la Ciencia y Tecnología, 2009/2.
CONACYT-INEGI (2003), *Indicadores de Actividades Científicas y Tecnológicas*, Mexico.
Danzón, P.M. and M.K. Furukawa (2003), "Prices availability of pharmaceuticals. Evidence from nine countries", Health Affairs Web exclusive PP 3521-WB-526, http://contenthealthaffairs.org/cgi/reprint/hlthaff.w3521V1.
De la Mora, J. (2005), "Las reformas de la leyes de patentes en la industria farmacéutica de México", in Guzmán, A. and G. Viniegra (eds), *Industria farmacéutica y propiedad intelectual: los países en desarrollo*, Miguel Angel Porrúa-Universidad Autónoma Metropolitana, Mexico: 323–350.
Edquist, C. (1997), "Systems of innovation approaches – their emergence and characteristics", in C. Edquist, *Systems of Innovation*, Pinter, London.
Frenkel, J. (1978), *Tecnología e competição ma indústria farmacêutica brasileira*, Rio de Janeiro: Finep/CEP/Gepetec.
Gay, J.G., V. Paris, M. Devaux and M. De Looper (2011), "Mortality amenable to health care in 31 OECD countries: estimates and methodological issues", OECD Health Working Papers, No. 55 OECD Publishing.
Gereffi, G. (1986), *Industria farmacéutica y dependencia en el tercer mundo*, Fondo de Cultura Económica, Mexico.
Gonzáles-Pier, E. and A. González (2004), "Regulación saludable del sector farmacéutico", Competencia Económica en México, Comisión Federal de Competencia, Mexico.
Guzmán, A. (2005), "El sistema de innovación del Cluster Farmacéutico en México: Universidad-Empresas-Gobierno" capítulo 6, en Centro de Capital Intelectual y Competitividad, Competitividad internacional para la articulación de la cadena productiva y desarrollo de cluster de la industria farmacéutica de la región centro país, Estudio de Diagnóstico de CANIFARMA.

Guzmán, A. and F. Brown, (2004), "Diseminación tecnológica en la industria farmacéutica mexicana", Comercio Exterior Vol. 54 (11) November: 976–987.

Guzmán, A. and R. García (2009), "University–Enterprise Knowledge Generation and Spillovers: Patents and Technology Transfer in the Bio-pharmaceutical Sector in México", in *The Intellectual Property Economy in Mexico*, World Intellectual Property Organization, Geneva, forthcoming in 2011.

Guzmán, A. and M.V. Guzmán (2009), "¿Poseen capacidades de innovación las empresas farmacéuticas de América Latina? La evidencia de Argentina, Brasil, Cuba y México", Economía: teoría y Práctica, Número especial, vol. 1, November.

Guzmán, A. and M.P. Zúñiga (2004), "Patentes en la industria farmacéutica de México: los efectos en la I&D y la innovación", Comercio Exterior, 54, No. 12: 1104–1121.

IMS, Intelligence Applied (2010), "Oportunidades en el mercado del gobierno mexicano", paper, March 23.

Jaffe, A. and M. Trajtenberg (2002), *Patents, Citations and Innovations: A Window on the Knowledge Economy*, The MIT Press, London.

Katrack, H. (1994), "In house technological efforts, imports of technology and enterprise characteristics in newly industrialising countries: the Indian experience", *Journal of International Development*, 263–276.

Katz, J. (1997), "Los países latinoamericanos con capacidad farmoquímica propia: Argentina, Brasil y México", in Jorge Katz (ed.), *Apertura económica y desregulación en el mercado de medicamentos*, Argentina, CEPAL/IDRC Alianza Editorial.

Kim, L. (1997), *Initiation to Innovation*, Harvard Business School Press, Boston, Massachusetts.

Lall, S. (2003), "Indicators of the relative importance of IPRs in developing countries", ICTSD-UNCTAD, Issue Paper No. 3, Geneva.

Lee, J. (1996), "Technology imports and R&D efforts of Korean manufacturing firms", *Journal of Development Economics*, 50 (1): 197–210.

Lundvall, B.A. (1993), "National systems of innovation", in C.I. Bradford (ed.), *The New Paradigm of Systemic Competitiveness: Toward More Integrated Policies in Latin America*, Paris, OCDE.

Malerba, F. (2002), "Sectoral systems of innovation and production", *Research Policy*, 31 (2), 247–274.

Malerba, F. (2004), *Sectoral Systems of Innovation: Concepts, Issues and Analyses of Six Major Sectors in Europe*, Cambridge University Press, Cambridge.

Martínez, E. (2010), "Evolución del Mercado de medicamentos: público y privado", paper, Ministry of Health database.

Moïse, P. and E. Docteur (2007), "Pharmaceutical pricing and reimbursement policies", OCDE Health Working Papers 25, Paris.

MOITI (2006), "Mexican pharmaceutical industry", www.mass.gov/moiti.

Mowery, D.C. and N. Rosemberg (1989), *Technology and the Pursuit of Economic Growth*, Cambridge University Press, Cambridge.

Nelson R. (1993), *National Innovation Systems: A Comparative Study*, Oxford University Press, Oxford.

OECD (2005), OECD Reviews of Health Care Systems, México, Paris.

Palmeira, F. and P.L. Pan (2003), "Cadeia farmacéutica no Brasil: avaliacão preliminar e perspectivas", Rio de Janeiro, BNDES.

Pavitt, K. (1984), "Sectoral patterns of technological change towards a taxonomy and a theory", *Research Policy*, 13 (6), 343–373.
Schmookler, J. (1966), *Invention and Economic Growth*, Harvard University Press, Cambridge, MA.
Scripps, Pharmaceutical Industry League Tables, 2004.
WHO, World Health Statistics, 2009, Geneva, NLM: WA 900.1.
WHO, World Health Statistics, 2010, Geneva, NLM: WA 900.1.
World Pharmaceutical Markets, Outlook, Mexico (2005 and 2006), "Mexico: accessing the pharmaceutical market", Espicom Business Intelligence, West Sussex.
Zúñiga, M.P., A. Guzmán and F. Brown (2007), "Technology acquisition strategies in the pharmaceutical industry in Mexico", *Comparative Technology Transfer and Society (CTTS)*, 5 (3), December: 274–296.

6. Corporate power and state resistance: Brazil's use of TRIPS flexibilities for its National AIDS Program[1]

Matthew Flynn

Brazil provides one of the most unique cases for exploring the impact of intellectual property on sustaining a social program based on social democratic principles. In 1996, Brazil passed legislation mandating the state to provide expensive anti-retroviral (ARV) medication to its citizens who have contracted the human immunodeficiency virus (HIV) that causes the acquired immunodeficiency syndrome (AIDS). Also in 1996, Brazil was one of the first countries to change its domestic patent laws as a result of the Agreement on Trade-Related Aspects of Intellectual Property (TRIPS), one of the pillars of the global trading system governed by the newly created World Trade Organization (WTO). In terms of both TRIPS and universal AIDS treatment, Brazil was ahead of its time. The country subsequently became one of the first countries to begin resorting to the use of the humanitarian safeguards outlined in the TRIPS accord. Specifically, Brazil began using compulsory licenses to drive down the price of medicines. By allowing other producers to enter the market, this legal device allows states to remove the market exclusivity a patent holder retains to set monopoly prices.

A close review of the Brazilian experience with the TRIPS accord and use of its flexibilities provides insight into the different forms of corporate power and state resistance related to intellectual property (IP). Brazil's experience with using TRIPS flexibilities reveals the importance of institutionalizing a universal public health system and construction of state

---

[1] This chapter is based on original field research involving over 50 interviews with policymakers, activists, and managers and representatives of private and public sector drug companies in Brazil carried out from October 2007 to September 2008.

organizations responsible for its administration. The legal and political commitments to universal health care are best illustrated by the establishment of the National AIDS Program. Having to sustain a long-term commitment to AIDS treatment with a limited amount of resources is what shapes policymakers' interests, drives them to use humanitarian flexibilities, and lays the groundwork for alliances with civil society. The right to health shapes a human rights discourse that is shared by both committed public servants and civil society activists. Domestic economic interests and threats by foreign economic forces may result in local industry vetoing initiatives by public health officials and/or resistance by other government ministries. But without the commitment to universal access to essential medicines, the Brazilian case suggests that the struggle for and use of TRIPS flexibilities would have been minimal. In the Brazilian case, coping with AIDS in Brazil has enhanced state powers.

THE POWER OF TRIPS

The Agreement on Trade-Related Aspects of Intellectual Property is the most impressive attempt to construct a worldwide patent regime. TRIPS stipulates that all WTO member countries must provide the same patent protection of twenty years, and domestic patent authorities cannot discriminate against foreign patent applications in favor of local applicants. Since TRIPS also mandated the inclusion of pharmaceuticals, the accord represents a qualitative shift in the role of IP in domestic legislation. Many countries, including Brazil, provided patent protections for other goods but not for pharmaceuticals due to the importance of a local drug industry in economic development and provision of medicines for health systems (Bermudez and Oliveira 2004).

Owing to the increasing economic competition in the world economy beginning in the 1970s, the salience of intellectual property in a knowledge-based economy has grown. The US's Section 301 of the Trade Act of 1974, for example, authorizes the United States Trade Representative (USTR) to impose tariffs on goods from countries engaging in unfair trade practices including infringements on intellectual property. Corporations not only from the US, but also from Europe and Japan, mobilized their governments to push for strong intellectual property rules through the WTO. While some developing countries hoped that after the creation of the WTO US bilateral trade pressure would end, industry associations continued to lobby the USTR to apply pressure on countries with regard to their IP laws (Sell 2003).

Despite the tremendous pressure brought to bear on developing countries to conform to the IP standards employed by wealthy nations, several flexibilities and humanitarian safeguards were included in the final TRIPS accord. Countries must adhere to the minimum obligations of TRIPS but could still determine the criteria of patentability based on claims of novelty, inventiveness and industrial applicability. WTO member states could also determine which government agency would adjudicate patent applications, whether other government bodies or civil society organizations could participate in the process, and how many flexibilities outlined in TRIPS could be included in domestic legislation (see Appendix 1 for a list of TRIPS flexibilities).

Just as there is great diversity across the levels of economic development and capabilities of state institutions throughout the developing world, compliance with the TRIPS accord and use of TRIPS flexibilities have also varied. There are a number of countervailing forces scholars have highlighted concerning the incorporation of TRIPS flexibilities and their use. The first concerns the presence of a weak, domestic-owned pharmaceutical industry. Since drug makers in the developing world tend to produce generic medicines, patents do not play an important role in their business strategies and often operate as a market barrier. Consequently, domestic drug firms lobby their government to include more TRIPS flexibilities. Thus countries like India and China, which are home to robust generic pharmaceutical firms, waited until the 2005 TRIPS deadline before changing their patent laws.

Another factor is civil society pressure. Health activists, for example, have become increasingly aware of the impact that patents have on access to essential medicines. Global outrage against the 39 pharmaceutical companies that sued the South African government for changing its patent laws to allow for parallel importing of cheaper AIDS medicines galvanized transnational advocacy networks across the world. Closely associated with the civil society pressure are issue area discourses or the framing of social conflicts. On the one hand, intellectual property is framed as a fundamental right to ownership of property; but on the other, health activists have coalesced around the frame of access to medicines as the fundamental right to life.

Additional related factors are the balance of needs between corporate investors and host countries, as well as pressures from hegemonic countries, for example the United States. Foreign investors seek out opportunities in developing countries based on the size of domestic markets, availability of cheap labor, and/or natural resource endowments. Host countries, depending on the degree of integration in the world economy and reliance on export markets for growth, seek to attract foreign companies for technology, capital, and foreign exchange. The balance of power varies depending on the size of the host country, the nature of the industry, and potential returns. Also weighing in on this relation is the ability of the corporation to elicit the support of the United States to support its interests. The degree to which a host country is dependent on the US market or susceptible to US trade or diplomatic threats will affect the balance of power.

These are important factors regarding the degree to which developing countries are affected by intellectual property regimes, as many of the chapters in this book detail. But one factor that has been under-emphasized in the literature on TRIPS compliance and use of humanitarian safeguards is the importance of social-democratic commitments by states. This institutionalist or state-centered approach argues that the *substantive* fulfillment of social policies empowers state actors, especially those state organizations responsible for carrying out successful programs, who then become the main proponents for the use of humanitarian safeguards. As Skocpol (1992, 59) describes: "a policy is 'successful' if it enhances the kinds of state capacities that can promote its future development, and especially if it stimulates groups and political alliances to defend the policy's continuation and expansion." The "lock-in" mechanism, in the case of successful AIDS policies, is the effective roll-out of treatment to all those requiring medicines. It is not just the *de jure* or legal mandate to provide medicines; it is also the *de facto* achievement that transforms the fulfillment of a social right into a powerful mobilizing force.

Much of the literature about the new institutionalism in the social sciences focuses on the constraints that institutions impose on actors. But institutions empower as well as constrain. Institutions are the formal and informal rules, as well as the systems of meanings, governing relationships among individuals and groups. The substantive fulfillment of a social program not only imbues certain values, such as 'the right to access to medicines,' amongst the members of the state organizations responsible for its execution, but also provides a platform for these actors to affect policy arenas that impinge on their mandate.

Two additional concepts underlie the state-centered approach. First is the concept of bureaucratic autonomy. According to Carpenter (2001), bureaucratic autonomy develops when state organizations develop strong reputations based on efficacy, professionalism and uniqueness of service. "It occurs, further, when [managers] ground this reputation in a diverse coalition wrought from the multiple networks in which they are engaged. These coalitions, suspended in beliefs and in networks, and uncontrollable by politicians, are the stuff of autonomous bureaucratic policy innovation" (Carpenter 2001, 353). The social power of a bureaucratic agency involves the active support and participation of numerous stakeholders both inside and outside of government.

Reinforcing bureaucratic autonomy are the actions of institutional activists. Santoro and McGuire (1997, 504) define institutional activists as "social movement participants who occupy formal statuses within the government and who pursue movement goals through conventional bureaucratic channels." The 'revolving door' not only occurs between government and industry, but can also arise between government and social movement organizations. Social movement insiders leading highly successful agencies responsible for a health program can be empowered to act in other government arenas such as foreign relations and industrial policies often viewed as outside their purview.

In relation to intellectual property, state agencies that have developed strong reputations for excellence in implementing universal drug policies and that are staffed by social movement activists would lead the charge in the incorporation and use of TRIPS safeguards. In sum, the success of a health program based on universalistic criteria drives the government agenda on medicines policies, lays the groundwork for alliances with civil society and/or the private domestic drug industry, and shapes discourses concerning human rights. Countries with weak social-democratic commitments in their health systems tend not to defend the inclusion of humanitarian safeguards in domestic IP legislation or take advantage of these TRIPS flexibilities once incorporated, while countries committed to the provision of universal care and state agencies that have powerful reputations lobby for more TRIPS flexibilities and use of compulsory licenses.

The Brazilian case demonstrates close co-variation between increasing success of its AIDS treatment program with the increasing "flexibilization" of its intellectual property laws backed by aggressive price tactics threatening the use of compulsory licenses. A close study of the Brazilian experience through a state-centered lens helps explain why the country passed highly restrictive patent legislation in 1996 and then pursued its subsequent flexibilization in following years. The next section explains the passage of that law along with the growing success of its national treatment program for people with HIV/AIDS.

INCORPORATING TRIPS INTO BRAZILIAN LEGISLATION

As mentioned, the irony of the Brazilian case is that in the same year, 1996, two laws – one providing patent protections for medicines and the other mandating the state to provide free and universal AIDS treatment – were passed. Had the successful and costly treatment program already been in place, resistance against reforming intellectual property laws would have been greater and probably have led to incorporating more TRIPS flexibilities instead of piecemeal changes at later dates when the high price of patented medicines began to threaten the sustainability of its treatment program (see Appendix 6A for a list of Brazilian legislation related to TRIPS flexibilities).

In May, 1996, Brazil passed Industrial Property Law 9.279 which reinstated patent protection for all pharmaceutical processes and patents. Since 1969 when all patents on pharmaceuticals were abolished to encourage the growth of the domestic industry, firms could legally copy medicines and sell them on the market. Patents existed for other industries – just not for pharmaceuticals. Why then did Brazil pass new IP legislation that went beyond the minimum requirements of the TRIPS accord? In particular, why did the country not wait until the deadline of 2005 like China and India in order to become TRIPS compliant? US pressures, beginning in the 1980s, had a direct impact on early compliance with TRIPS. In 1988, President Reagan, using Section 301 of the Trade Act of 1974, imposed a 100 percent tariff on imports of Brazilian paper products, consumer electronics and Brazilian medicines.[2] In the view of Rubens Ricupero, Brazil's ambassador to the General Agreement on Tariffs and Trade (GATT), which preceded the WTO, the US could never prove that its pharmaceutical companies were losing profits due to the lack of patent protection on pharmaceuticals, and furthermore the unilateral trade sanctions were illegal under international trade law. "We lost out because of power politics," summed up Ricupero.[3]

Foreign pressures were important and came at a time when the Brazilian political economy was vulnerable to trade threats and was undergoing important structural changes. Brazil abandoned a program of import substitution and liberalized trade in the early 1990s. The effect on the pharmaceutical industry was devastating. As tariffs on pharmo-chemicals and fine chemicals fell from 65 to 20 percent and state petrochemical firms were privatized, several upstream plants established to produce active pharmaceutical ingredients were phased out. In the first half of the 1990s, 1,700 production lines of synthetic intermediates and inputs were

---

2   "We regret that it is necessary to take this step. Retaliation should be an action of last resort in any trade dispute; that has not been the case here. The administration has made every effort to resolve this issue over the past two years . . . We hope that it will be possible to lift these sanctions in the near future," US Trade commissioner Clayton Yeutter is quoted as saying in Silverman et al. (1992, 53).

3   The ambassador believes that the US' strategy was to pressure Brazil to its side concerning intellectual property in order to obtain concessions from other countries like India and China (Ricupero 2007).

shut down (Orsi et al. 2003). The economic basis of the nationally owned drug sector and thus its ability to withstand the early adoption of TRIPS had been undercut. In China and India, by contrast, trade liberalization proceeded at a slower pace and industrial policies to support the domestic drug industry were maintained.

US pressure on Brazil to change its patent legislation on pharmaceuticals explains part of the reason for Brazil's early adoption of TRIPS. Domestic factors and political ideologies also weigh in on the decision. Brazilian policymakers began discussing a new patent law in the early 1990s as part of the adoption of new neoliberal economic policies. Fernando Henrique Cardoso, Brazil's president at the time of passage and chief sponsor of the legislation, refused to comment on his motivations for pushing the bill (see Nunn 2007). But two factors stand out. First, Cardoso and other members of his economic team believed that embracing IPR would be a positive step for Brazil's economic liberalization, reduce Brazil's dependence for importing technology, and attract foreign investment (Nunn 2007; Palmeiro Filho and Capanema 2004). Second, policymakers believed that it would improve trade with the US. Since many members of Congress are tied to export-agriculture industry in Brazil and the US is one of the main destination markets, deputies and senators were susceptible to US trade threats. In the view of Abifina, an industry association representing the domestic pharmochemical industry and directly affected by the new patent law on pharmaceuticals, US pressure resulted in a patent law incorporating fewer safeguards outlined in the TRIPS accord.[4]

Apart from political economy considerations, there were few activist groups mobilized to resist early adoption of TRIPS. The one exception was the public health reform movement, whose members are also known as *sanitaristas*. These public health advocates raised awareness of the potential impact of patent protection on access to medicines and may have stalled the passage of earlier legislation (Pinheiro 2008). In terms of civil society, they acted alone. One important group that was unaware of the implications of IP on drug access were AIDS activists. Without the input

---

[4] "The initial bill was approved by consensus in the House of Deputies in 1993–1994 and was very good – Abifina had taken part in the negotiations with (then President) Itamar Franco and (then Minister of Foreign Relations) Cardoso. But when it went to the Senate, which at the time Cardoso had become president and had other commitments, the bill changed form. Because of pressure from the US, such as in 1995 and 1996, Lampreia, the Minister of Foreign Relations, warned that if Brazil did not pass the TRIPS-plus legislation, there would be trade sanctions on steel, orange juice, among items," said Nelson Brasil (2008), Vice President of Abifina.

of public health advocates who did not have any backing from AIDS activists or other mobilized sectors of civil society, new IP legislation had few of the flexibilities outlined by TRIPS designed to protect consumers and curtail industry abuses. The ties between these two important groups – *sanitaristas* acting as "institutional insiders" and AIDS activists outside of government – only crystallized when the country's National AIDS Program had been established and treatment scaled up.

ESTABLISHING THE UNIVERSAL AIDS TREATMENT PROGRAM

Brazil's model AIDS policies grew out of the country's democratic transition in the 1980s. A coalition of *sanitaristas* and progressive forces established health as a human right guaranteed by the state in Brazil's new Constitution of 1988. Two years later, Congress passed the Health Act of 1990 which established the operating principles of the Unified Health System (*Sistema Único de Saúde-SUS*). While SUS provides access to 90 percent of the population and 29 percent rely exclusively on the public health system, some 40 million Brazilians feel obliged to purchase additional health care through a system of private insurance and hospitals. Extending SUS coverage and improving service delivery continues to strain budgets. Jadib Jantene, Minister of Health during the 1990s, said that SUS should have a budget of R$120 billion (approximately US$60 billion) a year, but current amounts barely reach R$50 billion (US$25 billion) (Martins 2008). In the view of Weyland (1995), the *sanitaristas* failed to achieve their objectives of a robust universal health care system due to the intractable problems of political clientelism and the failure of establishing alliances with mobilized civil society.

In spite of the problems associated with Brazil's underfinanced public health system, the National AIDS Program stands out as an exception. It has overcome entrenched political interests, established strong civil society partnerships, and achieved worldwide fame and recognition for curbing incidence, rolling out treatment, and reducing morbidity and mortality rates. Since Brazil first established its National AIDS Program in 1985, modelled after successful efforts at the sub-national level in São Paulo state, it has retained a high degree of autonomy and has been staffed with dedicated social movement insiders. The organization represents a high degree of professionalism and commitment in comparison to other state institutions, many of which suffer from the country's chronic political clientelism.

The success of the Brazilian model has attracted significant scholarly attention. A full review of that literature is beyond the scope of this study, but it is necessary to highlight a few factors. First, social movements and societal pressures were important for the establishment of Brazil's AIDS program (Nunn 2007; Teixeira et al. 2003; Passarelli and Júnior 2003). In the words of former president Fernando Henrique Cardoso, the "state and the social movement practically fused" (quoted in Biehl 2004, 114). The social origins of AIDS groups capable of pressuring the state resulted from contextual factors of Brazil's transition to democracy as well as the middle class position of AIDS activists capable of filing successful lawsuits for treatment (Parker 1997; Bastos 1999). Second, there is a tradition of state leadership in responding to communicable diseases (Gomez 2006) that transcends racial boundaries (Gauri and Lieberman 2006). My argument follows the tradition of other scholars who have employed a state-centrist approach when explaining Brazilian AIDS policies (Nunn 2007; Gomez 2006), but extend the analysis to the topic of intellectual property.

Why did this coalition of institutional insiders and AIDS activists not resist IP reform in 1996? At that time, the directors of the National AIDS Program and activists focused their efforts on obtaining universal access to treatment. Even after the passage of Sarney's Law 9.113 in 1996 mandating the state to provide AIDS medicines, the main challenge was to transform the formal law into substantive programs on the ground. Activists continued public protests; patients kept filing lawsuits to guarantee access; and the directors of the National AIDS Program stepped up criticism of ministers who failed to transfer sufficient resources to fund treatment. These actions were particularly evident in 1998–99 when the country suffered an economic crisis and the economic team imposed austerity measures. Despite the fiscal restraints, pro-treatment efforts prevailed, and efforts to scale up the program continued unabated. Only after successful treatment roll-out did intellectual property appear as a threat to the sustainability of universal treatment, and mobilization increased towards the inclusion of more humanitarian safeguards in domestic patent legislation and pressure build to make use of compulsory licenses to lower the price of patented ARVs.

Brazil's Department of DST/AIDS and Hepatitis[5] reported that some 200,000 patients were in treatment in 2010, out of a total seropositive population estimated at 630,000. According to UNAIDS (2008), access to anti-retroviral (ARVs) medicines in Brazil reaches 80 percent of those who require treatment – one of the highest rates of coverage in the developing world and comparable to wealthy country standards. Brazilian authorities

---

[5] In 2009 the National DST/AIDS Program and National Hepatitis Program were merged into a single department under the Secretary of Health Surveillance.

have also made an effort to incorporate the latest AIDS medicines into their treatment regimens. Specialists meet annually to evaluate best treatment practices and consider new drugs for incorporating into the therapeutic consensus. When legislation was passed in 1996 mandating that AIDS patients should receive free and universal access to treatment, the Ministry of Health mobilized federal drug maker Farmanguinhos, part of the Oswaldo Cruz Foundation (FioCruz) and other labs operated by state governments to supply the public health system (Flynn 2008; Cassier and Correa 2003). At the start of free and universal care in the 1990s, few of the medicines were protected by patents. Now 13 of the 20 medicines employed are patent-protected thus increasing the cost of the program.[6] Since anti-retroviral therapy does not cure the disease but transforms it into a chronic condition, patients must be provided with a continuous supply of medicines. As viral resistance develops and/or adverse reactions occur, users migrate to more expensive second- and third-line treatments protected by patent.

The TRIPS accord, stipulating exclusive marketing rights to pharmaceutical firms, has had a direct impact on Brazil's social program. If the Brazilian government had waited until the 2005 deadline to change national legislation, the cost of Brazil's AIDS program would be less and local industry would have had more time to develop local formulas of patented medicines, or procure supplies from Asian countries that had not yet incorporated patent protections for pharmaceuticals. The politics surrounding AIDS treatments and patents is thus illustrative of the factors contributing to TRIPS compliance and the role played by 'institutional insiders' in promoting increased use of humanitarian safeguards, especially the use of compulsory licenses, in order to drive down prices.

FIVE INSTANCES WHEN A COMPULSORY LICENSE WAS THREATENED DURING PRICE NEGOTIATIONS

Brazil's use of compulsory licenses stems from the fact that health officials must balance the ministry's available resources with necessary inputs

---

6   As of 2010, ARVs produced in public and national labs included didanosine, estavudine, indinavir, lamivudine, nevirapine, ritonavir, saquinavir, zidovudine, efavirenz and zidovudine+lamivudine. Imported and patent-protected ARVs include abacavir, amprenavir, atazanavir, darunavir, etravirine, enfuvirtide, fosaprenavir, lopinavir/ritonavir (Kaletra), and raltegravir. The production of tenofovir, whose patent request by Gilead was denied in 2008, is being scaled up locally.

Table 6.1   *Use of compulsory license and results of ARV negotiations,*
              2001–2007

Year	Medicine (brand name)	Patent holder/licensee	Result
2001	Efavirenz (Sustiva)	Merck	59% discount
	Nelfinavir (Viracept)	Hoffman-LaRoche	40% discount
2003	Efavirenz (Sustiva)	Merck	25% discount
	Nelfinavir (Viracept)	Hoffman-LaRoche	10% discount
	Lopinavir/ritonavir (Kaletra)	Abbott	13% discount
2005	Lopinavir/ritonavir (Kaletra)	Abbott	46% discount
2006	Tenofovir (Viread)	Gilead	51% discount
2007	Efavirenz (Stocrin)	Merck	Compulsory license 75% price reduction

for its health system.[7] Interviewees from Brazil's Ministry of Health and National AIDS Program consistently repeat that the overall objective is to ensure the sustainability of universal access without interruption (Costa 2008; Alvares 2008; Chequer 2008). Sustainability also includes the program's medium- and long-term financial viability. To this end, negotiators from the Ministry of Health have sought commodity prices. That is, policymakers want a price offering reduced premiums (i.e. profits) to the seller based upon Farmanguinhos' cost-of-production parameters or lowest available prices on the international market. The institutionalized commitment to providing universal ARV therapy has driven the Ministry of Health to propose legislative changes in IP law and use compulsory licenses in price negotiations.

Since the time when Jose Serra was Brazil's Minister of Health (1999–2002), negotiators have on several occasions threatened to issue compulsory licenses during price talks with foreign patent holders of AIDS medicines. Table 6.1 provides a list of the different episodes, the drugs and patent holders involved, and the results of the negotiation. A negotiated settlement resulting in a price discount occurred in every instance

---

[7]   Many other articles have highlighted how limited fiscal resources threaten the sustainability of important health programs such as free and universal access to AIDS treatment (Biehl 2004; Cassier and Correa 2007; Cassier and Correa 2003; Grangeiro et al. 2006; Greco and Simão 2007; Teixeira et al. 2003; Wogart and Calcagnotto 2006; Cohen and Lybecker 2005; Bermudez and Oliveira 2004; Serra 2004; Passos 2008; Coriat 2008; Orsi et al. 2003).

except one in 2007 when Brazil followed through with its threats against Merck. Analyzing the use of this legal instrument will allow us to explore the social forces involved in the use of TRIPS flexibilities. These factors include civil society support; presence of a weak, domestic-owned pharmaceutical industry; balance of needs between corporate investors and host countries; pressures from foreign governments; and issue area discourses, or how certain issues are framed.

Role of Domestic Pharmaceutical Sector

Brazil had the ninth largest pharmaceutical market in the world in 2007 with sales totaling US$15.7 billion (IMS Health 2008). Brazil's pharmaceutical sector consists of four distinct players: (1) foreign-based pharmaceutical companies which account for about 70 percent of the market; (2) 18 public labs, responsible for less than five percent of production (mainly sent to the public health sector); (3) local, privately owned firms which produce generic formulations; and (4) a local pharmochemical sector that produces the raw materials and active pharmaceutical ingredients for drug production. Generic medicines comprise almost 20 percent of the entire market, up from zero when the legislation regulating generics was passed in 1999. Of the generic medicines market, Brazilian companies account for 80 percent of sales (Pro-Genericos 2009). Few domestic drug makers are vertically integrated, that is, produce both APIs and finished dosage forms. The one notable exception is São Paulo-based Cristália, which has an ARV product line.

Brazil's market remains heavily dependent on imports. In 2006, medicine imports of US$1.7 billion surpassed exports of US$435 million; and imports of pharmaceutical raw materials such as active pharmaceutical ingredients amounted to US$1.3 billion compared to US$272 million in exports (Gadelha 2007). Currently, there are only 23 Brazilian pharmochemical producers in Brazil which supply about 20 percent of the domestic market (Chamas 2005). As a result of persistent external dependency, Brazilian officials included the pharmaceutical sector in new industrial policies implemented during the government of President Luis Inacio Lula da Silva (2003–2010).

Shadlen (2009) argues that the presence of an indigenous pharmaceutical sector that is weak relative to large transnational drug firms, but strong enough to lobby lawmakers, plays a significant role in pressing for TRIPS flexibilities. A domestic generic drug industry seeks weak IP legislation as opposed to strong laws that would benefit foreign-based companies. In the case of Brazil's use of CLs, the indigenous private drug industry has played an important supportive role. But the Ministry of Health has only purchased a small fraction of the ARVs used in its treatment program from the domestic private sector (Flynn 2008). Although Brazilian private company Microbiologica was the first to reverse-engineer AZT (zidovudine) in the early 1990s, the government's decision to produce ARVs in public labs (in effect, state nationalization of production) has kept the participation of private domestic drug makers to a minimum.

By the end of 2002, there were 19 national drug makers registered with ANVISA to sell ARVs. Only Laob, Eurofarma, Neo-Quimica and Cristália had closed large contracts during the early years of the program (Orsi et al. 2003). Most private domestic drug makers see few economic benefits to investing in ARVs, if the government crowds out their participation. Even public labs run by state governments are hesitant to dedicate resources to produce medicines for the national program if production is concentrated in Farmanguinhos and there are no firm purchase guarantees. The same logic affects upstream industries. Brazil's pharmochemical sector, including Microbiologica, has not benefitted from the billions spent on ARV procurement. Instead of purchasing raw materials from domestic producers, the drive to reduce costs, and strict tender laws, have forced public labs to source inputs from lowest-priced Asian producers (Marques and Hasenclever 2006).

Brazilian private sector producers said that government officials consulted them every time a compulsory license was threatened during price talks with foreign drug makers, except on the last occasion in 2007 when one was actually issued (Maçiara 2007; Neto 2008). Pedro Chequer, the former director of the AIDS program, is credited for reaching out to local industry to produce Kaletra during the tense 2005 confrontation with US-based Abbott. When a CL was finally issued in 2007, however, the Ministry of Health imported the drug from WHO pre-qualified Indian suppliers until its public labs ramped up production. The latest policy innovation following the CL is that Farmanguinhos has subcontracted production of the API of efavirenz to three domestic suppliers (Nortec, Globe, and Cristália) instead of obtaining inputs from foreign firms.

Having domestic pharmaceutical capabilities strengthens the bargaining hand of Brazilian negotiators. But apart from Farmanguinhos' managers, they have not played a proactive role in pressing for TRIPS flexibilities. The most dynamic indigenous drug sector is Brazil's generics industry, but they have been sidelined as a result of government monopolization of ARV production. Domestic firms did not object to changes to IP legislation to use of compulsory licenses because their interests were not threatened. Rather, they have played an important supportive role as Shadlen's (2009) account suggests. This is especially true for the domestic pharmochemical sector which has sought out increased government support over the past decade.[8]

Civil Society Pressure

Civil society support has been important in Brazil's battles with companies over the use of compulsory licenses. The Consumer Project on Technology (2009), a US-based consumer rights group,[9] lists on its website numerous examples of declarations from activists around the world in support of Brazil's AIDS program and right to use compulsory licenses. Domestic groups[10] are also networked in with other international health activists in both the global South and North. Globalization in this sense has empowered states in their relations with transnational corporations. My review suggests that support from health activists, though perhaps necessary, is not sufficient to explain the use of humanitarian safeguards.

The tradition of proactivity by the Brazilian National AIDS Program in establishing alliances with civil society through formal institutional and informal channels to fight the disease (Rich 2009) has been extended to the case of patents. During the 2001 WTO dispute with the US concerning the use of a compulsory license when a product is not "worked" locally, Brazilian officials enlisted the support of civil society for the country's defense. According to Paulo Teixeira (2008), the director of Brazil's National AIDS Program at the time, health officials took the initiative to reach out to local and foreign activists. The strategy worked, and the

---

[8] Shadlen highlights the importance of Brazil's pharmaceutical sector for promulgating more TRIPS flexibilities. Indeed, Brazil's pharmochemical industry association Abifina helped pen the 2003 legislation related to the use of compulsory licenses (Shadlen 2009; Maçiara 2007). While Abifina representatives have defended the government's use of humanitarian safeguards and criticized early adoption of TRIPS, few other pharmaceutical industry associations have because, in part, the market is dominated by foreign companies. In either case, my interviews with public health officials said they took the initiative to review laws regarding parallel importing, compulsory licenses, and other drug-related IP issues in 2003 after the election of Luiz Inacio Lula da Silva (Grangeiro 2008).

[9] The NGO is also known as Knowledge Ecology International – KEI.

[10] The most prominent is the Working Group on Intellectual Property from the Brazilian Network of Peoples Integration (Grupo de Trabalho em Propriedade Intelectual da Rede Brasileira pela Integração dos Povos – GTPI/ Rebrip). The group, established in 2001, is comprised of local NGO groups ABIA, CONECTAS, GAPA – SP, GAPA – RS, Gestos, GIV – Grupo de Incentivo a Vida, INESC, INTERVOZES, and Pela Vida, as well as international groups MSF and OXFAM.

US removed the WTO panel.[11] Indeed, price negotiations with Merck and Roche occurring at the same time as the panel dispute resulted in a negotiated settlement with steep discounts.

Pressure from the activist community to "break patents"[12] was greatest in 2005 during negotiations with Abbott over the price of Kaletra. In August of 2005 in the midst of price talks, Brazil's National Health Council (Conselho Nacional de Saúde) – the highest instance of societal participation in the public health system – unanimously voted in favor of compulsory licenses for patented ARVs that burdened Brazil's health system. Brazil's Minister of Health at the time, Saraiva Felipe, dismissed the motion and completed price negotiations without decreeing the CL. In the aftermath, several Brazilian organizations filed a lawsuit against the government for not rescinding Abbott's exclusive marketing rights.[13] But the efforts were in vain, and Abbott did not lose its monopoly on Kaletra, although it did provide a price discount.

When Brazil's current Minister of Health finally decreed a CL for Merck's efavirenz in May 2007, many activists were surprised (as well as many other observers and Merck itself), especially since many previous threats had never materialized. Nevertheless, domestic and international health rights groups voiced their support and educated the public about the measure (Chaves 2008). In terms of the use of compulsory licenses, civil society pressures have been important but not determinative in their effective implementation. One could rightly argue, though, that Brazil's National AIDS Program represents the institutional manifestation of a powerful social movement.

Issue Area Discourses

The way in which issues concerning intellectual property rights and the legitimate employment of compulsory licenses are framed have the potential to augment state power vis-à-vis corporations (Blanchard 2004; Greenhill and Busby 2008). For Brazilian health officials, this discourse is rooted in notions of collective rights and institutionalized in a public health system. In every instance in which Brazil has threatened to use a

---

[11] Brazilian AIDS activists interviewed for this research said they began to become aware about and mobilize against TRIPS during the WTO dispute.

[12] The "breaking of a patent" is a misnomer when a compulsory license is decreed since the patent remains in place. Only market exclusivity is revoked.

[13] Pedro Chequer (2008), the director of Brazil's National AIDS Program at the time, said he provided NGOs all the information necessary to proceed with a lawsuit.

compulsory license, negotiators based their arguments on international human rights treaties and domestic laws upholding these social rights. Additional frames have been used, but these have shifted over time. In the first episode, Brazil declared that its model AIDS program represented a case of urgency and public emergency. But on later occasions, the Ministry of Health employed the public interest clause (or public non-commercial use) in intellectual property legislation instead of emergency use. Since Brazil's AIDS program is considered one of the most successful in the developing world, it is difficult to classify AIDS as an out-of-control epidemic.[14]

The frames employed by patent holders have been less consistent, less coherent across the different groups of IP defenders, and evolved more over time. Indeed, industry has grudgingly adapted to the new reality after the Doha Declaration on TRIPS and Public Health of 2001. Although some industry advocates such as USA for Innovation call Brazil's and Thailand's actions 'theft' (USA for Innovation 2007) and strong IP defenders advocate a forceful US response (Kogan 2006), spokespeople for drug companies and industry associations concede that they are not against compulsory licenses per se. Rather, they argue that the measure should only be used in the last instance, specifically for national emergencies such as after the 9/11 terrorist attacks. A Pharmaceutical Research and Manufacturers of America (PhRMA) representative said that the Brazilian government acted within the TRIPS agreement but "against the spirit of the law" when issuing its first compulsory licenses for efavirenz in May 2007 (Singer 2007). Brazilian drug industry spokespeople also uphold this normative view that CLs should only be used in times of public emergency and not as a form of price regulation (Mortella 2008). For Brazilian health officials, however, the use of humanitarian safeguards remains important as a tool for market regulation since other governmental bodies responsible for enforcing antitrust legislation remain weak and fragmented (Rech 2008).

In the more recent price negotiations and compulsory license threats, the issues of differential pricing schemes and the necessity of funding research have become more salient. Industry argues that Brazil's effective treatment program would not be possible without innovations carried out in the private sector that result from strong IP protection. In order to ensure a steady stream of new medicines into the future, even developing countries should pay for part of the R&D expenses. Additionally, when Brazil

---

[14]   UNAIDS (2008) estimates Brazil's prevalence rate (adults aged 15 to 49) at 0.7 percent, compared to Thailand (1.5 percent) or South Africa (21.5 percent).

requested during 2007 talks that Merck reduce unit prices from US$1.65 to the price offered to Thailand of US$0.65, the company responded that it would undo its tiered pricing scheme. Merck's formula for pricing the medicine in developing countries is based on a country's score on the Human Development Index and HIV prevalence rates. In Thailand, prevalence is three times greater than Brazil. Brazilian negotiators countered that since they purchase larger quantities of efavirenz they should receive a deeper discount. Merck initially provided a discount of 5 percent, which increased to 30 percent in its last proposal, effectively reducing the unit price to US$1.10. But the amount was not compatible with commodity prices sought by Brazilian negotiators (Passarelli 2007; Passos 2008).

The last means by which the use of compulsory licenses has been framed is the impact on a country's industrial development. Negotiations also included offers to transfer technology to produce efavirenz. In the 2007 Merck negotiations, Brazilian officials rejected company proposals because the transfer was only to be concluded a year before the patent expires in 2012 and with the condition that the active pharmaceutical ingredient be provided by the company. For Brazilian officials, offers of technology transfer in the area of ARVs have never been acceptable.[15] An additional factor weighing in on Brazil's decision to use a compulsory license was Merck's efforts in the courts to block Farmanguinhos' access to the API of efavirenz to develop the drug.

Since there were no local producers registered to supply efavirenz after a compulsory license was issued, Brazil decided to import it from three WHO pre-qualified Indian companies until Farmanguinhos scaled up production. The measure left the Health Ministry open to charges by Merck's president, Tadeu Alves, that "Brazil is creating jobs in India" (Borsato 2007). Asked about the potential impact of the compulsory license on pharmaceutical research in Brazil, José Temporão responded that "when they say that multinational industry is going to stop doing research in Brazil, there the history is different: it never has done research in Brazil" (Lago 2007). The Minister of Health was referring to the high-end R&D of discovering new chemical entities. In the area of clinical testing, Brazil has a long history of volunteering its bodies for evaluating the effects of ARVs and other medicines.[16]

---

[15] There are cases in which foreign drug firms have joint ventures with Brazil's public labs. FioCruz has joint projects with GlaxoSmithKline and the Butanta Institute, another government research institute with Sanofi Pasteur.

[16] Transnational drug companies carry out clinical testing in Brazil, in part, to market their product. Brazil is the third largest market in ARVs after the United States and South Africa.

Tracing the discourses related to CLs reveals the importance of human rights trumping the intellectual property rights of drug companies during battles over prices. However, in later confrontations, concerns over the sustainability of the treatment program were subsumed under the state's interest in promoting economic and technological development.

Balance of Needs

Brazil's need for investment versus a company's need for markets affects the power plays involved in using humanitarian safeguards (Blanchard 2004). As the Brazilian economy has strengthened during the administration of Lula, it has become less vulnerable to drug company threats. Consequently, AIDS officials have become more successful in lobbying for support from other government ministries.

Brazil changed its IP legislation nine years before the expiration of the TRIPS transition period because of its susceptibility to US trade pressure. This was due to the fragile economy undergoing macroeconomic stabilization and embracing of neoliberal policy initiatives. During the first confrontation over prices and patents in 2001, Brazil faced down a WTO panel brought against it by rallying world support, yet in the end achieved a negotiated settlement. During the 2003 and 2005 negotiations in President Lula's first term, the primary concern was placating foreign investors who were worried about the macroeconomic policies of the left-of-center president. When negotiations with Abbott in 2005 came to a head, for example, ministries related to trade and finance voiced concerns about the possible ramifications of trade sanctions if Brazil were to issue a compulsory license for Kaletra.[17] Members of the US Congress urged the USTR to withdraw Brazil's trade privileges provided under the General System of Preferences.[18] Estimates of Brazilian exports affected by the possible trade retaliation range from US$48 million (Boletín Farmacos 2005) to US$3.6 billion (Kogan 2006).

In the lead-up to the compulsory license of efavirenz which happened in May 2007, the situation had changed. All ministries agreed that Merck was being intransigent during negotiations and thus provided key support in the Ministry of Health's decision (Passarelli 2007). After the decree, Tadeu Alves, the president of Merck's Latin American division, said

---

[17]   In fact, Minister Fernando Furlan from the Ministry of Development, Industry and Trade broke ministerial protocol by convening meetings concerning the issue that was the prerogative of the Ministry of Health (Alvares 2008).

[18]   General System of Preferences provides additional market access beyond what is stipulated in the World Trade Organization.

that "the perception of Brazil will not be the same" and declared that the company was reviewing its investment plan in the country (Borsato 2007). The following year, however, Merck announced plans to invest in clinical testing and was willing to work with the Ministry of Health on common projects, including the local production of efavirenz (Vieira 2008). The company also had another ARV, raltegravir (brand name Isentress), for which it lobbied and obtained inclusion in Brazil's AIDS program in 2008. Another factor weighing in Brazil's favor was its consumer reputation. Several executives from foreign drug companies mentioned in interviews: "Brazil is a good client that pays in full and on time."[19]

A critical issue concerning the balance of needs is whether a country has access to alternative drug suppliers where a compulsory license is issued. While Brazil's economy has strengthened, its local ARV production has not. This fact has tilted the balance of need in favor of patent holders. In the first round of negotiations in 2001 with Roche, Farmanguinhos provided information on production costs and produced samples of the drug. But due to organizational changes and obstacles in obtaining patented raw materials to produce medicines, its capability to rapidly reverse-engineer and scale up production had declined. Health officials who concluded the Abbott negotiations without issuing a compulsory license for Kaletra said during interviews that one factor that influenced their decision was the lack of guarantees from FioCruz's laboratory to scale up production fast enough to supply the critical ARV.[20] Having pre-qualified Indian suppliers by the World Health Organization, as in the case of efavirenz, improved the government's bargaining position.

The changing balance of needs varies at the macroeconomic level from a position of weakness to increasing strength. But at the microeconomic level, the capabilities of public labs have declined as a result of IP barriers to patented APIs and organizational changes. This factor remains contradictory in terms of its effects on Brazil's promulgation of TRIPS flexibilities. Policymakers, nonetheless, as a result of the requirements of its AIDS program, have pushed for industrial policies to develop local pharmaceutical-making capacity and overcome upstream weaknesses in local pharmochemical production.

---

[19]   Personal interviews with corporate government relation managers (Sanches 2008; Salles 2008).

[20]   Personal interviews with Ministers of Health (Felipe 2008; Alvares 2008). The question about Brazil's capacity to produce ARVs resulted in a flurry of studies and evaluations including UNDP (2006), Clinton Foundation (2006), and NGO-sponsored reviews (Fortunak and Antunes 2006).

Support of Home Governments

Another factor having an impact on the use of compulsory licenses is the role of the US government. In the first negotiations in 2001, price talks occurred in the midst of a WTO panel against Brazilian IP legislation related to the 'local working' provision. Although the US complaint had been brewing since Brazil's new Industrial Property Law was passed in 1996 and would have reached the WTO regardless of the price negotiations, that the two disputes coincided underscored US influence. In the 2005 price talks, cables between US diplomats in Brazil and the State Department reveal the US' direct involvement of the negotiations between the Ministry of Health and Abbott over the price of Kaletra.[21] One top Brazilian official involved in the price negotiations said that a US diplomat threatened to terminate all Brazilian scientific projects and studies at US universities if Brazil were to use a compulsory license (Alvares 2008).

A review of US diplomatic cables and interviews with a US diplomat and Brazilian participants suggests that the US Embassy was far less involved in the efavirenz negotiations in 2007 as compared to previous confrontations. Only after efavirenz was decreed in the public interest did US officials voice their concerns and warn Brazilian health authorities of the 'political storm' if a CL was issued. In fact, the USTR (2007) had removed Brazil from its Priority Watch list owing to the country's efforts to protect intellectual property, although it continued to highlight concern over the use of compulsory licenses. Furthermore, the US has not applied any trade sanctions nor carried out any out-of-cycle reviews of Brazil's IP protection, despite pressure from PhRMA.

This leads to two possible conclusions: either Abbott has more influence than Merck in obtaining the support of the US government in IP disputes, or the US has become more permissive towards the use of CL in the case of medicines used to treat AIDS. Concerning the latter possibility, the US again may be susceptible to "rhetorical entrapment" (Greenhill and Busby 2008). How could the US, while providing billions of dollars to fight HIV/AIDS through the Presidential Emergency Plan for AIDS Relief (PEPFAR), not allow a country that has become a model in fighting AIDS to economize resources? Here again, the success of Brazil's social policy of universal treatment may have undercut US pressure related to the use of a compulsory license. The US continues to back industry-favorable

---

[21] The cables made available through a Freedom of Information request are available at http://www.keionline.org/index.php?option=com_content& task =view&id=134.

positions in regional and bilateral trade agreements and global IP-related frameworks, but in individual cases concerning AIDS medicines, there may be a thawing.

CONCLUSION

The Brazilian case suggests that the TRIPS accord has had a significant impact on the political decision-making process in Brazil. The international IP framework has set up major obstacles and increased the political and economic costs of carrying out universal-based social policies. Patent monopolies have undoubtedly increased the bargaining power of TNCs. On balance, foreign drug firms have profited handsomely from Brazil's universal AIDS program. Between 1996 and 2007, the Brazilian government spent a total of US$2.71 billion on ARVs. Of this amount, foreign firms received US$1.85 billion[22] or 68 percent of the total.

Nonetheless, a strong health agency responsible for the substantiation of social rights, such as in the case of domestically driven AIDS policies, played an important role for incorporating more TRIPS safeguards in domestic legislation and resorting to their use. Policymakers responsible for maintaining the universal social programs sector must seek innovative ways between balancing limited budgets and increasing social demands. The right to health shapes a human rights discourse that is shared by both committed public servants and civil society activists. The interests of domestic drug companies and threats by foreign economic forces may result in local industry vetoing initiatives by public health officials and/ or resistance by other government ministries. But without the bulwark of a strong federal agency to fight AIDS, my review of the Brazilian case suggests, the struggle for universal access to essential medicines, incorporation of more TRIPS flexibilities in local legislation, and their subsequent use would have been minimal.

After the compulsory license issued for efavirenz in 2007, Brazil was able to achieve favorable prices for tenofovir and Kaletra. In recent price negotiations, market exclusivity of patent holders of ARVs has not been threatened by Brazilian negotiators. Additional factors have kept the use of compulsory licenses from being employed. After years of delayed analysis, Brazil's intellectual property office finally made a ruling denying Gilead's patent request for high-priced tenofovir, and public labs are gearing up to produce the medicine locally. Brazil's Ministry of Health has

---

[22] In 2005 US dollars, based on data from Brazil's National AIDS Program.

also adopted new price control regulations. When a new patented medicine demonstrates therapeutic advantages over existing treatment, the Ministry of Health sets a price ceiling based on the lowest price of the drug in several countries[23] including the country of origin (PAHO 2009). These efforts allowed Brazil to reduce treatment expenditures by 12 percent or some US$60 million in a recent round of negotiations (Brazil 2010).

The Brazilian case suggests that when a social program achieves success in rolling out medicines, a strong constituency develops to ensure its continued success. In looking towards the future, flashpoints along the IP landscape are likely to occur where public commitments and national organizations that provide ARVs remain strong, but the global economic crisis has reduced donor budgets. As budgets decline, stakeholders in universalizing treatment will demand that corporations reduce prices and will insist on using more TRIPS flexibilities so as to allow for more generic competition. Brazil will surely play an important part in this on-going struggle.

REFERENCES

Alvares, Agenor. 2008. Personal interview, Minister of Health, Mar. 2006–Jan. 2007. July 12.

Bastos, Cristiana. 1999. *Global Responses to AIDS*. Bloomington and Indianapolis: Indiana University Press.

Bermudez, Jorge, and Maria Auxiliardora Oliveira. 2004. *Intellectual Property in the Context of the WTO Trips Agreement: Challenges to Public Health*. Rio de Janeiro: ENSP.

Biehl, João. 2004. The Activist State: Global Pharmaceuticals, AIDS, And Citizenship in Brazil. *Social Text* 22, no. 3.

Blanchard, Jean-Marc. 2004. Corporate Hegemony in Remission: The Pharmaceutical Industry and the HIV/AIDS Crisis. Annual meeting of the International Studies Association, Montreal.

Boletín Farmacos. 2005. Brasil, Abbott Y Sida: Continúan las Negociaciones. El Consejo Nacional de Salud Recomienda Quebrar Patentes. *Boletín Farmacos*, September.

Borsato, Cintia. 2007. O Brasil criou empregos na Índia. *Veja*.

Brasil, Nelson. 2008. Personal interview, Vice President, Brazilian Fine Chemicals Industry Association (Abifina). June 30.

Brazil, Departamento de DST, Aids e Hepatites Virais. 2010. Contratos para compra de antirretrovirais ficam R$118 milhões mais baratos. January 25. http://www.aids.gov.br/noticia/contratos-para-compra-de-antirretrovirais-ficam-r-118-milhoes -mais-baratos.

---

[23] Specifically, Australia, Canada, Spain, United States, France, Greece, Italy, New Zealand, and Portugal.

Carpenter, Daniel P. 2001. *The Forging of Bureaucratic Autonomy*. Princeton University Press.
Cassier, Maurice, and Marilena Correa. 2003. Patents, Innovation, and Public Health: Brazilian Public-Sector Laboratories' Experience in Copying AIDS Drugs. In *Economics of AIDS and Access to HIV/AIDS Care in Developing Countries: Issues and Challenges*, 89–103. Paris: Agence Nationale de Recherches sur le SIDA. Economics of AIDS and Access to HIV/AIDS Care in Developing.
Cassier, Maurice, and Marilena Correa. 2007. Intellectual Property and Public Health: Copying of HIV/Aids drugs by Brazilian public and private laboratories. *Electronic Journal of Communication, Information and Innovation in Health* 1, no. 1: 83–90.
Chamas, Claudia Ines. 2005. Developing Innovative Capacity in Brazil to Meet Health Needs. In *Commission on Intellectual Property Rights, Innovation and Public Health*. Geneva: World Health Organization.
Chaves, Gabriela. 2008. Personal interview, Coordinator, Brazilian Interdisciplinary Aids Association (ABIA). Working Group on Intellectual Property (GTPI). March 27.
Chequer, Pedro. 2008. Personal Interview, Director of National AIDS Program, 1996–2000 and 2004–2006. July 12.
Clinton Foundation. 2006. Analisis da Situacao da Producao Local de ARVs: Precos, Custos, Planejamento de Producao e Competitividade Internacional. Powerpoint presented at the Seminário Nacional: Produção de Anti-retrovirais na Indústria Brasileira, August 8, Brasilia. http://www.aids.gov.br/data/documents/stored Documents/percent7BB8EF5DAF-23AE-4891-AD36-1903553A3174percent 7D/percent7BD51846A2-744D-4D83-B324-A3E2E553EC1Apercent7D/RNP 2.pdf.
Cohen, Jillian Clare, and Kristian M. Lybecker. 2005. AIDS Policy and Pharmaceutical Patents: Brazil's Strategy to Safeguard Public Health. *The World Economy* 28, no. 2: 211–230.
Consumer Project on Technology. 2009. Compulsory Licenses in Brazil. http://www.cptech.org/ip/health/c/brazil/.
Coriat, Benjamin. 2008. *The Political Economy of HIV/AIDS in Developing Countries: TRIPS, Public Health Systems and Free Access*. Cheltenham, UK and Northampton, MA, USA: Edward Elgar Publishing.
Costa, Humberto. 2008. Personal interview, Minister of Health, 2003–2005. July 22.
Felipe, Hayne. 2008. Personal interview, Farmanguinhos employee, former Director of Production at IVB, and Coordinator of Basic Pharmacy Program. Digital recording. September 22.
Flynn, Matthew. 2008. Public Production of Anti-Retroviral Medicines in Brazil, 1990–2007. *Development and Change* 39, no. 4: 513–536.
Fortunak, Joseph M., and Otavio Antunes. 2006. *The ARV Production in Brazil – An Evaluation*. Rio de Janeiro: MSF/ABIA. http://www.abiaids.org.br/_img/media/ARV.pdf.
Gadelha, Carlos. 2007. A indústria Farmacêutica no Contexto do Complexo Industrial da Saúde: Perspectivas Políticas. In *ENIFarMed*. São Paulo.
Gauri, Varun, and Evan S. Lieberman. 2006. Boundary Institutions and HIV/AIDS Policy in Brazil and South Africa. *Studies in International Comparative Development* 41, no. 4: 47–73.
Gomez, Eduardo. 2006. *The Politics of Government Response to HIV/AIDS in*

Russia and Brazil: Historical Institutionalism, Culture and State Capacity. Working Paper #4, Harvard Initiative for Global Health.

Grangeiro, Alexandre. 2008. Personal interview, Director of National AIDS Program, 2002–2003. May 7.

Grangeiro, Alexandre, Luciana Teixeira, Francisco I. Bastos, and Paulo Teixeira. 2006. Sustainability of Brazilian Policy for Access to Antiretroviral Drugs. *Revista Saúde Púbica* 40: (Supl).

Greco, Dirceu B., and Mariangela Simão. 2007. Brazilian Policy of Universal Access to AIDS Treatment: Sustainability Challenges and Perspectives. *AIDS* 21 (suppl 4): S37–S45.

Greenhill, Kelly, and Josh Busby. 2008. Have You No Shame? Hypocrisy, Punishment, and Weak Actor Influence in International Politics. Unpublished manuscript. http://www.utexas.edu/lbj/faculty/busby/wp-content/uploads/isqjune2008id.pdf.

IMS Health. 2008. IMS Health Reports Global Prescription Sales Grew 6.4 Percent in 2007, to $712 Billion. April 16. http://www.imshealth.com/portal/site/imshealth/menuitem.fc2127a7c34504dc88f611019418c22a/?vgnextoid=38bd482 2d7699110VgnVCM10000071812ca2RCRD&cpsextcurrchannel=1.

Kogan, Lawrence A. 2006. Brazil's IP Opportunism Threatens US Private Property Rights. *Inter-American Law Review* 38, no. 1: 1–139. http://www.itssd.org/Publications/IAL105-II(frompublisher) percent5B2 percent5D.pdf.

Lago, Rudolfo. 2007. Entrevistas: José Gomes Temporão. *Isto É.*

Maçiara, Lelio. 2007. Personal interview, former partner, Microbiologica, November 28.

Marques, Felipe, and Lia Hasenclever. 2006. Política de Compra Governamentais: O caso das compras de anti-retrovirais e seus efeitos nocivos à indústria nacional. Rio de Janeiro: UFRJ – Instituto de Economia.

Martins, Rodrigo. 2008. Política com P maiúsculo. *Carta Capital*, March 4.

Mortella, Ciro. 2008. Personal interview, Executive Director, Brazilian Federation of Pharmaceutical Manufacturers (Febrafarma). September 3.

Neto, Marchado. 2008. Personal interview, José Machado de Campos Neto, former Director, Labogen, July 7.

Nunn, Amy. 2007. The Politics of Life and Death: A Historical Institutional Analysis of Antiretroviral Drug Policy in Brazil. Dissertation, Harvard University, Department of Population and International Health.

Orsi, Fabienne, Lia Hasenclever, Beatriz Fialho, Paulo Tigre, and Benjamin Coriat. 2003. Intellectual Property Rights, Anti-AIDS Policy and Generic Drugs. In *Economics of AIDS and Access to HIV/AIDS Care in Developing Countries: Issues and Challenges*, 109–135. Paris: Agence Nationale pour Recherche sur le Sida.

PAHO. 2009. *O accesso aos medicamentos de alto custo nas Américas: contexto, desafios e perspetivas.* Brasilia: Pan American Health Organization, Brazil Ministry of Health, Brazil Ministry of Foreign Affairs. http://new.paho.org/bra/index2.php?option=com_docman&task=doc_view&gid=1082&Itemid=423.

Palmeiro Filho, Pedro, and L. X. Capanema. 2004. A cadeia farmacêutica e a política industrial: uma proposta de inserção do BNDES. *BNDES Setorial.*

Parker, Richard. 1997. *Políticas, Instituicões e AIDS: Enfrentando a Epidemia no Brasil.* Rio de Janeiro: Jorge Zahar/ABIA.

Passarelli, Carlos André. 2007. Personal interview, International Coordinator, National AIDS Program. December 13.

Passarelli, Carlos André, and Veriano Terto Júnior. 2003. Non-governmental Organizations and Access to Anti-Retroviral Treatments in Brazil. *Divulgação em Saúde pare Debate* 27: 252–264.

Passos, Cristina. 2008. Compulsory Licensing in the Real World: The Case of ARV Drugs in Brazil. In *The Political Economy of HIV/AIDS in Developing Countries*, 150–165. Cheltenham, UK and Northampton, MA, USA: Edward Elgar Publishing.

Pinheiro, Eloan. 2008. Personal interview, Director of Farmanguinhos, 1994–2002. June 4.

Pro-Genericos. 2009. Mercado. http://www.progenericos.org.br/mercado.shtml.

Rech, Norberto. 2008. Personal interview, Director of Department of Pharmaceutical Assistance, 2003–2004. September 10.

Rich, Jessica. 2009. Mobilizing the Grassroots from Above: Political Engagement among AIDS Associations in Democratic Brazil. Breslauer Symposium, University of California International and Area Studies, UC Berkeley. May 7.

Ricupero, Rubens. 2007. Personal interview, Brazilian Ambassador to GATT. October 15.

Salles, Antonio. 2008. Personal interview, Director of Corporate Relations, Bristol Meyers Squibb Brazil. May 8.

Sanches, João. 2008. Personal interview, Communications Director, Merck Brazil. April 1.

Santoro, Wayne A., and Gail M. McGuire. 1997. Social Movement Insiders: The Impact of Institutional Activists on Affirmative Action and Comparable Worth Policies. *Social Problems* 44, no. 4 (November): 503–519. doi:10.2307/3097220. http://www.jstor.org.ezproxy.lib.utexas.edu/stable/3097220.

Sell, Susan K. 2003. *Private Power, Public Law: The Globalization of Intellectual Property Rights*. Cambridge: Cambridge University Press.

Serra, José. 2004. The Political Economy of the Brazilian Struggle Against AIDS. An Institute for Advanced Study Friends Forum.

Shadlen, Kenneth. 2009. The Politics of Patents and Drugs in Brazil and Mexico: The Industrial Bases of Health Policies. *Comparative Politics* 42(1): 41–58.

Silverman, Milton, Mia Lydecker, and Philip Randolph Lee. 1992. *Bad Medicine*. Stanford University Press.

Singer, Chris. 2007. Personal interview. Executive Vice President, Pharmaceutical Research and Manufacturers of America (PhRMA). August 5.

Skocpol, Theda. 1992. *Protecting Soldiers and Mothers: The Political Origins of Social Policy in the United States*. Cambridge, MA: Belknap Press of Harvard University Press.

Teixeira, Paulo. 2008. Personal interview. Director of National AIDS Program, 2000–2002, May 7.

Teixeira, Paulo, Marco Antônio Vitória, and Jhoney Barcarolo. 2003. The Brazilian Experience in Providing Universal Access to Antiretroviral Therapy. In *Economics of AIDS and Access to HIV/AIDS Care in Developing Countries: Issues and Challenges*, 69–86. Paris: Agence Nationale pour Recherche sur le Sida. http://www.iaen.org/files.cgi/11066_part_1_n2_Teixeira.pdf.

UNAIDS (the Joint United Nations Agency on HIV/AIDS). 2008. *Report on the Global AIDS Epidemic 2008*. Geneva: UNAIDS.

UNDP. 2006. Avaliação da capacidade de produção de ARV genéricos no Brasil August, Brasilia.

United States Trade Representative. 2007. *2007 'Special 301' Report*. USTR Reports and Publications, Watch List.

USA for Innovation. 2007. Letter from Ambassador Ken Adleman, Executive Director, USA for Innovation, to Ambassador Condoleezza Rice, Secretary of State, Carlos M. Guierrez, Secretary of Commerce, Michael O. Leavitt, Secretary of Health and Human Services, Ambassador Susan Schwab, US Trade Representative. http://www.usaforinnovation.org/news/050907_USAFI_Adelman percent20Letter.pdf.

Vieira, André. 2008. Merck diz que 'quebra de patente' é passado e sinaliza produção local. *Valor Economico*. September 8. http://www.febrafarma.org.br/index.php?area=cf&secao=clip&modulo=clipping&id=8410.

Weyland, Kurt. 1995. Social Movements and the State: The Politics of Health Reform in Brazil. *World Development* 23, no. 10: 1699–1712.

Wogart, J.P., and G. Calcagnotto. 2006. Brazil's Fight Against AIDS and Its Implications for Global Health Governance. *World Health & Population*: 1–16.

APPENDIX 6A TRIPS FLEXIBILITIES AND RELATED BRAZILIAN INTELLECTUAL PROPERTY LEGISLATION

TRIPS FLEXIBILITY	BRAZILIAN IP LEGISLATION
(1) **Transition period**: The deadline that member countries have for making domestic laws compliant with TRIPS varies depending on their level of development. High-income countries had until 1996 to change their laws; middle-income countries, including Brazil and India, 2005; and least developed countries have until 2016 (Arts 65 and 66).	Brazil approved Industrial Property Law 9.279 in 1996 and implemented it the following year, several years before the 2005 deadline.
(2) **Experimental exception**: The patent will not prohibit the experimental use of an invention by third parties for scientific purposes.	Included in Industrial Property Law 9.279.
(3) **'Bolar'/early working exception**: Third parties may carry out all the necessary tests and procedures required for the registration of generic medicines before their patent expires (Art. 30).	Law 10.196 passed in 2001 amends Art. 43 in Law 9.279 to provide for this exception.
(4) **Parallel imports or exhaustion of rights**: Without the consent of the patent holder on the domestic market, a product may be resold or imported from another country where the patent holder has authorized it to be placed on the market (Art. 6).	Decree 4.830 of 2003 amends Decree 3.201 to allow parallel importing of patented products when a compulsory license is issued.

(5) **Prior use**: If a person uses an invention before a patent is filed for the product, s/he may be granted the right to continue using the invention despite the granting of the patent (Art. 30).

Included in Industrial Property Law 9.279.

(6) **Compulsory license**: The main legal instrument for correcting abuses by patent holders is the compulsory license (CL), which allows for the exploitation of a patent by third-parties without the consent of the patent holder. Use of a CL is permitted in six instances: (a) refusal to deal; (b) cases of emergency or extreme urgency; (c) to remedy anti-competitive practices; (d) failure to obtain voluntary license under reasonable terms; (e) public non-commercial use; and (f) dependent patents for innovations requiring patented inputs. Before issuing a CL, a government must first attempt to reach a negotiated settlement with the patent holder, who, in the case of the CL, still has the right to receive royalties. There are two exceptions. First, prior negotiations are not required in cases of a national emergency and public, non-commercial use. Second, royalty payments may not be necessary when a CL is issued to correct anti-competitive practices.

Industrial Property Law 9.279 states a CL can be issued for the following reasons: failure to exploit patent; public interest; national emergency; remedy for anti-competitive practices; and failure to produce locally and dependent patents.

Decree 3.201 of 1999 specifies the criteria for issuing a compulsory license in cases of national emergency and public interest.

Decree 4.830 of 2003 amends Decree 3.201 to allow parallel importing of patented products when a compulsory license is issued.

(7) **Prior consent and pre-grant opposition:** Countries can determine the appropriate method of implementing the provisions of TRIPS within their legal system; consequently, domestic legislation may allow other government agencies or members of society to participate in patent application process (Art. 1.1).

Law 10.196 of 2001 amends Art. 229 in Law 9.279 stating that National Health Surveillance Agency (ANVISA) must give prior consent before patents are granted on all pharmaceutical products and processes. (Prior consent was first established by Presidential Directive in 1999.)

(8) **Pipeline versus mailbox:** A pipeline patent is a form of retroactive protection for drugs already patented in other countries but not marketed at the time TRIPS comes into force. Otherwise, a mailbox system allows applications for patents for pharmaceutical product inventions to be filed but not examined until the end of the transition period (Art. 70.8).

Industrial Property Law 9.279 of 1996 allows for pipeline patents.

(9) **Data exclusivity**: Grants protection for undisclosed data that drug firms provide to regulatory officials in order to obtain marketing approval. Extending the timeframe for protecting undisclosed data, a TRIPS-plus measure, restricts competition from generic drugs makers that could lower prices (Art. 31).

Law 10.603 of 2002 provides protection to up to 10 years for drugs that include new chemical entities and 5 years for all other drugs for undisclosed test data that drug firms provide to ANVISA.

7. The politics of patents and drugs in Brazil and Mexico: the industrial bases of health policies

Kenneth C. Shadlen[1]

Intellectual property (IP) policies influence trajectories of industrial development and capacities to address humanitarian concerns. As pillars of national systems of innovation, IP regimes drive technological change through their effect on knowledge-creation and knowledge-diffusion. By affecting access to technologically intensive goods, such as pharmaceuticals, IP regimes influence national public health programs. This chapter bridges these dimensions. Analysis of the politics of drug patents in Brazil and Mexico shows that how IP affects the industrial sector – particularly the pharmaceutical industry – establishes the political economic parameters affecting countries' abilities to use IP to promote public health.

Prior to the 1990s, neither Brazil nor Mexico (nor many other developing countries) granted patents on pharmaceuticals.[2] Local firms could produce "generic" versions of new drugs – drugs that typically were patented in developed countries that offered pharmaceutical patents.[3]

[1] The British Academy and Nuffield Foundation financed research for this chapter, which was first published as an article in *Comparative Politics* (Vol. 42(1) (October 2009), 41–58). It is reprinted with the permission of the journal. Rodrigo Martinez assisted in Mexico; Eduardo Fernandez provided invaluable support in Brazil. I thank Sarah Brooks, Matthew Flynn, Kevin Gallagher, Cori Hayden, Lawrence King, Ariane McCabe, Tim Power, Diego Sanchez-Ancochea, Andrew Schrank, and Pamela Starr for suggestions, and the journal's referees for their constructive reviews.

[2] Until the 1970s and 1980s many developed countries did not issue pharmaceutical patents either.

[3] By "generic" I refer to drugs unprotected by patents. Some definitions also stipulate that the drug be unprotected by trademark. Although "generic" does not mean the same thing everywhere, Brazilian and Mexican regulations share a common definition. Núria Homedes and Antonio Ugalde, "Multisource Drug Policies in Latin America: Survey of 10 Countries," *Bulletin of the World Health Organization*, 83 (January 2005), 64–70.

In the 1990s, both countries introduced pharmaceutical patents to comply with new international obligations. The World Trade Organization's (WTO) Agreement on Trade-Related Aspects of Intellectual Property Rights (TRIPS) and the IP provisions of the North American Free Trade Agreement (NAFTA) prohibit countries from declaring pharmaceuticals non-patentable; and the agreements require countries to provide patent-holders with strong rights of exclusion over the knowledge contained in the patent.

Providing market exclusivity to owners of drugs can raise prices, place drugs out of consumers' reach, and strain governments' health budgets.[4] Not surprisingly, the introduction of drug patents was followed by backlash, and by the late 1990s policymakers in many developing countries faced subsequent pressures to modify their new IP systems.

Policy in Brazil and Mexico took different courses in response to this changing scenario. Brazil adjusted the IP system to ameliorate the effects that drug patents can have on prices and access; Mexico introduced few adjustments, and where changes were introduced they tended to reinforce and intensify the effects of drug patents. Variation in IP policy can be considered along three dimensions: what knowledge can be owned as property, the rights of owners vs. users of property, and the effective duration of property owners' rights. In Brazil, obtaining private ownership over knowledge in the realm of pharmaceuticals has become more difficult, and the rights of third parties to use knowledge simplified. In Mexico, impediments have been raised to third parties' rights to use knowledge, and the effective length of protection extended.

One seemingly obvious explanation for these differences is that Mexico is in NAFTA, while Brazil has no external obligations beyond its membership in the WTO. Although NAFTA places greater restrictions on IP policy, reliance on NAFTA as an explanatory factor is inadequate. Differences in the two countries' international legal obligations cannot explain the subsequent divergence. If it were the case that the reforms introduced by Brazil would, were they transferred to Mexico, violate NAFTA, then NAFTA could partially account for the divergence – it could tell

---

[4] World Health Organization, "Intellectual Property Protection: Impact on Public Health," *WHO Drug Information,* 19 (August 2005), 236–241; Commission on Intellectual Property Rights (CIPR), *Integrating Intellectual Property Rights and Development Policy* (London: CIPR, 2002), ch. 2; Brigitte Granville, ed., *The Economics of Essential Medicines* (London: Royal Institute of International Affairs, 2002); Julio Nogués, "Social Costs and Benefits of Introducing Patent Protection for Pharmaceutical Drugs in Developing Countries," *The Developing Economies*, 31 (March 1993), 24–53.

us that Mexico could not take the same path as Brazil on account of its "WTO-Plus" commitments. But the reforms introduced by Brazil would not violate NAFTA; legally, Mexico could imitate Brazil. Moreover, a strict emphasis on NAFTA cannot explain why Mexico reformed its IP system by moving in the opposite direction to Brazil. Mexico did not simply fail to emulate Brazil's IP move away from "TRIPS-Plus" but rather moved to an extended version of TRIPS-Plus.

Nor can the outcome be explained by focusing on political bias.[5] To be sure, the Brazilian governments in the period under study (Cardoso 1995–2002; Lula 2003–2010) were more "left-leaning" than their Mexican counterparts (Zedillo 1994–2000; Fox 2000–2006), which perhaps might lead us to expect Brazil to prioritize health. Yet the major health-oriented reforms occurred under President Cardoso, the more centrist of the two Brazilian presidents. This is the same Cardoso that championed the original TRIPS-Plus patent law in 1996, and the subsequent policy shift is not linked to prior changes in ideological disposition or political bias. In Mexico, the "right-leaning" Fox government introduced progressive reforms to the health system, initiating reforms to make access to healthcare a citizen-based rather than employment-based right.[6]

A political economy explanation for Brazil's and Mexico's divergent trajectories of patent policy focuses on the actors pushing for reform and subsequent patterns of coalitional formation and political mobilization. In both countries, drug patents and high prices yielded initiatives for health-oriented IP reform. What varies is who led these initiatives and the extent to which important actors in local pharmaceutical sectors were available as coalition partners. In Brazil, the existence of an economically and politically more autonomous local pharmaceutical sector allowed the Ministry of Health to build a coalition in support of IP reform. In Mexico, fundamental transformations of the pharmaceutical sector yielded a different terrain. In fact, the reform project in Mexico became commandeered by IP owners and ultimately had the perverse effect of reinforcing the system that was challenged.

Of course, the transformation of Mexico's pharmaceutical sector that I emphasize is not unrelated to NAFTA, which implied substantial tariff reduction and revisions to government procurement practices that previously afforded special treatment to local firms. These broad shifts in

---

[5]   Maria Victoria Murillo, "Political Bias in Policy Convergence: Privatization Choices in Latin America," *World Politics*, 54 (July 2002), 462–493.

[6]   In fact, Fox's appointment as Health Secretary was well known for his long-standing call for universal health coverage.

policy, including pharmaceutical patent protection, induced changes to Mexico's industrial sector that would ultimately restrict the realm of feasible policy alternatives. NAFTA is indeed significant, then, but in a broad political economy sense. A lesson of this chapter for scholars of international and comparative political economy is that we need to reorient our attention from the legal to the political economy aspects of international agreements, i.e. not the rules per se but how such agreements unleash economic and social changes that, in turn, affect subsequent policy choices.

This chapter also presents lessons for analysts relying on models of policy diffusion.[7] Diffusion models depict policymaking as an interdependent and interactive process, in which the likelihood that a given policy will be adopted in one country is a function of its adoption (or non-adoption) in other countries. Some analysts apply this logic to the case of IP and drugs. Nunn et al. suggest that Brazilian officials learned from Thailand's example of using IP regulations to challenge transnational pharmaceutical firms' pricing practices.[8] Cohen and Lybecker suggest that the Brazilian example of health-oriented IP reform can lead other countries to act similarly, even citing Mexico as a country so inspired by Brazil.[9] Indeed, learning from members of countries' "peer groups" is a principal mechanism of diffusion in this literature.

Although the *idea* of reforming the IP system for public health purposes diffused from Brazil to Mexico, the *policy* did not. The legislative initiative proposed to modify Mexico's patent system made explicit reference to the Brazilian experience that was to be replicated, but once the diffused idea placed IP on the political agenda in Mexico, the initiative became commandeered by those who did not want Mexico's patent rules to be made

---

[7] Special issues dedicated to the theme of policy diffusion of *Annals of the American Academy of Political and Social Sciences*, 598 (March 2005) and *International Organization*, 60 (October 2006). See also Beth Simmons and Zachary Elkins, "The Globalization of Liberalization: Policy Diffusion in the International Political Economy," *American Political Science Review*, 98 (February 2004), 171–189; Jeffrey Chwierorth, "Neoliberal Economists and Capital Account Liberalization in Emerging Markets," *International Organization*, 61 (Spring 2007), 443–463; Sarah Brooks, "When Does Diffusion Matter? Explaining the Spread of Structural Pension Reforms Across Nations," *Journal of Politics*, 69 (August 2007), 701–715.

[8] Amy S. Nunn et al., "Evolution of Antiretroviral Drug Costs in Brazil in the Context of Free and Universal Access to AIDS Treatment," *PLoS Medicine*, 4 (November 2007), 1–13.

[9] Jillian Clare Cohen and Kristina M. Lybecker, "AIDS Policy and Pharmaceutical Patents: Brazil's Strategy to Safeguard Public Health," *The World Economy*, 28 (February 2005), 226.

more useful for the government to negotiate price reductions, but rather more useful for patent-holding firms to strengthen their property rights and ward off competition. The product of diffusion was not Mexico adopting policies that worked in Brazil, but rather policies that were the mirror image of those in Brazil. The explanation for this difference is in the identity of the actors receiving and attempting to implement the diffused idea of health-oriented IP, and the availability of powerful alliance partners for those actors advocating reform. The chapter, thus, provides a caution against overstating the significance of ideas and policy communities, and calls for renewed attention to traditional variables such as interests and resources.

In the next section I present a framework for comparing health-related aspects of national patent regimes, which I use to illustrate commonalities between Brazil and Mexico in the mid-1990s. I then explain subsequent divergence in the health-related aspects of these two countries' patent systems. In the final section I conclude, synthesizing the key findings and pointing to broader implications for analysis of the political economy of late development.

PATENTS, PHARMACEUTICALS, AND HEALTH POLICY

Prior to explaining the different policy trajectories experienced by Brazil and Mexico in health-related dimensions of IP, we need to understand the range of variation. In this section I provide a framework that allows us to conceptualize variation with regard to patents, pharmaceuticals, and health policy.[10]

Patents confer limited rights of exclusion over inventions that are new, non-obvious, and have industrial use. Although the grant of a patent constitutes turning knowledge into private property, the subsequent rights of owners over their property are limited in that they are not automatic, not absolute, and not permanent. Patents are granted only where applicants demonstrate that their inventions satisfy the criteria of patentability. With application and examination central – and prior – to the process of establishing ownership, governments can control what knowledge becomes private property within their territory. Another limitation is that patent

---

[10]   For detailed discussion, see Carlos Correa, *Integrating Public Health Concerns into Patent Legislation in the Developing Countries* (Geneva: South Centre, 2000); CIPR, ch. 2.

Table 7.1   Law, politics, and health policy

Limitations	Political conflict	Health-related policy areas
Not automatic	What can be owned	Pharmaceutical patents "Pipeline patents"
Not absolute	Rights of owners vs. users	Compulsory licenses Parallel imports
Not permanent	Duration of rights	Post-patent generic entry (early working provisions, drug registration procedures)

rights include various exceptions to patent-holders' ability to control the use and distribution of their property. Patent regimes include provisions by which third parties can – without requesting permission – use knowledge that is owned by someone else, and they also include provisions that allow third parties to receive permission from the state to use other actors' privately owned knowledge in ways that would otherwise constitute violations of patent-holders' rights. Lastly, patents expire: at some point the private property enters the public domain, where access to and use of the knowledge is unrestricted.

These three limitations map onto lines of political conflict over what can be owned privately, between the rights of owners and users of private property, and over the duration of rights. These lines of conflict, in turn, map roughly[11] onto axes of policy variation. The rows in Table 7.1 take us from a limitation to a political conflict and then provide health-related policy examples.

With regard to conflicts over what sort of knowledge can be owned privately, the most important policy issue is whether or not countries grant pharmaceutical patents. As indicated, many developing countries did not do so prior to the 1990s, but TRIPS (and NAFTA) requires that countries grant patents on pharmaceutical products and processes.[12]

A second policy issue regards how to deal with inventions that are not new but that were not patented when they were new because the previous regime did not allow the sort of knowledge to be patented. If a country began granting pharmaceutical patents in 1995, for example, a drug that was invented in 1990 would not have been eligible for a patent when it was new. The novelty requirement would also make the drug unpatentable in

---

[11] In fact, some policy areas are relevant to multiple lines of conflict.

[12] Countries that did not grant pharmaceutical patents prior to 1995 had until 2005 to begin doing so.

1995, even with the introduction of pharmaceutical patents, because it was no longer new. Since drugs are patented before marketing authority is secured, the 1990 drug would most likely be undergoing clinical trials in 1995 – it would be in the "pipeline." How do countries introducing pharmaceutical patents treat drugs in the pipeline? On this dimension NAFTA exceeds TRIPS by obligating countries to offer "pipeline patents."[13]

Policy areas that correspond to conflicts over the rights of owners vs. users regard compulsory licenses (CLs) and parallel imports. CLs allow domestic entities (public or private) to import, produce, and distribute patented goods without the patent-holders' consent. TRIPS and NAFTA allow countries to determine the grounds on which they grant CLs, provided that a set of procedural conditions (e.g. prior negotiations with the patent-holder, payment of royalties, are met).[14] In the case of CLs granted during times of national emergency or for government use, countries are released from the obligation of prior negotiations.[15] Because potential delays introduced by negotiations are removed with this latter type of CL, they are easier and quicker to grant and, arguably, of most relevance for discussions of health.

Parallel importation consists of allowing patented goods to enter the market once patent-holders have placed the goods on the market elsewhere. Parallel imports can help ensure affordability of patented products by facilitating arbitrage and thus constraining patent-holders' ability to set monopoly prices. TRIPS allows countries to engage in parallel importation by adopting *international* doctrines of patent exhaustion, i.e. once products are placed on the international market, patent-holders' exclusive rights are exhausted. NAFTA prohibits parallel importation by requiring *national* doctrines of patent exhaustion.

Health-related policy areas corresponding to conflicts over the length of rights regard post-patent generic entry. When patents expire and knowledge enters the public domain, new actors gain rights to participate in markets that were reserved for patent-holders. How quickly new actors

---

[13]   In addition to stretching the definition of "novelty," the problem with pipeline patents is that they are not examined but rather revalidated.

[14]   Compare the nearly identical CL provisions of TRIPS Article 31 (http://www.wto.org/english/tratop_e/trips_e/t_agm3c_e.htm#5) and NAFTA Article 1709.10 (http://www.sice.oas.org/Trade/nafta/chap-171.asp).

[15]   This provision, that when CLs are issued on grounds of national emergency countries are released from procedural obligations, is often misrepresented to suggest that countries can only issue CLs in national emergencies. To repeat: countries can issue CLs on whatever grounds they establish in national legislation, but in times of national emergency (and government use) they can bypass negotiations.

enter markets and the subsequent competitive effects are felt in terms of reduced prices depends on a number of important policies, particularly early working provisions and procedures for registering generic drugs. Early working provisions allow firms to use patented knowledge and produce generic versions of patented drugs to obtain marketing approval once patents expire.[16] Without such provisions firms might be infringing patents by producing generic versions prior to the patents' expiration. Yet if firms must wait until patents expire to produce generic versions and apply to health authorities for authorization, patent terms are effectively extended by the amount of time it takes to complete these not-insignificant steps. Early working provisions, then, by allowing generic firms to use patented knowledge to prepare for market entry, can expedite competition at the point that patents expire. TRIPS and NAFTA both permit early working provisions.[17]

Some pharmaceutical firms opt to launch generic versions prior to the end of patent terms, believing that their follow-on products do not infringe existing patents or that the patents in question are invalid. Since marketing drugs depends on authorization from health authorities, the subsequent question is whether and how the activities of IP and health officials are coordinated. Neither TRIPS nor NAFTA addresses this. More recently, as we shall see, the US has pushed strongly for a form of coordination known as "linkage," whereby health authorities consult with IP authorities and deny registration to drugs when patents are in force. While this form of coordination seems unproblematic on the face of it (if the drug is patented, then the sale of generic versions would be illegal), many developing countries resist pressures to proceed in this direction, arguing that linkage inappropriately transfers the burden of defending patents from the private rights-holder to the public. In any case, this form of linkage, though included in more recent regional and bilateral trade agreements (RBTAs) that the US has negotiated, is not in NAFTA.

Table 7.2 contrasts the WTO and NAFTA with regard to the health-policy dimensions of the two agreements' IP provisions. While it is clear that there are differences, such as pipeline patents and parallel imports, the similarities are certainly greater.

---

[16] Formally, early working (also called "Bolar") provisions are examples of limiting owners' rights of exclusion, but where they most matter regards the effective duration of owners' rights.

[17] Such provisions do not shorten patent terms but rather eliminate the effective extension of terms that is yielded by leaving a single firm with market exclusivity despite the patents' expiration. I am not addressing data exclusivity.

Table 7.2   IP and health policy: WTO vs. NAFTA

Policy issue	WTO (TRIPS)	NAFTA (Chapter 17)
Pharmaceutical patents	Required (product and process)	–
Pipeline patents	Not required	required
Compulsory licenses	Permitted; ample discretion	–
Parallel imports	Permitted	not permitted
Early working provisions	Permitted	–
Drug registration procedures	Not addressed	–

Note: – indicates the absence of substantial difference between NAFTA and TRIPS.

The WTO's and NAFTA's provisions indicate the parameters of what countries can and cannot do, but not what they *do* do. Table 7.3 presents the main characteristics of the Brazilian and Mexican patent regimes implemented in the 1990s. Both countries greatly exceeded their new obligations, making ownership easy to obtain over a wide variety of pharmaceutical and pharmo-chemical products and processes, and giving owners strong – and effectively long – rights of exclusion. From a public health perspective, both countries' patent regimes were worrisome. For example, both countries offered pipeline patents, neither allowed parallel imports, both had only rudimentary mechanisms for compulsory licenses to deal with health concerns, and neither had early working provisions. As a result of these "TRIPS Plus" patent regimes, more drugs would become patented in both countries and it would be difficult to rely on generic competition to reduce prices. Beginning in the late 1990s, however, the two countries diverge in dramatic fashion. The subsequent sections explain this divergence, drawing our attention to the important role of local pharmaceutical industries in coalitions for health-oriented patent reform.

BRAZIL: FROM TRIPS PLUS TO "TRIPS JUST"

In the late 1990s and early 2000s, health-related aspects of Brazil's patent regime underwent substantial modifications. Obtaining pharmaceutical patents was made more difficult, the patent law was modified to facilitate government efforts to lower prices through compulsory licensing, and the government enacted measures to encourage competition with generics. The nature of the Brazilian government's demand for patented and expensive drugs made health-oriented IP reform a high priority, and the political

Table 7.3   Health-related IP policy: common origins

Policy	Brazil	Mexico
Pharmaceutical patents	Yes (1997)	Yes (1991)
"Pipeline patents"	Yes (1996)	Yes (1991)
Compulsory licenses for government or public use*	Yes (basic, Art. 71)	Yes (basic, Art. 77)
Parallel imports	No	No
Early working provisions	No	No
Linkage	No	No

Notes:
The shaded text indicates important differences.
*   In other areas of compulsory licensing, particularly the requirement to "work" patents locally, there are important differences in that Mexico explicitly accepts importation as local working whilst Brazil does so only under certain conditions (such as when local production is deemed to be not economically viable). As indicated below (note 25), this provision of Brazil's LPI has been a subject of controversy in the WTO.

organization and structure of the Brazilian pharmaceutical industry made reform politically feasible.

The Brazilian government's demand for drugs was strong – and relatively inelastic to price – on account of the Ministry of Health's (MH) extensive obligations to provide free medicines. These obligations are rooted in the 1988 Constitution, which establishes the right to health, including access to essential medicines through the new national health-care system (SUS), as a universal right. Government demand was particularly shaped by the HIV/AIDS epidemic. Although Brazil's adult prevalence rate of 0.6 percent is not particularly high by international standards, the country stands out for its early (since the late 1980s) and comprehensive approach toward prevention and treatment. Importantly, a 1996 law guaranteed free anti-retroviral (ARV) treatment through the MH's National HIV/AIDS Program, and intense social mobilization further reinforced the government's obligations.[18]

---

[18]   Guido Carlos Levi and Marco Antonio A. Vitória, "Fighting Against AIDS: The Brazilian experience," *AIDS*, 16 (2002), 2373–2383; Paulo Teixeira et al., "The Brazilian Experience in Providing Universal Access to Antiretroviral Therapy," in Moatti et al., eds, *Economics of AIDS and Access to HIV Care in Developing Countries* (Paris: ANRS, 2003), 69–88; Jane Galvão, "Brazil and Access to HIV/AIDS Drugs: A Question of Human Rights and Public Health," *American Journal of Public Health*, 95 (July 2005), 1110–1116; Alexandre Grangeiro et al., "Sustentabilidade da política de acesso a medicamentos anti-retrovirais no Brasil,"

Brazil's approach to HIV/AIDS treatment affected the government's demand in such a way as to make IP reform an imperative. Because ARVs treat but do not cure HIV/AIDS, they need to be taken indefinitely; and patients need to change treatment regimens as immunities develop. By the late 1990s the annual per patient cost of treatment in Brazil was nearly US$5000 and ARVs already consumed one-third of the MH's drug budget – and this was at a time when treatment featured almost exclusively unpatented drugs. As more people began treatment and as patients migrated to expensive second-line regimens based on drugs that were patented under Brazil's new IP law, the program would be unsustainable.[19]

Since 1999, then, the government took a range of measures to improve the capacity of the National HIV/AIDS Program (and the SUS more generally) to acquire less-expensive, generic versions of newer drugs from both foreign and local suppliers. The MH's initiative to lower costs via promotion of generics led to three important modifications of Brazil's new IP system: health authorities gained prominence in reviewing patent applications, compulsory licensing provisions were made more flexible and easier to use, and regulatory reforms were introduced to expedite post-patent generic entry.

Any pharmaceutical patent application that is approved by the National Institute for Industrial Property (INPI) is sent to the MH for review. The patent is issued only after IP officials in the ministry's health surveillance agency (ANVISA) issue "prior consent."[20] This reform, introduced by decree by President Cardoso in 1999 and converted into law in 2001,

---

Revista de Saúde Pública 40 (Supplement 2006), 60-69; João Biehl, *Will to Live: AIDS Therapies and the Politics of Survival* (Princeton: Princeton University Press, 2007); Anne-Christine d'Adesky, *Moving Mountains: The Race to Treat Global AIDS* (New York: Verso, 2004), ch. 3; Mathew Flynn, "Public Production of Anti-Retroviral Medicines in Brazil, 1990–2007," *Development and Change* 39 (July 2008), 513–536. Thus, in the context of persistent inequities in health services (Kurt Weyland, *Democracy Without Equity: Failures of Reform in Brazil* [Pittsburgh: University of Pittsburgh Press, 1996], ch. 7), the National HIV/AIDS Program offers an exception.

[19]   Levi and Vitória; Grangeiro et al.; Ministry of Health, "The Sustainability of Universal Access to Antiretroviral Medicines in Brazil," 157th Ordinary Meeting of the National Health Council, Brasília, August 2005. The former Minister of Health also emphasizes that an overvalued currency cheapened drug imports, a situation that changed with the real's devaluation in 1999. José Serra, "The Political Economy of the Brazilian Struggle Against AIDS," Institute for Advanced Study, Occasional Paper 17, 2004, 9.

[20]   ANVISA's IP division, established in 2001, was housed in INPI's Rio office building.

Table 7.4   ANVISA's prior consent

Decision	Number of cases	Percentage
Approvals	752	68.9
Denials	53	4.9
Pending (as of July 2008)	122	11.2
Other*	165	15.1
Total	1092	100.0

Note: *   Includes applications returned to INPI for further documentation and because determined not to be pharmaceutical patent applications.

Source: ANVISA.

aimed to provide the MH with an instrument to influence the patent-examination process, influence that it would otherwise lack on account of INPI being situated within a different ministry.

The prior consent requirement makes it more difficult to obtain private rights of exclusion over knowledge for pharmaceuticals. Many patent applications are not for new molecular entities (NMEs) but rather revised versions of NMEs that are already patented, raising the question of how patent examiners define "novelty."[21] ANVISA's health-focused criteria are significantly stricter than INPI's.[22] Whereas INPI is criticized by health activists and lawyers for adopting an overly broad definition of novelty, ANVISA denies patents to drugs that lack "genuine" novelty and where it adjudges that providing exclusive rights would be harmful to public health. Typically ANVISA uses its authority to prevent patents that, by its judgment, would extend the terms of existing patents.[23] As Table 7.4 indicates, 53 applications approved by INPI have been rejected by ANVISA since the prior consent process was initiated in 2001. Perhaps more critically, of the 68.9 percent of the applications that ANVISA has

---

[21]   Does showing a "second use" for an existing drug constitute "novelty" and warrant a patent?

[22]   Maristela Basso, "Intervention of Health Authorities in Patent Examination: The Brazilian Practice of the Prior Consent," *International Journal of Intellectual Property Management*, 1 (2006), 54–74; Maristela Basso and Edson Beas Rodrigues, "Direitos de Propriedade Intelectual, Desenvolvimento Humano e Tecnológico Local: Desafios para o Brasil no Cenário pós-TRIPS/OMC," Unpublished UNDP working paper, 2006, Annex 1.

[23]   This policy corresponds to two types of conflicts, what knowledge can be owned and also the duration of private rights.

approved, in 42 percent of these cases the applicant first had to reduce the breadth of the patent's claims.[24]

No aspect of the global politics of IP has received as much attention as compulsory licenses, and Brazil has been at the forefront of these debates. The 1996 patent law (formally the Lei de Propriedad Industrial, hereafter LPI) includes multiple articles that address CLs, the most significant for our purposes being Article 71 covering national emergencies and situations of "public interest." Presidential directives in 1999 and 2003 reformed Article 71 to make it more useful and thus increase the MH's capacity to leverage price reductions from patent-holding pharmaceutical firms.[25] These revisions gave clearer definitions of national emergency and public interest and simplified the mechanism for issuing CLs by giving the MH greater authority to act. Importantly, the 2003 directive stipulates that private firms supplying the government constitutes "public use" and is thus acceptable under Article 71, and also requires patent owners to transfer technological knowledge in the case of CLs.[26]

The threat of a CL is a bargaining tool used to entice patent-holders to make their products available at lower prices. The effectiveness of the bargaining tool, however, depends on the credibility of the threat. The reforms to Article 71 make the Brazilian government's threats more credible by making CLs easier to issue and less vulnerable to appeal, and by increasing the government's ability to secure the relevant drugs from alternative suppliers.

Since 2001 the MH has repeatedly used the CL instruments to obtain price reductions on second-line ARVs that consume a disproportionate share of the MH's drug budget. The key ARVs (patent-holders) are efavirenz (Merck), lopinavir/ritonavir (Abbott), and nelfinavir (Roche), which account for roughly 60 percent of the government's ARV expenditures. In August 2001, for example, the MH announced it would issue

---

[24]   Helen Miranda Silva, *Avaliação da análise dos pedidos de patentes farmacêuticas feita pela Anvisa no cumprimento do mandato legal da anuência prévia*, Masters Dissertation, National School of Public Health, 2008. One important hitch with the process is how INPI reacts when ANVISA rejects a patent. See Kenneth C. Shadlen, "The Political Contradictions of Incremental Innovation: Lessons from Pharmaceutical Patent Examination in Brazil," *Politics & Society* 39, 2 (2011), 143–174.

[25]   Although presidential directives are meant to establish implementation guidelines and not formally reform laws, they are often substantive, as in this case.

[26]   A different article (Art. 68, which authorizes CLs where a patented good is not manufactured locally) was the subject of a WTO case that the US filed and later withdrew.

a compulsory license on nelfinavir, and Roche responded by reducing the price. Similar episodes occurred with Roche and also Abbott, and Merck in 2003, and then again with Abbott in 2005. In 2007, following protracted negotiations with Merck, Brazil issued a CL on efavirenz. Note that these drugs are patented in Brazil because of the inclusion of pipeline patents in the 1996 LPI. Thus, to an important extent, the reforms to – and exercise of – the CL provisions can be understood as efforts to ameliorate the effects of the "TRIPS Plus" LPI.

Negotiations have not always been entirely successful: the 2005 agreement with Abbott left the price of lopinavir/ritonavir well above Abbott's most-discounted international price, for example, and the MH is widely criticized for not issuing more CLs.[27] Yet the MH's strategy, its shortcomings notwithstanding, has resulted in significant cost savings, even as patented second-line treatments play increasingly greater roles in the national treatment program.[28] In fact, while the affordability of second-line ARVs provided the main impetus for IP reform, the modifications have yielded lower drug prices across the board.[29]

The Brazilian strategy to introduce generic competition also included amending the 1996 LPI to introduce an early working provision, which allows generic firms to prepare for market entry at the moment of patent expiration.[30] Importantly, Brazilian authorities refuse to adjust terms for patents granted under the pipeline mechanism. That is, if a patent had a priority date from its USPTO application of 31 January 1987, for example, and was granted in Brazil under the pipeline mechanism in 1999, the patent would be due to expire in both the US and Brazil on the same day, 30 January 2007. And even if the USPTO were to extend the expiry date by two years, so that the patent expired in January 2009 in the US, it would still expire in 2007 in Brazil. The transnational sector pushes strongly for adjusting patent terms in this way and regularly demands this in court, but doing so is not the norm in Brazil.[31] The bias against adjustments of patent terms provides generic producers with incentives

---

[27]   Rebrip, "Acordo do Governo Brasileiro com a Abbot Frustra Expectativas dos Brasileiros," 13 July 2005 (http://www.rebrip.org.br/_rebrip/pagina.php?id= 659); Grangeiro et al. See the comments of Pedro Chequer, former director of the National HIV/AIDS Program, in Jon Cohen "Brazil: Ten Years After," *Science*, 313 (28 July 2006), 484–487.

[28]   Nunn et al.; Cohen and Lybecker; Galvão; Cohen, "Brazil: Ten Years After."

[29]   Nunn et al.

[30]   Introduced by presidential decree, then converted into law in 2001.

[31]   "Patent Term Extensions in Mexico Buck Latin American Trend," *Global Insight*, 2 January 2008 (http://www.globalinsight.com/SDA/SDADetail11297.htm).

to utilize the early working provision. The effectiveness of the system is further enhanced by ANVISA's policy of granting rapid approval of products that satisfy health criteria, leaving questions of potential patent infringement to be contested in courts.

While the nature of demand has driven the Brazilian government to introduce these health-oriented IP reforms, the support of the Brazilian pharmaceutical sector makes doing so feasible. The reforms have, not surprisingly, drawn strong criticism from the transnational pharmaceutical sector, both its representatives in Brazil (INTERFARMA) and the US (PhRMA). Actors that once heaped praise on Brazil for its "modern" 1996 LPI now complain of piracy and theft.[32] But these attacks do not isolate the government, which can rest on the support of a coalition of actors representing the national pharmo-chemical (ABIFINA) and pharmaceutical (ALANAC, ALFOB, and ProGenéricos) producers. These organizations – some of which unsuccessfully resisted the 1996 LPI – act as a bulwark against INTERFARMA, consistently presenting positions contrary to those of the transnational sector. When INTERFARMA assailed the reforms introduced in 1999 and 2000 or the 2007 CL, for example, ABIFINA quickly came to the MH's defense.[33]

The existence of a coalition supportive of health-oriented IP reforms is partially a function of state policy. After all, the local pharmaceutical sector benefited from significant government investment in research and production, much of it through the MH itself.[34] The ministry, acting as

---

[32] These complaints and accusations were repeated in multiple interviews with representatives from INTERFARMA, patent lawyers in Brazil, and USTR officials. See, as examples, Frederico Vasconcelos, "Mudanças na lei desagradam múltis," *Folha de São Paulo*, 21 February 2000; Lawrence A. Kogan, "Brazil's IP Opportunism Threatens US Private Property Rights," *Inter-American Law Review*, 38 (Fall 2006), 1–139; Igor Leonardo Guimarães Simões, "A Guerra das patentes farmacêuticas," *Jus Navigandi*, 9 (28 May 2005). See also the USTR's annual "Special 301" reports on IP, and PHARMA's submissions to these reports.

[33] See, for example, Vasconcelos, "Mudanças na lei desagradam múltis"; Marcos Oliveira, "A falácia da quebra de patente," *Jornal do Commercio*, 10 April 2006 (column by ABIFINA's vice-president published in newspapers throughout Brazil); Eduardo Costa and Nelson Brasil, "A Emancipação do Programa anti-Aids," *Jornal de Brasilia*, 15 November 2007. Brazilian industry's position is not uniform, of course, nor its support rock-solid. On some issues, particularly those affecting patenting of incremental innovations, local firms are ambivalent and divided. Shadlen, "The Political Contradictions of Incremental Innovation: Lessons from Pharmaceutical Patent Examination in Brazil," *Politics & Society* 39, 2 (2011), 143–174.

[34] Of Brazil's 18 government-linked pharmaceutical producers, the most important is part of the MH: Farmanguinhos, in Rio de Janeiro. Public-sector labs

"health entrepreneur," does not just purchase drugs but also takes an active role in their production.[35] Public-sector labs are important suppliers to the government, and, earlier in the production chain, the state works with private firms to help them develop synthesis technologies, produce necessary intermediates, and acquire capacities for reverse-engineering active principal ingredients (APIs).

Economic and technological collaboration between the public and private sectors created conditions for a political alliance and hospitable ground for the government's health-oriented IP reforms. The transnational sector opposed the government at nearly every step, but INTERFARMA does not monopolize the sector politically. The existence of a national pharmaceutical sector with interests distinct from the transnationals and with productive capacity retained from an earlier period of industrialization presented the MH with friendly and cooperative interlocutors. Indeed, the 2003 presidential directive on CLs was drafted by a lawyer who works as an advisor to ABIFINA.[36]

It is essential to emphasize that the virtuous circle – the government invests in industry and industry supports the government's IP reforms – is possible because of the condition of the local pharmaceutical sector. Even with the introduction of pharmaceutical patents and in the context of trade liberalization and an overvalued currency, Brazilian firms retained market share in the 1990s. By the time health-related IP reforms became politically salient, local firms still accounted for roughly one-quarter of sales and dominated the nascent generics market, and pharmo-chemical firms retained twice the market share of Chinese and Indian combined imports.[37] A critical point here regards the remaining capacity to produce final drugs and APIs – capacity that is a legacy of the import-substituting period, particularly the push for backward integration of the

---

mostly engage in formulation of final dosages, and to a lesser degree on pharmo-chemical inputs. Flynn 2008.

[35] Maurice Cassier and Marilena Correa, "Intellectual Property and Public Health: Copying of HIV/Aids Drugs by Brazilian Public and Private Pharmaceutical Laboratories," *RECIIS Electronic Journal of Communication, Information and Innovation in Health* 1 (January 2007), 84. See also, Claudia Chamas, "Developing Innovative Capacity in Brazil to Meet Health Needs," World Health Organization, Commission on Intellectual Property Rights, Innovation and Public Health, 2005; Eduardo Costa, "Política de medicamentos: tecnologia e produção no país," *ABIFINA Informa*, No. 216, March 2006.

[36] Confidential interview, 18 May 2008 (Rio de Janeiro). For further illustration of this collaboration, see Cassier and Correa, "Intellectual Property and Public Health"; Costa and Brasil, "A Emancipação."

[37] IMS and MH data; Chamas 2005.

pharmaceutical sector in the 1980s.[38] Furthermore, the "late" introduction of pharmaceutical patents in 1997 meant that the potential denationalizing effects had not yet materialized.[39] Because Brazilian firms were still capable of benefiting from the government's strategy they were available alliance partners.

MEXICO: FROM TRIPS PLUS TO NAFTA PLUS

Policy in Mexico followed a fundamentally different trajectory. Whereas Brazil implemented reforms to ameliorate the effects of patents on drug prices, Mexico introduced policy changes that reinforce these effects. Reforms to Mexico's patent law make use more difficult and complicate the process by which CLs can be issued. In addition, the modest steps to encourage post-patent generic competition were introduced in a self-undermining fashion. The explanation for this different path is rooted in the Mexican government's less comprehensive response to the HIV/ AIDS epidemic, which made IP reforms less compelling, and the transformations of the pharmaceutical sector, which not only made coalition-building for health-oriented IP reform less feasible but facilitated a counter-mobilization on the part of patent owners.

Although the affordability of medicines became a prominent issue in Mexico in the late 1990s, as prices increased significantly above the rate of inflation in the years following the 1994 devaluation of the peso, the nature of government demand reduced the sensitivity to such changes. State provision of discounted and free medicines was far from universal, extending only to workers in the formal sector (IMSS) and government employees (ISSSTE). Nor, importantly, did Mexico's Secretariat of Health (SH) face Brazilian-like obligations with regards to ARVs. Most HIV/AIDS treatment was provided outside of the state system and the uninsured generally

---

[38]   Sérgio Queiroz, "La Industria Farmacéutica y Farmoquímica Brasileña en los Años 90," in Jorge Katz et al., *Apertura Económica y Desregulación en el Mercado de Medicamentos* (Buenos Aires: Alianza Editorial, 1997), 125–165; José Eduardo Cassiolato et al., "Avaliação Econômica da Capacidade do Brasil para a Fabricação dos Medicamentos para HIV/AIDS," unpublished UNDP working paper, 2006; Joseph M. Fortunak and O.A.C. Antunes, *ARVs Production in Brazil: An Evaluation* (Rio de Janeiro: Associação Brasileira Interdisciplinar de AIDS, 2006); Lelio A. Maçaira, "A Capacitação Productiva Brasileira para Anti-Retrovirais," ABIFINA Informa 216, March 2006.

[39]   Introducing pharmaceutical patents in 1997 is still early, since Brazil had until 2005.

lacked access.[40] The SH, thus, had less cause for alarm in the face of higher prices and less motive to reform the patent system.

Rather than coming from within government, the initiative for health-oriented patent reform came from a segment of the local pharmaceutical sector that emerged in the 1990s in response to economic crisis and the limited coverage of IMSS/ISSSTE. In the late 1990s and early 2000s a chain of pharmacies selling non-bioequivalent generics under the mark Similares (Similars) expanded in low-income areas throughout the country.[41] The emergence of Farmacias Similares gave local firms that had traditionally supplied the state sector opportunities to sell to private pharmacies. The actors in the chain were closely related, in fact, with the leading producer of non-bioequivalent generics (Laboratorios Best) owned by the same person who owned the Farmacias Similares chain, a physician-pharmacist-industrialist named Victor González Torres, aka "Dr. Simi."[42]

The Similares sector and its allies in Congress spearheaded the initiative to reform the patent system. In December 2002 "Dr. Simi's" nephew, a Green Party (PVEM) member of the Chamber of Deputies, presented an initiative that would reform the 1991 patent law by reducing patent terms to ten years in the case of serious health situations. The PVEM initiative would have violated Mexico's TRIPS and NAFTA requirements for 20-year patent terms, but instead of rejecting the proposal out of hand, the Science and Technology Commission (CCyT) modified it. For all the proposal's faults, its motivations and context were not to be ignored: escalating drug prices were making access to medicines a growing problem, and, as the initiative's authors emphasized, other developing countries (such as Brazil) were demonstrating the feasibility of health-oriented patent reforms. Thus, the president of the CCyT acknowledged the concerns expressed by the bill's sponsors and decided to rewrite the proposal with proper legal assistance.[43] While the original proposal addressed patent terms (Article 23), the revised bill addressed CLs (Article 77), an area

---

[40] Patricia Uribe Zúñiga et al., "AIDS in Mexico," *The Body,* November 1998; d'Adesky, ch. 7; Sergio Bautista et al., "Antiretroviral Treatment Costs in Mexico," WHO/UNAIDS Workshop on Strategic Information for Anti-Retroviral Therapy Programmes, June 2003.

[41] Bioequivalent medicines feature the same APIs as reference drugs, and they perform identically in the human body. "Similars" may not satisfy the second criterion.

[42] For analysis of Farmacias Similares and the Dr. Simi phenomenon, see Cori Hayden, "A Generic Solution? Pharmaceuticals and the Politics of the Similar in Mexico," *Current Anthropology,* 48 (August 2007), 475–495.

[43] Interview, former President of CCyT, 10 August 2007 (Mexico City).

where Mexico had discretion under TRIPS and NAFTA. In March 2003 the CCyT approved a modest reform that would increase the capacity of the SH to issue CLs in the case of health emergencies. The key elements were to make a state of "serious illness" declared by the SH a ground for CLs, to simplify the process by which "serious illness" is declared, and to assure rapid issue of CLs at low royalties.

The March 2003 bill, similar in many ways to Brazil's 1999 CL reform, drew a sharp reaction from the transnational pharmaceutical industry and its local representatives. Government officials and legislators found themselves besieged by letters, faxes, emails, phone calls and personal visits from the transnational sector's trade association (AMIIF), Mexico's leading law firms, the USTR, and foreign embassies (e.g. US, Switzerland).

The transnational sector did not just react defensively but went on the offensive, converting the threat into an opportunity. AMIIF had attempted to terminate the patent-reform project, though once it was kept alive by the CCyT, AMIIF and its allies mobilized to secure a reform that would make the granting of CLs less likely than under the original patent law from 1991.[44] The campaign was successful, as the transnational sector essentially commandeered the initiative. The Fox government, never compelled by IP reform in the first place, joined the counter-offensive: the Secretary of Government's legislative liaison insisted that the March 2003 version could not proceed and provided the CCyT with a revised text.[45] This new version, which was passed by the full Chamber of Deputies and Senate and then signed into law by President Fox in 2004, *increases* the obstacles to issuing compulsory licenses by making the process by which "serious illness" is declared more complicated, removing serious illness as a ground for a CL, and requiring high minimum royalty rates.[46]

The transnational sector also secured favorable changes with regard to post-patent generic entry. In September 2003, at the same time as the reform to the patent law was in the Senate, the Fox government announced a new linkage system that requires health authorities to consult with the IP office and deny marketing authority to drugs where patents remain in effect. Thus, while Brazil's prior consent measure integrates health criteria into patent policy, Mexico's linkage system subordinates health policy to patent criteria.

---

[44]   Interview, Director General of AMIIF, 14 August 2007 (Mexico City).

[45]   CCyT archives; interview, former official in Secretaría de Gubernación, 14 August 2007 (Mexico City).

[46]   As an illustration of the perversity of this legislative process, note that the original sponsors of the initiative to reform Mexico's CL system (PVEM) ended up actively opposing the final bill that was passed in Congress.

Mexico also introduced an early working provision at this time, but this is largely undermined by the transnational sector's ability to secure routine adjustment of the expiration dates on pipeline patents.[47] The Mexican IP law stipulates that pipeline patents expire in Mexico on the same date as they expire in the first country where the patent was filed. These clauses, though contested in courts, essentially commit Mexico to adjust expiry dates. Because patent terms are adjusted in Mexico when they are adjusted in the original country, industry actors cannot know when a drug's patent will expire, which makes it difficult to take advantage of any opportunities created by the early working provision.

The changes introduced to Mexico's IP system (and health regulatory structure more generally) mean that the prices of patented drugs remain higher in Mexico. Patent-holding pharmaceutical firms do not fear CLs, and thus feel little compulsion to reduce prices. Abbott, for example, prices its patented version of lopinavir/ritonavir at more than five times the Brazilian price, but the Mexican government lacks the instruments to negotiate price reductions. More accurately, such instruments, as they previously existed, were dulled by the reforms of 2003–04.

To make sense of the perverse experience of IP reform in Mexico, where an initiative to enhance the rights of knowledge-users ended up yielding a set of changes that strengthen the rights of knowledge-owners, it helps to consider the changing political economy of the pharmaceutical sector. In contrast to Brazil, where INTERFARMA's positions are regularly countered by rival actors, in Mexico AMIIF dominates the sector economically and politically. Of course, individual Mexican firms would benefit from Brazilian-style patent reforms, as originally approved by the CCyT, yet outside of Farmacias Similares (and its subsidiary firms and suppliers) not even the local pharmaceutical sector provided support for the favorable version of the CCyT's initiative or opposed the revised and unfavorable version. Nor did they much contest the linkage system.

The early – and, with the inclusion of pipeline patents, retroactive – introduction of pharmaceutical patents transformed Mexico's pharmaceutical sector. Through the mid-1980s the national pharmaceutical sector thrived on reverse-engineering unpatented drugs.[48] By the late 1990s, however, trade liberalization had undermined the pharmo-chemical

[47] "Patent Term Extensions in Mexico Buck Latin American Trend."

[48] Gary Gereffi, *The Pharmaceutical Industry and Dependency in the Third World* (Princeton: Princeton University Press, 1983); Joan Brodovsky, "Industria farmacéutica y farmoquímica mexicana en el marco regulatorio de los años noventa," in Jorge Katz et al., *Apertura Económica y Desregulación en el Mercado de Medicamentos* (Buenos Aires: Alianza Editorial, 1997), 167–199.

sector and patent protection transformed the industrial structure. The decline of local firms in Mexico was much more accentuated than in Brazil. Mexican firms account for less than 15 percent of sales. In fact, nearly two-thirds of Mexico's pharmo-chemical firms disappeared from 1987 to 1998 as the sector became subject to import competition and patent protection.[49]

The transformation in industrial structure is reflected in the realm of politics. Whereas AMIIF and the principal association representing local firms (CANIFARMA) were arch-enemies during the IP debates of the 1980s and early 1990s, by the early 2000s they were speaking with one voice. Indeed, the organizations were formally fused, with the president of CANIFARMA an invited member of AMIIF's board and CANIFARMA's two-year presidency alternating between Mexican and foreign firms. Nor does Mexico have an equivalent to Brazil's ABIFINA. Instead the pharmo-chemical sector's representative body consists of a small unit within a broader multi-sectoral industrial chamber of manufacturing industries (CANACINTRA), which itself experienced dramatic decay in this period.[50] In short, Mexico's pharmaceutical and pharmo-chemical producers could not articulate positions independent from the transnational sector's because the local sector was neither economically nor politically independent.

A potential source of support for the CCyT's initiative was from the segment of industry that focuses on bioequivalent generics, represented by the National Pharmaceutical Association (ANAFAM). Yet this organization found itself in stark decline in the late 1990s and early 2000s, with a shrinking membership. In fact, ANAFAM did not represent a "national" pharmaceutical sector either, for this segment was undergoing transnationalization of its own, with international generic firms purchasing long-established Mexican firms.[51] ANAFAM's strategizing in response to the CCyT initiative reflects this politically precarious position: ANAFAM advised CANIFARMA that, despite the likelihood that members of the two organizations would benefit from the proposed reform, they should lie low and refrain from showing support to avoid the appearance of con-

---

[49]   CEPAL, "Las Industrias Farmacéutica y Farmoquímica en México y el Distrito Federal," LC/MEXL.400, 1999, 49; María Fabiana Jorge, "Efectos de la Globalización en la Industria Farmacéutica en México," in ANAFAM, *La Industria Farmacéutica Mexicana* (México, D.F.: Editorial Porrúa, 2006).

[50]   Kenneth C. Shadlen, "Orphaned by Democracy: Small Industry in Contemporary Mexico," *Comparative Politics* 35 (October 2002), 43–62.

[51]   The leading generics firms in Mexico are Israeli, British, French, and Canadian.

flicts of interest.[52] Fighting on two fronts – against AMIIF and Similares – and politically unstable on account of its own transnationalization, the bioequivalent generics sector was in no position to lend its support to the CL initiative, nor to oppose the revised pro-AMIIF version.

CANIFARMA and ANAFAM's economic and political weakness meant that AMIIF came to dictate the positions of the "pharmaceutical industry" on matters of policy. The lone alternative voice came from the Similares sector – purveyors of non-bioequivalent medicines (which most countries, including Mexico, are eliminating from the market) and closely tied to the fringe PVEM. AMIIF, thus, was able to do better than prevent Mexico's patent law from being reformed – à la Brazil – to simplify CLs. The transnational sector engineered reforms to Article 77 and the health regulatory system that strengthen the rights of knowledge-owners.

CONCLUSION

In this chapter I have introduced a framework for comparing countries' patent systems, and I have explained Brazil's and Mexico's distinct trajectories of patent policy since the late 1990s. On each of the three dimensions presented above – what knowledge can be owned as property, the rights of owners vs. users of property, and the effective duration of property owners' rights – the Brazilian tendency has been to increase the capacities of knowledge-users while the Mexican tendency has been to reinforce the rights of knowledge-owners.[53]

The chapter brings politics to bear on a topic that has been dominated by analyses of laws and formal international agreements. Comparing Brazil and Mexico, for example, a focus on external legal obligations calls attention to NAFTA, which includes IP provisions that differ from TRIPS (Table 7.2). Yet this is an insufficient explanation: as of the late 1990s the health dimensions of the two countries' patent systems were similar, and the subsequent divergence did not conform to unique obligations that Mexico had under NAFTA.[54] All the reforms implemented in Brazil would be acceptable under NAFTA too.

---

[52] CCyT archives, letter on file with author; interview, ex-President of ANAFAM, 21 August 2007 (Mexico City).

[53] Space prevents discussion of data exclusivity, but the same pattern prevails.

[54] Although neither restrictions on CLs nor the type of linkage introduced in Mexico are required by NAFTA, both sorts of provisions feature in many recent RBTAs.

I attribute the divergence to distinct interests and alliances over IP policy. In Brazil, the nature of government demand for patented and expensive drugs made health-oriented IP reform a high priority, and the political and economic characteristics of the pharmaceutical sector facilitated the creation of a coalition for IP reform. In Mexico, however, a less comprehensive response to the HIV/AIDS epidemic made IP reforms less compelling, and a transformed pharmaceutical sector not only prevented coalition-building for health-oriented IP reform but facilitated a counter-mobilization that strengthened the rights of patent owners. The argument is not that local pharmaceutical sectors drove policy change, but that their economic and political characteristics affected the receptiveness to such policy initiatives. The Brazilian reforms were state-led, but they were feasible because the government could elicit the support of local actors that had retained valuable economic and political assets. Different legacies of industrialization combined with Brazil's comparatively later retiring of industrial policies and introduction of pharmaceutical patents meant that Brazil was less advanced along the pharmaceutical-denationalization curve than Mexico.

To the extent that the argument rests on the actions of Brazilian and Mexican health officials, it is not a matter of institutional structure but power vis-à-vis society. Brazil's IP reforms were spearheaded by Health Minister José Serra, a close ally of the President who would run for the presidency in 2002, and Brazil's health activism certainly needs to be understood in this larger political–electoral context. Yet Mexico's Health Secretary Julio Frenk was a prominent figure within President Fox's cabinet as well. Mexico moved toward universalizing of health coverage under Frenk's tutelage, a measure that reflects the Secretary's authority. Yet state power is situational and relational, depending on what societal allies are available and against what opponents. The nature of Mexico's transnationalized pharmaceutical sector meant that Frenk could not – and therefore would not – attempt to go down the Brazilian path.

To understand the importance of industrial structure, consider a counter-factual: the Mexican government was not motivated to pursue health-oriented IP reform, but suppose that it were so inclined. It is difficult to imagine how the SH could have created the sort of pro-reform coalition that Brazil's MH did, because the early introduction of pharmaceutical patents and the subsequent transformation of the sector deprived it of potential allies. Indeed, on a number of issues related to health provision, Mexico's SH sought the collaboration of local producers only to be stymied by AMIIF's dominance of the sector and the absence of local interlocutors. Industrial transformation and denationalization have political and policy consequences.

My emphasis on industrial structure aims to supplement (not substitute) prevailing emphases on Brazilian civil society's role in pushing government to make AIDS treatment a high priority and introduce health-oriented IP reforms. Whatever inspired the Brazilian government to act, local industry was crucial in not blocking – and, indeed, eventually supporting – the reforms. The difference with Mexico, where domestic industry ended up actively opposing health-oriented IP reforms and effectively supporting a strengthening of patent-holders' rights hand-in-hand with the transnational sector, is stark.

To conclude, it is worth returning to the two areas where IP matters, as the chapter began: technology and industrialization, and health and humanitarianism. My analysis bridges these two realms, for the key variable explaining differences between Brazil and Mexico has been the existence of indigenous pharmaceutical and pharmo-chemical capacities. An earlier generation of scholarship argued that promotion of local pharmaceutical sectors may be important for industrial development, but that because promotional measures may also raise the final prices of medicines, such strategies were less beneficial on the humanitarian axis of development.[55] The argument and findings in this chapter invert this line of reasoning: to use IP to achieve humanitarian goals, countries also need to use IP to achieve industrial goals – they need local pharmaceutical industries that can act as a countervailing political force to the transnational sector. Indeed, whereas previous scholars have depicted pharmaceutical development as good for industrialization but not for humanitarianism, I show how pharmaceutical development may be good for both, because it makes humanitarianism *politically* feasible in a world of strong IP. My analysis suggests that the key to reforming patent systems to increase access to drugs is the presence of economically and politically autonomous, national pharmaceutical industries that are available as coalition partners for those advocating such reforms.

---

[55] Gereffi; Daniel Chudnovski. "The Challenge by Domestic Enterprises to the Transnational Corporations' Domination: A Case Study of the Argentinean Pharmaceutical Industry" *World Development*, 7 (January 1979), 45–58.

8.   Pharmaceutical patent policy in developing countries: learning from the Canadian experience[1]

Jean-Frédéric Morin and Mélanie Bourassa Forcier

It is often believed that Canada is in a delicate position as regards adopting a strongly different patent policy from the United States. It is true that the Canadian economy is still greatly, although decreasingly, dependent on its southern neighbor. The Canadian government intentionally strengthened these economic and industrial ties by signing a bilateral free trade agreement (FTA) with the US in 1987, followed by the North American Free Trade Agreement (NAFTA) in 1992. In 2008, 78 per cent of Canadian exports were destined for the US market and 58 per cent of foreign direct investment stock in Canada was owned by American investors (Canada 2009). Few other countries, including in Latin America, are as dependent on the US economy and therefore vulnerable to US trade pressures regarding their pharmaceutical patent policy.

Nevertheless, Canada did not hesitate to depart from the US model to design a unique patent policy for pharmaceutical products. The history of the Canadian pharmaceutical patent policy, although increasingly imprinted by US influences, reveals a Canadian philosophy for justice in access to health care services. One could even argue that universal access to health services is a symbol of the Canadian identity and a source of national pride, enabling Canadians to distinguish themselves from Americans. In 2004, Tommy Douglas, a politician known as Canada's father of Medicare, was named the Greatest Canadian of all time in a nationwide contest casting over 1.2 million votes. Few other nations, if any, treat health care policy as a key component of their national identity.

This continuous concern to provide access to pharmaceutical products, combined with a heavy dependence on the US economy, contribute to the

---

[1]   This chapter borrows from Bourassa Forcier and Morin (2009).

uniqueness of the Canadian patent policy. On the one hand, Canada has always accepted the patentability of pharmaceutical processes and has accepted the patentability of pharmaceutical products since 1987. On the other hand, Canadian lawmakers demonstrated a strong sense of legal creativity by continually conceiving new limitations and exceptions for these pharmaceutical patents.

The Canadian experience could be of interest to large developing countries with significant generic manufacturing capacities, foreign investment in the pharmaceutical sector, modest private investment in drug discovery, numerous international IP obligations and constant pressure from the US.[2] These countries should find in this study a sign that, even in the presence of international trade agreements, there is room to make medicines more accessible.

Each of the seven following sections presents distinctive features of the Canadian patent policy, following a roughly chronological order.[3] In the next section, we provide an overview of the history of compulsory licenses in Canada.[4] For a length of time, compulsory licenses were considered an essential tool for containing drug expenditures in Canada. In the third section, we describe the uniqueness of the Canadian price regulations scheme and focus on the role of the Patented Medicine Prices Review Board (PMPRB), a federal organization created to control patented drug prices. Following this analysis, we highlight the 'early working' and 'stockpiling' exceptions introduced to limit the negative impact of restricted compulsory licenses on access to medicines. In the fifth section, we draw attention to the Canadian Patented Medicines (Notice of Compliance) Regulations (NOC Regulations). These regulations, sometimes associated

---

[2] In 2008, the pharmaceutical sector employed 28,697 people, accounting for 1.5 per cent of total employment in manufacturing. That year, R&D expenditures in Canada were $1.3 billion. It is worth noting that 74.6 per cent of this sum was for applied research. The Canadian market for drugs is quite small. In 2008, it accounted for 3.8 per cent of total major-market sales, a share comparable to that of Italy (Canada 2008).

[3] For the purpose of the chapter, the 'Canadian patent policy' includes not only direct pharmaceutical patent policies but also the data protection policy in Canada. When adopted, this last policy has been presented as closely linked to patent rights for the pharmaceutical industry.

[4] Compulsory licensing is when a government allows someone else to produce the patented product or utilize the process without the consent of the patent owner. The principal requirement for the issue of a compulsory license is that attempts to obtain a license under reasonable commercial terms must have failed over a reasonable period of time. Specific situations in which compulsory licenses may be issued are set out in the legislation of each patent system and vary between systems.

with an 'automatic injunction tool' available to the pharmaceutical industry, were created in response to the 'early working' and 'stockpiling' exceptions in an effort to keep the balance of the Canadian patent policy. The sixth section of this chapter provides a review of the history of the different patent terms that have existed in Canada. In contrast with its American and European counterparts, Canada has not provided the industry with a patent term restoration to compensate for delays in drugs' approval. However, as explained in the following section, the Canadian government has recently granted the industry an eight-year clinical data protection period. This chapter ends as it started, with a review of the Canadian compulsory licenses policy. While the earlier regime was abandoned to comply with NAFTA requirements, the federal government amended its patent law in 2004, to authorize compulsory licensing for exports to countries with insufficient manufacturing capacities. Although this chapter has a clear legal perspective on the issue of access to medicines, one of its main conclusions is that outcomes depend more on politics, especially international politics, than international law.

A SPECIAL REGIME OF COMPULSORY LICENSES

Past and present Canadian policies regarding compulsory licenses are often put forward as an example to follow. Jerome Reichman and Catherine Hasenzahl from Duke University suggest that Canada's historical use of compulsory licenses could inspire policy makers in developing countries (Reichman and Hasenzahl 2002). However new international rules forced the Canadian policy to undergo radical changes in the early 1990s and those rules would make it difficult for developing countries to draw from the Canadian experience.

During most of the twentieth century, Canada had few international obligations with respect to compulsory licensing. The only restriction prescribed by the Paris Convention (Article 5A) was a minimum period of time before a compulsory license could be applied for. Since no international treaty prohibited discrimination in the field of technology, Canada could develop an aggressive policy for compulsory licenses on pharmaceutical products. The initial conceptualization of this policy dates back to 1923 when the Parliament adopted a bill, modeled on British patent law, to keep the price of medicines reasonably low and encourage the domestic generic drug industry. Under the regime of the Patent Act, any person with an interest in exploiting a patent on foods and medicines was virtually entitled to a 'license of right' for manufacturing purposes. To obtain a compulsory license, it was not necessary to demonstrate any abuses of the patentee's rights, failures to work locally, or anticompetitive practices. The only requirement was to manufacture the chemical ingredients in Canada (Orlhac 1990).

This single requirement was, in fact, a major impediment and contributed to the modest results of the regime. Since the Canadian market was relatively small, the generic producers had neither the capacity nor the willingness to manufacture the chemical ingredients in Canada (McFetridge 1998, 81–82). In consequence, until 1969, only 49 applications were submitted, of which 22 were granted (Canada 1985, 14–15). Some innovative companies even took advantage of their favorable position and prices of patented medicines became significantly higher in Canada than in other industrialized countries. This failure of the Canadian regime became a major public crisis in the 1960s when Canadian provinces were nationalizing their medical services and beginning to pay for pharmaceuticals. A Royal Commission established by the government and a special Parliamentary committee investigated the issue and concluded that the regime needed to be reformed (Canada 1963; Canada 1964; Canada 1966).

This reform occurred in 1969 when the Canadian Parliament amended its Patent Act. According to the amendment, any person could apply for a compulsory license to import medicines or bulk active ingredients produced with patented processes. The Commissioner of Patents was required to grant the license unless he saw 'good reasons' not to, with the result that most license applications filed and not abandoned were granted.

The 1969 reform had immediate consequences. In the two decades following the enactment of these provisions, 1030 applications were filed and 613 licenses were granted (Reichman and Hasenzahl 2002, 38). The generic industry significantly increased its market share and drug prices decreased substantially. For example, according to the report of the Eastman Commission of Inquiry on the Pharmaceutical Industry (Eastman Report), Canadians saved more than 210 million dollars in 1983 as a result of the 1969 amendment (Canada 1985, xvii). More surprisingly, investments in R&D in the pharmaceutical sector did not experience major fluctuations (Canada 1985, 62–63).

Despite these positive results, Canada was under diplomatic pressure to move away from its policy. At the end of the 1980s, while the FTA was under negotiation, the Reagan Administration used the access to the large American market to pressure the Canadian government (French 1987, 341–342; Harrison 2000). It also threatened the Canadian government with trade sanctions by adding the Canadian compulsory licensing regime for pharmaceutical products to the Special 301 Watch List.

Consequently, Bill C-22, amending the Canadian Patent Act, was introduced and adopted in 1987. It extended patent protection to pharmaceutical products themselves, as opposed to merely protecting processes by which these products were made. As a result, a generic producer could not anymore circumvent the patent protection by finding a way to manufacture the medicine by a different process. In addition, Section 46 of Bill C-22 provided that generic producers could not obtain a compulsory license on a pharmaceutical product until a deferral period of exclusivity had elapsed. Patents covering a new process of manufacturing a known drug were excluded from this period of exclusivity. But it was only a modest exclusion since a compulsory license with immediate effect was effective on a process patent if, and only if, the drug itself was not protected by another patent.

On the other hand, Bill C-22 included two discriminatory measures that were heavily condemned by the US government. First, the deferral period varied according to whether the generic drugs would be imported or locally manufactured. It could be reduced from ten to seven years if production occurred in Canada. Second, the amendment excluded patented pharmaceutical products invented or developed in Canada from the application of the compulsory licenses regime. This 'Made-in-Canada' policy was obviously adopted to encourage local investment more than to alleviate criticism from the US and transnational corporations.

Not surprisingly, 'the Canadian reform of 1987 became emblematic of the type of regime the United States Trade Representative would challenge in the course of regional and international trade negotiations' (Reichman and Hasenzahl 2002, 42). Pressure on the Canadian government reached an unprecedented level during the negotiation of NAFTA (Lexchin 2001, 2–3; Robert 2000, 298). The US government especially condemned the less favorable treatment given by the Canadian regime to pharmaceutical products, inventions made outside Canada and imported generics. Accordingly, Canada traded a privileged access to the US market against a reinforced protection of its intellectual property rights, including a provision that made patents 'available and patent rights enjoyable without discrimination as to the field of technology, the territory of the Party where the invention was made and whether products are imported or locally produced' (NAFTA, Art. 1703). This provision forced Canada to abolish its special regime of compulsory licensing for patented medicines, which it did in 1993.

The Agreement on Trade-Related Aspects of Intellectual Property Rights (TRIPs) was adopted in April 1994, 16 months after NAFTA. This new multilateral agreement duplicated NAFTA's rule on non-discrimination with the consequence that, legally speaking, no other WTO member could duplicate Canada's former regime of compulsory licenses. In reality however compliance with the non-discrimination rule depends more on WTO politics than on WTO law. Indeed, several countries do not fully comply with a rigid interpretation of the non-discrimination rule. One could even argue that the US itself maintains several discriminatory measures, advantaging for example Patent Cooperation Treaty (PCT) applications written in English, oral disclosure made in US territory, or undisclosed invention made in the US (see Section 102(a)(e) and (g) of the United States Code title 35). But few of the discriminatory measures found in several WTO member states are challenged through the dispute settlement body. Formal complaints must be raised by a government rather than a private entity and therefore are subject to strategic considerations and political transactions. A good illustration is the Brazilian measure favoring compulsory licenses on imported rather than locally produced pharmaceutical drugs (Brazil Law no. 9279, Art. 68). When the US argued that this measure was contrary to the WTO rule of non-discrimination, the Brazilian government immediately responded that the US law was equally discriminatory (Brazil 2001a). Soon after, the American and the Brazilian delegations at the WTO announced that they had reached a mutual understanding and the dispute was never submitted to a WTO panel (Brazil 2001b). This is only one illustration that domestic patent law depends greatly on international politics, arguably more than on international law. But as the next section establishes, foreign political pressures, even coming from powerful actors, do not fatally prevail over domestic priorities: Canada was able to establish and maintain drug price regulations ensuring lower prices than in the US.

THE UNIQUENESS OF THE CANADIAN DRUG PRICE REGULATIONS

What particularly distinguishes the drug price control scheme in Canada from those of other countries is the federal government's direct price control regulation. This regulation is supplementary to provincial indirect price regulations and exclusive to patented drugs (Paris and Docteur 2006).

Theoretically, drug price regulations in Canada are part of the provincial constitutional jurisdiction. Provincial drug price regulations only apply for public drug coverage. Although there are no incentives to do so, private insurers may thus decide not to follow the different provincial pricing schemes. Each province has a distinct drug coverage policy. Some provinces, such as Quebec, offer comprehensive public drug coverage while others only offer catastrophic drug insurance (Paris and Docteur 2006). Each province determines the criteria for reimbursing (or not) a new drug under the public coverage. For example, British Columbia has created a reference pricing scheme. In this scheme, drugs with the same therapeutic effects are clustered into different groups. A drug will be fully reimbursed by the province if its price is equal to, or below, the reference price. This reference price is, in British Columbia, that of the most cost-effective drug within each group (a reference price could also be an average price of the lowest price for a drug within a group). Other provinces, such as Ontario or Quebec, have decided not to follow the British Columbia model and have preferred to limit their policy to the reimbursement of generic drugs, once marketed (Paris and Docteur 2006: 20–21). However in order to provide the brand-name industry with an incentive to invest in R&D, Quebec has implemented a '15-year rule'. This rule allows the reimbursement of a brand-name drug for 15 years after it is marketed in Quebec even if a generic drug is already available on the market. This policy is highly criticized by the generic industry and it is not clear whether it effectively helps the province to attract R&D investments (Bahan et al. 2005). Finally, most provinces use positive drug reimbursement lists and have established a 'lowest price' policy. According to this policy, a province will not reimburse a drug if its price is not the lowest among all Canadian provinces. Considering the foregoing, the provincial drug price control schemes are generally qualified as 'indirect' since they do not directly impose a price on drugs but provide an incentive to the industry to provide its products at a price that will allow them to be reimbursed by the different provincial insurance plans.

As previously mentioned, in Canada, in addition to being regulated at the provincial level, patented drug prices are controlled by a federal, independent and quasi-judicial board, the PMPRB. This board was created by the 1987 amendments to the Patent Act, concomitantly to the introduction of limited rights to compulsory licenses. Its creation was a clear attempt to limit the negative impact that restrictive compulsory licenses would have had on drug prices, that is, by limiting generic entry (Paris and Docteur 2006, 12).

The PMPRB's mandate is to protect Canadian consumers from excessive prices for patented drugs prior to or after their marketing. When determining whether a drug is being sold or has been sold at an excessive price, the PMPRB takes different factors into consideration. Only off-factory prices are considered (as opposed to retail prices). In the presence of a breakthrough drug, particular attention is given to the median price for this drug in seven comparable countries: France, Germany, Italy, Sweden, Switzerland, the UK and the US. If the drug represents just a modest improvement on already existing drugs, the board will first compare its price with one of the drugs in the same therapeutic class. This price comparison system is, in fact, very similar to those used in other countries, such as in France, Spain or Greece, when determining what brand-name drug (patented or not, in this case) can be listed in drug formularies. According to the Patent Act (sections 79ss), patented drug prices cannot, in any case, exceed changes in the Consumer Price Index.

In contrast with some other countries, where a drug is not reimbursed if its price exceeds a ceiling price, a Canadian patented drug cannot be marketed if its price is not first approved by the PMPRB. If, once marketed, a drug price becomes excessive in the opinion of the PMPRB, the board may either direct the patentee to reduce the price of the drug or any of its marketed drugs in Canada, or order the patentee to compensate the government for the excess in profits having resulted from the sale of the high-priced drug.

It is generally acknowledged that the creation of the PMPRB has been effective in controlling and keeping the price of Canadian patented drugs low. In 1987, before the board was created, the price of patented drugs was 23 per cent higher than the international median price. After 1987, patented drug prices were reduced considerably and have become, on average, below the international median price (Paris and Docteur 2006: 15). According to the PMPRB's 2008 Annual Report however, Canadian prices for patented drugs that year were below those of the US but relatively close to those of the UK, Germany, Sweden and Switzerland.

Although the PMPRB's creation in 1987 was relatively 'accepted' by the pharmaceutical industry, this industry now imposes a constant pressure on the Canadian government to eliminate the review board. This pressure has particularly emerged owing to US consumers' growing interest in cheap Canadian drugs, which can be up to 40 per cent less expensive than in the US. In fact, some Canadian provinces, particularly Manitoba, are now recognized for the success of internet pharmacies whose main business is cross-border trade of drugs between Canada and the US (Skinner 2006, 9). Even though the pharmaceutical industry has deployed lobbyists in Canada to urge the government to free up drug prices, the government keeps sending the signal that the PMPRB will survive.

Considering the pharmaceutical industry's general dissatisfaction with restrictive marketing rights, it has occasionally been pointed out that, although effective in controlling drug prices, the PMPRB might have chilled R&D investments in Canada. This argument lacks empirical data owing to the difficulty in isolating the specific impact of the 1987 amendments to the Patent Act which introduced at the same time both the PMPRB and limited compulsory licenses. This last amendment was precisely aimed at promoting R&D in Canada. Considering the dichotomist effects these amendments might have had on R&D, we are confronted with uncertainty as to the impact one or the other has had on R&D. From the PMPRB's 2008 Annual Report, we note that after 1987, R&D investments have increased (although they seem to be now decreasing). We may wonder however if these investments would have been higher without the existence of the PMPRB. In any case, considering the fact that most developing countries already have a low investment rate in R&D from the brand-name industry, it might be pertinent for them to consider the benefits attached to the implementation of a price control scheme if their goal is to circumvent the negative impact of the TRIPs on drug prices and access. The Canadian experience certainly demonstrates that this goal is realistic and viable.

EXCEPTIONS TO RIGHTS CONFERRED

When the special regime for compulsory licenses on medicines was completely abolished in 1993 to comply with the NAFTA and TRIPs requirements, the Canadian government sought to maintain the equilibrium of its patent system and ensure access to low-cost drugs. The need to find another policy tool to address cost control in the health care system was especially crucial as the expenditures on therapeutic drugs had dramatically risen between 1975 and 1993 (Canada 1996). With this objective in mind, the Canadian Parliament introduced two new exceptions to rights conferred by a patent.

The first exception authorized the production, use and sale of a patented invention for the purpose of seeking regulatory approval in Canada or any other country (sometimes referred to as the 'early working' exception). This exception is similar to what is known in the US as the 'Bolar' exception, introduced in 1984 by the Hatch-Waxman Act. Since the regulatory approval process needed to demonstrate that a generic drug is equivalent to the brand-name drug takes about two or three years, this measure could significantly accelerate the market entry of generic drugs. The second exception, called the 'stockpiling' exception, was a unique Canadian measure, having had no equivalent in European or American law. It allowed generic producers who used the regulatory approval exception to manufacture and store, during the last six months of the patent term, the drugs intended for sale. With these exceptions, generic producers were able to market and sell their products the day after the patent expired.

The 'early working' and 'stockpiling' exceptions were, predictably, heavily criticized by innovative pharmaceutical companies (United States 2001). Nevertheless, they did not succeed in convincing the US government to bring the matter under the WTO dispute settlement mechanism.

Drug pricing was a sensitive issue in American politics and the government did not want to put its own 'Bolar exception' at risk (Matthews 2002, 101). Therefore, European and US companies, through their European branches, turned to the European Commission, which requested the establishment of a WTO panel in 1998.

Canada acknowledged that its exceptions conflicted with the patent rights granted in accordance with Article 28 of TRIPs, but it claimed that they were exceptions authorized by Article 30 of the Agreement. Consequently, the main task of the panel was to determine if the two exceptions fulfilled the triple test of Article 30. Inspired by Article 9(2) of the Berne Convention, this provision authorizes exceptions to rights conferred as long as they are limited, do not unreasonably conflict with the normal exploitation of the patent and do not unreasonably prejudice the legitimate interests of the patent owner.

In its report issued in March 2000, the panel concluded that the exception for regulatory approval could be covered by Article 30. For greater clarity, the US government provided in its most recent free trade agreements that the 'Bolar exception' is a legitimate but voluntary exception to patent law (Morin 2007: 433). Despite the panel decision and the US clarification, several developing countries do not provide an exception to patent rights to support an application for marketing approval of a pharmaceutical product (Thorpe 2002).

The panel found however that the 'stockpiling' exception did not fulfill the triple test. It failed to be limited, as evidenced by the first requirement for authorized exceptions: 'With no limitations at all upon the quantity of production, the "stockpiling" exception removes that protection [on making and using] entirely during the last six months of the patent term, without regard to what other, subsequent, consequences it might have' (Canada – Patent Protection of Pharmaceutical Products 2000, para 7.34). The panel dismissed Canada's argument that the curtailment was limited because it preserved the exclusive right to sell, it could only be used by those having utilized the regulatory approval exception and it only applied for six months. It agreed with the European Community that 'six months was a commercially significant period of time, especially since there were no limits at all on the volume of production allowed, or the market destination of such production' (para 7.37).

Canada did not refer the dispute to the Appellate Body, complied with the panel report and amended its Patent Act. Canada probably felt that it had little political support and legitimacy to bring the 'stockpiling' exception to the Appellate Body since, in contrast with the situation regarding the 'Bolar exception', it was one of the few developed countries to provide such a generous exception. However, since the 'stockpiling' exception was introduced to compensate for the abandonment of its compulsory licensing regime for drugs, with its abrogation, Canada once again faced the prospect of an unbalanced patent system. This was even more the case if one considers the parallel maintenance of the NOC Regulations, initially adopted to limit the effect of the 'early working' and 'stockpiling' exceptions.

NOTICE OF COMPLIANCE (NOC) REGULATIONS

The NOC Regulations were adopted in 1993 in order to limit the likelihood of patent infringements by generic companies facilitated by the newly introduced 'early working' and 'stockpiling' exceptions. These regulations are essentially based on the US linkage regulations model. They are, from time to time, referred to as 'linkage regulations' because they require the Minister of Health (Minister) to take into consideration the registered patents before issuing a notice of compliance (NOC) to a generic drug company. These regulations exclusively apply when this company files an abbreviated new drug submission (ANDS).[5] By filing an ANDS a generic drug company can only demonstrate the bioequivalence of its product with the brand-name drug to prove its safety and efficacy. The company is thus exempted from undertaking the complete clinical trial process normally required to prove the safety and efficacy of a new drug.

According to the NOC Regulations, when a brand-name company submits a NOC application, it can join a list of patents to be registered on a patent register administered by the Minister. When a generic company files its ANDS it must inform the Minister of the existing registered patents, if any, pertaining to the brand-name drug to be copied. When the brand-name drug is still under patent, the generic company must either state that it is willing to wait until the patent expires before a NOC is issued for the generic drug or file a notice of allegation alleging that the registered patents have expired, are invalid or will not be infringed by the NOC's delivery to the generic company.

Once the brand-name drug company is notified, it can request the Tribunal to issue an order prohibiting the Minister from delivering a NOC until after the expiration of the registered patents. The simple deposit of this request by the brand-name company triggers a 24-month stay before

---

[5] This prohibition does not apply if the generic company has filed a complete NDS. In such case, the Minister would thus not be tied up by the existence of patents applying to the brand-name product (*Bristol-Myers Squibb Co. v. Canada*, 2005).

the NOC can be issued to the generic drug company except if, during that time, the patent expires or the Tribunal issues its order. Because the Tribunal is only competent to assess the validity of the patent registration, and not the validity of the patent *per se* (*Merck Frosst Canada Inc v. Canada*, 1994), it is possible, following this order, that a generic company market its product and infringe an existing and valid patent according to the Patent Act. *Vice versa*, an order from the Tribunal may restrain a generic company from marketing its product, the patent being well registered but, in fact, invalid according to the Patent Act criteria for patentability. The likelihood of such contradictory judgments provides high incentives for pharmaceutical companies to occupy the judicial system in Canada (*Janssen-Ortho inc. v. Novopharm*, 2006).

Because the brand-name company's request to prevent the Minister from issuing a NOC to the generic company triggers a 24-month stay, its effect can be compared to that of an automatic interlocutory injunction. This makes the Canadian patent policy particularly interesting for the brand-name companies, considering the fact that interlocutory injunctions are rarely granted to pharmaceutical companies in Canada. Effectively, in contrast to European courts, Canadian courts do not generally consider a loss of profit to be a criterion for granting an interlocutory injunction (*American Cyanamid v. Ethicon*, 1975). Nevertheless, during this suspension period, the Minister will examine the generic company's ANDS. This factor is crucial because it allows the generic company to obtain a NOC as soon as the 24 months have elapsed.

Since their creation, the regulations have been highly criticized owing to the existence of significant pitfalls leading to *evergreening* practices by brand-name drug companies: rapidly, as also happened in the US, some pharmaceutical companies developed different strategies for registering additional patents for marketed drugs or abused the opposition process to prevent generic companies from obtaining a NOC approval.[6] Also, due to the lack of clarity in their writing, the NOC Regulations have triggered different judicial interpretations that did not always fit with their original purpose. Considering the foregoing, in October 2006, the government introduced important clarifications to the regulations.

In particular, it is now clear that to be listed in the patent registry, the patent list submitted by the patentee must be linked to the drug subject

---

[6] These practices artificially extended their patent protection (*evergreening* practices). In 2002, the Commission on the Future of Health Care in Canada (Canada 2002) reported persistent concerns about still existing *evergreening* practices in the pharmaceutical industry.

to the NOC application. Previously, it was unclear whether a company could submit a new list of patents when it filed a supplementary drug application for cosmetic changes to the drug, name change, or changes in manufacturing facilities (*Ferring Inc. v. Canada*, 2003). Some companies benefited from this lack of clarity to continually file new patents and thus prevent generic drug companies from obtaining a NOC (*Ferring Inc. v. Canada*, 2003; *Hoffmann-La Roche Ltd v. Canada*, 2005). The new amendments also limit the type of patents that can be included in the registry. Since 2006, the patent must relate to: (1) a claim for the approved medicinal ingredient, (2) a claim for the approved formulation containing that medicinal ingredient, (3) a claim for the approved dosage form, or (4) a claim for an approved use of the medicinal ingredient. The delay for registering new patents in the registry is also limited to 30 days after the patent is issued if the patent application was submitted to the patent office before the NOC application. This time limit was introduced in order to prevent brand-name companies, who had forgotten to register the patents attached to their drug at the time they had filed their NOC, from adding these patents to the registry. Finally, the amendments provide that the register will be 'frozen' from the time a generic drug company files a NOC application. Consequently, this modification impedes brand-name companies from submitting new patents after the generic company's NOC application to force it to constantly send new notices of allegation.

By clarifying the NOC Regulations, it is the Canadian government's hope that they will finally reach their objective of creating a balance between the promotion of R&D in the pharmaceutical industry, through strong IP protection, and access to generic and affordable drugs. Only the future can tell whether or not this will occur. For now, it can be noted that discrepancies still exist within the regulations. In particular, nowhere in the regulations is the Minister granted the power to withdraw a patent from the registry if it is deemed invalid by a court. Consequently, this forces generic companies to file a notice of allegation for a drug although the patent registered for it has previously been judged to be invalid.

Until recently, linkage regulations only existed in the US and in Canada. This situation has changed however over the last few years, particularly since some other countries, such as Morocco, Jordan and Chile, have entered into bilateral agreements with the US.[7] Under the terms of these agreements, these countries must make sure that a generic drug is

---

[7]   However, we underline that some countries, such as Mexico in 2003, may have implemented linkage regulations without having any obligations to conform with bilateral, regional or international agreements.

not marketed if a patent still exists on the brand-name drug to be copied (Sanjuan 2006). This requirement is certainly open to modulations. Before nationally modeling and implementing linkage regulations, or even before contemplating their introduction, developing countries should certainly consider the *evergreening* practices that have occurred both in Canada and in the US following their implementation. Also, a critical assessment of the positive impact of the last amendments adopted in Canada to reduce such practices would certainly be appropriate.

TERM OF PROTECTION

Members of the Paris Union are free to determine the term of protection. In the 1980s, the duration varied extensively from one country to another, and sometimes between fields of technology, ranging from three to 20 years and calculated either from the filing date of the application or the date of the grant. Canada and its southern neighbor had offered a protection of 17 years, calculated from the grant of the patent in any field of technology. But the Canadian legislation was amended twice to modify this term of protection.

The first and most important amendment entered into force in 1989. It introduced a term of protection of 20 years from the filing date for patents filed after 1 October 1989. In other words, these 'New Act patents' could benefit from a longer effective term of protection if the period between the filing and the granting was less than three years. For 'Old Act patents', filed before 1 October, the term remained unchanged.

Unlike most legislative amendments to the Canadian Patent Act, this change in term of protection was not externally dictated. Even NAFTA, signed in 1992, left some flexibility to its signatories by providing that the term of protection should be 'at least 20 years from the date of filing or 17 years from the date of grant' (section 1709(12)). The US took advantage of this flexibility and adopted the 20-year standard only in 1995, to comply with the TRIPs. In fact, the 1989 change in the term of protection was adopted, together with the first-to-file principle, early publication of applications and deferred examination, to simplify administrative procedures and increase the predictability of the patent system.

The Canadian term of protection came under the international spotlight in 1999 when the US filed a complaint with the WTO dispute settlement mechanism. The US claimed that the term of protection available for the 'Old Act patent' did not comply with Article 33 of the TRIPs, which requires that 'the term of protection available shall not end before the expiration of a period of twenty years counted from the filing date'. It argued that Canada should protect patents filed before 1 October 1989 for a duration of 20 years from the filing date or 17 years from the grant date, whichever is longer. It estimated that over 66,000 'Old Act patents', including 33,000 from US applicants, would expire sooner than would be the case if Canada had provided a term of 20 years from filing (*Canada – Term of Patent Protection*, Panel Report 2000, para 6.60). Despite these impressive numbers, the real issue in this dispute was related to some 30 commercially significant drugs (Canada 2001).

Canada's main argument was that an 'effective' term of protection of 17 years is equivalent to a nominal term of 20 years and, therefore, consistent in substance with Article 33. Canada made this assertion based on the fact that the administrative procedures between the filing date and the issuance date could exceed three years, making a term of 20 years 'available' to patent holders. The Panel and Appellate Body dismissed Canada's arguments, stating that the notion of an 'effective' term of protection was not supported by Article 33 and that making a term of protection 'available' is a matter of legal right and certainty (*Canada – Term of Patent Protection*, Appellate Body Report 2000, paras 80–101). They concluded that the term of protection for 'Old Act patents' was inconsistent with Article 33 of the TRIPs. In 2001, Canada complied with the Appellate Body's recommendations and amended its Patent Act to entitle 'Old Act patents' to the longer term of 17 years from the date of the grant or 20 years from the date of filing.

Since the time period between the filing date and the grant date is sometimes longer than three years, the effective patent term could be shorter than it would have been prior to the 1989 amendment (Canada 2001, 16). To avoid this problem, the US adopted the Patent Term Guarantee Act in 1999 and extended the term of protection in the event that issuance was delayed due to a secrecy order, interference, or successful appellate review. This measure has the effect of ensuring an effective term of 17 years from the granting of the application, even though the US has formally converted to a standard term of 20 years from the application's filing.

The case *Canada – Term of Patent Protection* (2000) made it clear however that WTO members do not have an obligation to ensure an effective term of protection and therefore do not have to offer an extension in case of administrative delay. Developing countries are free to not adjust the term of a patent to compensate for delay that could occur in granting the patent or the drug's marketing approval. In that respect, the Canadian legislation could serve as a reassurance to developing countries that at least some OECD countries consider that patent term extensions are neither a legal obligation under TRIPs nor a wise policy for ensuring access to patented medicines. As the next section shows, Canada is less a model to follow in respect of data protection.

DATA PROTECTION

Data protection in Canada was intended to implement Canada's NAFTA (sec. 1711(5)(6)) and TRIPs (Art. 39(3)) obligations, which require signatories to provide protection against the unfair commercial use of undisclosed tests or other data submitted by a pharmaceutical company in order to obtain a new drug submission (NDS) approval. The main objective of this measure is to protect the investments made by a brand-name company by ensuring a minimal period of market exclusivity. This market exclusivity must however be distinguished from the one resulting from patent rights. The result of such protection is to prevent generic drug companies from obtaining an ANDS approval until the period of protection expires. The underlying reasoning is that, to prove the bioequivalence of its product with the brand-name one, a generic company must refer to the data submitted by the brand-name company in its NDS (these data demonstrate the safety and efficacy of the new drug). Therefore, until the data protection expires, this comparison is impossible.

Before 2006, Canada granted a five-year data protection period to brand-name companies from the date of their first NOC. This protection was however considered ineffective as a result of the Federal Court's interpretation of the protection given in *Bayer Inc. v. Canada (Attorney General)*, 1998. Precisely, it was held by this court that the protection was not triggered if the generic drug company could demonstrate the bioequivalence of its product without requiring the Minister to consult the data submitted by the brand-name company. Since this situation was common, the protection was seldom applied.

At the end of 2006, following pressures from the pharmaceutical industry and allegations that Canada was not following its international obligations (Pharmaceutical Research and Manufacturers of America 2003) the government modified its regulations and introduced an eight-year data protection period with the possibility for generic companies to file an ANDS two years before the expiration of the protection. In the case of pediatric drugs, the protection is extended by six months. The possibility for a generic drug company to file an ANDS two years before the protection ends reflects the Canadian government's effort to facilitate generic entry. During these two years, it is possible for the Minister to review the ANDS application, thus making possible the marketing of the generic drug immediately after the data protection expires.

The Canadian data protection model is somewhat peculiar. It is difficult to trace the impetus for the choice to grant an eight-year data protection period, when NAFTA requires a minimum of five years (and it is still unclear whether the previously existing five-year data protection period in

Canada, as applied by the *Bayer* decision, effectively contradicted NAFTA). Actually, the Canadian data protection period seems to result from somewhat of an average of the data protection periods existing in the US and in European countries. The former offers a five-year data protection period to its industry, while the latter offer ten years. It would have been interesting to compare cost–benefit analyses demonstrating the positive impact of an eight-year data protection period, versus five years, on R&D investments in Canada. If these analyses exist, the government has not published them.

Fortunately, in Canada the negative impact of data protection in term of access to medicines is still fairly limited, but nonetheless present (Pugatch 2006, 120). In practice, the protection grants a period of market exclusivity for non-patented drugs or for drugs for which the patent expires before the end of the eight-year data protection. In the former case, data protection might however eventually represent a problem due to the emergence of out-of-patent biologic drugs, for which companies now increasingly rely on trade secrets.

It must be stressed that no minimum protection time for clinical data is required by the TRIPs. The TRIPs requirement for data protection is actually particularly vaguely defined. At the risk of being included on the 301 Watchlist and until this requirement is defined by the WTO Dispute Settlement Body, developing countries should take advantage of the TRIPs flexibility (ICTSD 2005). The original data protection that existed in Canada before the 2006 amendments could actually represent a source of inspiration for them.

CANADA'S ACCESS TO MEDICINES REGIME

This chapter begins and ends with an analysis of two different Canadian regimes for compulsory licensing in the pharmaceutical sector. As mentioned earlier, the first regime was intended to improve access to medicines for Canadians and was abolished in 1993 in order to comply with Canada's international obligations. In contrast, the second regime, described in this section, is intended to improve access in developing countries and was established to implement a WTO decision.

The WTO decision that Canada implemented was adopted on 30 August 2003, on the eve of the Cancun Ministerial Conference. Although the TRIPs allows WTO members to issue compulsory licenses, countries with insufficient manufacturing capacities in the pharmaceutical sector cannot make effective use of them. WTO members also face difficulties importing pharmaceutical products manufactured under compulsory licenses because Article 31(f) of TRIPs provides that they must be 'authorized predominantly for the supply of the domestic market of the Member authorizing such use'. The 30 August 2003 decision 'waived', under specific conditions, this restriction on exports to countries that cannot manufacture the pharmaceuticals themselves.

On 26 September 2003, the Canadian government was the first WTO member to announce its intention to implement the 2003 WTO decision. This announcement was partly the result of pressure from the Canadian Generic Pharmaceutical Association and Canadian activists, including Stephen Lewis, the UN Special ambassador for HIV/AIDs. It was above all the result of a few individual leaders inside the Jean Chrétien government which, in the last months of its ten-year reign, wanted to leave a positive legacy, including assistance for African countries. The government promptly drafted a bill, sought advice from the industry and selected NGOs and made sure that the Bill C-9, oddly named the Jean Chrétien Pledge to Africa, would be enacted prior to the 2004 general elections.

The Canadian government had little flexibility in the drafting of its bill since it was bound by the numerous conditions already negotiated in the 2003 WTO decision. Nevertheless, the Canadian legislation resolved some ambiguities and included additional restrictions (Elliott 2006; Rimmer 2005). With the objective of improving access to medicines in developing countries, the royalty rate is linked to the ranking of the importing country on the UNDP Development Index; the requisite negotiations over a possible voluntary license between the generic producer and the patent holder are limited to 30 days; the regime is open to least-developed countries and other developing countries that are not WTO members; and NGOs authorized by the government of the importing country are considered eligible purchasers. On the other hand, to maintain the integrity of the country's patent system, pharmaceutical products that can be manufactured and exported under this regime are restricted to a specific list; the term of compulsory licenses is limited by a two-year cap with the possibility of one easily obtained renewal; and patent holders may apply for a court order terminating a compulsory license or ordering a higher royalty on the grounds that a generic company's contract with a purchaser is commercial in nature. Another controversial provision of the Canadian legislation is the requirement that a drug manufactured solely for export undergo a Canadian regulatory approval process while ignoring the WHO approval process that is presumably more appropriate for drugs needed in developing countries. These features are the most significant ones that do not typically appear in legislations of other WTO members which implemented the 30 August 2003 decision, including Norway, India, Korea, China and the European Union.

Canada is not only the first country to have announced its intention to implement the 30 August 2003 decision, but also the first to effectively use its legislation. On 20 September 2007, the Federal Commissioner of Patents granted a compulsory license to Apotex to produce and export 260,000 packs of TriAvir, an HIV/AIDS combination therapy, to Rwanda. To date, no other WTO member has issued a compulsory license for export. The WTO has not even received any other notification from an exporting or importing country of their intention to use the so-called 'paragraph 6 system'.

The fact that Canada's Access to Medicines Regime was used only once in five years raised some criticisms, especially from the NGO community. Among the explanations frequently mentioned for its ineffectiveness are the procedural burdens that dissuade generic producers, the lack of capacity and information in potential importing countries and the competition from other exporting countries, including India and China. These issues and potential amendments are currently under discussion by the Canadian Parliament. Two private bills were introduced in 2009 to facilitate the issuing of compulsory licenses by simplifying the conditions and requirements. Although Canada's Access to Medicines Regime is one of the most recent innovations of the Canadian patent system, it may well be the target of the next amendment to the Patent Act.

CONCLUSIONS

Canadian patent policy history is rich with examples demonstrating the Canadian government's efforts in promoting the equilibrium between R&D investments and consumers' access to medicines. Limits to compulsory license rights, NOC Regulations and data protection are all different components of Canadian patent policy aimed at promoting the interests of the pharmaceutical industry with, as justification, positive effects on R&D investments. On the other hand, other components of the policy – such as the PMPRB, the Canadian refusal to adopt a patent term restoration, the possibility for a generic company to file an ANDS two years before the end of the data protection, and the 'early working' exception – all exist to promote access to medicines in Canada.

The fact that R&D in Canada is increasingly focused on clinical trials, combined with the relatively small size of the Canadian market (Paris and Docteur 2006), leaves us questioning whether the patent policy could ever, in practice, represent an effective tool for promoting R&D. However, it certainly contributed to promoting access to pharmaceutical drugs. Canadian prices for patented medicines consistently decreased from 1987 to 1994, when prices stabilized up to 10 per cent below the median in seven comparative countries (Paris and Docteur 2006, 15). Simultaneously, the generic industry flourished and increased the export of its products to the US (Paris and Docteur 2006, 69).

Given the priorities of Canadian society for access to pharmaceutical products, the modest amount of investment in pharmaceutical R&D, and the growing domestic industry of generic drugs, it appears that Canada shares significant characteristics with large developing countries. Like most of their governments, the Canadian government had a defensive approach at the WTO and strengthened its patent system mainly to comply with international trade treaties. Given these similarities, it is surprising that Canada does not actively cooperate with Brazil, Argentina, India and other countries to influence the global patent regime.

Canada's cooperation with developing countries has focused on the unilateral design of a mechanism for the export of generic drugs under compulsory license. The Canadian government should consider however exporting its expertise in health and patent policy in addition to exporting generic drugs. Canada has developed a unique legal environment for pharmaceutical products that reflects its social values, economic priorities and industrial ambitions. Unfortunately, several developing countries lack the necessary expertise to exercise the same legal and policy creativity. They simply transplant into their domestic legal systems strategies developed for the most advanced economies, missing opportunities to increase their access to cheap drugs of good quality. Canada can and should provide advice on the regulatory environment necessary to ensure quality production of drugs, price control and access to generics.

REFERENCES

Case Law

American Cyanamid v. Ethicon, [1975] A.C. 396 (H.L.).
Bayer Inc. v. Canada (Attorney General) (1998), 84 C.P.R. (3d) 129, [1999] 1 F.C. 553 (F.C.T.D.).
Bristol-Myers Squibb Co. v. Canada (Attorney General), [2005] 1 S.C.R. 533, 2005 SCC 26.
Canada – Patent Protection of Pharmaceutical Products (Complaint by the European Communities and their Member States) (2000), WTO Doc. WT/DS114/R (Panel Report).
Canada – Term of Patent Protection (2000), WTO Doc. WT/DS170/R (Panel Report).
Canada – Term of Patent Protection (2000), WTO Doc. WT/DS170/AB/R (Appellate Body Report).

Ferring Inc. v. *Canada (Attorney General)* (2003), 26 C.P.R. (4th) 155, 2003 FCA 274.
Hoffmann-La Roche Ltd. v. *Canada (Minister of Health)* (2005), 40 C.P.R. (4th) 108, 2005 FCA 140.
Janssen-Ortho inc. v. *Novopharm Ltd.* (2006), 57 C.P.R. (4th) 6, 2006 FC 1234.
Merck Frosst Canada Inc. v. *Canada (Minister of National Health and Welfare)* (1994), 55 C.P.R. (3d) 302 (F.C.A.).

Legislation and Regulations

Brazil, Law no. 9279 Diario Oficial, 15 May 1996.
Canada, Patent Term Guarantee Act of 1999, Pub. L. No. 106-113, § 4401-4405, 113 Stat. 1501.
Canada, Regulations Amending the Patented Medicines (Notice of Compliance) Regulations, Canada Gazette 2006.I.1611.
Canada, Act to Amend the Patent Act, the Trade Marks Act and the Food and Drug Act, S.C. 1968–69.
Canada, An Act to Amend the Patent Act and to Provide for Certain Matters in Relation Thereto, S.C. 1987.
Canada, Patented Medicines (Notice of Compliance) Regulations (NOC Regulations) SOR 93/133.
Canada, Regulations Amending the Patented Medicines (Notice of Compliance) Regulations, Canada Gazette 1998.II.1051.
European Community, Council Regulation (EEC) No. 1768/92 of 18 June 1992 concerning the creation of a supplementary protection certificate for medicinal products, [1992] O.J. L. 182/1.
United States of America, Drug Price Competition and Patent Term Restoration Act of 1984, Pub. L.No. 98-417, 98 Stat. 1585 (codified as amended 21 U.S.C. §355 (1994)).

International Treaties

Agreement on Trade-Related Aspects of Intellectual Property Rights, Annex 1C of the Marrakesh Agreement establishing the World Trade Organization, 15 April 1994.
Berne Convention for the Protection of Literary and Artistic Works, 9 September 1886.
Free Trade Agreement between the Government of Canada and the Government of the United States of America, 2 January 1988.
North American Free Trade Agreement Between the Government of Canada, the Government of Mexico and the Government of the United States, 17 December 1992.
Paris Convention for the Protection of Industrial Property, 20 March 1883.

Studies, Books and Articles

Bahan, David et al. (2005), *Les impacts économiques de la 'règle des 15 ans' appliquée au remboursement des médicaments innovateurs au Québec*, Québec: Direction des communications du ministère des Finances.

Bourassa Forcier, Mélanie and Jean-Frédéric Morin (2009), 'Canadian Pharmaceutical Patent Policy: International Constraints and Domestic Priorities' in Ysolde Gendreau (ed.), *An Emerging Intellectual Property Paradigm: Perspectives from Canada*, Cheltenham, UK and Northampton, MA, USA: Edward Elgar, pp. 81–104.

Brazil (2001a), Measures Affecting Patent Protection – Request for the Establishment of a Panel by the United States. United States – US Patents Code – Request for Consultations by Brazil, WTO Doc WT/DS224.

Brazil (2001b), Measures Affecting Patent Protection – Notification of Mutually Agreed Solution, WTO Doc. WT/DS199/4.

Canada (1963), Department of Justice, Restrictive Trade and Practices Commission, *Report Concerning the Manufacture, Distribution and Sale of Drugs*, Ottawa: Queen's Printer.

Canada (1964), Royal Commission on Health Services, *Report of the Royal Commission on Health Services*, Ottawa, Queen's Printer.

Canada (1966), House of Commons, Special Committee on Drug Costs and Prices, *Report of the Standing Committee on Drug Costs and Prices*, Ottawa: Queen's Printer.

Canada (1985), Minister of Supply and Services, Commission of Inquiry on the Pharmaceutical Industry, *The Report of the Commission of Inquiry on the Pharmaceutical Industry*, Ottawa: Queen's Printer.

Canada (1996), Health Canada, Policy and Consultation Branch, *National Health Expenditures in Canada, 1975–1994*, Ottawa: Supply and Services Canada.

Canada (2001), 'Government Tables Amendments to Bring Patent Act Into Conformity with WTO Agreement', available at http://www.ic.gc.ca/cmb/welcomeic.nsf/ffc979db07de58e6852564e400603639/85256779007b82f4852569f900 6a56c7!OpenDocument (accessed 1 October 2009).

Canada (2002), Commission on the Future of Health Care in Canada, 'Building on Values – The Future of Health Care in Canada', available at http://www.hc-sc. gc.ca/english/care/romanow/index1.html (accessed 1 October 2009).

Canada (2008), Patented Medicine Prices Review Board, *Annual Report*, Ottawa: Patented Medicine Prices Review Board.

Canada (2009), 'Canada's State of Trade', available at http://www.international. gc.ca/economist-oconomiste/assets/pdfs/DFAIT_SoT-2009_en.pdf (accessed 1 October 2009).

Elliott, Richard (2006), 'Pledges and Pitfalls: Canada's Legislation on Compulsory Licensing of Pharmaceuticals for Export', *International Journal of Intellectual Property Management* 1(1), 94–112.

French, David J. (1987), 'Patent Law Reform in Canada', *Canadian Intellectual Property Review* 4(2), 337–342.

Harrison, Christopher Scott (2000), 'Protection of Pharmaceuticals as Foreign Policy: The Canada–US Trade Agreement and Bill C-22 Versus the North American Free Trade Agreement and Bill C-91', 26 *North Carolina Journal of International Law and Commercial Regulation*, 457–528.

ICTSD (International Centre for Trade and Sustainable Development), *Resource Book on TRIPS and Development*, Cambridge: Cambridge University Press.

Lexchin, Joel (2001), *Globalization, Trade Deals and Drugs: Heads, the Industry Wins; Tails, Canada Loses*, Ottawa: Canadian Centre for Policy Alternatives.

Matthews, Duncan (2002), *Globalising Intellectual Property Rights: The TRIPs Agreement*, New York: Routledge.

McFetridge, Donald G. (1998), 'Intellectual Property, Technology, Diffusion, and Growth in the Canadian Economy' in Robert D. Anderson and Nancy T. Gallini (eds), *Competition Policy and Intellectual Property Rights in the Knowledge-Based Economy*, Calgary: University of Calgary Press, pp. 64–104.

Morin, Jean-Frédéric (2007), *La nouvelle frontière du droit international des brevets: Les traités bilatéraux américains*, Bruxelles: Larcier.

Orlhac, Thierry (1990), 'The New Canadian Pharmaceutical Compulsory Licensing Provisions or How to Jump Out of the Frying Pan and Into the Fire', available at http://www.robic.com/publications/Pdf/167E-TO.pdf (accessed 1 October 2009).

Paris, Valérie and Elizabeth Docteur (2006), *Pharmaceutical Pricing and Reimbursement Policies in Canada*, available at http://www.oecd.org/dataoecd/21/40/3786818.pdf (accessed 1 October 2009).

Pharmaceutical Research and Manufacturers of America (2003), *Special 301 Submission*, Washington: PhRMA.

Pugatch, Meir Perez (2006), 'Intellectual Property and Pharmaceutical Data Exclusivity in the Context of Innovation and Market Access' in David Vivas-Engui, Geoff Tansey and Pedro Roffe (eds), *Negotiating Health*, Geneva: ICTSD, pp. 97–132.

Reichman, Jerome H. and Catherine Hasenzahl (2002), 'Non-voluntary Licensing of Patented Inventions: The Canadian Experience', http://www.iprsonline.org/unctadictsd/docs/reichman_hasenzahl_Canada.pdf (accessed 1 October 2009).

Rimmer, Matthew (2005), 'The Jean Chrétien Pledge to Africa Act: Patent Law and Humanitarian Aid', *Expert Opinion on Therapeutic Patents* 15(7), 889–909.

Robert, Maryse (2000), *Negotiating NAFTA: Explaining the Outcome in Culture, Textiles, Autos, and Pharmaceuticals*, Toronto: University of Toronto Press.

Sanjuan, Judit Rius (2006), 'Patent–Registration Linkage', Consumer Project on Technology, available at http://www.cptech.org/publications/CPTechDPNo2Linkage.pdf (accessed 1 October 2009).

Skinner, Brett J. (2006), 'Price Controls, Patents and Cross-Border Internet Pharmacies, Risks to Canada's Drug Supply and International Trading Relations', available at http://www.fraserinstitute.org/commerce.web/publication_details.aspx?pubID=3121 (accessed 1 October 2009).

Thorpe, Phil (2002), 'Study on the Implementation of the TRIPS Agreement by Developing Countries', available at http://www.cipr.org.uk/papers/pdfs/study_papers/sp7_thorpe_study.pdf (accessed 1 October 2009).

United States of America (2001), *Special 301 Report*, Washington: United States Trade Representative.

9. Access to Indian generic drugs: emerging issues

N. Lalitha

The focus of this chapter is on access to generic drugs[1] produced by the Indian pharmaceutical industry. Globally, about 60 developing countries have no pharmaceutical industry and 87 have capacity to make finished products only (Cullet, 2005). The Indian pharmaceutical industry (IPI), with its 8 per cent share in global pharmaceutical production, over the years has grown to become an important generic supplier to such countries. India now accounts for 20 per cent of the world's generic supply (IDMA, 2010). Two thirds of the drugs produced in India are exported, with destinations in North America, the European Union, CIS countries and West Africa in that order (Table 9.1).

Drugs produced in India satisfy 95 per cent of the domestic demand (EXIM Bank, 2007). Though production of drugs is not an issue in India, access to drugs is an issue of concern since health cover is limited to a small percentage of the population in India. Private out of pocket health expenditure is estimated at 84 per cent of the total health expenditure, because of the limited public health expenditure which is estimated at less than one per cent of GDP. The National Sample Survey on Consumer Expenditure (55th Round) reports that, respectively, 77 and 70 per cent of the health expenditure in rural and urban areas is on medicines. Therefore, out of pocket medical costs alone may push 2.2 per cent of the population below the poverty line in one year in India (World Bank, 2001).

In that scenario, the government would be better off controlling the drug prices and/or providing access to drugs in the government health care. India has been following some form of control of prices of select essential drugs since the early 1970s. Government provision of drugs is more often drawn from the list of national essential drugs and is limited to about 400 drugs. This list does not include the new and innovator drugs

---

[1] Throughout the chapter, the terms 'drugs' and 'medicines' have been used interchangeably.

Table 9.1   Pharmaceutical exports from India (US$ million)

Region	1996–97	2000–01	2003–04	2006–07	2007–08
EU countries	156.67	138.09	265.09	450.7	657.86
Other western European countries	8.8	16.82	26.04	58.97	47.47
Southern Africa	10.39	25.51	64.11	161.56	210.35
West Africa	49.12	110.76	152.88	297.92	367.16
Central Africa	19.22	26.42	27.5	59.18	83.67
East Africa	20.69	36.47	61.11	137.16	186.74
North America	52.35	63.8	251.73	563.44	984.96
Latin America	23.37	70.38	116.16	283.01	295.58
East Asia	4.99	13.09	15.44	39.67	50.58
ASEAN	60.23	86.98	123.47	198.62	242.18
WANA	40.8	66.07	123.97	167.72	223.18
NE Asia	62.07	71.56	59.23	68.48	58.67
South Asia	51.1	79.71	124.72	225.36	223.95
CARs countries	3.15	8.35	17.51	47.72	62.96
Other CIS countries	108.99	130.56	179.69	411.28	446.57
Unspecified	0.11	0.55	11.44	4.69	10.99
Total	672.05	945.12	1620.09	3175.48	4152.87

Source: Compiled from data provided by the Directorate General of Foreign Trade, Government of India, available at www.dgftcom.nic.in.

that are protected by intellectual property rights (IPR). In the product patent regime, it is estimated that 10 to 15 per cent of the drugs in the Indian market would be affected because of patenting (Grace, 2005). Newer biotech based drugs, innovative drugs for HIV/AIDS, cancer, diabetes, and other diseases where the existing drugs have become ineffective, come under this category. The uniform standards of IPR adopted by the WTO member countries ensure that IPR protected drugs are accessible only in extraordinary circumstances and through complicated procedures.

This chapter discusses both the non-IPR and IPR issues that have an impact on access to drugs and is divided into five sections. In the next section, we present the government initiatives to provide access to essential drugs. IPR is not an issue as far as these drugs are concerned, though price and availability are subjects of concern. These two issues are addressed by the government through (a) drug price control mechanisms (b) provision of drugs in the government health care and (c) selling non-branded generic drugs in the retail market. Next, we discuss two types of situations where the IPR on the drug matters. In the first type of situation, the heavily export oriented generic companies compete to file an Abbreviated New

Drug Application (ANDA) to launch their generic drugs. Besides the cost that will have to be incurred to meet the international regulatory standards that are associated with launching the drugs in the regulated markets, the domestic industry will also have to certify that no patents are infringed or the patents are invalid. If the effort is successful, while the generic company gets the market exclusivity, consumers gain by the availability of a generic drug that is priced lower than the innovator drug and the generic company reaps substantial profits through market exclusivity. In the second type of situation, highlights of a few of the drug patent cases won by IPI by utilising the Section 3d provisions in the Patent Act of India that ensure the availability of drugs are discussed. This is followed by a highlight on policy initiatives at the international level to provide access to drugs. Lastly, we present the possible issues that could prevent access to generic drugs in general.

ACCESS-TO-DRUG INITIATIVES IN THE GENERICS SEGMENT BY THE GOVERNMENT OF INDIA

Price Control

Almost all the countries in the world have some form of control on drug prices to ensure access to medicines. Administrative pricing systems for drugs were first introduced by the Government of India (GOI) in 1962, in the wake of Chinese aggression and declaration of emergency, to curb the spiralling prices of medicines. Subsequently, the Drug Price Control Order was formulated in 1970 and was revised substantially in 1979, 1987 and 1995. We briefly mention here the scope of each of the control orders and the reaction of the industry.

The first ever price control on drugs was introduced by the Drugs (Display of Prices) Order 1962 and the Drugs (Control of Prices) Order, which had the effect of freezing the prices of drugs as of 1st April 1963 (Srinivasan, 2006). This control order was effective for a long time, though the emergency situation ended in 1966. The industry, however, took the view that the freeze on sale prices, without a similar control on the prices of raw materials would hamper the long term growth of the industry by reducing profitability (Narayana, 1984).

The Drugs Prices Control Order 1970 (DPCO 1970) was to build up a rational system of price control. The DPCO 1970 divided the bulk drugs[2]

---

[2]   Bulk drugs are the basic raw materials, or the active pharmaceutical ingredients essential for making a drug.

into essential and other bulk drugs. Prices of the essential drugs would not be allowed to rise without prior approval of the government and prices of the 'other bulk drugs' were frozen at the level prevailing immediately before the announcement of the DPCO. But consequent upon the oil price hike in 1973, prices of petroleum products began to rise and the government evolved guidelines to compensate for the cost escalations and granted price revisions.

The Hathi Committee, which was set up in 1974 to suggest various measures to promote the growth of the domestic industry, observed that

> any scheme of price/production regulation should be: (1) to ensure that the country's dependence on imports of basic drugs is reduced as quickly as possible by encouraging, wherever possible, an economically viable domestic production of such bulk drugs. The primary objective of policy in this field should be larger production and lower costs so that in the long run, these may be reflected in adequate availability and lower prices. (2) In the field of formulations, the main thrust of policy should be to take measures which will reduce or eliminate the social costs involved in comparative product adaptation or aggressive selling. (GOI, 1975, 180)

It was in this context that the Committee recommended abolition of brand names and a rational price policy that was beneficial for both consumers and producers. It recommended a reduced mark-up for essential drugs and for the non-essential drugs a liberal margin. While the ceiling for the bulk drugs was decided on the net worth or capital employed, prices of the formulations were fixed by applying the concept of maximum allowable post manufacturing expenses (MAPE), which is similar to the mark-up on the ex-factory cost of the products that includes the cost of distribution.

The successive revision orders also adopted the same strategy, though the percentage of net worth varied. As the price of bulk drugs used in the production of price controlled formulations were also fixed by the government, in effect, the DPCO 1979 brought 370 drugs or 90 per cent of the drugs under control. These drugs were classified into categories 1, 2 and 3 with a MAPE fixed at 40, 55 and 100 per cent respectively. Categories 1 and 2 included the life saving drugs and category 3 included vitamins and supplements. Drugs that did not belong to the three categories belonged to category 4 (Narayana, 1984; Chaudhuri, 2005; Srinivasan, 2006).

DPCO 1979 had the overall impact of reducing the profitability of companies as the contribution to sales as well as the profitability came from a few formulations and depended on the type of drugs produced (Narayana, 1984). The noticeable effect of this price control was the shift in the output behaviour of the industry, which shifted to production for exports and production of decontrolled items (Narayana, 1984; Chaudhuri, 2005).

As a result of stiff opposition from the industry the DPCO of 1979 was revised in 1987. This reduced the number of drugs under control to 145 (70 per cent of the drugs), with two categories that had a mark-up of 75 and 100 per cent. Further, a price hike of up to 25 per cent was allowed in the case of essential drugs. This was more favourable for the industry compared to the earlier DPCO, as it reduced the number of drugs under control and the two categories had a higher mark-up, thus addressing both public health and profitability criteria in the control mechanism.

With the onset of liberalisation policy measures which reduced the control of government in sectors including pharmaceuticals, the DPCO was further revised to reduce the number of drugs under control to 78 in 1995, and the revision in 1997 finally fixed the number at 74 drugs based on the market competition in those drugs. These 74 drugs covered 40 per cent of the market. This list continues to be under control up to the present day.[3] One important change that occurred between the 1979 DPCO and the 1995 DPCO was that while the essentiality of the drug determined the basis of the price control in the former, in the latter case it was decided on the percentage of market competition in a particular drug (Centad, 2009). Also some of these 74 drugs became outdated and were replaced by newer drugs which are not under any price control mechanism. Hence, in real terms fewer than 50 common drugs are under price control (GOI, 2010).

The GOI established the National Pharmaceutical Pricing Authority (NPPA) in 1997 to fix/revise the prices of the controlled drugs and to enforce prices and availability of essential medicines in the country. There are no official guidelines to fix the prices of other medicines, which are fixed through free market competition (Kotwani et al., 2007). However, NPPA monitors the drugs that are not under price control and price increases of more than 20 per cent are subject to government action and recovery. But, over the years, several companies have filed cases, protesting the price fixing measures of NPPA, thus paralysing its functions. NPPA was due to recover over US$20 million from leading pharma companies for overpricing drugs. As ceiling prices are often fixed for standard size packs, NPPA found that companies were altering the ingredients in formulations as well as selling non-standard-size packs to avoid price control, thus defeating the purpose of price control. Several large companies have either

---

3   This list of drugs under control is available at www.nppaindia.nic.in/index1. html. Ironically, the Drugs Price Control Review Committee, 1999 that was appointed to look at the pricing policies of pharmaceuticals in different countries and suggest a suitable model for India, suggested continuation of price control especially in the absence of health cover for the majority of people. However, the industry lobby has resisted any such move.

discontinued the production or drastically cut the production of these controlled items (Francis, 2006).

Studies on drug prices in the context of India show varied results because of the differences in the methodology and the time points considered. While a few argue that price controls have been ineffective (Rane, 1999 and 2002; Guha, 2002), price analysis of the fifty largest-selling drugs which accounted for 15 per cent of the total retail formulations between 1995 and 2003 shows that prices of decontrolled drugs have indeed risen substantially (Chaudhuri, 2005). Studies carried out by the Indian Drug Manufacturers Association and Organisation for Pharmaceutical Producers in India pointed out that the rise in prices of drugs including those of decontrolled items had been modest as compared to the overall price rise as reflected in the Wholesale Price Index (Chaudhuri, 2005). The basic premise of removing price controls has been that competition would lower prices. But in the Indian scenario, where branded generics are plentiful in the retail market, the top selling brand is also the highest priced drug and competition seems to bring down the prices of the monopoly producer in the early stages of the products (Srinivasan, 2006; Srinivasan and Bhargava, 2006). As a result of this, different prices prevail for the same drug. A study that surveyed the variation in prices of 84 formulations used in the management of cardiovascular diseases concluded that variation in retail prices ranged from 2.8 per cent to 3406 per cent (Srinivasan, 2006).

In countries where health insurance is widely prevalent, companies strive to include their drugs in the reimbursement lists. But where there is no insurance and consumers depend on the private market, companies thrive on price differentials. Existence of price differentials even in controlled items is one of the weaknesses of the Indian price control system.

At present, patented medicines are not under price control. GOI has been toying with the idea of controlling patented drugs through a separate agency on the lines of the Patented Medicines Price Review Board (PMPRB) of Canada. This board categorises the drugs into three groups. Category 1 comprises those drugs which are comparable with an existing medicine; category 2 drugs are the new drugs to treat effectively a particular illness or which provide a substantial improvement over existing drug products, often referred to as a breakthrough drug; and category 3 drugs are new dosage forms of an existing medicine that provide moderate, little or no improvement over existing medicines and accordingly prices are fixed (Lalitha, 2005).

Government Intervention in Providing Medicines

In India health comes under the jurisdiction of the states' governments. Though there is a list of national essential drugs, the list followed by each state differs according to its health needs. The health expenditure of each state varies according to its development status. Central government also spends on health through centrally sponsored programmes relating to tuberculosis, malaria, AIDS and a few other diseases.

Public provision of health care is plagued by issues such as limited allocation for drugs by the government. Lack of prioritisation of drugs and absence of data regarding the demand for the right medicines often restrict the availability to a brief period during the fiscal year forcing the consumers to buy the drugs from the market.

Since the mid 1990s various state governments have been introducing health reform measures in order to provide better services to people dependent on public health care. Some of the measures particularly with reference to drugs have been the adoption of (1) an essential drug list, (2) a pooled procurement procedure for all government health care and (3) streamlining drug procurement as well as the supply process so that the objective of access to medicines is served. Though there is a national drug list in India, states have their own list of the formulary that may not necessarily be based on the list of essential drugs but reflects more of the local needs. The advantage of adopting an essential drug list is that it weeds out the non-essential drugs from the procurement procedure and thus helps in focusing the expenditure on essential drugs alone.

Studies show that the autonomous supply models[4] as adopted by Tamil Nadu and Delhi have resulted in rationalisation of the budget and that drug supplies to the government health care have improved (Srinivasan, 2006; Lalitha, 2009). Both these states have drawn up a list of essential drugs taking into account the needs ranging from primary to tertiary health care. Most importantly, the different health providers within the government health care prescribe drugs only from this list. The Tamil Nadu model has demonstrated that adopting an essential drugs list and the pooled procurement procedure have resulted in availability of quality medicines in the government health care. This model has been studied by different state governments and a few state governments such as Rajasthan and Andhra Pradesh have adopted the Tamil Nadu model of identifying, procuring and distributing the essential drugs.

---

[4] Autonomous supply agencies are constituted as parastatals either under the Ministry of Health or as independent organisations. The purpose of establishing an autonomous supply agency is to achieve the efficiency and flexibility associated with private management and private sector employment conditions. Their primary and priority client is government health services and they may or may not operate on a non-profit basis (Essential Drugs Monitor, 1998).

Sale of Non-branded Drugs in the Retail Market

While the above-mentioned efforts do improve access to medicines in the government health care, as these are not widely prevalent or the norm for every other state government, the larger issue of non-accessibility remains. Since the early 1980s, the All India Drug Action Network, a non-governmental organisation promoting the use of essential drugs, has taken an initiative to sell generic drugs through the Lokayat Medical Centre in Pune and Shramik Aushadalaya in Kolaphur district of Maharashtra. The former, managed by a professionally trained physician, provides generic substitutes produced by standard companies for the branded drugs prescribed by physicians, for consumers who want to have a 'second opinion' on the prescription, and are willing to take generic drugs. This results in substantial savings for consumers and the success is creating more awareness among consumers about the use of generic drugs. Shramik Aushadalaya is a regular chemist shop selling only non-branded generic drugs. Consumers go to the shop with whatever prescription their health provider has given. Though the sales are not widespread, the NGO concerned is determined to spread awareness of the concept of the stores.

In Chittorgarh district of Rajasthan, the district administration has taken efforts to set up a co-operative medical store. A medicines list was arrived at by taking cognisance of the drugs frequently prescribed by the health providers and consumed by the consumers. This list comprises 564 generic medicines including 100 surgical and intravenous fluids. These medicines were procured by inviting tenders and was sold to consumers at a profit margin of 20 per cent compared to more than 100 per cent charged in the retail trade. The co-operative runs six such stores in Chittorgarh town and also supplies to the community health centres and district hospital in Chittorgarh (Srinivasan, 2009). Price lists of drugs are displayed to educate the consumers about the differences in prices. A seven day therapy for pneumonia which would cost US$25.67 (approximately) in the retail market is made available at a cost of US$3.15 (approximately) at the co-operatively run drug stores in Chittorgarh (GOI, 2010). Bihar, which is one of the less developed states of India, has also adopted a similar strategy. 'Every medical college, district hospital and the primary health centre in the state has a shop where generic medicines at less than 50 per cent of the maximum retail price are sold and yet Bihar government is earning 45 per cent revenue on the project' (GOI, 2010).

Taking its cue from the success of these isolated efforts and with the purpose of reaching out to the people without health cover in a wider geographical region, the Department of Pharmaceuticals of the Government of India introduced the Jan Aushadhi scheme in November 2008. Under this scheme, the central government procures unbranded quality generic drugs from a panel of producers adhering to good manufacturing practices with production experience of at least three years. A drug list based on the national essential drug list as well as drugs that are commonly used in chronic and other diseases are sold in these outlets. The states would also be able to add to this list. The products carry the logo 'Jan Aushadhi-24X7 drug store' and are sold at half the market rate[5,6] through outlets in public hospitals. The first such store was opened in Chandigarh in November 2008 and as of July 2010, 44 stores have been opened in Punjab, Delhi, Rajasthan, Andhra Pradesh, Uttaranchal and Orissa. The government has plans to open such stores in each district hospital of the country. In May 2010, the government also announced its plan of providing cancer drugs at discounted rates in its Jan Aushadhi outlets.[7] Success of this scheme depends on the number and location of such shops in different states and uninterrupted supply to these stores. Unlike the localised efforts of the few state governments and NGOs, this broad based scheme would have a wider reach if the concept of selling drugs in their generic names is well received by the physicians and consumers.

Discussion in this section showed the efforts by the government of India using mechanisms such as (a) control of the prices of drugs, (b) provision of essential drugs in government health facilities and (c) selling generic drugs in their generic names to provide access to drugs. But the price control has only 74 drugs under its jurisdiction and government provision of essential drugs depends on resources, adoption of an essential drug list and procurement policy and several other factors. However, the Jan Aushadhi is a novel initiative to provide generic drugs in their international nonproprietary or generic names. As the consumers and the physicians have got used to buying the branded generics in the retail market in India and certainly the Jan Aushadhi scheme lacks the advertising and promotions that go with retailing, the success of this model depends on the acceptance of the concept among consumers and the assurance that generic drugs are not inferior drugs. If the concept becomes popular and accepted by physicians, it would definitely bring down the drug expenditure of consumers and provide more access to drugs.

---

5   As per the price information accessed on 8 July, 2010 at http://janaushadhi. gov.in/, a pack containing 10 tablets of azithromycin 500 mg costs $1.57 in the Jan Aushadhi store, while in the retail market one of the companies sells the same drug for approximately $4.93 per pack.

6   The prices of drugs have been converted to US$ at the rate of 1$=48Rs.

7   http://www.dancewithshadows.com/pillscribe/india-to-supply-cancer-drugs-at-discounted-rates-through-jan-aushadhi-stores/ accessed on 3 May, 2010.

IPR ISSUES IN ACCESS TO PATENTED MEDICINES

Generic Entry into Regulated Markets

The IPI is heavily export intensive, and this is particularly true of the companies in the top 50. In 2005–06, exports as a percentage of sales were at 44.9 for the top 27 companies. Of India's total exports in 2005–06, these 27 companies' exports accounted for 54.39 per cent (Chaudhuri, 2009). Realising the scope for generics in north America, Europe and Japan where the unaudited and audited drug sales account for 82 per cent of global drug sales (PricewaterhouseCoopers, 2010), the IPI started focussing on gaining a market share in those countries in the 1990s. Thanks to the efforts to promote domestic industry by the GOI, India has a number of vertically integrated companies that can produce active pharmaceutical ingredients (API) as well as the formulations. This feature makes it easier for the companies to demonstrate that they have sound manufacturing practices to produce a quality product, which is a pre-requisite for regulatory approval[8] to enter the regulated markets. R&D expenditure since the late '90s has been directed to facilitate this entry. R&D which was estimated to be 1.8 per cent of the sales turnover in 1993–94 improved to 5 per cent by 2004–05 (EXIM Bank, 2007), major contributors being companies like Ranbaxy, Dr. Reddy's, Sunpharma, and Piramal Healthcare[9] (see also Table 9.2). The positive results of improving R&D is obvious from the number of (1) patents filed by Indian companies, (2) plants with international regulatory approvals, (3) Drug Master Files and (4) Abbreviated New Drug Applications (ANDA).[10]

India has 119 US Food and Drug Administration (FDA) and 84 UK Medicines and Healthcare products Regulatory Agency (MHRA) approved plants. In Europe between 2001 and 2005, Ranbaxy had 204

---

[8]   The cost index of a plant (a) without good manufacturing practices, (b) with good manufacturing practices, (c) EU and (4) US FDA would be 50, 100, 200 and 300 respectively (Chaudhuri, 2005: 190).

[9]   Dr. Reddy's, Glenmark, Lupin and Piramal Healthcare are working on about 50–70 drug candidates, with a view to becoming the first Indian drug maker to come out with at least one original molecule in the commercial stage by 2010–11. While Glenmark had out-licensed the potential drug candidates to multinationals for further development, Dr. Reddy's have adopted a different strategy of cost sharing and joint development of the product with the multinationals (Chaudhuri, 2009).

[10]   DMF and ANDA are required for selling the generic drugs in the US. A DMF contains details of the manufacturing plant, process used in the manufacture, storage and packaging of the API. An ANDA is required for getting market approval for a product in the US.

Table 9.2   Percentage share of R&D expenditure of selected companies

Name of company	1999–2000	2005–06
Ranbaxy Laboratories	2.93	17.21
Dr. Reddys	2.69	10.85
Sunpharma	3.92	11.93
CIPLA	3.89	5.01
Cadila Healthcare	4.45	8.87
Nicholas Piramal	1.89	6.04
Wockhardt	4.17	8.73
Aurobindo	1.92	5.22
Orchid	1.26	6.95
Glenmark	3.58	7.52
Jubiliant	0.53	2.61
IPCA	1.75	4.61

Source: EXIM Bank (2007).

approvals from MHRA, while Dr. Reddy's and Aurobindo had 57 and 19 approvals respectively (Dhar and Gopakumar, 2007). Between 2000 and 2007, India filed 1155 DMFs, which is higher than the number filed by China, Italy and Japan during the same period in the US. India accounted for one quarter of ANDAs in the years 2007 and 2008 and more than one quarter of DMFs filed with the US FDA, the largest share in registrations in the world including the USA (GOI, 2009).

Upon filing an ANDA, companies have to file a paragraph IV application stating that the innovator patent is either invalid or is not infringed by the ANDA. This is where the R&D expenditure in developing new processes for generics supports Indian companies. If the application is in favour of the ANDA applicant then this applicant gets 180 day market exclusivity, during which no other generic company is allowed to market their product. Aurobindo, Cipla, Dr. Reddy's, Ranbaxy and Matrix have filed more than 100 DMFs each. Ranbaxy holds 170 ANDAs in the US,[11] besides those of Glenmark and Sunpharma. Of the following four companies, Ranbaxy obtained the 180 day market exclusivity for four products[12] followed by

---

[11]   Ernst and Young (2009) and company websites.
[12]   In September 2010, Ranbaxy obtained 180 day exclusivity to launch a generic version of Aricept, to treat Alzheimers, which is expected to provide $300 million to Ranbaxy (http://www.fiercepharma.com/story/ranbaxy-nabs-exclusive-aricept-rights/2010-09-21?utm_medium=nl&utm_source=internal, accessed on 22 September, 2010).

three for Sunpharma and one each for Dr. Reddy's and Glenmark. The number of generic drugs launched by Indian companies in the US increased from 93 in 2003 to 250 in 2008, benefiting consumers. But it is a market with a lot of risks. If a company gets the 180 day exclusivity, then it hits the jackpot and it benefits consumers as well. According to the Generic Pharmaceutical Association's estimate early generic competition following successful patent challenges of just four products (prozac, zantac, Taxol and Plaitinol) has saved consumers US$9 billion (in the US) (Leibowitz, 2009).

However, such patent challenges involve lots of financial resources. For instance, in 2004, Dr. Reddy's lost the case of amlodipine to Pfizer and could not launch its generic drug. It lost more than US$10 million in defending its case. In early 2009, Pfizer filed patent infringement suits against Sunpharma, Wockhardt Ltd and Lupin Ltd to prevent these companies from securing marketing approvals for the generic equivalents of its high selling neuropathic pain management drug Lyrica in the US. The suit was against the alleged violation of patents granted to Pfizer in 1996, 1999 and 2001 respectively. Pfizer's move came after the Indian companies filed the abbreviated new drug applications (ANDA) seeking marketing approvals for generic versions of Lyrica, which had sales of US$1.05 billion sales in the US alone. Besides the Indian companies, Pfizer has also sued three other generic firms: Teva, Sandoz and Actavis (compiled from various articles of Pharmabiz available at www.pharmabiz.com).

It is also not uncommon to find the innovator companies influencing the generic companies to delay the launch of the first generic products as the first generics can take away a substantial part of the market of the innovator product. The Federal Trade Commission (FTC) of the US has been investigating such 'pay for delay' deals. Such deals have been said to cost US citizens $3.5 billion a year in high drug costs (Leibovitz, 2009).

In 2008, 16 settlements included both compensation to the generic drug company and a restriction on the company's ability to market its product. These 16 agreements resolved patent disputes on 13 different pharmaceutical products with combined sales of US$10 billion (Leibovitz, 2009). A few of the Indian companies' patent litigation settlements may also come under the scanner of the FTC. Glenmark,[13] Sunpharma, Dr. Reddy's[14]

---

[13]   In May 2010, Merck and Glenmark entered into an agreement to settle their patent litigation by which Glenmark would be able to launch the generic version of Zetia in December 2016, before the patent expiration in April 2017 with 180 day exclusivity. http://www.business-standard.com/india/news/glenmark-settles-patent-litigationmerck/394566/ (accessed on 8 July, 2010).

[14]   The letter sent by FTC to the legal counsel of Dr. Reddy's on March 10, 2009, however indicates that Dr. Reddy's had not engaged in any unfair

and Ranbaxy have entered into patent litigation settlements with Merck, Medicis, Mediimmune, Schering and Pfizer between 2008 and 2009, which they however feel would not be categorized as 'pay for delay' deals.[15]

Mergers and acquisitions is a recent strategy adopted by the Indian pharma industry to gain entry to the regulated markets. These acquisitions are made with the purpose of getting access to the brands, intellectual assets and manufacturing facilities so that generics can be launched with ease. As regards the regional acquisition pattern of the Indian pharma industry, it is reported that 51 per cent of the acquisitions were made in Europe, 29 per cent in North America, 10 per cent in Asia, 5 per cent in Africa, 3 per cent in Latin America and 2 per cent in Australia (EXIM bank, 2007).

It emerges from this section that launching generic products in the lucrative regulated markets is a strategy adopted by companies with a larger net worth and by companies that have spent a sizeable amount of their R&D budget in the process of adhering to international regulations. Obviously the companies will have to study the patent landscape thoroughly and ensure none of the patents is violated. If the condition is met, then it benefits both consumers and the company.

Patents and Access to Life-saving Drugs

Though GOI adopted product patents in the pharmaceuticals industry, it has taken a few measures that would protect the interest of consumers and the domestic generic industry. Important among these measures are: (1) opposing the patent either before or after the grant; (2) preventing frivolous patent applications; (3) allowing generic companies to continue with their production through the provision of automatic licences and (4) not allowing data exclusivity. The post-grant opposition can be filed within one year of the grant of the patent but before the expiry of one year from the date of publication of grant of a patent in the official journal. A post-grant opposition can be filed by an interested person alone. The Patents Act defines a 'person interested' as a person engaged in or in promoting research in the same field as that to which the invention relates. A pre-grant opposition can be filed by any person by giving a written representation and the patent rules do not prescribe any fee or specific form.

---

means of selling Keppra or its generic equivalents: http://www.ftc.gov/os/closings/090310ucbkepprasilber.pdf, accessed on 9 July, 2010.

[15] http://www.business-standard.com/india/news/us-to-curb-delay-in-entry generic-drugs/383145/ accessed on 28 April, 2010.

However, the Patent Act specifies the grounds on which the pre- and post-grant opposition to the patent can be made.

Section 3 restricts the scope of subject matter eligible for patentability by listing what are not inventions. Section 3(d) specifically does not allow patents on mere discovery of a new form of a known substance, unless such form demonstrates significant efficacy over the original substance. In simple terms Section 3(d) defines what are not inventions[16] and through this restricts the 'evergreening' of the patent. Of the 2734 product patents granted between 2005 and 2008 in India, 58 patents were opposed. Of these, 33 cases were filed before the grant of the patent and one case was filed after the patent was granted. Twenty out of the 25 patent applications were rejected on the grounds of 3d.[17] Twenty-four oppositions were based on other options. Some of these rejections have become very controversial and the companies concerned have appealed to the higher courts. The grounds of conflict between the innovator companies and the generic competitors seeking entry by challenging the 'protected segment' are highlighted in the following paragraphs.

In the following five cases, four cases were contested based on Section 3d. The last one is related to the patent linkage case.

Cases Contested based on Section 3(d)

Gleevac As a developing country India had availed itself of the transitional period from 1995 to 2005 to make amendments to the Patent Act. Through the first amendment in 1999 it had set up the mailbox[18] which facilitated receiving of patent applications during the period 1995–2004,

---

[16] The mere discovery of a new form of a known substance which does not enhance the known efficacy of that substance is not patentable. Similarly, the mere discovery of any new property or new use for a known substance or of a mere use of a known process, machine or apparatus, unless such known process results in a new product or employs at least one new reactant, shall not be a subject matter of patent (Khader, 2007, 47). For the purposes of this clause, salts, esters, ethers, polymorphs, metabolites, pure form, particle size isomers, mixtures of isomers, complexes, combinations and other derivatives of known substance shall be considered to be the same substance, unless they differ significantly in properties with regard to efficacy.

[17] http://www.livemint.com/2009/09/07234455/3-provisions-helped-India-cull.html?h=A1 accessed on 16 September, 2010.

[18] One of the requirements under TRIPS during the transitional period. The mailbox system facilitates accepting patent applications in India from 1 January, 1995 for pharmaceutical and agricultural chemical products. These were to be examined from 1 January, 2005 onwards.

that were to be examined from January 2005. The second amendment paved the way for the provision of exclusive marketing rights[19] (EMR) for those products that had already been granted a patent in another WTO country and also been granted marketing approval. Gleevac (imatinib mesylate) by Novartis, used in chronic myeloid leukaemia, and Nadoxin, an anti-bacterial drug by Wockhardt were the two drugs that came up for EMR. In both cases, infringement suits were filed by the innovator against the competitors after the grant of EMR. While Wockhardt lost the EMR after the patent was rejected by the Controller of Patents in 2006, Novartis is still battling in the court. At the time Novartis was granted EMR, a generic version of Gleevac was available in the Indian market.[20] Immediately after the EMR in January 2003, six companies, namely Sun Pharmaceuticals, Cipla, Ranbaxy, Intas, Hetero and Emcure were asked to stop the manufacture, sale, marketing and export of imatinib mesylate, thus forcing consumers to be dependent on the expensive Gleevac.

In 2005, the generic producers filed a pre-grant opposition against Novartis stating that the product should not be granted a patent as it lacked novelty and an inventive step (Novartis had filed the patent for the beta crystalline polymorphic form derived from imatinib mesylate, which is an improved form of imatinib). In 2006, the Chennai patent office rejected Novartis's application on several grounds including Section 3(d) of the Indian Patent Act. The patent office held that Gleevac lacked novelty and inventive step and also failed to show increased efficacy. Novartis urged that Section 3(d) of the Indian Patent Act was not TRIPS compliant.

Novartis argued that the use of the expressions 'enhancement of known efficacy' and 'differ significantly in properties with regard to efficacy' without the appropriate guidelines specifying their scope made Section 3(d) ambiguous. Further, it gave uncontrolled discretion to the patent controller to apply his own standards (Banerjee and Roy, 2009).

Due to changes in law, the set of appeals was transferred from the Madras High Court to the Intellectual Property Appellate Board (IPAB). The IPAB held that Novartis was not entitled to a patent on imatinib mesylate as the product did not meet the requirement of increased therapeutic efficacy. IPAB held that though the product was novel and inventive, Novartis could not demonstrate that the beta crystalline form

---

[19] Exclusive marketing rights is another requirement to be complied with by countries availing themselves of the transitional period. However, EMR will end once a decision on whether to grant patent or not is taken by the Indian patent office.

[20] Gleevac, which has to be taken life-long by patients, as manufactured by Novartis would cost US$2500, while the generic version would cost US$166.6 a year.

was significantly more efficacious than imatinib mesylate and hence Gleevac could not be patented (Banerjee and Roy, 2009). Now Novartis has approached the Supreme Court of India, appealing against IPAB's decision.[21] If the Supreme Court rejects the IPAB's finding on therapeutic efficacy and grants the patent in favour of Novartis, the patients would not have access to the cheaper generic versions of Gleevac. Though Novartis promises to cover many patients under its Gleevac International Patient Assistance Programme, which provides Gleevac free of cost to the patients, it has covered only 7000 patients in India from 2002–2007, whereas closer to 30,000 patients are diagnosed with chronic myeloid leukaemia every year in India alone (Srinivasan, 2007).

Valganciclovir   This drug, used for organ transplants and treating eye infections in AIDS patients, is sold by the innovator Roche as Valcyte and by Cipla as Valcept. The Chennai patent office had granted a patent to Roche in 2007, which was challenged by an Indian NGO that had filed a pre-grant opposition which was allegedly not heard by the patent office. According to the NGO, Valcyte is (1) a pre-1995 molecule and (2) lacks inventive step and hence cannot be granted patent. While the Madras High Court remanded the case back to the Chennai patent office, Roche decided to move the Supreme Court. Meanwhile, Cipla launched its generic version in 2008, which was again challenged by Roche in Bombay High Court on account of patent infringement and trademark violation. After this, Cipla agreed to change the name of the drug. The Supreme Court ruling in March 2009 favoured Roche, but asked Roche not to pursue the patent violation case against Cipla till the Chennai patent office re-examines the case.

In May 2010, the Indian patent office refused patent on valganciclovir on the grounds that the ester gancyclovir was already present in the market and was being administered intravenously for HIV infections and hence did not meet the criteria of patentability. Owing to problems with intravenous administration, a person skilled in the art would have been motivated to look out for an oral dosage form with increased bio-availability and this would have resulted in the L-valinate ester of gancyclovir, a combination with hydrocholoric acid to result in valgancyclovir hydrocholoride (Valcyte by Roche). The more interesting part of this case is that the court verdict is clear on the lack of inventive step, as compared to the IPABs contentious decision on Gleevac based on therapeutic efficacy.[22]

---

[21]   www.lawyerscollective.org.
[22]   http://spicyipindia.blogspot.com/2010/05/breaking-news-roche-loses-valcyte-case.html accessed on 23 May, 2010.

Tenofovir Tenofovir disoproxil fumarate (TDF) is highly recommended by the WHO for the treatment of HIV/AIDS. Gilead's patent-protected tenofovir was sold at a cost of US$5718 per patient per year in developing countries. Gilead entered into agreement in 2007 with 11 Indian companies (which included Aurobindo Pharma, Matrix Laboratories, JB Chemicals, Alchem Hetero and Emcure) for the manufacture and sale of tenofovir in 95 countries using Gilead's technology. Under the voluntary licence, local producers could produce tenofovir subject to payment of royalties and on the condition of not selling the drug in countries such as Brazil and China (IDMA, 2009). Licensed sellers of tenofovir were also required to buy the active pharma ingredients from Gilead-affiliated licensed suppliers. Concerned by these restrictive clauses in the licence, Cipla refused Gilead's licensing offer and filed a pre-grant opposition on the grounds of ever-greening and that granting of the patent would lead to non-affordability of the drug worldwide.[23] The main opposition to the patent was that TDF is created by the addition of a salt (fumaric acid) to the already existing compound tenofovir disproxil and hence should not be granted patent. Civil society groups had also filed a pre-grant opposition. For the first time, a foreign advocacy group from Brazil, the Brazilian Interdisciplinary AIDS Association, joined forces with the Indian civil society groups to fight the patents on tenofovir, since India granting the patent would have affected Brazil's access to tenofovir.

The US patent office revoked the patent on tenofovir in January 2009 after the evidence provided by the contesting parties clearly proved that it was a known substance even at the time Gilead filed application for the patent.[24] In September 2009, the patent office in New Delhi refused patent for the AIDS drug tenofovir filed by Gilead Sciences of the US[25] on the grounds of evergreening. Cipla is selling the product at around US$700 per patient per year.

Erlotinib Yet another case involved Cipla and Roche. The drug in question was Tarceva, a chemotherapy drug to be taken once a day that is used to treat non-small-cell lung cancer and pancreatic cancer. Roche sold Tarceva (erlotinib) for approximately US$94 a tablet, while Cipla sold it for US$33 per tablet. The dispute started when Cipla announced its decision to sell the generic version of erlotinib as Erlocip ($33 a

---

[23] http://www.internationaldrugmart.com/news-section/cipla-generic-hiv-drug-tenofovir-receives-usfda-approval.shtml accessed on 24 April, 2010.
[24] http://beta.thehindu.com/health/article15145.ece accessed on 3 May, 2010.
[25] 'India Refuses Patent Protection for AIDS drugs of US Company', *Business Standard*, 2 September, 2009.

tablet), sold in the name of Tarceva by Roche, which obtained the patent in India in February 2007. Roche sued Cipla for patent infringement in 2008. Cipla filed a post-grant opposition plea in the Delhi High Court and asked for revocation of the patent on the grounds that the drug was a derivative of an older drug and contended that the price as charged by Roche ($94) for a single tablet was almost double the per capita monthly income of an average Indian. Cipla also argued that Tarceva corresponded to polymorph b of erlotinib hydrochloride, the patent application on which was rejected following the opposition filed by Cipla primarily under Section 3(d). The Supreme Court in August 2009 rejected Roche's plea to stop Cipla from selling the generic version of Tarceva, so as to ensure access to medicines at a lower cost till the Delhi High Court decided on Cipla's patent challenge plea. The temporary injunction heard at Delhi High Court allowed Cipla to continue with the generic production and sales; however the company was told to keep records of the sales, so that the innovator could be compensated should the generic manufacturer lose the case.

Encouraged by the court's decision, Natco, another Indian company, which has the licence to manufacture and sell the product in Nepal at US$29 a tablet, also launched its generic version Erleva in India. However, in April 2010, Roche initiated legal proceedings against Natco for infringing its patent on Tarceva. Natco on the other hand claimed that Tarceva does not conform to the specification claimed in Roche's patent application. Hence, neither Erlocip nor Erleva infringe Roche's patent. Roche's claim is a paper patent and cannot be worked (manufactured).[26] The legal outcome of this case is awaited.

The rejection of cases based on Section 3(d) indicates that a large number of drug applications that seek product patents may not relate to purely innovative drugs but improvements over existing drugs. Such challenges indicate the enormous responsibility with the different stakeholders such as civil society groups, generic manufacturers and patent offices to examine each application carefully.

However, critics regard it as essential to distinguish between evergreening and incremental innovations. The National Research Council has pointed out that the cumulative effect of numerous minor incremental innovations can sometimes be more transforming and have more economic impact than a few radical innovations or technological breakthroughs (cited in Banerjee and Roy, 2009). Section 3(d) could go against the interests of the IPI, which has grown because of reverse-engineering

---

[26]   Compiled from www.spicyipIndia.blogspot.com.

skills. Also, Indian companies follow both positive and defensive patenting strategy – a strategy to secure their own products as well as to prevent others from obstructing their R&D activities (Gehl, 2005). But removal of this provision would be detrimental to access to medicines. In line with TRIPS Articles 8 and 27.2 India has adopted the 3(d) route to exclude certain innovations from patentability to provide for public health (Banerjee and Roy, 2009).

Patent Linkage Case

The ongoing patent linkage[27] case has lots of implications for the introduction of generic drugs in India. Patent linkage is prevalent in China, Canada and the US, wherein marketing approval for a generic product is linked to the patent status of the product. Patent linkage prevents marketing approval for a generic product during the term of the patent. In other words, a generic manufacturer will not get approval to market his product as long as the patent on the innovator product is effective. Marketing approval for generic products is essential if a country has to produce the generic under compulsory licence for domestic use or for export purposes. If a generic is not registered, time loss would be incurred in getting the approval to conduct the bio-equivalence studies and the final approval to launch the product.

In India, the right of the patentee does not extend to preventing the registration of generic medicines. Under Section 107A of the Indian Patent Act, relating to Bolar exemptions and parallel imports, 'any act of making, constructing, using, selling or importing a patented invention solely for uses reasonably relating to the development and submission of information required under any law for the time being in force, in India or in a country other than India that regulates the manufacture, construction, use sale or import of any product' shall not be considered as an infringement of patent rights (Khader, 2007: 624). At present in India two separate regulations, viz the granting of the patent through the patent office and marketing approval through the Drug Controller General of India (DCGI), are in operation. Linking the patent status with the marketing approval is a 'TRIPS plus' requirement and it delays the entry of generics and use of generics under compulsory licence provisions.

In the present case, Bayer filed a suit against the Union of India, DCGI and Cipla for granting marketing approval for the generic version of

---

[27] In some countries, the patent owner's rights are extended to block the regulatory approval of marketing for the competing generic products.

sorefenib tosylate on which Bayer has a valid patent till 2020. Sorefenib tosylate is used for treatment of kidney cancer and costs approximately US$5937.50 for 120 tablets for a month's dosage. Bayer filed a writ petition in the Delhi High Court stating that DCGI should consider the patent status of sorefenib tosylate before granting approval to any generic company, which resulted in the court ordering an interim injunction in favour of Bayer, stopping DCGI from granting approval to Cipla. At the intervention of the Cancer Patients Aid Association, which pointed out that because of the High Court's order DCGI wasn't accepting any application for marketing approval, the court clarified that the interim injunction was only with reference to sorefenib tosylate. In August 2009, the Delhi High Court rejected the appeal of Bayer and refused to sanction patent linkage through a court direction.

Automatic Licence

The above-mentioned cases bring out the controversies around those product patent applications that were filed during the 1995–2005 period, and accessibility to the generics purely depends on the legal outcomes. However, for those drugs that came up for patent consideration during the transitional period between 1995 and 2005, where a generic manufacturer was already engaged in production, the amendment made to the Indian Patent Act 1970 by Section 11A(7),[28] relating to automatic licences, facilitates continuation of generic production subject to the payment of royalty. It is essential that the generic producer should have been engaged in the production and marketing of the drug before 2005 and also should have invested in the said drug significantly.

Data Exclusivity

GOI also does not provide for protection of the data outlined in Article 39.3 of the TRIPS Agreement, which is eagerly demanded by the multinationals. The executive vice president and chief operating officer of Pharmaceutical Research and Manufacturers of America (PhRMA) who

---

[28]   Section 11A(7) of the Indian Patent Act 1970 facilitates this: 'Provided also that after a patent is granted in respect of applications made under sub-section (2) of section 5, the patent holder shall only be entitled to receive reasonable royalty from such enterprises which have made significant investment and were producing and marketing the concerned product prior to 1.1.2005 and which continue to manufacture the product covered by the patent on the date of grant of the patent, and no infringement proceedings shall be instituted against such enterprises.'

along with other delegates visited India in October 2010 said, 'We welcome the Patent law of India but there are many concerns . . . India has to build on the law with regard to the enforcement. Another crucial thing was about the data protection so that the companies who spent huge sums on research should not lose out by parting with the data' (Pharmabiz, 23 October, 2010).[29]

Protection of data for a period of five or ten years after the expiry of the patent would effectively extend the monopoly position and will delay the entry of competition. The Satvant Reddy committee (GOI, 2007) set up to look into data exclusivity has recommended that data exclusivity not be required for pharmaceuticals. However the committee recommended changes in the Drugs and Cosmetics Act of India to ensure that no data leaks out of the drug controller's office, so that competitors will not be able to acquire such data.

INTERNATIONAL INITIATIVES TO IMPROVE ACCESS TO MEDICINES

While the outcome of these cases would be curiously watched by the different stakeholders, some initiatives have been taken to improve access to medicines which merit mention here. The US President's Emergency Plan for AIDS Relief (PEPFAR), launched in 2003, is the largest programme committed to fighting HIV/AIDS in any nation. PEPFAR aims to support treatment for at least 3 million people, prevention of 12 million new infections, and care for 12 million people including 5 million orphans and vulnerable children by the year 2013. The success of the programme depends on the continuous availability of cost effective, safe generic HIV/AIDS medicines in the developing world. For this purpose, the US Food and Drug Administration (FDA) has introduced the 'tentative approval' procedure to allow anti-retrovirals (ARVs) from any part of the world to be rapidly assessed for quality standards and subsequently purchased for PEPFAR. The number of drugs cleared under the tentative approval has increased from 15 in 2005 to 78 in 2008. Of the 78 generic formulations that have been approved under the expedited process, 20 ARVs are meant for paediatric use. This approval also includes 16 fixed dose combinations (FDC) that contain two drugs in the same capsule or tablet and seven FDCs which have three drugs in the same capsule or tablet. This process

---

[29] www.pharmabiz.com, 'PhRMA objects to compulsory licence idea, shows concern over enforcement of patent laws', accessed on 25 October, 2010.

has also expedited the approval for seven generic versions of ARV in the US, where the patent has expired.[30] Aurobindo, and Ranbaxy from India have already had their ARV drugs cleared by the US FDA for the supply for PEPFAR. Cipla has also received US FDA approval for tenofovir under PEPFAR.

Global health care aid agencies such as UNITAID and Médicins Sans Frontières (MSF) have begun to lobby for a 'patent pool' of HIV/ AIDS drugs. Through this, patent holders, companies or universities will voluntarily offer the intellectual property related to their inventions to the pool and any company that wants to use the IP will be able to seek a licence from the pool against the payment of a royalty, without waiting for the patent to expire. GlaxoSmithKline has said it will create a pool of about 300 patents related to neglected diseases such as malaria and TB. However, pooling patents in pharmaceuticals, particularly biotechnology-related patents, will be a difficult task as the primary institutional mechanisms to set guidelines, manage and transfer patents and know-how from the pool will have to evolve. As immunity development to the older drugs is already reported in several parts of the world, this patent pool should help the generic companies such as Cipla, Natco, Hetero Drugs, Emcure, Strides Arcolab and Aurobindo, which are presently producing the first line HIV/AIDS drugs, to also produce the newer drugs. Though the patent pool or compulsory licence options would be beneficial for consumers, the companies may not be enthused about focusing on the developing and least developed country markets alone.

The Government of India itself through the Council of Scientific and Industrial Research has launched the Open Source Drug Discovery Project (OSDD). This is a project with the purpose of providing affordable health care particularly in the area of neglected diseases afflicting the developing world. The idea is to provide an open platform for scientists and researchers with diverse expertise to work on drug discoveries relating to neglected diseases. The project presently focuses on tuberculosis as it is the leading cause of death in developing countries. OSDD aims to discover new chemical entities through global collaborative effort and make it accessible to everyone to expedite the process of drug discovery. The Government of India has committed US$35 million for the project and already made available $12 million (www.osdd.net).

---

[30] http://www.pepfar.gov/press/fifth_annual_report/113725.htm, accessed on 6 October, 2009.

IN LIEU OF A CONCLUSION

The Indian pharmaceutical industry has established itself well in the generic field as the main supplier of essential drugs to developing countries. But in the uniform patent regime, the future journey for the IPI does not appear to be smooth. Within the domestic market, competition from multinationals is increasing. As the number of new chemical entities is dwindling, multinationals are setting their sights on the emerging markets.

In 2007–08, Indian companies made 14 acquisitions abroad at a cost of US$1354.1 million. In 2009, overseas companies were shopping in India for pharmaceutical acquisitions and alliances. Daichii acquired Ranbaxy in 2009. In August 2009, US based Perrigo, one of the largest OTC pharmaceutical producers in the world, acquired an 85 per cent stake in Mumbai based Vedanta Drugs and Fine Chemicals to make India its major global production base. Sanofi Pasteur, a French vaccine maker, acquired the Hyderabad based vaccine major Shantha Biotechnics for over $781 million. In May 2010, Abbott acquired one of the leading generic manufacturers of India, Piramal Healthcare, for $3.73 billion. The bigger loss for India is that in order to give a running start to this deal, Piramal has agreed not to make generic drugs for sale in India or for emerging markets for a period of eight years.[31]

In the top ten companies ranked according to their sales turnover, the number of Indian companies has reduced from nine to six, giving place to the multinationals[32] and almost indicating the pre-1980s scenario. Besides the acquisitions, alliances are also being formed with domestic companies. GlaxoSmithKline has formed a strategic alliance with Dr. Reddy's Laboratories, a significant market leader in oncology and cardiovascular drugs. Through this alliance, GSK would get a licence to sell about 100 drugs of Dr. Reddy's (some of which are still being developed). Similarly Pfizer has formed alliances with Aurobindo and Claris Life Sciences. In these alliances the Indian companies under contract manufacturing would produce specific drugs to be sold in the US and Europe by Pfizer. In the latest alliance with Biocon, Pfizer would have the exclusive right to sell the recombinant human insulin and insulin analogues produced by Biocon.[33]

---

[31] http://www.fiercebiotech.com/press-releases/abbott-become-no-1-pharmaceutical-company-india-acquisition-piramals-healthcare-solut, accessed on 22 May, 2010.

[32] http://www.livemint.com/2010/05/23233618/Hold-of-foreign-firms-on-India.html, accessed on August 16, 2010.

[33] http://www.pharmabiz.com/article/detnews.asp?articleid=57893 accessed on 19 October, 2010.

Acquiring stakes in the vertically integrated Indian companies offers scope for contract manufacturing to contain manufacturing expenses for the multinationals. But such strategies could perhaps completely alter the product profile of the Indian manufacturer to target the export market and neglect the domestic market.

The seizure of Indian generics in 2009 by customs authorities at different European ports warns of the extremes to which the intellectual property laws could be stretched. These drugs were exported to Mexico, Brazil, Ecuador, Peru, Venezuela and Colombia. An EU directive gives authority to customs officers to control goods suspected to be infringing intellectual property rights, particularly those goods that are destined for EU countries as well as those that are merely passing through EU ports on their way to another country outside the EU. This IP maximalist strategy in effect denies access to medicines to the least developed and developing nations that are dependent on such goods, particularly the hybrid generics.[34]

Being branded as 'counterfeit' is another threat that the generics face in the export market. The 66th meeting of the WHO regional committee for South East Asia has rejected the WHO-IMPACT definition of counterfeit drugs. Recognizing the need to separate the IP issues from quality, safe medical products, the draft resolution urged the member countries to refrain from IP enforcement that compromises access to medicines.

A campaign by multinationals in several African countries to ban generic medicines is already under way. According to Kenya's anti-counterfeit law passed in early 2009, generics exported to Kenya, from any country, which are under patent anywhere else can be considered counterfeit. Kenya is the third-largest African market for Indian generics[35] and African countries together account for 14 per cent of India's generic exports. A ban on the import of generics would adversely affect the manufacturers in India and could severely jeopardise access to drugs in those countries.

Within the domestic market, the issue of access to medicine arises owing to the prices and non-availability of adequate drugs in the government health care. The GOI initiated an insurance programme for people below the poverty line in 2008. Many of the states have adopted the programme which is being tried on a pilot scale in select districts of different states.

---

[34]   Hybrid generics as defined by Shadlen (2007) refer to those that are under patent in some countries but not where they are produced, or produced under CL. The anti-retroviral produced by India and supplied to various least developed and developing countries falls into this category.

[35]   http://www.theeastafrican.co.ke/news/-/2558/519156/-/view/printVersion/-/5pgdaz/-/, accessed on 24 April, 2010.

Wider coverage of this programme would depend on the resources of the different governments. The need of the hour therefore is to increase the reach of the Jan Aushadhi scheme. The present small number of 44 stores as against the 300,000 chemical drug stores in the country is a drop in the ocean. The Jan Aushadhi shops will have to spread wide in the country and their success depends on the continuous supply of quality drugs to these shops. The plan to open as many as 275 stores by the end of March 2010 has not been fulfilled, because of the weak supply chain link (Jayaraman, 2010).

The loopholes in the price control mechanisms encourage companies to shift away from the production of essential drugs. This criticism apart, the government has a huge responsibility to evolve policy guidelines to control the price of these new patented drugs. The few litigation cases cited in this chapter provide evidence of the fact that the entry of Cipla and other generic manufacturers has reduced prices, but these drugs would still not be accessible to those without health cover. With the increasing role of multinationals in the country, the chances are that the prices of the drugs would be rising.

India in future will have to resist the pressures that come from developed countries and through the free trade agreements to remove the 3(d) provision and to provide for data exclusivity, to protect the interest of the consumers.

After India adopted a product patent regime, 3488 product patents in pharmaceuticals were granted by the Indian patent office from 2005 to 2009.[36] It is likely that important life-saving drugs are in this list of granted patents. In such cases, compulsory licences would be the only option to get access to these patented drugs both within the country as well as for exports, and such licences have been provided for under the Indian Patent Act. Under Section 84, the three grounds for seeking a compulsory licence are: (a) reasonable requirements of the public with respect to the patented invention have not been satisfied; or (b) the patented invention is not available to the public at a reasonably affordable price; or (c) the patented invention is not produced in the territory of India (Khader, 2007: 717). Section 91 provides for issue of compulsory licences for related patents. Section 92 provides for issue of compulsory licences for government purposes and to control national health emergencies and epidemics. In the wake of the Doha Declaration, the Patents (Amendment) Act 2005 introduced a new provision under Section 92A for the grant of compulsory

---

[36] http://www.ipindia.nic.in/iponew/Patent_PharmaProduct_2005_06_2009_10.pdf, accessed on 15 September, 2010.

licences for the export of patented pharmaceutical products[37] to countries without manufacturing facilities.

Exercising compulsory-licence powers for government purposes would be particularly apt in the case of expensive life-saving drugs without alternatives. Such medicines should be brought under the list of drugs procured under the Jan Aushadhi scheme and in the government health care to provide access. While domestic policy reforms are required to extend access to patent-expired drugs, for patented drugs, India should be prepared to use compulsory licensing for the government use option to provide access to medicines.

REFERENCES

Banerjee, Meghna and Roy, Yajnaseni (2009), 'Patentability of Incremental Innovation vis-à-vis S 3(D) of the Indian Patents Act: Striking a Balance', *NUJS Law Review,* October–December, **2** (4) 607–636.

Centad (2009), 'Glaring Disparities', *Trading Up,* **5** (1), 25.

Chaudhuri, Sudip (2005), *The WTO and India's Pharmaceutical Industry – Patent Protection, TRIPS, and Developing Countries,* NewDelhi: Oxford University Press.

Chaudhuri, Sudip (2009), 'Is Product Patent Protection Necessary in Developing Countries for Innovation? R&D by Indian Pharmaceutical Companies after TRIPS', in Netanel, Neil Weinstock (ed.), *The Development Agenda, Global Intellectual Property and Developing Countries,* New York, Oxford University Press, 265–291.

Cullet, Philippe (2005), *Intellectual Property Protection and Sustainable Development,* New Delhi: Lexis Nexis Butterworths.

Dhar, Biswajit and Gopakumar, K.M. (2007), *Effect of the Product Patents on the Indian Pharmaceutical Industry,* NewDelhi: Centre for WTO Studies, Indian Institute of Foreign Trade.

Ernst and Young (2009), 'Taking Wings: Coming of Age of the Indian Pharmaceutical Outsourcing Industry', Organisation of Pharmaceutical Producers Association of India, Mumbai.

Essential Drugs Monitor (1998), **25** & **26**, Geneva: World Health Organisation.

EXIM Bank (Export Import Bank of India) (2007), 'Indian Pharmaceutical Industry: Surging Globally', Occasional Paper No. 119, Mumbai: EXIM Bank.

---

[37]   Section 92A stipulates the conditions under which this could be used: (a) the compulsory licence shall be solely for manufacture and export of patented pharmaceutical products; (b) the export should be to a country having insufficient or no manufacturing capacity in the pharmaceutical sector to address public health problems; (c) a compulsory licence should have been granted by that country or that country should have by notification or otherwise, allowed importation of patented pharmaceutical products from India (Khader, 2007: 732)

Federal Trade Commission http://www.ftc.gov/os/2010/01/100113mpdim2003rpt. pdf, accessed on 10 July, 2010.

Francis, P.A. (2006), 'An ACT to Replace DPCO', Pharma Biz, www.pharmabiz. com, accessed on 2 November, 2006.

Gehl, Sampath Padmashree (2005), 'Economic Aspects of Access to Medicines After 2005: Product Patent Protection and Emerging Firm Strategies in the Indian Pharmaceutical Industry', United Nations University–INTECH, http:// www.who.int/intellectualproeprty/studies/padmashreeGehlSampthFinal.pdf, accessed on 7 September, 2008.

Government of India (1975), 'Report of the Committee on Drugs and Pharmaceutical Industry', Ministry of Petroleum and Chemicals, New Delhi.

Government of India (2007), 'Report on Steps to be Taken by Government of India in the context of Data Protection Provisions of Article 39.3 of the TRIPS Agreement', available at http://chemicals.nic.in/DPBooklet.pdf, accessed on 8 September, 2008.

Government of India (2009), Annual Report, 2008–09, Department of Pharmaceuticals, available at http://pharmaceuticals.gov.in/ accessed on 24 April, 2010.

Government of India (2010), 'Forty-fifth Report on Issues Relating to Availability of Generic, Generic-Branded and Branded Medicines, Their Formulation and Therapeutic Efficacy and Effectiveness', Parliament of India, Rajya Sabha, August, available at http://164.100.47.5/newcommittee/reports/English Committees/Committee%20on%20Health%20and%20Family%20Welfare/45th %20report.pdf, accessed on 10 October, 2010.

Grace, Cheri (2005), 'A Briefing Paper for DFID: Update on China and India and Access to Medicines', London, DFID Health Resource Centre, available at http://www.dfid.gov.uk/aboutdfid/organisation/accessmedicines.asp, accessed on 10 July, 2007.

Guha, Amitava (2002), 'Recent Trends in Pharmaceutical Pricing and Marketing', Presentation at the workshop on TRIPS, Pharmaceutical Industry and Health, Kolkata: Indian Institute of Management, Calcutta, October, 7–8.

IDMA (2009), 'India Overturns HIV Drug Patents', IDMA Bulletin, **40** (34), 35–36.

IDMA (2010), 'India – The Generics Pharma Capital of the World', Mumbai, IDMA.

Jayaraman, K. (2010), 'Troubles Beset Jan Aushadhi Plan to Broaden Access to Generics', *Nature Medicine*, **16** (4), 350.

Khader, F.A. (2007), *The Law of Patents – With a Special Focus on Pharmaceuticals in India*, New Delhi, Lexis Nexis Butterworths.

Kotwani, Anita, Ewen, Margret, Dey, Dalia, Iyer, Shobha, Lakshmi, P.K., Patel, Archana, Raman, Kannamma, Singhal, G.L., Thawani, Vijay, Tripathi, Santhanu, Laing, Richard (2007), 'Prices and Availability of Common Medicines at Six Sites in India: Using a Standard Methodology', *Indian Journal of Medical Research*, **125**, 645–654.

Lalitha, N. (2005), 'Review of the Pharmaceutical Industry of Canada', *Economic and Political Weekly*, **40** (13), 1355–1362.

Lalitha, N. (2009), 'Access to Medicines in Public Health Care: Lessons from Tamil Nadu', in Kumar, Girish (ed.), *Health Sector Reforms in India*, New Delhi: Manohar Publishers and Distributors and Centre De Sciences Humaines, 87–113.

Leibowitz, Jon (2009), 'Pay for Delay Settlements in the Pharmaceutical Industry', available at http://www.ftc.gov/speeches/leibowitz/090623payfordelayspeech. pdf, accessed on 10 June, 2010.

Narayana, P.L. (1984), *Indian Pharmaceutical Industry Problems and Prospects*, NewDelhi: National Council for Applied Economic Research.

PricewaterhouseCoopers (2010), 'Global Pharma Looks to India: Prospects for Growth', available at http://www.pwc.com/en_GX/gx/pharma-life-sciences/publications/india-growth.jhtml, accessed 5 July, 2010.

Rane, Wishwas (1999), 'Essential Medicines and International Trade', *Economic and Political Weekly*, **34** (50), 3490–3491.

Rane, Wishwas (2002), 'Prices of Prescription Drugs', *Economic and Political Weekly*, **37** (33), 3402–3404.

Shadlen, Kenneth C. (2007), 'The Political Economy of AIDS Treatment: Intellectual Property and Transformation of Generic Supply', *International Studies Quarterly*, **51**, 559–581.

Srinivasan, S. (2006), 'A Lay Person's Guide to Medicines: What is in Them and What is Behind Them', Vadodara, Lowcost Standard Therapeutics.

Srinivasan, S. and Bhargava, Anurag (2006), 'Why is Paswan's Price Reduction a Let Down?', *Economic and political Weekly*, **41** (50), 5101–5105.

Srinivasan, S. (2007), 'Battling Patent Laws: The Glivec Case', *Economic and Political Weekly*, **42** (37), 3686–3690.

Srinivasan, S. (2009), 'Too Good to be True – But True Retail Sale of Generic Drugs at Low Prices by Government at Chittorgarh Dt', *Medico Friend Circle Bulletin*, August.

World Bank (2001), *India – Raising the Sights: Better Health Systems for India's Poor*, Washington DC: World Bank.

10. Sufficient but expensive drugs: a double-track system that facilitated supply capability in China

Mariko Watanabe and Luwen Shi

This chapter analyses access to essential drugs in China by focusing on institutions involved in the demand for and supply of drugs. With regard to the demand for drugs, the Chinese health care system is undergoing substantial change. Health care used to be an extremely underdeveloped sphere of China's public policy: most of the population was not covered by health insurance, so the general public had to pay a substantial share of drugs expenditure themselves. This situation generated significant social discontent, and the discontent compelled a reform of the health care system in the mid-2000s. A new health care system is now under discussion, which is likely to change the nature of demand for drugs drastically.

On the supply side, China adopted a double-track system of drug listing before joining the WTO in 2001. The drug patent system was introduced in the early 1990s in order to protect the innovators, most of which are big foreign pharmaceuticals firms. At the same time, local firms, which produce generic drugs, were provided an opportunity of entry under the principle of "New Drug Protection", which protects the first firm to enter the Chinese market regardless of patents. This double-track system allows many local firms to enter drug production, facilitating access to essential drugs for the general public. However, shortcomings on the demand side, particularly in hospitals, cause a problem of expensive drugs.

The chapter is organized as follows: Section 1 describes the nature of demand for drugs in China, where poor fiscal support for the health care system and incentives for hospitals to prefer prescribing expensive drugs tend to drive up the price of drugs. Section 2 describes price setting and drug listing institutions. The separation of drug patents and the license for the first firms to enter the market create the space for many firms to enter the industry. Then, Section 3 discusses the idea that expensive drugs with numerous suppliers are a feature of the accessibility of drugs in China due to the dual nature of demand and the double-track system in supply.

1   THE DEMAND FOR DRUGS AND THE HEALTH CARE SYSTEM IN CHINA

In this section, we look at the extent of demand and who pays what in China with reference to the complicated health care system under the gradual reforms from the 1990s to the present.

1.1   Size of Drug Demand

In 2007, the entire medical expenditure in China was 1,128.95 billion RMB (US$154.8 billion), which was about one half of Japan's expenditure, 3.313 trillion JPY (US$297.4 billion). The population of Japan is around 0.12 billion, which is about one tenth of the Chinese population. China's per capita medical expenditure, therefore, is almost one twentieth of Japan's.

Table 10.1 presents some basic health statistics. Indices for health achievement reveal that China has seen relatively good performance as a developing economy: life expectancy is considerably lower than in Japan and the US (although it is at almost the same level as that of Thailand). Infant mortality substantially decreased from 34.7 per mil in 1980 to 1.8 per mil in 2008. The proportion of the population aged 65 or above is smaller than in Japan and the US, but it is expected to grow faster. As a whole, China is still a long way from Japan or the US in terms of these indices. China's health spending is smaller than that of these countries in terms of ratio to GDP, per capita spending or as a proportion of total fiscal expenditure. China's share of drug expenditure out of total health expenditure (52 per cent) is much higher than that of Japan (20 per cent) or the US (11 per cent) (see Table 10.2).

The burden on the individual of health care spending is much larger than in the two developed economies. The Chinese government sector only

Table 10.1   Basic health statistics for China, Japan and the US (2008)

	China	Japan	US
Health achievement			
Life expectancy	Male: 72	Male: 79	Male: 76
	Female: 76	Female: 86	Female: 81
Infant mortality	1.8%	0.3%	0.7%
Proportion of the population aged over 65	7.1%	21.9%	12.4%

Source: Life expectancy, infant mortality: World Health Organization, *World Health Statistics 2010*. Aged population: United Nations, *Demographic Yearbook 2008*.

Table 10.2   Medical expenditures of China, Japan and the US (2007)

	China	Japan	USA
Expenditure			
TME/GDP	4.6%	8.0%	15.7%
Medical fiscal expenditure/total fiscal expenditure	9.9%	17.9%	19.5%
Drug expense/total medical expenditure	52%	20%	11%
Per capita medical spending	US$108	US$2,751	US$7,285
Burden sharing			
Distribution by agents	Government 20.3%	Government 36.6%	
	Society 34.5%	National health insurance 49%	Government 36.5%
	Individual 45.2%	Individual 14.4%	Private 63.5%
Public medical insurance coverage	88% of nation	Almost all the nation	–
Ratio of individual disbursement	Urban 45% Rural 79%	30%	–

Source: WHO, World Health Statistics; People's Republic of China, Department of Health, Reform and Development of Health Sector in China (2008) (年我国卫生改革与发展情况)

bears 20 per cent of the cost, while the Japanese government and compulsory medical insurance cover 86 per cent of medical fees. Furthermore, about 12 per cent of the population has no public medical insurance (Table 10.2). What needs to be stressed here is that the share of private expenditure is high and fiscal expenditure is limited, so that medical institutions cannot help pursuing profit maximization.

1.2   Structure of Demand

1.2.1   OTC drugs and prescriptions

The channel for drugs sales consists of prescriptions at hospitals and OTC (Over the Counter) drugs. For OTC sales, the State Drug Administration has regularly announced since 1999 that OTC drugs should be registered in the "Catalogue of OTC Drugs", which is separate from the control over prescription drugs, which must be registered under the "Drug Registration Management Law". OTC drugs are required to be sold to

Table 10.3   Sales routes for drugs

	Prescription	OTC
Sales route	Manufacturer→wholesaler →hospital	Manufacturer→wholesaler →drug store
Who prescribes?	Physicians No. of Physicians 1,555,658 (2005) No. of Hospitals 65,000 (2005)	Pharmacists No. of Pharmacists 349,533 (2005)
Who pays?	Medical insurance/patients	Patients
No. of drugs	3,214*	4,279 (2005)
Sales volume	150.4 billion RMB (2005)	78.2 billion RMB (2005)

Note: * Number of prescription drugs is the number of drugs in the China Pharmaceutical Catalogue.

Source: China Health Statistics.

patients by pharmacists over the counter. However, as Table 10.3 shows, the number of pharmacists is far smaller than that of physicians, and so in practice OTC drugs are sold in the same way as ordinary commodities in supermarkets.

The proportion of prescription drugs is around 70 per cent of total pharmaceutical sales in China, with OTC taking up around 30 per cent (interview with Chemical Drug Manufacturers' Association in November 2006), although the latter has been steadily increasing over the years. Thus, for most pharmaceutical firms in China, physicians in hospitals are the buyers who decide whether the hospital should order a particular drug, and they also prescribe the drugs as an agent of the patient.

1.2.2 Medical insurance plans

There are two categories of ultimate drug purchasers: medical insurers and patients. Currently, there coexist about seven types of medical insurance plans: in 2008, 12.8 per cent of the population remained uninsured, though this represents great progress compared to 2003 when as much as 78 per cent of population was uninsured (Table 10.4).

In 1997, the Central Committee of the Communist Party and the State Council announced the "Decision on Health Sector Reform and Development". Based on this political commitment, the Urban Employee Basic Medical Insurance (城镇职工基本医疗保险: UEBMI), or the National Basic Medical Insurance, was launched by the State Council in

Table 10.4   Social medical insurance plans and their coverage

Item	Total %		Urban %		Rural %	
	2008	2003	2008	2003	2008	2003
Urban Employee Basic Medical Insurance	12.7	8.9	44.2	30.4	1.5	1.5
Government Officials Medical Insurance	1.0	1.2	3.0	4.0	0.3	0.2
Basic Medical Insurance of Residents	3.8	–	12.5	–	0.7	–
New Rural Cooperative Medical Insurance	68.7	–	9.5	–	89.7	–
Others	1.0	12.0	2.8	15.2	0.4	10.9
No social medical insurance	12.8	77.9	28.1	50.4	7.5	87.3

Source: National Survey on Health Service in 2003 and 2008.

1998. This is the country's compulsory medical insurance plan, but it has not yet been legislated, even as of early 2011, and its coverage is still limited as corporations are reluctant to pay the premiums. However, the UEBMI is currently the largest medical insurance plan in China, although it covers only 30 per cent of the urban population (or less than 10 per cent of the total population). Serious Disease Medical Insurance provides a complement to those insured under the UEBMI, covering expensive medical services. For the urban population, there used to be two medical insurance plans: the Public Expense Medical Insurance (公费医疗保险) and Labor Medical Insurance (劳保医疗保险), both established in 1951. The former was disbursed by the local government's fiscal budget, while the latter was disbursed by government department and state owned enterprises. Both covered 100 per cent of medical fees for the insured and a proportion of the fees for their families. After the UEBMI was set up in 1998, these two insurance plans were intended to gradually merge with the UEBMI. In 2007, the Urban Residents Basic Medical Insurance (城镇居民基本医疗保险: URBMI) was introduced to cover non-working urban residents, such as children, students and people over 65, on a voluntary basis. Until the URBMI was introduced, households with children or elderly people, who are actually heavy users of medical services, had to meet all the medical expenses themselves.

In rural areas, cooperative medical insurance plans were set up in the 1940s accompanying the People's Commune (人民公社), but they declined in the 1980s. The State Council announced the "Decision on Strengthening the Health Care System in Rural Areas" in 2002, and the

"Announcement on the New Rural Cooperative Medical System（新农村合作医疗制度". By the end of 2006, 0.508 billion people in the 1,451 counties had joined the insurance plan. In that year, the participation ratio was 80 per cent, although it was on a voluntary basis, and the insurance plan reimbursed 15.581 billion RMB. Currently, UEBMI, URBMI and the Rural Cooperative Medical Insurance are the main social medical insurance plans covering the population of China. See Table 10.5.

1.2.3   Drug catalogues and purchasers of drugs
These multi-track medical insurance systems provide multiple drug catalogues, creating a complicated demand structure for drugs in China. There are three basic drug catalogues: the China Pharmacopoeia, the State Basic Drug Catalogue (issued by the State Food and Drug Administration) and the SFDA Import Drug Catalogue. UEBMI compiles an insurance reimbursement list consisting of 1,031 chemical drugs and 832 Traditional Chinese Medicines (2004 version). Rural cooperative insurances or the urban community also compile their own drug catalogues. In practice, from the viewpoint of pharmaceutical firms, the insurance reimbursement list of UEBMI is the most important drug catalogue. See Table 10.6.

Figure 10.1 presents a rough depiction of drug demand, to show who purchases what proportion of drugs in China. Though there is no exact data for this, we have estimated the share of costs borne by medical insurance and by the patients as follows: OTC drugs, whose share of the drug market is 30 per cent as we saw in Section 1.2.1, is 100 per cent self-paid by the patients. The share of individual payment in this drug market is $0.3*1 = 30$ per cent. The payment for prescription drugs, which have a 70 per cent share of the market, is shared by insurance reimbursement and the patients themselves. In 2008, medical insurance covered 88 per cent of the population, i.e., 50 per cent of prescription drugs. Furthermore, the insurance reimbursement ratio is less than 100 per cent, but we have no exact data – we have assumed here 80 per cent. Thus, medical insurance purchases are $0.7*0.88*0.8 = 49.5$ per cent of total drug sales in 2008. The remainder of the prescription drug cost is borne by the patients themselves.

Here we can see that roughly 50 per cent of drug sales are paid for out of the patient's own pocket. Coverage by medical insurance plans is around only 50 per cent (it will rise to around 70 per cent when all the population is insured). As already pointed out universally in China, the limited coverage of medical insurance plans is the main reason why the general public complains that hospital services are far beyond their ability to pay.

Table 10.5   Targets and burden sharing of social medical insurance plans

Insurance	Started	Target	Burden Sharing
1 Urban Employee Basic Medical Insurance (UEBMI)	1998	Compulsory for current and retired workers in urban areas	Corporation pays 6% of total wage and individual pays 2% of own wage A list: insurance pays 100% B list: individual also pays a fixed ratio (fixed by the local governments)
2 Major disease insurance		Insured by insurance 1	Corporation and employee (different amounts according to administration)
3 Labor medical insurance	1951	Employees, retired staff of SOEs and their families (transition to 1)	Corporation (100%)
4 Public expense medical insurance	1951	Public servants, party leaders and cadets (transition to 1)	Local fiscal (100%)
5 Urban Residents Basic Medical Insurance (URBMI)	2007	Voluntary for students, children and non-workers in urban areas who are out of target of insurance 1	Household bears most, government subsidizes some (not less than 40 RMB every year, additional subsidies are given to households with people aged over 65, the disabled and those on lower incomes)
6 New Rural Cooperative Medical System (NRCMS)	2002	Revived in 2002	Individual (10 yuan), central and local fiscals (20 yuan respectively)
7 Other social medical insurance		1) Labor injury insurance 2) Urban welfare medical assistance 3) Maternity medical insurance	1) Corporation pays 0.5%, 1% and 2% of wages 2) Local fiscal: deducts 20–30% of medical expenses 3) Corporation pays 1% or below of wages of female workers
8 Commercial medical insurance 9 Not insured		Individuals	Individuals

Source: Author.

Table 10.6   Drug catalogues

	By	Insurance	No. of drugs
Basic drug catalogues			
China Pharmacopoeia	Pharmacopoeia committee	–	3,214
State Basic Drug Catalogue	SFDA	–	CD 773, TCM 1260
SFDA Import Drug Catalogue	SFDA	–	
Insurance reimbursement catalogues			
State Basic Medical Insurance Drug Catalogue	MLSS	1	CD 1031, TCM 832
A list: basic, generic drugs	MLSS	1	CD 315, TCM 135
B list: optional, new drugs	MLSS	2, 3	CD 712, TCM 688
Basic Drug List	MOH	1, 5, 6	CD+TCM 307
Rural Cooperative Insurance Drugs Catalogue	MOH	5	
Urban Community Drug Catalogue	–		
Important Base Drug Catalogue	–		

Note: CD = chemical drugs, TCM = traditional Chinese medicine, SFDA = State Food and Drug Administration, MLSS = Ministry of Labor and Social Security, MOH = Ministry of Health.

Source: State basic drugs list, State Food Drug Administration. State Basic Medical Insurance Drug Catalogue, Ministry of Labor, Social Securities. Wikipedia, Medicine (China).

1.3 "Feeding Hospitals with Drugs (以药养医)": Agency Problem Between Hospitals, Drug Retailers and Patients

1.3.1 Overview of "feeding hospitals with drugs"

The demand for drugs in China is characterized as follows. 1) The ultimate purchasers of the drugs are the medical insurers or the patients; the former cover about 50 per cent of the population. 2) The direct purchasers of the drugs from manufacturers are primarily hospitals. Hospitals and physicians are expected to act as patients' agents. However, hospitals in China are not necessarily good agents for patients as they themselves suffer from the following problems: 1) though there is strong demand for better medical services, the utilization rate of medical services remains low because hospi-

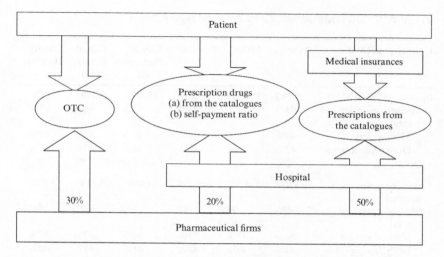

Note: Figures in three pillars are sales ratios estimated by the authors. The formula for estimation is stated in the text.

Source: Authors.

Figure 10.1 Who purchases what proportion of drugs in China?

tal charges are far beyond the means of the general public. 2) The hospitals' revenue structure largely depends on the revenue earned from dispensing drugs. All types of hospitals depend on drugs for more than 40 per cent of their revenue. Medical services are loss-making for all types of hospitals, but this is alleviated by profits from drug sales (see Table 10.7).

The figures are consistent with the public perception that drug price margins between sales to the patient and procurement from the manufacturers is the main profit source of hospitals. Hospitals and physicians have a strong preference to prescribe more expensive drugs. In our interviews with the management of pharmaceutical firms that also run private hospitals, it was confirmed that "no hospital can afford to operate without depending on the drug margins" (interview in June 2007). The high dependency of hospitals on drug price margins is often attributed to poor fiscal support. As we can see from Table 10.8, subsidies from the government are limited to only 5–7.5 per cent. This poor support from the government or public sector is attributed to fiscal decentralization provoked by the central government's huge deficit during the reform period since 1978 (Uchimura and Jutting, 2007).

So hospitals maximize their revenues by increasing drug price margins. Meng (2006) conducted a detailed data collection on the impact of the

Table 10.7   Revenue structure by hospital type (2008)

Unit: 10,000 RMB	Average	MOH	Province	City at Prefecture Level	City at County Level	County Hospital
Income per hospital	9,283	116,818	47,023	15,285	5,510	3,530
Medical operation total	93%	93%	93%	92%	93%	92%
Medical service	49%	49%	49%	49%	49%	49%
Drug prescriptions	42%	42%	43%	42%	42%	41%
Others	2%	2%	1%	1%	2%	2%
Expenditure per hospital	8,988	114,102	45,499	14,888	5,313	3,378
Medical operation total	98%	98%	98%	98%	99%	98%
Medical service	56%	57%	55%	56%	57%	57%
Drug prescriptions	41%	40%	42%	41%	41%	40%
Others	1%	1%	1%	1%	1%	1%
Profit per hospital	295	2,716	1,523	397	197	152
Medical operation total	–193	–2,630	–491	–403	–109	–85
Medical services	–510	–7,766	–2,226	–874	–327	–179
Drug prescriptions	249	3,717	1,404	373	166	78
Expense per outpatient	146	282	220	153	118	99
for drugs	74	158	117	78	57	44
Expense per inpatient	5,464	13,981	11,084	6,557	4,115	2,712
for drugs	2,400	5,678	4,849	2,845	1,852	1,236
for examination and treatment	1,361	3,761	2,712	1,739	946	632

Source: China Health Statistical Yearbook (2009).

medical reform on medical service demand. A study on the introduction of price regulations on drugs in 2000 found that the hospitals prescribed new drugs under the price regulation, with prices being two times higher than pre-reform. This result suggests a preference on the part of hospitals toward higher-priced drugs, which is the opposite of the response towards other goods.

1.3.2   Hospitals have an incentive to prescribe expensive drugs

Due to the income structure described above, hospitals have an incentive to prescribe more expensive drugs. Bao (2008: 56) introduces a story about aspirin, a classic drug for fever and headache. This chemical entity

Table 10.8 *Historical change of revenue structure (general hospitals)*

	1980	1998	1999	2000	2001	2002	2003	2004	2005
Share (%)									
Subsidy	48.8	6.0	6.8	6.3	7.1	7.3	7.5	6.2	5.0
Medical consultations	n.a.	38.2	43.7	43.6	44.2	45.3	46.0	44.9	47
Drug prescriptions	n.a.	46.2	46.8	46.3	45.3	43.5	43.7	40.0	48

Note: Statistics show a fourth channel of revenue, "other channel", but we do not include this here because its size is insignificant.

Source: 1998–2005: China Health Statistical Yearbook 2005; 1980: Bao (2008: 85).

Table 10.9 *Price structure from fieldwork by Bao (2008)*

Unit: RMB	A	B	C	D	E
Retail price	68	68	65	34	22.7
Back margin	5	–	10	–	–
Wholesale price	42	59	46	–	19.6
Price at factory	50	50	36	24.58	16.46
Production cost	7	17	6.7	6.5	2.32

Note: Figures of production costs are estimated in Bao (2008). Other prices are based on information gained in interviews with medical representatives of pharmaceutical firms.

Source: Price structures in five case studies in Bao (2008) Chapter 3 are summarized here.

was discovered more than a century ago, and there is a huge production capacity in China. Thus, its price is as cheap as 0.03 RMB per tablet. It is an effective drug even now. However, physicians in China rarely prescribe this drug, but prescribe Bamyl because its retail price is as high as 0.63 RMB per tablet. The higher retail price provides a bigger income for physician and hospital. This structure still exists even after the government started reducing maximum retail prices. A lot of pharmaceutical companies stopped producing aspirin, which is irrational from the point of view of patients because they cannot buy cheap, effective and safe drugs on the market (interview by one of the authors in 2006).

1.3.3 High margin in distribution leads to high retail price of drugs
Bao (2008) presented raw information on price structures in distribution obtained from interviews and media: see Table 10.9. The difference

between price at factory and production cost includes all non-production costs such as advertising, interest payments, back rebates. The remainder is actually very low. Bao (2008: Chapter 8) attributed the high margins in the distribution channel to incentives of hospitals, not pharmaceutical companies or wholesalers. An analysis in Watanabe (2006) also concluded that high retail prices are a result of the monopoly power of hospitals in the drug distribution channels in China, and the pharmaceutical firms gain little profit in a very competitive environment created by the government.

2   SUPPLY: DOUBLE TRACK IN DRUG LISTING AND PRICE SETTING REGULATION

The double track in drug listing which consists of drug patent protection and the "new drug document" license is a very special feature of the drug supply system in China. Patents have protected drug innovators since 1993 in China. In addition to this patent protection, the first supplier of the new drug in the market was also able to get market exclusivity regardless of patents. The latter license was introduced in order to promote active entry into the market to satisfy demand for drugs. In this section, we will describe the two-track drug listing up to 2002 and the price setting regulations.

2.1   Drug Listing Control 1: Patent Protection

2.1.1   Historical development of the patent system in China
In China, new chemical entities were not patented until 1993, though the Patent Law was enacted in 1985. As in other countries, drugs were originally excluded from patent protection to secure public welfare; however, following lobbying by the big international pharmaceutical companies, they started to be patented in 1993.

In the Patent Law enacted on 1st April 1985, the 25th clause clearly stated that a "patent will not be provided for a drug or new chemical entity". In other words, the Patent Law did not give patent protection to drugs and chemical entities themselves, but only to the process and methods used. In legislation, the weak innovation capacity of pharmaceutical firms in China because of its position as a developing economy is taken into greater consideration.

Nearly eight years after the introduction of the first version, the Patent Law was revised on 1st January 1993. The revised Patent Law added protection for drugs and new chemical entities, and extended the scope of protection to include products that were produced by a patented process, in order to keep the Chinese economic system consistent with international customs and in particular to facilitate China's membership to the World Trade Organization. This was also consistent with China's Reform and Open-Door Policy. Revisions in 2000 confirmed the 1993 Patent Law, clearly providing all drugs in China with patent protection.

2.1.2 Objects of patent protection and conditions

Drug patents consist of (1) the innovation itself, (2) the drug's practical use and (3) the product's appearance and design. The subject of the protection is the discovery of a new chemical entity, in other words innovation; the new form and compound of drugs, and any new and revised process. Of these, the most important conditions for patent protection are novelty, creativity and practicality. "Novelty" shows that a similar drug has not been published in domestic or foreign publications prior to the patent application, has not yet been used in public or announced in any other form, and patent administration has not been applied for or publicized by other persons. "Creativity" shows that the new drug demonstrates substantial features and progress compared to the technology that existed before its application. "Practicality" indicates that it should actually be possible to manufacture and use the innovative drug and that it generates a positive effect. Likewise, patent protection on a drug or process is provided for the products of innovative efforts. In terms of practicality, the patent only requires that the drug or the process be applicable in commercialization, or the prospect of commercialization. Application in commercialization indicates that not only is the drug or new process capable of curing a disease, but also that is has been rigorously inspected regarding toxicity and/or safety (Chen et al., 2006: 30).

2.1.3 Time period and instruments of patent protection

The Patent Law clearly provides that an innovation patent is protected for 20 years from the date of application. Practically speaking, those 20 years are classified in three stages, and the protection is strengthened step by step. Because China's patent system employs the principle of "publishing earlier, and investigating slowly", during the period that a drug patent is applied for but has yet to be published it is impossible for the other parties to know the details of any innovation, and thus they cannot be held to be infringing the patent. If an identical drug were innovated during this period, the innovator could not claim compensation, because patent protection would not yet have come into effect, but the competition could neither apply for a patent nor destroy the novelty inherent in this innovation. Therefore, this transitional period can be regarded as a period of "mutual non-intervention".

In the second period, when the patent has been applied for but not yet approved, the general public is able to know detailed contents of the particular innovation. Thus, if another party were to utilize the same innovation, he would have to make payment to the innovator for the appropriate costs. This can be regarded as the period of "transitory protection". During the third period, when the patent has been approved, no institution or individual can utilize the patent to manufacture for sale, use, license, sell or import the patented products or use the patented process, nor can they use, sell, license or import products that directly rely on that particular patent. During this period, if somebody uses the patent without the approval of the patent holder, the patent holder or another stakeholder can file a complaint with the courts, or ask the patent administration to require the violator to stop and to pay compensation. This is the period of "complete protection".

According to clauses in the Patent Law, only one patent is approved for each innovation. Because of this provision, patent protection provides exclusive marketability. In other words, each patent protects only one new drug. This exclusivity can lead to monopolized profit from the market, including production, sales, use and importation of the new drug (Chen et al., 2006: 30–31).

2.2   Drug Listing Control 2: New Drug Protection Policy

2.2.1   Laws, regulations and incentive structure
When the economic reform started in China, the first priority of the government was to secure a sufficient supply of pharmaceuticals to maintain the existing level of health of the population. To meet this target, the government set the production of generics as the first priority: the first Drug Management Law, enacted in 1985, provided "new drug protection" independent of patent protection. No new pharmaceutical entity could be patented until the Patent Law was revised in 1993. Even after new chemical entities in drugs could be patented, "new drug protection" provided "market exclusivity" for the protected pharmaceutical firms, independent of "patent protection".

Under this scheme of new drug protection, market exclusivity was given to the introduction of new technology, so to speak, but not to research and development into new chemical entities. This was a unique industrial policy for China, which contrasts with India. In India, patent protection for pharmaceuticals has been rejected, because it is not ethical to allow a firm to monopolize pharmaceutical production and the ensuing profits when people's lives may be at stake. China accepted patent protection and, simultaneously, provided market exclusivity to technology introduction by domestic firms, which remains consistent.

Table 10.10 shows the development of new drug protection: from 1999 to 2002, market exclusivity given to a new chemical entity (Class 1) was as long as 12 years. This could be longer than patent protection on some occasions, as the patent protection period runs from the filing date of application, not the product listing date. Usually, the patent is applied for when research and development is under way, and it will take several years to list the new drug products after completing clinical tests. Thus, the protection period for new drugs could be longer than the patent protection.

In 2002, "New Drug Protection" was replaced by the "New Drug Monitoring Scheme". When China joined the WTO, new drug protection became inconsistent with the intellectual property protection systems under TRIPS. Because of these circumstances, the Act was revised to comply with international norms. Firstly, market exclusivity was not provided for manufacturers' introduction of a new technology, but instead was provided when responsibility to monitor the safety and effectiveness of the drugs was undertaken in exchange for market exclusivity. Secondly, the definition of "new drugs" was changed from "those not produced in China" to "those not listed in China". The New Drug Monitoring Scheme was planned to monitor new drugs for safety and effectiveness, by providing market exclusivity to the supplier of that new drug. However, the period of market exclusivity was reduced from 12 years to five years for Class 1 new chemical entities, and raw materials and active/intermediate products were taken off the monitoring list (Table 10.11). Thirdly, data on new drugs, submitted by the drug's developer, became legally protected, which had not been the case previously. On the whole, property protection for pharmaceuticals was strengthened and made consistent with current international standards.

2.3 The Principles of Price Setting

In China, the price of drugs had been kept low until the mid-1980s so that basic medical care would be affordable for the general public. The medical care system was decentralized as a result of the process of fiscal reform in China. Fiscal reform requires the local government to be responsible through their budget for the social security system. Thus, fiscal subsidies for the hospital and health care sector are limited, and as a result they are also required to operate by means of their own revenues. In this way, since the middle of the 1980s, the prices for medical services have been adjusted to compensate for the operating costs of the health care sector.

The current price-setting mechanism has the following principles: (1) the State Development and Reform Committee (SDRC) sets a price cap on the retail price of drugs in the medical drug catalogues. (2) There is a

Table 10.10   Market exclusivity under the new drug protection versus patent protection (chemical drugs)

Classification	1985	1999	2002	Patent protection
	Drug Controlling Law	New Drug Registration Act and Notice on New Drug Protection and Technology Transfer	New drug protection in Revised Drug Management Law, Drug Management Act[1]	
Class 1: new chemical entity that has not been listed anywhere in the world	8 years	12 years	Transitory protection 5 years	15 years (–1993) 20 years (1993–)
Class 2: Listed abroad, but not listed in the foreign pharmacopoeia, nor imported to China	6 years	8 years	4 years	None
Class 3: New combination of registered drug	4 years	8 years	3 years	None
Class 4: Listed on the foreign pharmacopoeia, imported into China but not produced in China (not listed in China since 2002)[2]	3 years	6 years	3 years	None
Class 5: New use of already registered drug	3 years	6 years	3 years	None

Notes:

1 On introduction of the Revised Drug Management Law and Drug Management Act in 2002, new drug protection was abolished, and the new drug monitoring period was introduced in 2002. The following transitional measures were taken: 1) drugs that passed clinical tests on 15 September, 2002 were given market exclusivity for the period of new drug protection in the 1999 scheme; 2) Drugs that were applied for to the government, but had not passed a clinical test yet, nor sold in China, were given a "monitoring period" in the new 2002 scheme.

2 The Class 4 category is unique in China for protecting domestic firms in securing a sufficient supply of pharmaceuticals. The 1999 Drug Application Act listed 8 types in this category:

   (1) Raw materials, intermediates, and drugs listed on the foreign pharmacopoeia.
   (2) Raw materials and intermediates and/or drugs already imported into China (drugs manufactured using the raw materials or intermediates imported for research and development are categorized here).
   (3) Any drug or its optical isomer whose synthesis method is already know and registered abroad.
   (4) Any drug that utilizes an acid or alkali or replaces metal elements of a drug already sold in China, or has a similar pharmacology mechanism.
   (5) Compound or change of drug formation of a drug that is listed abroad.
   (6) Drug that is manufactured from imported raw materials.
   (7) Drug that has changed drug formation.
   (8) Drug that has changed use.

Source: Documents on the related regulations and Deng and Kaitin (2004).

*Table 10.11   Monitoring period in "Notice Related to Revised Drug
Registration Act"*

Monitoring period	Classification

5 years	• Among drugs not listed in the world, drugs that contain
	  (1) New chemical entities
	  (2) New biological pharmaceuticals
	  (3) Optical isomers of an already known entity

4 years	• Among drugs not listed in the world, drugs that contain
	  (1) Compound of a known entity where the amount of the effective entity is reduced but retains the same effectiveness
	  (2) New compounds of a known entity
	  (3) New delivery systems
	• Among drugs that were listed abroad, but not in China, drugs that
	  (1) Are listed abroad for 2 years, changed drug formation

3 years	• Among drugs that were listed abroad, but not in China, drugs that
	  (1) Are listed abroad more than 2 years ago, or changed drug formation
	  (2) Contain new compound of known entity
	  (3) Changed drug formation
	  (4) Have new delivery systems
	• Drugs that utilize new salt* of known pharmaceuticals, with a similar pharmacological effect, as raw materials
	• Drugs that changed formation, but not delivery systems, with special technology (slow delivery system etc.)

Out of monitoring	• Among drugs not listed in the world, drugs that
	  (1) Were listed in China, but had added a new therapy that was not approved globally
	• Among drugs that were listed abroad, but not in China, drugs that
	  (1) Added a new therapy that was approved abroad
	  (2) Drugs that changed the formation of drugs listed in China, but saw no change in use
	  (3) Raw materials and active intermediates

Note: *Salt is a material that is produced by an acid base reaction.

Source: State Food and Drug Administration, Notice on Revised Drug Registration Act, 23rd June, 2005.

price margin rule between forms of drug (差比价格规则). The SDRC also sets a price ratio among forms of drug, using a normal tablet as reference. (3) However, patented drugs are free to have the maximum retail price, being independent of government price regulations (sole setting price: 单独定价). (4) Auctions are used in the central tendering system of drugs at a provincial level. The firms are faced with a price controlling mechanism with several additional, and unnecessary, steps.

2.3.1 Retail price cap by the SDRC

From 1980 to the present day, the government has controlled every step of a drug's pricing: the manufacturer's shipment price, the wholesale price and the retail price. Currently, the SDRC sets official prices based on the "Announcement on Official Price Setting Mechanism on Pharmaceuticals" promulgated in 2000. That announcement laid out the following "cost plus pricing formula":

- Retail (maximum) official price = wholesaler's price + 15 per cent margin
- Wholesaler's price = manufacturer's shipment price + 15 per cent margin
- Manufacturer's price = production cost + sales fee + 5% sales margin

This pricing formula is applied for the "official prices" and "special prices" categories in Table 10.12, which shows the current pricing system of pharmaceuticals in China.

2.3.2 Auctions under the Centralized Tendering Drug Procurement Policy

In addition to the SDRC's price control on the medical insurance drug catalogue, there is another mechanism relating to drug prices: the Centralized Tendering Drug Procurement Policy, which operates at the provincial level. In 1999, centralized tendering drug procurement was initiated to overcome "high drug prices and problems of corruption". Firstly, the government hoped to reduce drug prices by monopolizing the purchasing power of hospitals over pharmaceutical firms and using an auctioning mechanism. Secondly, by using these auctions, the government expected to open up the drug procurement process.

It is true that by monopolizing both purchasing and auctions, one can expect to reduce the procurement prices of drugs. However, this does not mean a reduction in the retail prices for patients. As depicted in Figure 10.2, the hospitals and physicians have, by nature, an information advantage over the choice of drugs, and therefore the power of monopoly

Table 10.12 Retail drug price setting mechanism by purchasers

Price		Price setting mechanism	Drug catalogues/types	Insurance reimbursement ratio
Official prices	Officially set	SDRC set a national unified maximum retail price	UEMIL A list	100%
	Guideline	Local governments can adjust within a range of 5%	UEMIL B list	Fixed ratio set by the local governments (90% for Shanghai)
Special prices	Officially set	SDRC set a national unified maximum retail price	Special drugs such as anaesthetics, vaccines, etc.	If the drug is not on the UEMIL Catalogue, 0%
	Guideline	SDRC set a maximum retail price	Patent protected drugs	
Market adjustment price	Sole setting prices (单独定价)	If firms are not satisfied with the SDRC price and have sufficient reasons to set higher price, firms can apply		Depends on reimbursement ratio on the drug catalogues
Free pricing		Firms can set the price as they like	Drugs not in the catalogues	0%

Note: UEMIL: urban employment medical insurance.

Source: Japan Pharmaceutical Manufacturers Association, Information on China's pharmaceuticals (in Japanese).

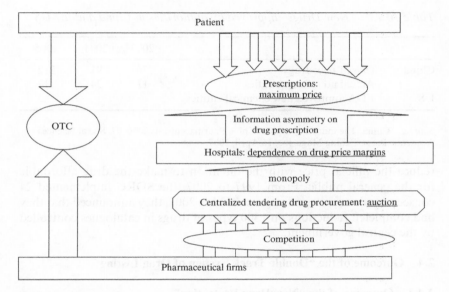

Figure 10.2 Duplicated drug price regulation

over patients. Furthermore, in China, hospitals are highly dependent on income from the drug price margin, and so they prefer to prescribe expensive drugs (the more expensive the drug, the larger the margin even though its margin ratio is fixed). As long as this factor exists, any reduction in a drug's procurement price from the pharmaceuticals companies will simply increase the profit margin of hospitals, and not reduce the drug's retail price. In addition to this problem of hospitals' incentives and motivation, the situation has become even more complicated as several price regulations regarding drugs are duplicated: the SDRC sets the maximum retail price and official margin, but on the other hand, the provincial government requires even lower prices to be bid in auction.

The pharmaceutical industry has continued to oppose this method of centralized procurement, and 13 pharmaceutical associations sent a letter to the government requesting that they discontinue this mechanism. They claim that, given the highly competitive situation in the pharmaceutical industry and hospitals' high dependence on the drug price margin in China, the current institutions are only strengthening the power of monopoly that hospitals have over suppliers. Furthermore, the current drug procurement scheme pays much less attention to the actual quality of drugs.

Regarding the retail price cap, the SDRC has started to aggressively

Table 10.13　"New Drugs" approved by authorities in China and the US

		2003	2004	2005
China	Class 1 new drugs	76	91	212
	Actual no. of new entities	11	24	17
US	FDA approved new chemical entities			3

Source:　China: The industrial map of China Pharmaceuticals 2006–07, Social Sciences
Academic Press. Caijing Magazine, 16 April, 2007, p. 66.

reduce the official price with the intention to make the drug affordable
for the general public. From 1997 to 2007, the SDRC implemented 24
consecutive drug price reductions. In May 2007, they announced that they
had completed reductions on 1500 types of drugs in catalogues controlled
by the central government.

2.4　Outcome of the "Double Track System of Drug Listing"

2.4.1　Outcome of the "New Drug Protection"
Criticism over inconsistencies in patent protection and the new drug protection was strong, and finally the new drug protection was removed in
2002. The policy had the following outcomes: firstly, numerous Chinese
firms invested in the industry, started to produce drugs and succeeded
in satisfying the demand for basic drugs. The first target set in the 1980s
was fulfilled. Secondly, however, "new drug" approval in China was
separate from the outcome of actual research and development, as the
policy designed to induce technological introduction was equally or more
profitable than the actual research and development.

Table 10.13 shows the number of "approved new drugs" in China
and the US. The number of new drugs approved in China is a great deal
higher than in the US, taking into account that these drugs were introduced as part of a program to catch up with the rest of the world. In
worldwide trends, the number of new drugs discovered is decreasing. One
respondent in our interview said that synthesis technology is reaching its
limit, and that a new technological breakthrough seems to be necessary
for the pharmaceutical industry. Table 10.14 relates to the development
of a number of new chemical entities (Class 1 new drugs). The number
of new drugs approved increased explosively in 2000, when 17 Class 1
drugs were approved; a total of 40 were approved between 1985 and 2000.
This implies that the explosion in the registration of new drugs might
be related to the corruption of the ex-Director of the SFDA, who was
arrested in 2006.

Table 10.14 New chemical entities approved as Class 1 drugs between 1985 and 2000

Developer of new drug	1985–2000	Approved in 2000	Notes
Chinese manufacturers	26	6	● Independently developed by 17 domestic research institutes: anti-malarial (6), anti-cancer (2), anti-platelet (1), anti-infective (2), anti-toxin (1), anti-AIDS (1), anti-allergen (1), anti-dizziness (1), abortifacient (2) and cardio-protective (1) ● Developed by domestic research institutes based on the information provided in foreign publications at the outset of the research program
Foreign manufacturers (including joint ventures with domestic firms)	12	10	
Outsourced development by domestic firms to foreign research and development firms	2	1	
Total	40	17	

Source: Deng and Kaitin (2004).

(a) Patent protection

Application   Listing date

(b) New drug protection

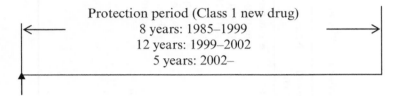

Listing date

Source: Authors.

Figure 10.3   Patent protection and new drug protection

A large number of new drugs have provided huge room for Chinese pharmaceutical firms to enter and operate in the industry, which has in turn brought about sufficient production capacity in the industry. However, as the new drug protection could be more profitable than research and development at a given moment, pharmaceutical firms are less interested in research and development, as focusing on R&D requires long periods and sensitive management to nurture scientists' inspiration and abilities. This could have induced the current reduction in investment in innovation that is greatly worrying the Chinese government.

2.4.2   Relationship between patent protection and new drug protection

New drug protection might render patent protection ineffective, if it is provided without any connection to patent protection. Figure 10.3 shows the "market exclusivity protection period" by patent protection and by new drug protection. In accordance with global practices, patent protection will be provided from the date of a new drug's application. Usually, the patent is applied for during research, and it takes several years for a product to be listed after completing the rest of the research work and clinical trials. If it takes 10 years between application and listing, 10 years of exclusive market protection remain for the patent. On the other hand, exclusive market protection based on new drug protection is provided from the date of listing. If the period for new drug protection is long enough, it effectively provides a longer protection period than patent protection.

This confusing situation seems to have actually occurred from 1999 to 2002, when the "Notice on New Drug Protection and Technology Transfer" was effective: the protection period of Class 1 drugs was as long as 12 years. Quite a few firms only applied for the new drug document, as its protection period was longer than the patent protection itself. Furthermore, as the new drug protection did not explicitly require patent application, generic manufacturers could apply for new drug protection by following the work of a published paper and any other publication written by the innovator. This effectively weakened patent protection.

When China joined the WTO, the "Notice on New Drug Protection and Technology Transfer" was invalidated, and currently market exclusivity is based on the "Monitoring Period of New Drug's Side Effects". The longer protection for new drugs that was provided between 1999 and 2002 is now expiring, but its impact on the industry remains.

3 ACCESS TO DRUGS IN CHINA: SUFFICIENT BUT EXPENSIVE

Here, we consider the situation that emerged in the drug market in China, and how it affects access to drugs for the general public in China.

3.1 Sufficient Entry Thanks to the Dual-Track Drug Listing System

The market facing Chinese pharmaceutical firms has the following features: (1) hospitals, who are the agents of the final consumers (patients) and the largest buyers of drugs, prefer more expensive drugs because they maximize income, which usually consists of a fixed share of the mark-up in the retail price of drugs. (2) Technical barriers to the listing of new drugs have been lowered by the New Drug Protection System, which is independent from patent protection.

Both of these factors – higher prices preferred by customers, lower technical requirements for new drug listing – make it very attractive to enter the industry. In reality, the number of pharmaceutical firms in China rapidly

Table 10.15   Number of pharmaceutical firms in China and India

	China	India	
	No. of firms	No. of firms	No. of manufacturing units
1969/70	–	–	2,257
1980	800	–	–
1990	1,761	250 large firms 800 small and medium	20,053
1995	5,300	–	–
1998	6,300	–	–
2003	–	5,877	–
2005	5,071 (3,959 passed GMP)	–	–
2006	4,682	–	–
2007	4,846	–	10,563

Source: China: Bao (2008) and Statistics at State Drug Administration home page. India: Ministry of Chemicals and Fertilizer, Annual Report, 1999/2000 for 1990. Report of the Expert Committee on A Comprehensive Examination of Drug Regulatory Issues, including the problem of spurious drugs, 2003 for 2003. Department of Pharmaceuticals Annual Report, 2007/08 for 2007.

increased during the reform and open-door policy era. Particularly, new chemical entities were not patented prior to a patent law revision in 2000. Thanks to these lowered technical barriers, new firms entered the industry in huge numbers. However, even after new chemical entities became patentable, the number of firms in the industry continued to increase, as the new drug protection system provided market exclusivity to domestic firms independent from patents, with a similar protection period. The number of firms started to decrease when new drug protection was abolished and strict Good Manufacturing Practice (GMP) examination was introduced in 2002, when China joined the WTO.

The number of firms in the industry increased to a level similar to India's, where new chemical entities were not patentable until 2005. China and India share common features: almost the same population size and weak patent protection for new chemicals in the 1990s, inducing the massive entry of suppliers (Table 10.15).

The impact of the double-track system can also be observed in a particular drug market. Table 10.16 shows the number of firms entering the market for the statin drug group, which is effective in lowering cholesterol. There exist seven types of statins in the world, and the first six types are sold in China. Among these six types, the oldest two are out of patent

Table 10.16   Number of statins and number of firms in the market

Derivation	Generic name	No. of brands (production document and firms) (document holder)	Global product patent holder	Effective patent	Effective new drug protection (latest)	State Basic Medical Insurance Catalogue
1st gen: Fermented	1 Lovastatin	51 documents, 36 firms	Merck	X	X	O
	2 Simvastatin	107 documents, 54 firms	Merck	X	X	O
	3 Pravastatin	14 documents (3 raw drugs), 6 firms Bristol-Myers/Sankyo/Huabei Haizheng/Shanghai Xiandai/Shanghai Tianwei	Bristol-Myers/Sankyo	O	O	O
1.5 gen: Semi-synthesis	4 Fluvastatin	3 documents, 2 firms Beijing Novartis (2 drugs) and Zhejiang Haizheng (1 raw drug)	Novartis	O	X	O
2nd gen: Synthesis	5 Atorvastatin	6 documents (1 raw drug), 3 firms Pfizer, Beijing Jialin (Honghui) and Henan Tianfang	Pfizer	O	O	X
	6 Rosuvastatin	Not produced in China	AstraZenecca	–	–	X
3rd gen.	7 Pitavasatin	Not produced, on sale since 2009	Kowa	–	–	X

Source: No. of production document holders and effective new drug protection was derived from the Database on Local Production Drugs, at China Medical Drug Webnet. Information on effective patents was obtained from the New Horizon Database/State Basic Medical Insurance Catalogue.

279

protection already. There is a much larger number of firms supplying the patent-expired drug than the patented drugs. It cannot be denied that the impact of patent protection in limiting market entry is substantial in China. However, we can also observe an interesting phenomenon. Even in the market for patented statins, up to five firms which do not have a patent are operating. They hold the Chinese style new drug protection documents. Nor can it be denied that the new drug protection policy, which is independent of innovation, is effective in allowing more firms to enter the drug market. The double-track system of drug listing control in China has helped to increase the number of firms entering the drug market.

In summary, government policies on the supply side have induced aggressive and active entry to the market, facilitating the sufficient supply of drugs in China. Particularly, the double-track system of drug listing licenses (patent protection and new drug protection) encourages firms to enter the drugs market and ensures sufficient supply of drugs. For the patent-holding pharmaceutical companies, mainly the large foreign ones, their patent drugs are protected by patent law and enjoy preferential pricing policy. Higher maximum retail prices are set for patented drugs than for generics. At the same time, the new drug protection policy has made room for Chinese generic pharmaceuticals to enter the market.

3.2   Agency Problem with Drug Prices

Under a normal demand system, the entry of more suppliers leads to fiercer price competition, because buyers prefer lower prices. However, pharmaceutical firms set prices as high as possible, because their main buyers, hospitals, prefer more expensive drugs, which make larger profits for the firms. This nature of demand and the response from suppliers has pushed up the retail price of drugs. The main cause of the high prices of drugs in China is the twinned incentive structure of hospitals. Thus, reforming the income structure of hospitals is necessary to remedy this detrimental situation.

Restricted coverage of medical insurance exacerbated the situation. Most patients must meet the high retail drug price out of their own pockets. Patients have very limited financial resources, but as the agents who intermediate between patients and drug firms have the incentive to prescribe more expensive drugs, the price of drugs stays high.

3.3   Drugs are Sufficiently Available but Expensive in China: "Difficult to See Doctor, Expensive to Buy Drug (看病难, 看病贵)"

The above discussion shows that drug prices in China are high even though there is sufficient entry to the market and competition due to the

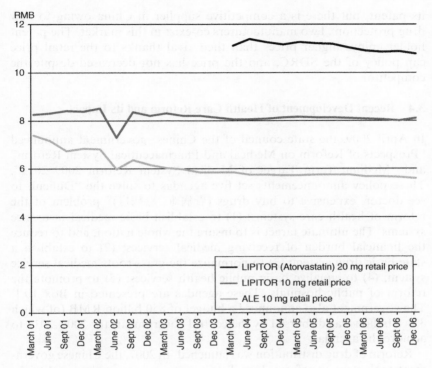

RMB

LIPITOR (Atorvastatin) 20 mg retail price
LIPITOR 10 mg retail price
ALE 10 mg retail price

Source: IMS Health.

Figure 10.4 Prices of Atorvastatin, Pfizer (patented) vs Beijing Jialin (no patent)

double-track system in drug listing control. The double-track system consisting of patent protection and new drug documents allows local firms who have no research and development capacity to list relatively new drugs in the Chinese market. Separation of patent and new drug protections could have contributed to reduce the price between pharmaceuticals and hospitals. However, this simply allowed hospitals to increase their profits, rather than leading to reductions in the retail price of drugs. This is because active entry on the production side does not change the incentive of hospitals, as agents of the patients. An appropriate demand system is necessary to bring hospitals' incentives in line with those of patients.

Patenting alone may not be a sufficient condition to restrict access to drugs in developing economies. Figure 10.4 shows a situation in the market for Atorvastatin, one of the statins and a profit-maker for Pfizer. In the global market, Atorvastatin is monopolized by Pfizer thanks to its patent, but there is a competitive supplier in China owing to new drug protection. Two manufacturers co-exist in this market. The patent holder enjoys higher prices than their rival thanks to the retail price cap policy of the SDRC, and the price has not decreased despite the competitor.

3.4   Recent Development of Health Care Reform and its Impact

In April 2009, the state council of the Chinese government announced "Prospects of Reform on Medical and Pharmaceutical System Reform" and "Medium Term Target of Medical System Reform 2009–2011". These policy announcements set five agendas to solve the "Difficult to see doctor, expensive to buy drugs (看病难, 看病贵)" problem of the reform of health care systems: (1) to establish basic medical insurance systems. The ultimate target is to insure the whole nation, and to reduce the financial burden of receiving medical services; (2) to establish a state basic drug system; (3) to normalize the grass-roots medical service system; (4) to equalize basic public health services; (5) to promote the reform of public hospitals. These agendas are presented in Box 10.1. The government also announced a budget of 850 billion RMB (of which 331.8 billion was disbursed by the central government) for 2009–2011 to achieve the agendas.

Reform of drug distribution was launched. In 2007, the Chinese government took steps to reform drug distribution and reported several trials. First, Nanjing City is testing the separation of hospitals and pharmacies. It is expected that hospitals will not set high prices when their income is separated from drug revenue. This has been effective in Japan since around 2000. However, it is reported that in Nanjing management and ownership of pharmacies has been separated, and management has been given over to drug trading companies, whereas ownership still belongs with the hospital. As no new revenues were arranged for hospitals, they consequently still need to rely on the drug margin, requiring the drug trading companies to pay back a margin for drug sales. The margin ratio is reported to be 36–45 per cent (Zhao and Zhao, 2006). Thus the separation of the management and ownership of pharmacies does not seem to be effective in reducing drug prices. Second, the Beijing Community Hospital Medical Reform has been taking place. In 2007, the Beijing City Government started to reimburse all the drug fees for 16 basic diagnoses at community health stations. This reform is targeted not only at reducing the general public's expenditure, but also at encouraging patients with mild diseases to go to the community health stations rather than the main hospitals that are already overburdened.

BOX 10.1   AGENDA IN THE MID TERM OF
MEDICAL SYSTEM REFORM
2009–2011

1. Basic
   Medical
   Insurance
   System

   1. To extend coverage of the basic medical insurances (UEBMI, URBMI and NRCMS) to more than 90 per cent in three years, 2009–2011. To include the retired and laid-off employees of bankrupt or struggling firms into the Urban Employee Basic Insurance. To start the Urban Residence Basic Medical Insurance in the whole nation in 2009, including college students into URBMI, employees of non-public enterprises, part-time workers and workers from rural area (UEBMI)
   2. To raise the insurance level
   3. To normalize management of medical insurance funds
   4. To establish medical rescue system in both urban and rural areas
   5. To improve management of basic medical insurances

2. State
   basic drug
   systems

   1. To set up the State basic drug list in 2009
   2. To establish a supply system of drugs in the list. The government sets the maximum retail price of drugs on the list
   3. To set up a prescription manual and a system to prioritize use of drugs on the list

3. To normalize
   grass-roots
   medical
   service
   systems

   1. To build 2,000 county level hospitals, 29,000 village clinics, to set up 1 to 3 medical organizations in every county. In urban areas, 3,700 community health centers, 11,000 health service stations in 3 years

4. To equalize
   public health
   services

   1. To start periodical health checks for the over 65s, children under 3, pregnant women and new mothers

5. To reform public hospitals	1. To reform the subsidy mechanism for public hospitals, which currently consists of three items: medical service, drugs prescription and subsidy

Source: Announcement by Health Department, Government of P.R. China, on 7 April 2009

4   CONCLUDING REMARKS

The main characteristic of China's pharmaceutical industry is "high drug prices despite the sufficient entry of suppliers". This situation can be attributed to the incentive structure of hospitals and a poorly designed, laissez-faire health care system. Hospitals have to finance themselves by prescribing expensive drugs because of poor financial conditions with few subsidies from the government, although they are state-owned. At the same time, the share of drug expenditure paid by the patients themselves is huge. Drugs are therefore very expensive for the general public. Patent systems have also contributed to some extent. Experience in China raises the universal problem of how to finance hospitals. The current situation in China reveals that it is very difficult and problematic to run hospitals on entirely profit-making principles.

REFERENCES

Bao, Shengyong (2008) *Why are the Expenses for Drugs so High: A Sociological Analysis on the Drugs Circulation of Urban China*, Social Science Academic Press (in Chinese).

Chen, Jing, Shi Luwen and Cao Jinyan (2006) "Patents, New Drug Protection and Innovation Promotion Policy" in Chen Xiaohong and Watanabe Mariko, eds, *Pharmaceutical Industry in China*, ASEDP 75, Institute of Developing Economies, Japan.

Deng, R. and K. I. Kaitin (2004) "The Regulation and Approval of New Drugs in China", *Drug Information Journal* 37, 29–39.

Kubo, K. ed. (2007) *Japanese Generic Drug Market and Pharmaceutical Industries in India and China*, Institute of Developing Economies (in Japanese).

Meng, Qingyue (2006) *Health Care Pricing and Payment Reforms in China: The Implication for Health Service Delivery and Cost Constraint*, Ph.D thesis, Karolinska Institute.

Uchimura, H. and Jutting, Johans (2007) "Fiscal Decentralization, Chinese Style: Good for Health Outcomes?" IDE Discussion Paper No. 111, July.

Watanabe, Mariko (2006) "Pricing Strategy: Theoretical Analysis, Data and Case Study" in Chen and Watanabe, eds, *Pharmaceutical Industry in China*, ASEDP 75, Institute of Developing Economies, Japan.

Zhao, Yanlin and Zhao Yaming (2006) "A True Story of the Separation of Management and Ownership of Pharmacies in Nanjing", *Capital Week* 41, 4 November.

11.   Access to essential drugs in Thailand: intellectual property rights and other institutional matters affecting public health in a developing country

Samira Guennif

Since the ratification of the Trade Related Aspects of Intellectual Property Rights agreement (TRIPS) in 1994 by country members of the new World Trade Organization (WTO), the effects of this agreement in developing countries have been relentlessly questioned. Doubts are persistent in response to incessant incantations from the North holding that the strengthening of intellectual property rights (IPR) in developing countries will foster greater access to the latest technological and therapeutic innovations, finally inducing an improvement in the social welfare of the population in these countries. Studies have been carried out by international organizations, nongovernmental organizations and other bodies to establish the effects of TRIPS in the South. These studies have investigated the chances of technology transfers and foreign direct investments (FDI) toward developing countries (Saggi, 2000; Lall, 2003; Gallagher, 2005; Maskus and Reichman, 2005) as well as the risks for drugs accessibility (Nogues, 1990; Desterbecq and Remiche, 1996; Boulet and Velasquez, 1999; Correa, 2000). In one case or another, IPR have invariably been scrutinized, celebrated or questioned.

Highlighting the role of patents as an element influencing the access of Southern countries to the latest technical and therapeutic innovations may lead to the neglect of an essential fact. The pharmaceutical industry is unique insofar as its primary mission is to provide an essential good, i.e. drugs which can help improve the health conditions of people and their life expectancy. As such, while analysing the effect of the introduction of a new regulatory standard as important as the drug patent in the South, no one should ignore other standards that developing countries establish to improve the efficiency, safety and quality of this essential good.

On this point, there is a lack of studies aimed at examining the major regulatory changes that have occurred in the pharmaceutical industry in developing countries and at assessing their effects on the accessibility of essential medicines. Therefore, this chapter precisely proposes to draw attention to the major institutional changes that have taken place in the pharmaceutical industry of a developing country, Thailand, and estimates their impacts on drug accessibility when the country is affected by a generalized epidemic of HIV/AIDS.

In doing this, first the content of the new institutional arrangement that regulates the production and marketing of medicines in Thailand will be characterized. Beyond the notable strengthening of IPR before and after the ratification of the TRIPS, the promotion of good manufacturing practices (GMP) and generic production will be sketched. Second, the effects of this new arrangement on domestic production, technology transfers and FDI will be analysed. One will see that it is rather difficult to put the entire blame on patents when there is a shrinking of the national production structure or a higher dependence of the country vis-à-vis foreigner supply. Finally in the last section, the accessibility of essential medicines in this new institutional context will be addressed. We shall see that it is easier to question the protection of IPR in the obstacles faced by Thai health authorities to improve access to anti-AIDS medicines and the sustainability of its universal access programme to these life-saving medicines.

1 RELEVANT INSTITUTIONAL EVOLUTION SINCE THE 1980s

To comprehend the elements that determine the functioning of the pharmaceutical industry, it is crucial to go beyond the simple patent aspect and to consider other institutional factors which globally regulate the quality of essential medicines supplied on the market.

1.1 Improving the Quality of Medicines

In the 1980s, Thailand initiated measures to improve the safety, efficacy and quality of drugs produced and marketed in the territory (FDA/MOPH, 1999). The objective was to eliminate substandard drugs on the market: drugs that "do not meet quality specifications set for them" (Caudron et al., 2008) and help the building of people's confidence needed to support the consumption of drugs, especially those locally produced.[1]

Accordingly, the Thai FDA, created in 1974, launched a campaign to promote GMP in 1984 (FDA/MOPH, 1999). But the inspection of local production units and sampling of drugs locally produced, imported or provided by retail pharmacies for analysis by the FDA could not effectively solve problems. Accordingly, producers, importers and distributors had to comply with GMP guidelines to ensure the quality of medicines produced and marketed, following WHO practices. Thus, in 1987, the Thai code of GMP was published and from the 6th (1987–1991) and 7th (1992–1996) National Plans for Economic and Social Development, the Thai authorities promoted, and helped local producers to comply with, these GMP guidelines. Among other things, annual training seminars for personnel from private firms and public institutions were organized, the production and dissemination of technical documents were provided, and audits were conducted in firms.

This project involved the implementation of development strategies, including technical, educational and financial resources to accelerate the implementation of GMP guidelines. However, there were considerable obstacles to the development of GMP such as requirements for investment, personnel and technical know-how. Besides, compliance with GMP guidelines was not made mandatory in 1984 but later, in 2003.[2]

In parallel, starting in 1989, the marketing of new drugs was made subject to more-stringent measures with the implementation of the Safety Monitoring Programme (SMP).[3] Prior to the granting of marketing

---

[1]   According to WHO, substandard drugs must be carefully distinguished from counterfeit drugs resulting from "deliberate criminal activity, deliberately and fraudulently mislabelled with respect to identity and/or source" (Caudron et al., 2008).

[2]   According to the new Drug Act of B.E.2546 (2003), "Manufacturers who are unable to comply with the good manufacturing practices (GMP) principles can no longer proceed with the drug business" (see www.fda.moph.go.th/eng/drug/laws. stm).

[3]   The origin of this programme is not clear. First, it may have arisen from the fact that Thailand joined the WHO international drug monitoring programme in 1984. This provides a forum for member states to cooperate in the monitoring of drug safety through the collection of reports of suspected adverse drug reactions and their storing in a common database, presently containing over 4.6 million case reports (see www.who-umc.org). Second, this programme may be traced back to the beginning of US pressure on Thailand in 1985 aimed at the strengthening of IP protection. Third, the tool may have been implemented under the aegis of the WHO and later being modified under US pressure and exploited for the granting of monopolies (Schoen-Angerer and Limpananont, 2001) (see below).

approval, drugs had to go through a pre-marketing protocol to ensure their safety, efficacy and quality. Under this protocol, a drug was supplied only in hospitals under the supervision of physicians who had to evaluate the potential side effects of the new drug. The programme covered new chemical entities, new combinations, new recommendations and new delivery systems. Besides, for the registration of new generics, bioequivalence studies were required from 1993:[4] copies marketed for the first time in Thailand had to go through bioequivalence studies while copies already marketed at that date did not have to do so (Teerawattananon et al, 2003).[5] Finally, control and rigorous supervision of drug producers, especially those without the GMP certification, were implemented in the transitional phase during which the certification was not made mandatory.

In addition, from 1992, the Ministry of Health required public hospitals to buy their drugs from GMP certified producers. The Thai FDA asked retail pharmacies to do the same. And health authorities published a list of essential drugs, following the model established by the WHO, and commended public hospitals to buy up to 80 per cent from this list.

Thus, public authorities sought to improve the quality of drugs produced and marketed locally by using essential regulatory tools: promotion of production conditions, requirement for firms to perform bioequivalence studies and linking access to the public market for life-saving and other essential drugs to the holding of the GMP certification.

1.2 Strengthening the Protection of Intellectual Property of Medicines

In 1992, while country members of the General Agreement on Tariffs and Trade (GATT) were still negotiating for six years the content of what would become two years later the TRIPS Agreement, from 1984 Thailand was involved in bilateral negotiation with the United States which brought about new standards for IP protection.

Thailand's first patent law dated from 1979 and provided patents for

---

[4]   Two pharmaceutical products are bioequivalent if they are pharmaceutically equivalent and their bioavailabilities (rate and extent of availability) after administration in the same molar dose are similar to such a degree that their effects, with respect to both efficacy and safety, can be expected to be essentially the same. Pharmaceutical equivalence implies the same amount of the same active substance, in the same dosage form, for the same route of administration and meeting the same or comparable standards.

[5]   For lack of a deadline for copies marketed before 1993, similars can still be found on the Thai market (interview with Dr. Jiraporn Limpananont, Faculty of Pharmaceutical Sciences, Chulalongkorn University, Thailand).

process for 15 years in the pharmaceutical sector (Supakankunti et al, 2001). In 1985, the International Intellectual Property Alliance identified Thailand as "a country with one of the worst piracy records in the world" (IPAA, 2005).[6] In 1987, a petition against Thailand was filed jointly by the Alliance, the Motion Picture Export Association of America and the Recording Industry Association of America. As a result, Thailand was designated a "Priority Watch country" under Special 301[7] in 1989 and excluded the same year from preferential trade benefits under the Generalized System of Preferences programme for failure to provide adequate and effective copyright protection (Sallstrom, 1994; USTR, 1994; Stewart, 1999).[8]

In 1991, the Pharmaceutical Research and Manufacturers of America (PhRMA) filed another petition deploring Thailand's inadequate and ineffective patent protection laws for pharmaceuticals. In particular, the association complained about several elements of the Thai Patent Law that caused the US pharmaceutical industry substantial financial harm: a lack of product patent protection, a short term of protection, requirements to manufacture a product or use a process in Thailand, and excessively broad compulsory licensing provisions. PhRMA requested that Thailand amend its patent law promptly to remedy these deficiencies (see www.cptech.org, Oxfam, 2004).

---

[6]   The IIPA is a lobby formed in 1984 and made up of trade associations representing US copyright-based industries in bilateral and multilateral efforts working mainly to improve international protection and enforcement of copyrights and open up foreign markets closed by piracy and other market access barriers (see www.iipa.com). With other lobbies from the US, Europe and Japan, IIPA worked actively for the introduction of the IP issue in the Uruguay Round GATT negotiating agenda and for the implementation of high standards for IP protection in the final draft of the TRIPS agreement (see for instance Matthews, 2002).

[7]   Since the 1980s, the US Trade Representatives (USTR) have played a key role in the expansion of IPR in the world by monitoring efforts made by governments of commercial partners to protect IPR. Concretely, the Special 301 report and mechanism were created in 1988 with the Omnibus Trade and Tariff Act. The report examines the adequacy and effectiveness of IPR protection in many countries around the world. Countries may be designated gradually in the categories "Watch List", "Priority Watch List" and "Priority Foreign Countries". And the Special 301 may be used to put commercial pressure on countries that affect US economic interests by electing standards deemed insufficient for the protection of IP. Ultimately, commercial sanctions may be imposed by the US (www.ustr.gov).

[8]   A scheme implemented first in 1971 under the aegis of the United Nations Conference on Trade and Development, the GSP programme provides for preferential tariff treatment for developing countries' exports of manufactured and semi-manufactured goods to increase their export earnings, promote industrialization and economic growth. In 1993, Thailand was the third largest beneficiary of the US GSP Program and its revocation cost the economy US$165 million (Sallstrom, 1994).

As a result of this petition and lobbying from the US, the same year, Thailand was given the worst classification under the Special 301: "Priority Foreign Country".[9] Consequently, under commercial pressures,[10] the country amended its patent law, which became effective in 1992, and implemented higher standards for the protection of IPR. First of all, patents were provided for process and product for 20 years. Medicines invented after 1992 were from this time forth patentable within the country. Further, Thailand conferred broad authority to issue compulsory licences particularly in cases where patents were not locally worked, i.e. patents were not effective on the basis of local production (Love, 1999). Finally, as a safeguard against the introduction of a temporary monopoly on drugs, the Pharmaceutical Patent Review Board was created with the role of controlling the price of patented products through the requirement of sensitive production cost and pricing information from firms (Wilson et al, 1999).

In 1992 and 1993, Thailand was confirmed as a "priority foreign country" as a result of its large provisions for compulsory licences, its Pharmaceutical Patent Review Board and its lack of pipeline protection. As a consequence, the Safety Monitoring Programme (SMP) became a useful pipeline protection in 1993. While its purpose was to ensure the safety, efficacy and quality of new drugs before the granting of marketing approval, this tool evolved under US pressure. It did not merely concern all drugs entering the Thai market, but specifically those which had been patented elsewhere between 1986 and 1991 and not qualified for patent protection under the non-retroactive 1992 Law (ASEAN, 2000, Kwa, 2001, Ford et al, 2007).

In practice, for two years a drug was put under a pre-marketing protocol. As stated earlier, during this period the drug was not available in pharmacies but only in hospitals. More importantly, during the protocol while awaiting formal marketing approval, any generic production of the drug was prohibited. It was only at the end of this pre-marketing surveillance and with the effective granting of marketing approval that the product was available on the whole market and then for copying by generic producers. To sum up, firms enjoyed exclusive marketing rights under the SMP.

---

[9]   "Priority Foreign Countries" are those countries that "have the most onerous or egregious acts, policies or practices that deny intellectual property protection and limit market access to US persons or firms depending on intellectual property rights protection" and "have the greatest adverse impact (actual or potential) on the relevant United States products" (www.ustr.gov).

[10]   The commercial pressure was all the more important given that the Thai economy was dependent on exports of 60 per cent and specifically on exports to the US market of 15 per cent (Kwa, 2001).

Whereas initially the granting of exclusive marketing rights lasted for two years, in 1993, Thailand modified the exclusivity period. Firms could then apply for two successive extensions of a year of the programme. After that, they had about six months to analyse the data collected on the safety, efficacy and quality of the product and submit them to the Thai FDA. The latter had six months then to make a decision on the granting of marketing approval. In total, the exclusivity period could last five years.

Yet, the Thai Patent Law did not include a "Bolar" provision.[11] As a consequence, generic producers were not allowed to start bioequivalence studies and file for marketing approval before the expiry of the pre-marketing protocol. Consequently, a copy could not be released as soon as the SMP expired. Instead, for lack of a Bolar provision, generic producers needed from six to twelve months to conduct bioequivalence studies, then submitted them to the Thai FDA in order to gain marketing approval. Finally, the SMP could provide a monopoly for 6 years (Kwa, 2001).

In addition to the introduction of product patent in IPR law, Thailand also abandoned some legal tools aimed at restoring competitive conditions and/or dealing with national emergencies: parallel imports were prohibited and compulsory licences limited.[12] If parallel imports were banned following US threats to restrict imports of Thai textiles in 1992, one year later, USTR insisted on the adverse effects of compulsory licensing and invited the Thai government to limit the scope for it. For instance, public authorities had first to negotiate with the patentee before issuing a compulsory licence (Huang, 2006). Still, the local working of patents was required. In return, preferential tariffs were promised for the export of jewellery and wood products to the US market. And the authority of the Pharmaceutical Patent Review Board was restricted (Love, 1999; Stewart, 1999).

By the end of 1993, after three years of continuing commercial pressure, Thailand was removed from the USTR Priority Foreign Country list and placed on the Priority Watch list. Then, the signing of the TRIPS agreement intervened at the WTO in 1994. As a new member Thailand amended again its patent law five years later. Patents on process and product were confirmed for 20 years in 1999. In compliance with TRIPS,

---

[11]   Following the US legislation, this early working provision enables firms to develop and test a generic product in order to obtain marketing approval before the patent of the product expires.

[12]   The former tool allows for the imports of medicines marketed at a lower price in a foreign country. The latter tool enables a country to circumvent patent and authorize a domestic firm (public or private) to produce a copy of a patented drug in order, for instance, to deal with a national emergency.

parallel imports were reintroduced. Because of US pressure, compulsory licences remained part of the Thai Patent Law and still usable under limited circumstances. It was thus entirely possible to circumvent life-saving-drugs patents and for the production of generics to be allowed in case of a national emergency. In compliance with TRIPS, the requirement to negotiate with a patentee before issuing a compulsory licence was no longer included under the Thai Patent Act. Finally, the failure of patent holders to fulfil the local working requirement provision was still a ground for issuing a compulsory licence.

In addition, petty patents were introduced: a utility model used in Germany or Austria, this tool provides shorter term protection for minor innovations that have industrial application (Supakankunti et al., 2001). As a result, the Government Pharmaceutical Organization (GPO), the public unit in charge of producing and distributing essential drugs in hospitals, filed for example a patent for its GPO-VIR, an anti-AIDS cocktail made of three antiretrovirals patented abroad and recommended as a first line regimen by the World Health Organization (WHO) in the treatment of HIV/AIDS (Guennif and Mfuka, 2003).[13] The process of obtaining such a patent is shorter compared to a regular patent filing and its duration is also shorter: six years.

If the pipeline protection was confirmed, changes were however introduced (Kwa, 2001). First, a Bolar provision was introduced as the TRIPS provides for such a legal possibility in Article 8.[14] Firms were thus allowed to undertake bioequivalence studies and file for a marketing approval before the SMP expiry for a drug. Second, the FDA decided to exclude drugs under SMP from the National List of Essential Drugs. Insofar as the safety, efficiency and quality of these drugs were not confirmed, they could not be included on the National List of Essential Drugs. As a result, even if drugs under SMP held a temporary monopoly, they had access to a limited market as hospitals were requested to fulfil their needs by buying drugs from the National List of Essential Drugs – up to 80 per cent as indicated above.[15] These decisions quickly raised the

---

[13] More precisely, a cocktail is a therapy consisting of two or more drugs combined in one single pill to be taken several times a day. This cocktail increases observance among patients and prevents resistance.

[14] A case filed by the European Communities against Canada in 1997 was decided in a way that permitted the WTO's Dispute Settlement Body to stipulate that the Bolar provision was in compliance with TRIPS and could be used in all country-members (See Morin and Bourassa Forcier in this volume).

[15] Later, with the implementation of the universal coverage scheme (30 baht Scheme in 2001), only medicines registered on the NLED will be reimbursed.

concern of the USTR, which considered this measure as a trade barrier and again threatened Thailand with commercial sanctions. Last but not least, the Pharmaceutical Patent Review Board was finally abolished in 1999 (Love, 1999; Wilson et al, 1999).

2   THE EFFECT OF THE NEW INSTITUTIONAL FRAMEWORK ON THE NATIONAL PHARMACEUTICAL INDUSTRY

As regards the impact of this new institutional framework regulating the production and marketing of drugs in Thailand, evidence suggests *inter alia* the contraction of the domestic pharmaceutical industry and the rise of imported drugs and the absence of FDI inflows under the new IPR regime.

2.1   Industrial Capability and Local Production

In 1989, 30.4 per cent of producers (58 firms) held the GMP certification, including GPO (see Figure 11.1). In 2000, 73 per cent of firms (130 units) held the certification. From 2004, there was a significant acceleration of the phenomenon as the GMP certification became a legal require-ment. In 2006, 94.4 per cent of producers held the GMP certification (Wibulpolprasert, 2007).

But these figures hide another trend: it seems that, unable to upgrade

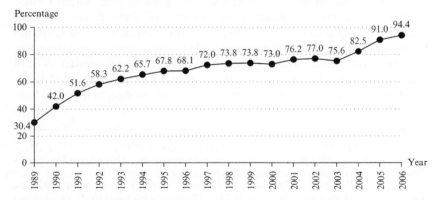

Source: Drug Control Division and Drug Administration, Ministry of Public Health, 2007, reprinted in Wibulpolprasert (2007).

Figure 11.1   Percentage of GMP-certified manufacturers, 1989–2006

their equipment, to recruit qualified staff or to face the economic crisis, a number of firms had to cease production. There were 191 producers in 1989 against 176 in 1999 after the financial crisis in Asia. Recently, there were 179 domestic firms.

Furthermore, the gradual implementation of GMP and the stipulation of new quality standards for drugs produced locally induced Thai firms to consider exporting their products. Indeed, the Thai market remains small compared to countries in the area such as India or China, or countries outside the zone like Brazil. There are growing export opportunities toward neighbouring countries, including the ones that are members of the Association of South-East Asian Nations, formed in the late 1960s.[16] Finally, the Thai market has become over time more and more dynamic as indicates the evolution of drug exports (see Figure 11.3). Between 1983 and 2005, exports multiplied by 24, from 255.6 million to nearly 6.2 billion baht.

Nevertheless, the increasing number of firms producing under GMP or the rising of exports should not mask the growing importance of the drugs imported into the Thai market. Indeed, the market had a value of US$1.32 billion in 2004, making it the 33rd largest in the world. As Figure 11.2 shows, between 1983 and 2004 the proportion of locally produced medicines steadily declined. It decreased from 65.2 to 50.9 per cent, having experienced a peak of 76.5 per cent in 1984 (in value), to the benefit of imported drugs. And from 2004, the sharing between locally produced drugs and imported drugs changed radically: imports dominated the market, at 56.3 per cent in 2005. In other words, policies and institutional changes carried out to

---

[16] ASEAN is a geo-political and economic organization of ten countries from South-East Asia. Formed in 1967 by Indonesia, Malaysia, the Philippines, Singapore and Thailand, it includes today Brunei, Myanmar, Cambodia, Laos, and Vietnam. It gives rise to the ASEAN Free Trade Area and an agreement was ratified in 2003. Working for the promotion of socioeconomic development among its members, ASEAN includes nearly 584 million people or 10 per cent of the global population and a total trade of US$1,700 billion. The gross domestic product reached US$1,500 billion with a growth of 4.4 per cent the same year (ASEAN, 2009). With the "ASEAN Plus Three" Forum institutionalized in 1999 following the financial crisis, there is a concern about the establishment of an East-Asia Economic Community made of present members of the ASEAN Free Trade Area with the joining of China, Japan and South Korea. This Asia Economic Community, building upon the existing free trade areas within the region, would include 2 billion people or almost a third of the global population and represent a gross domestic product of US$6.3 trillion or almost 20 per cent of global GDP in 2002. This economic community could bring new commercial opportunities to small countries in the region. In particular, access to the Chinese market could be in part a good substitute for the American market (Ahmad, 2003).

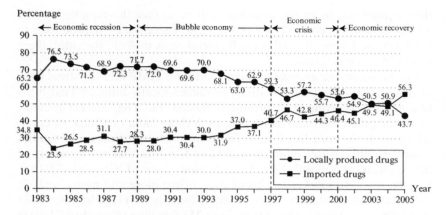

Source: Drug Control Division and Drug Administration, Ministry of Public Health, 2005, reprinted in Wibulpolprasert, 2007.

Figure 11.2   Percentage of locally produced and imported drugs, 1983–2005

introduce generics, to improve the safety, efficacy and quality of drugs produced by local firms, to foster the consumption of generics,[17] and the establishment of higher IPR standards meaning fewer opportunities for the copying of drugs, did not stop the rise of imported drugs.

Thus, the trade balance of the pharmaceutical sector has steadily deteriorated over the past two decades (see Figure 11.3). Certainly, the growth in imports of drugs partly explains this phenomenon. The Thai market is supplied by multinational firms producing locally up to 45 per cent, by importers up to 30 per cent, by domestic firms up to 15 per cent, and by GPO up to 10 per cent. In summary, the Thai pharmaceutical market is characterized by a strong involvement of importers and distributors of

---

[17]   In fact, following the Asian financial crisis of the late 1990s, the need for the Thai government to control health care spending led to the establishment of a public health policy, "Good Health at Low Cost". This policy gave rise to a campaign calling for the consumption of generics produced by local firms through the "Buy Thai" programme (see www.sandia.gov/policy/34s/pdf). Like the "Buy American Act" which provides that all US government organizations have to buy their finished products in preference from American producers rather than foreign suppliers when domestic products are of satisfactory quality and are available in sufficient quantity, "Buy Thai" strongly encourages government hospitals to buy local generic products whenever possible. This policy explains the rise of locally produced drugs observed briefly in 1998 and 1999.

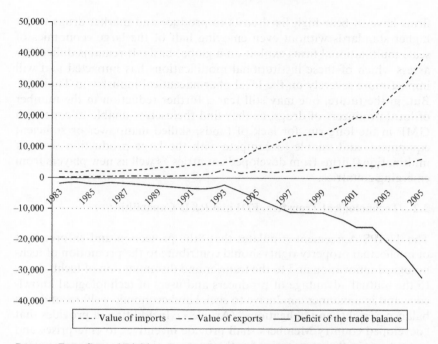

Source: Drug Control Division, Food and Drug Administration, MoPH, reprinted in Wibulpolprasert, 2007.

Figure 11.3   The trade balance of the pharmaceutical industry (in millions of baht, current prices)

drugs, in total 486 (Wibulpolprasert, 1999). This was due to a chronic lack of consumer confidence *vis-à-vis* the local production of generic drugs and a strong preference for branded drugs imported by multinational firms. Another significant element, which contributes to the large trade deficit of the pharmaceutical sector, is that fewer than a dozen private firms and GPO produce some raw materials (Kuanpoth, 2006). Thus, the dominant activity of firms, local and foreign, in the sector remains the formulation, even the packaging of imported medicines. Accordingly, the pharmaceutical industry in Thailand is still largely dependent on the import of active ingredients to the tune of 96 per cent (MOPH and NHSO, 2007).

Overall, it appears that measures taken to improve the quality of locally manufactured medicines and the strengthening of patent law bring about the consolidation of a market which brings less benefit to domestic firms and more to multinational ones. To put it differently, these institutional modifications act as entry barriers (Bain, 1956) in so far as local firms have to bear high fixed costs to produce and market drugs under higher standards without even enjoying half of the large economies of scale multinational firms exploit on a global basis. It remains difficult to assess which of these institutional modifications has impacted and will impact more severely on the local pharmaceutical industry in Thailand. But, in the future, one may still fear a further reduction in the number of local producers of drugs, as they find themselves unable to cope with GMP in the long run for lack of funds, skilled manpower or sufficient equipment, and unable to compete with the large production scale of multinational firms from developed countries as well as new players from emerging countries.

2.2   Technological Transfers, FDI and R&D Capabilities

The TRIPS Agreement stipulates that "the protection and enforcement of intellectual property rights should contribute to the promotion of technological innovation and to the transfer and dissemination of technology, to the mutual advantage of producers and users of technological knowledge and in a manner conducive to social and economic welfare, and to a balance of rights and obligations" (Article 7). In addition, it provides that "developed country Members shall provide incentives to enterprises and institutions in their territories for the purpose of promoting and encouraging technology transfer to least-developed country Members in order to enable them to create a sound and viable technological base" (Article 66.2). In other words, in exchange for the establishment of a strong IPR regime in compliance with the TRIPS, developing countries should see their access to the latest technical and therapeutic innovations improve thanks to a significant increase of technology transfers and FDI toward their territories.

Since the amendments of the Thai Patent Law in 1992 and 1999, evidence of a rise in technology transfers toward Thai pharmaceutical industry is weak. According to Supakankunti et al (2001), from 1984 to 1998, companies in Thailand were mostly of Thai nationality, leading the authors to conclude that little FDI has come into the local pharmaceutical industry since 1992. For Oxfam (2001), "many multinational pharmaceutical companies based on R&D have in fact relocated their offices in Singapore, despite a strengthening of patent law in Thailand". The argument put forward by Professor Chitman, the Executive Director of the Pharmaceutical Producers Association (PPA), is that Singapore offers more incentives than Thailand: tax reductions, fast registration procedures or work permits for expatriates (Oxfam, 2001). Besides, the introduction of GMP in the country did not encourage multinational firms in the sector to upgrade their production units when necessary. Instead, they took the opportunity to relocate their operations in countries where labour costs are lower, in Vietnam for example (MOPH and NHSO, 2007).

Basically, the amount of FDI has changed little for the reason that multinational firms still prefer exporting to Thailand rather than establishing local production, as shown by the increasing share of imported medicines in Thailand since 1992. When production units of multinational firms are located in Thailand, their activity is limited to the manufacturing or the packaging of finished products. Krisana Kraisintu, the former director of GPO's R&D unit, points out that the public unit has been approached by multinational firms. At these occasions, there was no discussion about technology transfer, technical assistance from multinational firms or FDI. For example, Boehringer Ingelheim (BI) offered to license to GPO the production of an antiretroviral, nevirapine, in dry syrup for children. The multinational firm knew GPO was technically capable of such an achievement. The public unit declined the offer saying simply that it was not interested by the proposition. Then, willing to take advantage of the GPO distribution network, the same multinational firm later asked GPO to be the distributor of Nevirapine in Thailand. Once again, GPO declined the offer (Guennif and Mfuka, 2003).

These circumstances, supported by a survey showing that 82 per cent of managers in the pharmaceutical industry believed that there were no technology transfers in the pharmaceutical industry in Thailand (Supankakunti et al, 2001), call into question the evidence of the link between IPR and technology transfers. It seems that multinational firms seek at best to exploit the formulation capacities of domestic firms and are not inclined to promote technology transfers to Thailand.

Unsurprisingly, the strengthening of IPR induces firms to expand trade towards Thailand instead of proceeding to technology transfers and FDI in order to establish local production units. The "market-expansion effect" (Maskus, 2004) is all the more marked in an industry where economies of scale are significant and does not necessarily support the argument of FDI inflows following the strengthening of IPR. Smaller compared to the Brazilian, Indian or Chinese markets, the Thai one does little to encourage multinational firms to establish production units in the sector. More logically, multinational firms are inclined to export finished products to Thailand or to carry out only minor, final-stage formulating activities in the country. Besides, IPRs are not the sole or main element which induces FDI. As indicated by Lall, "most studies suggest that IPRs come fairly low on the list of factors affecting [foreign direct investment] location decision" (2003, p. 12). Others elements matter such as "effective infrastructure and transparency and stability in government", and of course the market size (Maskus, 2004, p. 34).[18]

Moreover, despite the lack of consistent data on the subject, it seems that domestic firms do not engage in R&D (Kuanpoth, 2006). For its part, GPO allocates a small portion of its resources to R&D activities, which are more 'D' activities as suggested by the development of an anti-AIDS cocktail, the GPO-VIR, composed of three already known drugs, each patented by multinational firms abroad (Guennif and Mfuka, 2003). Similarly, some public institutions such as university laboratories conduct R&D activities, particularly with the aim of valuing traditional knowledge. For lack of financial resources and qualified personnel, R&D remains very low in the country.

In the end, the institutional changes initiated in the 1980s have resulted in a contraction of the domestic production structure and a rise in imports, without any counterparts in technology transfers and FDI. And the few efforts made by local actors in R&D do not permit one to define Thailand as a country holding innovation capabilities. The country certainly has capabilities in formulation, but it remains dependent on foreign suppliers for raw materials and the market is increasingly dominated by imported drugs.

In parallel, since the 2000s, the country has been strongly committed to the promotion of public health. This commitment led to the institution of universal health coverage in 2001 and the universal access programme to HIV/AIDS treatments in 2003, both aimed at improving drugs accessibility in a new regulatory environment but with the risk of an unsustainable rise in health expenditures for the future.

3 THE INFLUENCE OF THE NEW INSTITUTIONAL FRAMEWORK ON PUBLIC HEALTH: AVAILABILITY/ACCESSIBILITY OF ESSENTIAL DRUGS

As noted earlier, the HIV/AIDS epidemic constitutes a severe health crisis in Thailand. Today the prevalence rate is 1.4 per cent among adults aged between 15 and 49 (UNAIDS, 2008). In this context, the new institutional framework and particularly the strengthening of the IPR regime calls into

---

[18] This is a major argument in favour of public investment and the establishment of national or sectoral systems of innovation that encourage FDI and technology transfers (Maskus, 2004).

question the ability of public health authorities to address this national emergency.

As also mentioned, the TRIPS agreement and the 2003 Doha Ministerial Declaration provide for flexibilities with the purpose not to unconditionally subject public health to IPR protection. Therefore, the TRIPS enables a country to issue a compulsory licence and allows a domestic firm to produce a copy of a patented drug to ensure its accessibility. Furthermore, in case a country lacks domestic industrial capabilities for the manufacturing of a needed drug, it can proceed to import under compulsory licence: the country may issue a compulsory licence and ask a firm located abroad to produce and export the needed drug to its territory.

Despite these flexibilities, Thailand has been experiencing the greatest difficulties in providing affordable medicines. In the first place, the impact of the SMP on drugs accessibility was blatant. In 1998, the programme covered 700 medicines. A study published in 2000 by the ASEAN workshop on TRIPS and pharmaceuticals stated that between 1979 and 1992, a generic version came on the market one or two years after the introduction of an original drug. After 1992, the generic version was available five or six years later, only when the product was released from the pre-marketing protocol. With the amendment of the Thai Patent Law, a generic version of a patented drug is available up to 15 years after the expiration of the patent.

In particular, the SMP did not help Thailand to address the AIDS epidemic, by preventing the production of generic antiretrovirals. For instance, didanosine was released from the SMP in 1998, allowing GPO to envisage the production of a copy. In the same vein, stavudine, another antiretroviral, discovered before 1992, was not patentable in Thailand. However, the SMP permitted Bristol-Myers Squibb (BMS) to gain exclusive market rights for the drug till 1999. Soon after the expiry of exclusive market rights, the generic production began, enabling a substantial reduction in the price of the medicine (see Table 11.1).

An example of the difficulties faced by Thailand in improving drugs accessibility is provided by the emblematic didanosine case. GPO succeeded shortly before the ratification of the TRIPS agreement in developing a generic version of the antiretroviral. In 1998, BMS filed a patent for an improved formulation of didanosine. This improvement consisted in the combination of an antacid with the earlier formulation. According to the applicant, this new formulation increased the bioavailability of the medicine within the human body. The firm was granted a patent and GPO was no longer entitled to produce a generic. As a result of the temporary monopoly granted to BMS, the drug was marketed at US$2.5

Table 11.1   Comparison of some prices for HIV/AIDS drugs in Thailand (in US$, 2001)

Medicine	Branded drug price	Generics price	Decrease in %
Fluconazole (200mg caps)	6.20	0.26	95.8
Stavudine (40mg caps)	2.60	0.10	96
Zidovudine (100mg caps)	0.50	0.15	70
Didanosine (100mg tab/170mg powder)	1.20	0.62	48

Source: Oxfam (2001) and GPO (2001).

a tablet when the average daily wage was around US$3.84 dollars in the country.[19]

Resolute, GPO asked the government to issue a compulsory licence. Under pressure from the US,[20] the Thai government interrupted the proceedings for a compulsory licence. GPO persisted and finally proposed a new formulation: the didanosine in powder which did not infringe the BMS patent for its improved formulation. In 2001, civil society continued the offensive: two patients and a NGO decided to file a case against BMS demanding the withdrawal of its patent on several grounds. According to the complainants, the combination of an antacid with an already known substance does not constitute an inventive step but amounted to only a minor improvement which did not deserve patentability. The objection was so well founded that the US Patent and Trademark Office had refused twice to grant a patent to BMS on the same ground (ASEAN, 2000). The complainants claimed also that details of the patent were unlawfully altered: a dosage restriction was erased in the original patent application (Ford et al, 2007). Accordingly, the patent protection granted to BMS extended considerably the scope of the original patent application. The patent was not invalidated but its scope reduced, permitting GPO to produce a 100mg tablet, a formulation more convenient for patients and less expensive (Oxfam, 2004). The generic was finally sold at half the price of the branded drug. Ultimately, under pressure from civil society, BMS relinquished its patent.[21]

---

[19]   GPO marketed the drug in 2001 at US$0.62 per tablet. This will lead BMS to market its drug at US$1.2 per tablet the same year (see Table 11.1).

[20]   Thailand was placed again under "Special 301".

[21]   In 2006, a NGO filed a case against GSK's application for a patent for a cocktail composed of two antiretrovirals (zidovudine and lamivudine). The com-

Another example of the impediments Thailand faced while dealing with drug accessibility for people living with HIV/AIDS is provided by fluconazole. This is a treatment against cryptococcal meningitis, the first opportunistic infection, which affects about 10 to 25 per cent of people living with HIV/AIDS in Thailand. The drug was patented by Pfizer in 1983 and was not patentable under the Thai Patent Law enacted in 1992. Local firms were entitled to produce a generic. However, under international pressure, the Thai FDA put fluconazole under SMP. Therefore, Pfizer was granted exclusive marketing rights and generic production was forbidden. It was only in 1998, when fluconazole was released from the SMP, that two local firms invested in its production and marketed a generic version at a lower price than the branded one (Dubus, 2000). This competition led Pfizer to reduce its price by 50 per cent. As shown by Table 11.1, the price of the generic is still far lower than the price of Pfizer's branded drug (Guennif and Mfuka, 2003).

While with the support of GPO and civil society Thailand was trying to make progress in the field of drug accessibility, the country was again under pressure from the US Trade Representatives from 2006. According to them, the country was violating the patents of multinational firms: the Thai authorities announced their willingness to issue a compulsory licence for drugs against HIV/AIDS and cancer without prior negotiations with the patent holders, namely Abbott and Merck.[22]

In 2007, the Ministry of Health of Thailand and the National Health Security Office published a document in which they answered the accusations of the US. On the one hand, they noted their legitimate right to use the flexibilities provided by TRIPS, furthermore with the support of UNAIDS (PIJIP, 2008). On the other hand, they set out the efforts made to negotiate with the patent holders in order to obtain lower prices for some essential medicines. This is an important point since the procedures for issuing a compulsory licence for a public non-commercial use do not require prior negotiations with the patent holders; they must be informed and adequately compensated.[23]

---

plainants claimed the cocktail did not deserve a patent as the combining of two known molecules did not constitute an inventive step. The granting of a patent for this cocktail would have forced GPO to stop the production of its generic formulation sold at U$276 per year and per patient as against US$2436 for the branded cocktail (Ford et al, 2007). Under the pressure of Thai civil society, GSK withdrew the patent application.

[22] For a comprehensive presentation of the events that led Thailand to issue compulsory licences for several life-saving drugs, see Krikorian (2009).

[23] In compliance with TRIPS and Thai legislation, even the occurrence of a conflict between Thai authorities and firms' representatives concerning the

This document stated also that the Ministry of Health had set up in October 2003 a universal access programme to antiretrovirals, which was currently supplying treatments to 80,000 people infected with HIV/AIDS. The budget allocated for the treatment of people with HIV/AIDS rose from US$10 million to 100 million between 2001 and 2007, of which 20 per cent was funded by the Global Fund against AIDS, Tuberculosis and Malaria. In the coming years, the budget is expected to increase dramatically. Indeed, patients are initially receiving a first-line treatment recommended by the WHO (2006) mainly consisting of drugs that are not patented in Thailand. But patients are progressively developing severe resistance to these treatments and must switch to a second-line regimen involving drugs that are patentable and patented in Thailand. The price of these drugs is higher for lack of generic competition. They include efavirenz and the cocktail lopinavir/ritonavir. Causing a significant increase in public health spending, this therapeutic change could compromise the sustainability of the universal access programme.[24]

In response, the Thai government has been negotiating for two years with Merck and Abbott to obtain lower prices. In fact, Merck was marketing efavirenz at US$468 per year and per patient while the generic was offered by Indian producers at US$216. In November 2006 the failure of negotiations, symbolically a few days before the World Day against AIDS, and under civil society pressure, drove Thailand to announce its intention to issue a compulsory licence for five years to GPO to ensure the production of efavirenz and the cocktail lopinavir/ritonavir. The reactions were strong on the part of multinational firms and US Trade Representatives. The fact is that after the announcement about the issuing of compulsory licences, negotiations took a different turn.

In March 2007, Abbott announced the withdrawal of registration applications for seven medicines in Thailand, among which was a more suitable formulation of the cocktail lopinavir/ritonavir for hot countries. Then, the firm declared in April that the price of the cocktail would be halved for Thailand and forty other developing countries that agreed not to use compulsory licences: the treatment would be sold at US$1000 per year per patient as against US$2,200 previously. Abbott indicated that this price was lower than the one offered by Indian producers. Likewise, Merck proposed to lower the price of Efavirenz: the price of the bottle would

---

compensation (the value of the royalties paid to the patent holders) does not impede the issue of a compulsory licence.

[24]　According to the WHO (2005), the supply of a second-line regimen to 25 per cent of patients will absorb 75 per cent of the treatment budget by 2020.

decrease to US$23. The Thai authorities insisted that lopinavir/ritonavir was currently marketed by Abbott at US$500 per year per patient in the poorest countries and efavirenz was sold by Indian generic manufacturers at US$20 per bottle.

At last, imports from India began while GPO developed its ability to produce its own copy in large quantities.[25] So the issue is now whether the threat of compulsory licensing and the resort to cheaper imports will enable Thailand to achieve US$100 million in savings over five years and increase by up to 100,000 the number of patients covered by the universal access programme. To date, it seems that the only way to get these price cuts and savings is the formal use of compulsory licences resulting in production by GPO or exports to Thailand by Indian generic makers, this being comparable with the Brazilian experience.

In February 2008 it was feared that the Thai strategy of resorting to compulsory licensing was about to be interrupted. The new health minister announced his intention to reconsider the decision made by his predecessor to issue compulsory licences for four cancer drugs. The announcement was motivated by the threat to elevate Thailand to Priority Foreign Country status in the USTR Special 301 report, the most severe trade category, which can lead to significant commercial sanctions (PIJIP, 2008).

4 CONCLUSION

Since the 1980s, the pharmaceutical industry in Thailand has undergone several significant institutional changes. On the one hand, measures to

---

[25] Thanks to its R&D capabilities, mainly 'D' capabilities as mentioned earlier, GPO produces many drugs supplied to public hospitals and numerous ARVs provided to the universal access programme. However, the extent of GPO's capabilities has been questioned. The public unit failed to comply with WHO GMP requirements in 2006 for the production of its anti-AIDS cocktail, GPO-VIR. It failed also to pass a bioequivalence study for the cocktail. The drug's efficacy started to be questioned in 2005 when a study conducted by the faculty of medicine of Mahidol University revealed that resistance to GPO's cocktail had grown dramatically in the previous years (Bate, 2007). Therefore, Thailand passed a resolution approving a proposal to build a production unit that would meet international standards. To date, GPO is still not prequalified by WHO for the supply of antiretrovirals (WHO, 2010). These events put Thailand in a difficult situation since the Global Fund financially supported the universal access programme and required that drugs provided be manufactured according to WHO-GMP standards. Finally, for lack of safety, efficacy and quality of the cocktail, the Global Fund had to withdraw its financial support in 2007.

improve the quality of drugs produced and marketed locally have been implemented, including for instance the introduction of the GMP and the promotion of generics. On the other hand, owing to international pressure, the country has implemented a significant strengthening of its IPR standards before and after the TRIPS ratification, bringing about the introduction of product patents in the pharmaceutical sector.

As regards the effect of these institutional changes, some evidence has been put forward. There has been a contraction in the domestic production structure and increased dependence on the importation of drugs. However, we are still waiting for support over the occurrence of technology transfer and FDI into the Thai pharmaceutical industry. Moreover, the country has had to overcome many obstacles to promote public health, in particular to promote access to essential drugs such as antiretrovirals.

When questioning the underlying factors, the argument should be measured. Higher standards for IP protection and for the safety, efficacy and quality of drugs have deeply influenced the evolution of the Thai pharmaceutical sector since the 1980s. All these standards have acted as institutional constraints and entry barriers that national actors have had difficulties in overcoming to keep on producing and marketing drugs. Therefore, it is difficult at the end to assess which of these measures had a major impact on the evolution of the Thai pharmaceutical industry regarding the constant contraction of structure of the domestic production or the increasing domination of multinational firms on the market.

However, in the field of institutional impediments to drug accessibility, patents can be more easily questioned. First, the strengthening of the IPR regime in Thailand did not induce technology transfer and FDI. On the contrary, it has prompted multinational firms to export more to Thailand, causing a significant deterioration in the trade balance for pharmaceuticals. More problematically, this outcome is at odds with the argument of developed countries according to which higher IPR standards will foster FDI, technology transfers, ease access to the latest technical and therapeutic innovations, and promote in the end socioeconomic development in the developing world. Second, patents and other protections of IPR, namely pipeline protection or SMP, have had damaging effects on the accessibility of essential medicines and on public health expenditures. It is difficult to contend that some of the obstacles overcome to date by Thailand to improve the sustainability of its universal access to HIV/AIDS medicines have little to do with the strengthening of IPR standards and the granting of temporary monopolies in the country.

Now, Thailand has to face another challenge, the optimal mastering of the content of a free trade agreement presently negotiated with the US, which could further strengthen the protection of IP and greater undermine accessibility to essential drugs. In fact, Thailand needs to avoid "TRIPS plus provisions" that could prejudice its public health imperatives and ultimately hamper its socioeconomic development.

REFERENCES

Ahmad P. (2003), 'East Asia Economic Community: Prospects and Implications', ASEAN Plus Three: Perspectives of Regional Integration in East Asia and the Lessons from Europe, Conference, 30 November–1 December 2003, Seoul, South Korea, available at http://www.aseansec.org (accessed 31 August 2010).

ASEAN (2000), 'The TRIPS Agreement and Pharmaceuticals', Report of an ASEAN workshop on the TRIPS agreement and its impact on pharmaceuticals, Jakarta, 2–4 May, Directorate General of Drug and Food Control, World Health Organization.

ASEAN (2009), 'Selected basic ASEAN indicators', available at www.asean.org (accessed, 31 August 2010).

Bain J. (1956), *Barriers to New Competition: Their Character and Consequences in Manufacturing Industries*, Cambridge: Harvard University Press.

Bate R. (2007), 'The Cost of Cheap Drugs', *Economic Affairs*, June 1, available at http://www.aei.org/article/26345 (accessed 31 August 2010).

Boulet P. and G. Velasquez (1999), *Mondialisation et accès aux médicaments: les implications des Accords ADPIC/OMC*, Organisation Mondiale de la Santé.

Caudron J.M., N. Ford, M. Henkens, C. Mace, R. Kiddle-Monroe and J. Pinel (2008), 'Substandard Medicines in Resource-poor Settings: A Problem that can No Longer be Ignored', *Tropical Medicine and International Health*, 13(8), August, 1062–1072.

Correa C. (2000), *Intellectual Property Rights, the WTO and Developing Countries: The TRIPS Agreement and Policy Options*, UK: ZED-TWN.

Desterbecq H. and B. Remiche (1996), 'Les Brevets Pharmaceutiques dans les Accords du GATT: l'Enjeu?', *Revue Internationale de Droit Economique*, 10(1), 7–68.

Dubus A. (2000), 'Des Médicaments Antisida trop chers pour la Thaïlande. Les Multinationales Pharmaceutiques s'opposent aux Produits Génériques', *Libération*, 2 mars.

Food and Drug Administration/Ministry of Public Health (1999), 'Current Status and Practice in Pharmaceutical Regulations and Technical Requirements in Thailand', available at http://www.fda.moph.go.th (accessed 31August 2010).

Ford N., D. Wilson, G. Costa Chaves, M. Lotrowska and K. Kijiwatchakul (2007), 'Sustaining Access to Antiretroviral Therapy in the Less-developed World: Lessons from Brazil and Thailand', *AIDS*, 21 (suppl. 4), S21-S29.

Gallagher K. (2005), *Putting Development First*, UK and USA: Zed Books.

Guennif S. and C. Mfuka (2003), 'Impact of Intellectual Property Rights on AIDS Public Health Policy in Thailand', in Jean-Paul Moatti, Tony Barnett, Benjamin Coriat, Yves Souteyrand, Jérôme Dumoulin and Yves-Antoine Flori (eds), *Economics of AIDS and Access to HIV/AIDS Care: Issues and Challenges*, France: Edition de l'Agence Nationale de Recherches sur le Sida, pp. 137–151.

Huang Y.L. (2006), 'Negotiating Health in Thailand: AIDS, Global Patent Regime, and Health Social Movement', available at http://www.newpaltz.edu (accessed 3 July 2009).

International Intellectual Property Alliance (2005), 'International Intellectual Property Alliance 2005 Special 301 Report Thailand', available at http://www.ipaa.com (accessed 31 August 2010).

Krikorian G. (2009), 'The Politics of Patents: Conditions of Implementation of Public Health Policy in Thailand', in Sebastian Haunss and Kenneth Shadlen (eds), *Politics of Intellectual Property: Contestation Over The Ownership, Use, and Control of Knowledge and Information*, Cheltenham, UK and Northampton, MA, USA: Edward Elgar Publishing, pp. 29–56.

Kuanpoth J. (2006), 'Harmonisation of TRIPS-Plus IPR Policies and Potential Impacts on Technological Capability. A Case Study of the Pharmaceutical Industry in Thailand'. ICTSD Programme on Intellectual Property Rights and Sustainable Development, November.

Kwa A. (2001), 'Dying For "Free Trade", Dying at the Hands of "Free Trade": The Law of the Jungle Institutionalised', Focus on the Global South, July.

Lall S. (2003), 'Indicators of the Relative Importance of IPRs in Developing Countries', UNCTAD–ICTSD Project on IPRs and Sustainable Development, Issue Paper no. 3, June.

Love J. (1999), USTRE NTE Reports on Thailand pharmaceutical policies, available at http://www.lists.essential.org (accessed 31 August 2010).

Maskus K.E. (2004), 'Encouraging International Technology Transfer', ICTSD–UNCTAD Project on IPRs and Sustainable Development, Issue Paper no. 7, May.

Maskus K.E. and J.H. Reichman (2005), *International Public Goods And Transfer of Technology Under a Globalized Intellectual Property Regime*, Cambridge: Cambridge University Press.

Matthews D. (2002), *Globalising Intellectual Property Rights*, UK and USA: Routledge/Warwick studies in globalisation.

Ministry of Public Health and the National Health Security Office (2007), 'Facts and Evidences on the 10 Burning Issues Related to the Government Use of Patents on Three Patented Essential Drugs in Thailand', Document to support strengthening of social wisdom on the issue of drug patent, Ministry of Public Health and the National Health Security Office, February.

Nogues J. (1990), 'Patents and Pharmaceuticals Drugs. Undertanding the Pressures on Developing Countries', International Economics Department, the World Bank, September, WPS 502.

Oxfam (2001), 'The Impact of Patent Rules on the Treatment of HIV/AIDS in Thailand. Thailand Country Profile', OXFAM GB, March.

Oxfam (2004), 'Free Trade Agreement Between the USA and Thailand Threatens Access to HIV/AIDS Treatment', Oxfam Briefing Note, July.

Program for Information, Justice and Intellectual Property (2008), 'Timeline for Thailand's Compulsory Licenses', available at http://www.wcl.american.edu (accessed 31 September).

Saggi K. (2000), 'Trade, Foreign Direct Investment and International Technology Transfer. A Survey', *The World Bank Development Research Group*, Policy Research Working Paper, 2349, May.

Sallstrom L.R. (1994), 'US Withdrawal of Thailand's GSP Benefits: Real or Imagined?', *TDRI Quarterly Review*, 9(3), September, 15–22.

Schoen-Angerer T. and J. Limpananont (2001), 'US Pressure on Less-developed Countries', *The Lancet*, 358(9277), 245, 21 July.

Stewart D.P. (1999), *The GATT Uruguay Round: A Negotiating History (1933–1994), Volume IV: The End Game (Part 1)*, USA: Kluwer.

Supakankunti S., W. Janjaroen, O. Tangphao, S. Rahanawijnasini, P. Kraipornsak and P. Pradithavanij (2001), 'Impact of the World Trade Organization TRIPS Agreement on the Pharmaceutical Industry in Thailand', *Bulletin of the World Health Organization*, 79(5), 461–470.

Teerawattananon Y., V. Tangcharoensathien, S. Tantivess and A. Mills (2003), 'Health Sector Regulation in Thailand: Recent Progress and the Future Agenda', *Health Policy*, 63, 323–338.

UNAIDS (2008), 'Report on the Global AIDS Epidemic 2008', UNAIDS, available at http://www.unaids.org (accessed 31 August 2010).

United States Trade Representatives (1994), 'Intellectual Property Rights – US Trade Representative Investigation of Foreign Countries' Practices', available at http://www.fedbbs.access.gpo.gov (accessed 31 August 2010).

Wibulpolprasert S. (1999), 'Mobilization of Domestic Resources for Essential Drugs', Developing Countries: Case Study for Thailand, MOPH, Thailand.

Wibulpolprasert S. (2007), 'Thailand Heath Profile 2005–2007', available at http://www.moph.go.th (accessed 31 August 2010).

Wilson D., P. Cawthorne, N. Ford and S. Aongsonwang (1999), 'Global Trade and Access to Medicines: AIDS Treatments in Thailand', *The Lancet*, 354, November 27, 1893–1895.

World Health Organization (2005), *External Review of the Health Sector Response to HIV/AIDS in Thailand*, New Delhi: MOPH, WHOSEA, August.

World Health Organization (2006), 'Antiretroviral Therapy for HIV Infection in Adults and Adolescents in Resource-limited Settings: Towards Universal Access. Recommendations for a Public Health Approach', revision.

World Health Organization (2010), WHO List of Prequalified Medicinal Products, August, available at http://apps.who.int/prequal/ (accessed 1 October 2010).

12. The TRIPS agreement and health innovation in Bangladesh

Padmashree Gehl Sampath

As more and more countries are beginning to acknowledge the need to build science-based health innovation systems, Bangladesh is in a privileged position due to its established pharmaceutical sector. Local pharmaceutical firms dominate the production landscape with a wide range of generics that include antiulcerants, fluoroquinolones, antirheumatic non-steroid drugs, non-narcotic analgesics, antihistamines, and oral antidiabetic drugs. As a least developed country, Bangladesh is exempted from implementing the pharmaceutical patenting provisions of the TRIPS agreement until 2016, an exemption from which its own local pharmaceutical firms could benefit extensively.

The local pharmaceutical sector exports a wide range of pharmaceutical products (therapeutic class and dosage forms) to 67 countries, and firms are in numerous partnerships with Chinese, Indian and other international firms to expand their technological know-how. The prospect of TRIPS compliance by 2016 and the impending opening up of the local market to international competition (presently, only those drugs which are not locally produced can be imported) is transforming not only the local firm-level strategies for pharmaceutical production, but also increasingly the publicly provided healthcare services available in the country.

This chapter uses original empirical data collected by the author during a sector-wide survey in 2007, updated in 2010, to analyse the impact of patenting as under the TRIPS agreement on health innovation in Bangladesh. The analysis seeks to provide some answers to an important question in the global access to medicines debate: can Bangladesh's pharmaceutical sector gradually evolve to provide low-cost substitutes of important patented drugs to other developing and least developed countries in the short or mid-term? The next section presents the generic strengths of the sector, and this is followed by a section discussing the current patent landscape in the country. Despite the potential of the firms, hurdles to innovation capacity exist. These are analysed in the third section. The fourth section of the chapter concludes by presenting the key challenges and policy insights.

The research process was detailed and consisted of three main stages. In the first stage, a background report and a pilot survey on the state of innovation and the main incentives that play a role in driving innovation in the pharmaceutical sector in Bangladesh were conducted jointly with a local research team. The second stage consisted of 130 firm-level surveys, guided by data generated through the background report and the pilot survey. A total of 130 questionnaires were administered to firms, universities and public research institutes active in biomedical research, and hospitals. The third stage consisted of face-to-face interviews conducted with a cross-section of firms, as well as a variety of other actors, such as professional associations and agencies and the concerned government departments. These detailed interviews have been used as case studies to interpret the results of the survey. A total of 68 persons (including CEOs, and top level management, and government officials) were interviewed in 2007, followed by 22 interviews in 2010.[1]

INNOVATION TRENDS AND CAPACITY TO PRODUCE DRUGS OF IMPORTANCE TO PUBLIC HEALTH

The most prominent policy measure that led to building capacity in Bangladesh's pharmaceutical sector was the Drug Control Ordinance of 1982 that placed a ceiling on selling imported drugs in the local market in order to promote self-reliance. This policy is credited with having reversed the ratio of foreign supply versus domestic supply of drugs in the country. Whereas prior to this policy, local manufacturing companies provided only 20 per cent of the total health needs of the country, relying on foreign companies for the remaining 80 per cent of drugs, with foreign companies supplying 80 per cent. By 2007 local manufacturing companies were supplying 82 per cent of drugs, whilst subsidiaries of MNCs were supplying 13 per cent and the last 5 per cent were imported. According to official estimates, the local exports rose from US$0.04 million in 1985 to US$27.54 million in 2006 (Export Promotion Bureau, 2009).

---

[1]   The 2010 field interviews were conducted by the author as part of a study for the GTZ, Germany.

The local market comprises 237 companies registered with Bangladesh's Pharmaceutical Association, of which 150 are estimated to be operational. These companies manufacture approximately 450 generic drugs in 5,300 registered brands having 8,300 different presentations of dosage forms and strengths (data collected by author, 2007). The Bangladesh Association of Pharmaceutical Industries (BAPI) is the main professional association for the sector, and has 150 member companies that lobby the government for policy changes, among other activities. The local market is extremely concentrated with the top ten firms catering to about 70 per cent of the market and only two companies, Beximco and Square, holding 25 per cent of the entire market (Chowdhury et al, 2006). This highlights the extreme disparities in firm sizes and capabilities, as far as innovation as well as marketing capabilities is concerned.

The survey shows that many of the bigger firms are now venturing into the production of anti-cancer drugs, antiretroviral drugs for the treatment of HIV/AIDS and anti-bird-flu drugs. Local pharmaceutical firms in Bangladesh are presently in the process of mastering reverse-engineering skills that are a prerequisite to the production of active pharmaceutical ingredients (APIs). All local firms in Bangladesh import APIs; some do so in the finished form and several others import APIs at advanced intermediate stages and undertake the final production in-house. This lack of capacity to locally produce APIs reduces the competitiveness of the firms enormously, since between 40 and 90 per cent of the production price of the drugs is taken up by the cost of securing APIs from external sources. The top local firms (around six in total) are trying to secure skills and scientific infrastructure in order to venture into API production and reverse-engineering.[2] All firms interviewed confirmed that they produce APIs from an intermediate stage, wherein the intermediate stage varies from firm to firm and product to product, depending on the technical sophistication required. Box 12.1 summarizes the main competitive advantages and drawbacks of generics production in Bangladesh currently. While presenting a snapshot of the activities, the second half of the table sums up the impediments that local producers face in expanding production to more difficult and technologically challenging areas.

---

[2] Field interviews and joint meeting with the members of the Bangladesh Association of Pharmaceutical Industries (BAPI), April 2007.

BOX 12.1 ATTRIBUTES OF GENERICS PRODUCTION IN BANGLADESH

✓ Low labour costs
✓ Low electricity costs (by the use of gas generators)
✓ Technology transfer
✓ Concentration of large number of manufacturing firms
✓ Ability to do contract manufacturing for larger firms (including multinationals)
✗ Inability to reverse-engineer active pharmaceutical ingredients which account for anywhere between 40–90% of the total drug costs
✗ Lack of relevant human skills in process chemistry and process re-engineering
✗ Lack of manufacturing capacity for excipients, binders and primary packaging materials
✗ Low spending (both in the public and enterprise sectors) on acquiring reverse-engineering capabilities

Source: Gehl Sampath, 2010a.

THE CURRENT PATENT LANDSCAPE IN BANGLADESH: IMPLICATIONS OF THE TRIPS AGREEMENT

The present patent protection regime comprises the Patents and Designs Act of 1911 (last amended in 2003) and the Patent and Design Rules of 1933. The 1911 Act deems patents to be valid for a total of 16 years (Section 14), calculated from the date of application (Section 7), and allows a further extension of 10 years (Section 15(a)(1)).[3] Section 8 contains

---

[3]   Section 7 reads: "After the acceptance of an application and until the date of sealing a patent in respect thereof, or the expiration of the time for sealing, the applicant shall have the like privileges and rights as if a patent for the invention has been sealed on the date of the acceptance of the application." Section 15(a)(1) on "Patents of Addition" provides that "Where a patent for an invention has been applied for or granted, and the applicant or the patentee, as the case may be, applies for a further patent in respect of any improvement in or modification of the invention, he may in his application for the further patent request that the term limited in that patent for the duration thereof be the same as that of the original patent or so

Table 12.1   Patents granted in Bangladesh between 2001 and 2009

Year	Applications filed			Applications accepted		
	Local	Foreign	Total	Local	Foreign	Total
2001	56	239	295	21	185	206
2002	43	246	289	24	233	257
2003	58	260	318	16	206	222
2004	48	268	316	28	202	230
2005	50	294	344	21	161	182
2006	23	287	310	16	146	162
2007	27	269	296	6	211	217
2008	60	278	338	14	151	165
2009	55	275	330	28	103	131

Source: Department of Patents, Designs and Trademarks, Bangladesh.

provisions for opposition to grant of patent (within four months from the date of advertisement of acceptance of application). According to the Registrar of Patents, Designs and Copyrights, half of the patents granted continue to be in the pharmaceutical sector, making it an imperative to enact the draft patent law of 2010 (see below).

The present patent regime in Bangladesh does not contain a provision that enables firms to export to other LDCs in accordance with TRIPS flexibilities. Section 22 of the Patents and Designs Act of 1911 deals with the grant of compulsory licenses and revocation of patents. According to this section, any person can present a petition to the government of Bangladesh to the effect that the demand for a patented article is not being met, but this is presumably for the local market only. Under such circumstances, the government or the high court division may order the patentee to grant licenses on terms they see fit. A revocation can also be made within four years of the grant of patent, in case the patentee fails to give adequate reasons for his default (Section 22 (4)).

An update of the patent regime that took into account the flexibilities of the TRIPS Agreement was proposed under the Draft Patent Act of 2007, prepared by the Bangladesh Law Commission. The field investigation as part of this paper particularly tried to trace the status of this draft patent law. According to the Assistant Registrar of Patents, Design and Trademarks, the draft act has gone through a process of stakeholder

---

much of that term as is unexpired, and, if he does so, a patent (hereinafter referred to as a patent of addition) may be granted for such term as aforesaid."

consultation in the Ministries of Health, Culture, Law, Commerce and Industries, after receiving detailed comments from the WIPO.[4] Further interviews revealed that the draft patent law has been delayed due to some observations of the Ministry of Industries on a couple of clauses that were conflicting in the law, which were currently being reconciled.[5] According to all ministry officials interviewed in March 2010, the draft Act was expected to be enacted soon and contained several changes to the Draft Patent Act of 2007.[6] A clearer picture of the situation is yet to emerge. There is also some speculation that Bangladesh will request an extension of the 2016 TRIPS deadline for LDCs by another 15 years, but this has not yet been officially formulated. Despite the absence of a new patents law, Bangladesh makes use of several flexibilities granted by the TRIPS Agreement for LDCs.

Closer scrutiny of the patents that have already been granted within the country shows that the grant of patents may not have any particular ramifications for the activities of local firms. A major explanation for this lies in the technological intensity of local firms; their inability to reverse-engineer offers the best form of protection for the foreign firms who sell their products in the local market. Given this, one is forced to question the motivation of foreign firms to patent in the local market. An explanation for the patenting therefore could be that the patent-holder firms may wish to prevent competition from companies in other countries, such as India, which may still be keen on producing generic versions of patented drugs that they can no longer sell in the Indian market for exports to Bangladesh.

Previous studies show that it is highly unlikely that intellectual property protection will provide a direct incentive to innovate for local firms, since their activities are not at the technological frontier (see UNCTAD, 2007). An empirical analysis of the impact of intellectual property rights, both as a direct incentive for innovation as well as an indirect contributor to firm-level technological upgrading through avenues such as technology licensing, found very little support in the pharmaceutical sector in Bangladesh (Gehl Sampath, 2007a). Technology licensing to local firms is marginal and not a contributor to innovative efforts presently in the local pharmaceutical sector in Bangladesh (Ibid.). Although the new Drug Policy has

---

[4] Personal interview with Mr. Farhad Hossain Khan, Assistant Registrar, Department of Patents, Design and Trademarks, Ministry of Industries, and Mr. Binoy B. Talukder, Deputy Project Director, IPR, Department of Patents, Design and Trade Marks, Ministry of Industries.

[5] Personal interview with Jnanendra N. Biswas, Joint Secretary, Office of the (Permanent) Secretary, Ministry of Industries, 10 March 2010.

[6] The draft Act is not publicly available.

provisions for joint research and technology transfer between foreign firms and local firms, efficient technology transfer for the future, especially in the case of a knowledge-intensive sector like pharmaceuticals, will hinge upon transfer of know-how (Arora, 1995, p. 41). Successful transfer of know-how, which is uncodified and costly to transfer, will in turn depend on the technology absorption capacities of the recipient, and not just the willingness of the licensor.

SYSTEMIC CONSTRAINTS ON EXPANSION OF HEALTH INNOVATION CAPACITY

The dynamism of local firms in Bangladesh is stifled by lack of adequate scientific and physical infrastructure, and institutional failure to promote inter-linkages between innovation capacity and greater access to medicines. The lack of scientific infrastructure includes the absence of human resources as well as the incapacity of domestic research and development institutes (RDIs) and universities in assisting firms in developing chemical synthesis skills due to under-funding of research, disillusion of scientists and researchers and lack of a cogent focus amongst core university faculties that do work in medical sciences. Apart from this, a range of factors, including lack of common industry infrastructure, lack of capabilities to conduct bioequivalence tests in the country, and the lack of biotechnological capabilities to branch out into emerging options such as biogenerics, all curb firms' innovative capacity. The top Bangladeshi firms are keen on diversifying exports between regulated and unregulated markets, since sales in regulated markets can be huge once the initial hurdles of market entry are countered. Square Pharmaceuticals, for example, has invested huge sums in setting up production facilities just outside Dhaka that meet export requirements to the UK (and is planning to expand to the USA too). The absence of infrastructure support for the conduct of bioequivalence tests and the lack of biotechnological capabilities pose major barriers to such firms seeking to branch out into emerging options such as bio-generics or focus on exporting to regulated markets. Some of these factors and their impact on innovation capacity are discussed in detail here.

Disarticulation Within the Local Knowledge System for Pharmaceutical Research

The gradual transition from manufacture to knowledge-intensive reverse-engineering skills in the pharmaceutical sector assumed the availability of human skills and scientific and physical infrastructure. For developing

countries seeking to build capacity, this is a significant hurdle to sur-
mount. Bangladesh has very weak knowledge infrastructure, in terms of
secondary and tertiary enrolments, R&D investments and scientists per
million of the population. Specifically in the context of pharmaceutical
research, the survey reveals that the disarticulation between university
and public sector research and the enterprise sector is very strong, and one
of the largest impediments to building API skills. Bangladesh's success
in terms of near-universal primary school enrolment does not extend to
secondary and tertiary education. There is a drastic drop in enrolment
rates from primary to secondary and tertiary education, which presents
a bleak picture of the human skills available in the country with severe
repercussions for innovative capacity, a result that was corroborated by
data collected in the survey.

**Weak Public Sector Institutions of Relevance to the Pharmaceutical and
Health Sector**

University education of relevance to the pharmaceutical and health sector
in Bangladesh can mainly be divided into three fields: medical education, nutrition and biochemistry and pharmacy education. In the public
sector in Bangladesh, there are 13 governmental medical colleges, two
institutes of health technology, six postgraduate institutes, three specialized institutes and five medical assistant training colleges, all meant to
impart training of relevance to both the pharmaceutical and health sector
(field interviews). Among the university faculties, Dhaka University
is of high repute with very established departments that deal with
pharmaceutical sciences, followed by others such as Jehangir Nagar
University. Apart from these public universities, Bangladesh has recently
seen the mushrooming of several private universities, such as BRAC
University, North-South University, Stanford University, among others.
However, most students graduating from the universities specialize in
pharmacological aspects of drug production, specifically quality assurance
and quality control. University graduates in chemistry, biology and
biotechnology are scarce and in great demand within local firms seeking
to expand their production capacity (field interviews).

Similarly, although there are a number of R&D institutions under
the Ministry of Health and Family Welfare for various aspects of drug
research, they are under-funded. These institutions are mandated to
conduct study and research in specific areas. Some of these are: Institute
of Public Health; Bangladesh Medical Research Council; Bangladesh
National Research Council; Institute of Epidemiology, Disease Control
and Research; International Centre for Diarrhoeal Disease Research,

Table 12.2   Observable patterns of product and process innovations

New product develop-ment	New process development											
	Universities/ PRIs			Firms			Hospitals			All		
	No	Yes	Total	No	Yes	Total	No	Yes	Total	No	Yes	Total
No	39	2	41	2	0	2	48	1	49	89	3	92
%	90.70	4.65	95.35	4.44	0	4.44	96	2	98	64.49	2.17	66.67
Yes	1	1	2	29	14	43	1	0	1	31	15	46
%	2.33	2.33	4.65	64.44	31.11	95.56	2	0	2	22.46	10.87	33.33
Total	40	9	43	31	14	45	49	1	50	120	18	138
%	93.02	6.98	100	68.89	31.11	100	98	2	100	86.96	13.04	100

Source: Author's survey, 2006–2007.

Bangladesh (ICDDR,B); National Institute of Cancer Research and Hospital; National Institute of Cardiovascular Disease; National Institute of Ophthalmology and Hospital; National Institute of Population Research; National Institute of Preventive and Social Medicine; and Rehabilitation Institute and Hospital for the Disabled. However, lack of funding, incoherent mandates and lack of strategic policy direction all account for the lack of R&D in these public sector institutions.

Low Levels of Interactive Learning and Collaboration

Despite the presence of these institutions, very low levels of collaboration between firms and public sector institutions involved in R&D, teaching and delivery of health services are observed in Bangladesh. Table 12.2 shows the observable patterns of product and process innovations in Bangladesh's pharmaceutical sector based on survey data. These patterns of innovation among firms and public sector actors are quite different from what one would expect. More specifically, almost no universities and public research institutes and no hospitals are involved in new product development (4.65 per cent and 2 per cent respectively) and new process development activities (6.98 per cent and 2 per cent respectively). Furthermore, a very small percentage of universities and public research institutes (2.33 per cent) and none of the hospitals are involved in both product and process development. As for the pharmaceutical firms, a majority of them (95.56 per cent) are involved in new product development. While the percentage of firms involved in new process development is much higher than universities/ public research institutes and hospitals, it is much lower (31.11 per cent) than that of firms involved in new product development. When the sector is taken as a whole, 33.33 per cent of all actors are involved in new product development and 13.04 per cent are involved in new process development and 10.87 per cent are involved in both.

Firms tend to collaborate strongly with private laboratories and medical practitioners (for sale of their products), and moderately with industrial associations and governmental agencies (for lobbying). Similarly, universities tend to collaborate strongly with other universities and moderately with medical practitioners and governmental agencies.

These patterns of collaboration reveal the inherent incentives that overwhelmingly dominate transactions in the local health innovation system, thereby shaping its effectiveness (or the lack thereof). Fundamentally, these are not geared towards promoting greater technological learning in the pharmaceutical sector and access to medicines, and call for greater policy intervention. There is a relatively large mismatch amongst the qualifications of personnel as well as facilities available to enable them to perform in the various organizations and several of these accrue from the (dis)incentives to various actors in the local pharmaceutical sector. Aspects of the health sector in the country, especially those related to drug procurement and sales, interact perversely with pharmaceutical production incentives and contribute to low competitiveness of the Bangladeshi firms. Since local firms mainly engage in formulation activities, quality control and quality assurance personnel are in high demand. The country produces a large number of qualified pharmacists most of whom are absorbed by the pharmaceutical firms, and employed for quality assurance and quality control activities for the manufacture of drugs. As a result, most pharmacies in the country are run by pharmacy owners, or personnel who have very little professional training (field interviews).

Furthermore, the internal market is characterized by branded competition: each product essentially a generic, competing on the basis of brand names. In the absence of control mechanisms that check for good manufacturing practice (GMP) standards and bioequivalence of drugs marketed locally, the drug distribution system is organized solely around pharmacies (run by unqualified or inadequately qualified personnel) and doctors. This offers ample scope for the sale of low quality drugs at high prices, with firms relying solely on extensive distribution systems that promote their brand name products through medical practitioners, often in unethical ways. This is the reason for the skewed patterns of collaboration observed in Table 12.2: firms tend to collaborate very highly with medical practitioners for distribution of their products. Also, drug supplies through both institutional and private pharmacies proceed through suppliers and retailers in a market that is not well regulated and offers ample scope for price-fixing and other anti-competitive practices (World Bank, 2008).

The survey also found that there is an overlap of competencies between medical practice, teaching and research in the sector, due to the lack of relevant manpower to conduct these activities, as well as regulations that prevent professionals from being employed in conflicting activities. Practising doctors also teach at university departments (with very little time or effort spent on improving course curricula) and also are involved as research consultants with several large/medium scale firms in their formulations activities. This is once again confirmed by the collaboration patterns reported in Table 12.2: university researchers, for example, collaborate intensely only with other universities and medical practitioners. This creates inherent conflicts of interest, and is one of the biggest problems in the nexus of the health and pharmaceutical sector in the country.

Lack of a Coherent Policy Framework to Promote Pharmaceutical Innovation

The problems of disarticulation between public sector research and product development, as well as misallocation of skills owing to perverse overlaps between the pharmaceutical and health sectors, can all be credited to the lack of a coherent policy regime for the pharmaceutical sector. The Drug Control Ordinance of 1982 was in several ways very similar to India's policy initiative of a similar kind that triggered self-reliance in its pharmaceutical sector, but this policy has not been supported by complementary industrial policy measures to support the sector. Thus, although it promoted the growth of the sector, the present deficiencies of the sector can be traced back to the absence of a consistent, strategic policy framework that could steer it into a profitable and competitive trajectory. The missing investments in public sector research, common industry infrastructure services, university education of relevance to building up reverse-engineering skills as well as other industrial policy measures for technology transfer and investment all account for the difficulties faced by even the best firms in the country today.

The pharmaceutical sector falls under the Ministry of Health and Family Welfare (MHFW) in Bangladesh, rather than the Ministry of Industry and Commerce (or Ministry of Science and Technology), which is generally the case in other countries. The sector has not been a leading sector in the most recent economic policies that seek to provide a variety of incentives for exports, although the government has enacted a New Drug Policy (2005) and a National Biotechnology Policy (2005), and is in the process of establishing an API park. The New Drug Policy (2005) contains provisions for technology transfer and some other incentives to multinational corporations to set up production facilities in the country on both a joint venture or independent basis, although it is not clear how this alone will help in the absence of other institutional incentives that promote knowledge-intensive activities, such as human skills. The Directorate of Drug Administration is the key department in charge of the sector, and is supported by the Institute of Public Health, which has the mandate of supporting public health activities, quality control, and production of biomedicals, training and research. Both organizations are severely under-equipped and under-funded.[7] One of the few services offered by the Directorate is the Bangladesh National Formulary, produced by the Directorate of Drug Administration, which contains a list of all drugs available in the country, with manufacturing details and price. Empirical research conducted by the author elsewhere using the survey data (not reported here) shows that the only factors that contribute to present innovation efforts in the pharmaceutical sector are skilled manpower and quality of local infrastructure services (see Gehl Sampath, 2007b; 2010b). All other governmental policies and institutions, such as innovation incentives by the government and local research in the PRIs and universities, are very weak in promoting innovation activities in the sector.

PROMOTING ACCESS TO MEDICINES: KEY ISSUES AND CONCLUSIONS

The pharmaceutical sector in Bangladesh has received a lot of attention in the context of access to medicines and the TRIPS Agreement in recent times. With India becoming TRIPS-compliant in 2005, the sector in Bangladesh could potentially fill the vacuum created by Indian firms, if the local firms are able to produce generic versions of important medicines at globally competitive rates. There are however many reasons, analysed in this chapter, that may not work in favour of local pharmaceutical firms in Bangladesh that are seeking to capitalize on TRIPS provisions.

The analysis shows that a major impediment to enhancing competitiveness is firms' inability to produce APIs, as a result of which local firms tend to focus inwards. This is not necessarily a bad result; however, the protective local policy regime that was initially intended to boost local

---

[7] The Directorate of Drug Administration has only two laboratory facilities (in Dhaka and Chittagong) and these can test about 3,500 samples of medicines a year. About 12,000 samples of different brands of medicines remain without test every year, although the regulations require that medicines are tested for quality and efficacy twice every year (World Bank, 2008).

manufacture of drugs and enhance access to medicines in the local market is, in the absence of safeguards that regulate price of drugs and access, creating incentives for local firms to focus on extracting rents from local consumers. As a result, local pharmaceutical firms are largely focused on retaining the gains that accrue from their dominant positions in the domestic market, often at the expense of making cheaper drugs available to the poor and the needy. The survey noted several avenues through which firms tend to maximize their profits through price fixing, supplying medical practitioners, among others. This narrow focus, attenuated by the policy environment, fails to create appropriate incentives for firms to strategically invest in acquiring reverse-engineering skills required for production of APIs.

Currently, a very small percentage (less than 5 per cent) of the total production of even the biggest firms is exported, which is a very small amount for a sector of this size. At the same time, in the absence of an export focus, the relatively small domestic market does not provide the requisite economies of scale, which is an all-important factor for API skills development. The policy framework needs dynamism, and a re-orientation that balances local innovation with greater access to medicines. Industrial policy incentives that provide the requisite scientific and physical infrastructure support to the firms will need to be provided hand-in-hand with an enabling intellectual property regime that incorporates TRIPS flexibilities. Regulation of competition and pricing practices will also be important from an access to medicines perspective.

Some important policy changes are underway, as part of the new Industrial Policy of 2009 and the Science and Technology Policy of 2010. A new Drug Policy of 2010 is also expected to be enacted soon. These ongoing policy changes, the impact of which is currently unclear, offer much hope.

REFERENCES

Arora, A. (1995) "Licensing Tacit Knowledge: Intellectual Property Rights and the Market for Know-how," *Econ. Innov. New. Techn.* 4, 41–59.

Chowdhury, F., S. Gurinder, S. Raihanuddin and S. Hasan Nasir (2006) "A Strategy for Establishing the API Park," Interim Report. Bangladesh: Ministry of Industry.

Export Promotion Bureau (2009) Bangladesh Ministry of Commerce, available at http://www.epb.gov.bd/export_Policy_2009-12.php.

Gehl Sampath, P. (2007a) "Intellectual Property and Innovation in Least Developed Countries: Pharmaceuticals, Agro-Processing and Textiles and RMG in Bangladesh," Background Paper No. 9 for the Least Developed Countries

Report 2007 on "Knowledge, Technological Learning and Innovation for Development," UNCTAD, Geneva.

Gehl Sampath, P. (2007b) "Innovation and Competitive Capacity in Bangladesh's Pharmaceutical Sector," Working Paper Series, UNU-MERIT, Maastricht.

Gehl Sampath, P. (2010a) "TRIPS Flexibilities and Local Pharmaceutical Production Capacity in Bangladesh: An Update," GTZ Study, December.

Gehl Sampath, P. (2010b) *Reconfiguring Global Health Innovation*, Routledge, London.

UNCTAD (2007) "Knowledge, Technological Learning and Innovation for Development," Least Developed Countries Report, UNCTAD, Geneva.

World Bank (2008) "Public and Private Sector Approaches to Improving Pharmaceutical Quality in Bangladesh," Bangladesh Development Series Paper No. 23, March.

Index

Printed and bound by CPI Group (UK) Ltd, Croydon, CR0 4YY

16/04/2025

14658492-0005